Ethnic Leadership
and Midwestern Politics

ETHNIC LEADERSHIP
AND MIDWESTERN POLITICS

*Scandinavian Americans
and the Progressive Movement
in Wisconsin, 1890–1914*

JØRN BRØNDAL

2004
PUBLISHED BY
The Norwegian-American Historical Association, Northfield, Minnesota
DISTRIBUTED BY
The University of Illinois Press, Urbana and Chicago

Published with the support of:
Statens Humanistiske Forskningsråd
(The Danish Research Council for the Humanities)

CONTENTS

FOREWORD

If historians were once preoccupied with politics, they are no more. In the past century history has embraced the whole range of human activity. In the United States, Theodore C. Blegen and his colleagues in the early work of the Norwegian-American Historical Association were, in fact, among the pioneers of a broader conception of history than was then customary. Yet historians cannot, or at least ought not, avoid politics. Aristotle was right: humans are by nature political beings and politics is naturally an essential human activity. Whatever else history must do, then, it needs always to take politics into account.

The Norwegian-American Historical Association is therefore pleased to publish Jørn Brøndal's study of Scandinavian-Americans in politics. The author is currently an Associate Professor of American History at the University of Southern Denmark. His book, which originated as a dissertation submitted to the faculty of the University of Copenhagen, is noteworthy for its emphasis on the role played in American politics by cohorts of ethnic leaders. It is also an able contribution to an undeveloped field, the comparative study of Scandinavian ethnic groups in the United States. In these respects his work complements other studies, including a number published by the Association itself, that have emphasized popular involvement in Norwegian-American politics or the careers in politics of single individuals.

In addition to thanking Jørn Brøndal for his effort in transforming his dissertation into an engaging book, it is a privilege to join him in expressing appreciation to the Danish Research Council for the Humanities

(Statens Humanistiske Forskningsråd) for a grant which greatly assisted in the publication of this volume. Sylvia Ruud provided expert assistance in both editing and production. The typography and design of the book are her work, as is the dust jacket. Without the support of the Board of Directors of the Norwegian-American Historical Association and the gifts of members and friends, it would not be possible for the Association to publish books like this one. I thank them all.

Todd Nichol
Saint Olaf College
2 August 2004

PREFACE

When I visited the University of Wisconsin-Madison in 1989 as an exchange student and wrote a master's thesis on Robert M. La Follette's fight for the direct primary, I became intrigued by the role played by the Scandinavian Americans in Wisconsin's progressive movement. Five years later, I returned to Madison on a Fulbright Research Fellowship to undertake work on a PhD dissertation on that topic, a dissertation that I defended in 1999. The present book is the result of my effort to abbreviate and revise that bulky three-volume document. I should mention here that, unless otherwise noted, all translations from Scandinavian-language sources in this work are my own.

This book would never have materialized had it not been for help and support from numerous friends and colleagues. I am particularly grateful to Professor Inga Floto of the University of Copenhagen, who as my mentor not only guided me through the process of writing the dissertation but was always ready to support me, far beyond the call of duty. Had it not been for Inga Floto's encouragement, I would probably not have entered the PhD program. On the other side of the Atlantic, I feel deeply indebted to Professor John Milton Cooper Jr. of the University of Wisconsin-Madison, who during my stays in Madison in 1989–1990 and again in 1994–1995 was my adviser. He was ever willing to discuss whatever questions I brought up, and he gave me invaluable advice on the study of Wisconsin progressivism.

Along the way, many other people have also offered me help and encouragement. I am very grateful to Todd Nichol of the Norwegian-

American Historical Association for editing the present work and for always patiently being ready to discuss changes to the manuscript. I also feel indebted to Odd S. Lovoll, who from an early stage supported my work and was the first person to suggest that I submit it to the Norwegian-American Historical Association. Likewise, I am very grateful to Professor Glen Gendzel of Indiana University-Purdue University at Fort Wayne, who not only read parts of my manuscript, but after my return to Denmark time and again mailed me copies of important documents. Several of my present colleagues at the University of Southern Denmark have also been very helpful. Professors David Nye, Henrik Lassen, and Roy Sellars all read parts of the manuscript and offered valuable advice. I am grateful to Peter Rye Hansen for the same reason.

Still other colleagues inspired me through their work and our discussions: Professor Dag Blanck and Professor Harald Runblom, both of Uppsala University; Professor David Mauk of the Norwegian University of Science and Technology, Trondheim; Professor Thomas J. Archdeacon and Professor Leon D. Epstein, both of the University of Wisconsin-Madison; Torben Grøngaard Jeppesen, Director of Odense City Museums; Kristian Hvidt, former Head Librarian of the Library of the Danish Parliament; Jette Mackintosh of the University of Copenhagen; and Birgit Flemming Larsen, formerly of the Danes Worldwide Archives, Aalborg. I would like to add that the three referees who read my manuscript in connection with the planning of this book all offered insightful suggestions. I would also like to thank Sylvia Ruud of the Norwegian-American Historical Association for always being ready to give me concise answers to whatever technical questions arose concerning the manuscript.

Likewise, I am grateful to the staff of various institutions: the Library-Archives of the Wisconsin Historical Society in Madison; the Manuscript Division of the Library of Congress; the Archives of the Norwegian-American Historical Association at St. Olaf College in Northfield, Minnesota; the Swenson Swedish Immigration Research Center at Augustana College in Rock Island, Illinois; and the Danes Worldwide Archives in Aalborg, Denmark. I am also indebted to the personnel at the many libraries that I consulted.

I am very grateful to the Danish Research Council for the Humanities (Statens Humanistiske Forskningsråd) for publication support. Moreover,

I would like to thank the following institutions for giving me the financial aid without which I would not have been able to perform my research during two wonderful stays in the United States: the Fulbright Commission, the Danish Research Academy, the Denmark-America Foundation, Knud Højgaard's Foundation, the Politiken Foundation, Christian and Ottilia Brorson's Fellowship, and the University of Copenhagen.

In sum, I have many people and institutions to thank, yet whatever errors may still be found in the present work are all my own.

I dedicate the book to my dear family whose affectionate encouragement was crucial: my wife Hervør and our three children, Maria, Hanna, and Jóhan. When I began this project, there were only three of us. Now, Jóhan, our youngest child, is six years old. That says it all.

Jørn Brøndal
Kolding, February 2004

Introduction

THE PROBLEM:
ETHNIC LEADERSHIP AND MIDWESTERN POLITICS

Nils Pederson Haugen (1849–1931), the Norwegian-born Republican representative from Wisconsin's Eighth Congressional District, hit the nail on the head: "What you more particularly need would perhaps be good local correspondents in different parts of the state. There is no common natural center for our Wisconsin Scandinavians."[1] He wrote in reply to a query by A. C. Hurst, the newly appointed editor of the Norwegian-language *Fædrelandet og Emigranten*, who in the spring of 1890 wanted to learn more about the political mood among Wisconsin's Scandinavian Americans, now that that state was becoming embroiled in an ethnic controversy over an English-language school law. It may be that the Danish-born yet Norwegian-raised editor had hoped for a simpler answer to his inquiry than this, yet Haugen's reply was strikingly accurate, reaching as it did far beyond the immediacy of the situation and pointing to the complexities involved in being a Scandinavian American.

Haugen was right, on the one hand, in implying that many Scandinavian Americans had little in common with each other, typically orienting themselves inward toward their own native locality and tending to divide over cultural and religious values along parochial or regional rather than national, not to speak of pan-Scandinavian, lines.[2] Despite this lack of a common natural center, Congressman Haugen was also correct, on the other hand, in roughly categorizing the people he was referring to as "our Wisconsin Scandinavians." Americans of non-Scandinavian origins, after all, at most thought of their Nordic neighbors as Norwegians, Swedes, and

1

Danes, but more often just as Scandinavians. National epithets were hardly foreign to the Scandinavian immigrants, particularly not the latest arrivals, but these labels nevertheless took on new meaning in the ethnic clatter and noise of the New World, especially as some of the Scandinavian-American leaders themselves adopted those labels and began to develop positive notions about ethnic identity, while they built and maintained their churches, mutual-aid societies, temperance associations, and newspapers.

Haugen's double insight into the nature of being Scandinavian American has informed much of the migration research of recent decades. At a micro level, a number of historians and cultural geographers, responding to earlier calls for analysis of the migration process in its trans-Atlantic totality, began detailing how people of Old World communities formed human chains across the Atlantic Ocean that brought many of them together again in the New World in tightly knit ethnic settlements. This notion of chain migration not only replaced the older metaphor of the lonely, uprooted immigrant suffering rude culture shocks from the unsettling encounter with the strange New World, but also led to a more refined and flexible understanding of the concept of ethnicity.[3] Ethnic identity was now outlined in terms of locally defined, shared senses of peoplehood, subnational in character and transferred from the Old World to the New, only to enter into continued processes of transformation, innovation, and redefinition in the ensuing dialogue with the novel surroundings.[4]

Congressman Haugen's implicit proposition that *national* and *Scandinavian* attachments also mattered is likewise reflected in current historical research. In recent years, several ethnic historians, drawing inspiration from studies on the precarious nature of the nation-state and of nationalism, have argued that if the latter two concepts are to be viewed first of all as modern, invented constructs, then this perspective may be profitably applied to the analysis of ethnic groups in the New World. In other words, in America, ethnic leaders attempted to assert a "national" presence across the many inward-looking ethnic strongholds by making appeals to—and, indeed, to a large extent inventing—common sentiments of national belonging.[5]

This "national" perspective informs the present study, the aim of which is to investigate, from the point of view of Scandinavian-American political leaders in Wisconsin, how between 1890 and 1914 a very rough and constructed type of ethnic identity based on Old World national attachments played an important role in the political arena, the quintessentially "American" sphere of life in the United States. That arena had been defined by the Founding Fathers in terms of a universalist and individualist political creed that made precious little room for notions of ethnic group rights. By 1890, however, a system was in fact in place in the Middle West that accorded ethnicity a certain role in practical politics, to some extent recognizing citizens of foreign parentage on the basis of what was called their "nationality," yet also circumscribing some of their rights and responsibilities.[6] Even though many leaders of Scandinavian-American institutions embraced national attachments wholeheartedly and viewed them as a source of pride and inspiration, some Scandinavian-American politicians were more ambiguous in their celebration of this type of ethnicity, worrying about its potential for creating inequality. In 1892, Congressman Haugen, for one, sighed, "We belong to that class of citizens who are Americans in every country under the sun, except in the United States."[7]

The two main strategies of the present book are, first, to investigate the workings of this political system that accorded ethnic considerations a certain role in politics, arguably at the expense of disguising real, substantial political, social, and economic issues, and, second, to analyze the challenge to this politics of tradition mounted by the progressive movement of Wisconsin. By concentrating on Scandinavian-American political culture in the Middle West in the late nineteenth and early twentieth centuries, and on the nature of Wisconsin progressivism, this study will also address the questions of why so many Scandinavian-American spokesmen joined Wisconsin's progressive movement under the charismatic leadership of Robert Marion La Follette (1855–1925) and what kind of appeal they made to the ethnic grass roots who likewise tended to back the cause.

I will focus on people who in political matters were lumped together into one category, the Scandinavian Americans, but who in fact consisted of Norwegian Americans, Swedish Americans, and Danish Americans. These various labels always remained in a certain state of flux, and the epithet "Scandinavian" had a rather precarious existence by 1890.[8] On the one hand, the rise in immigration in the recent decades worked as a centrifugal force, allowing many Scandinavian Americans the luxury of basing their ethnic institutional commitments on *national* rather than broader pan-Scandinavian foundations. On the other hand, the American context had a continuously centripetal effect, as people of non-Scandinavian background tended to group the Norwegian Americans, Swedish Americans, and Danish Americans into one Scandinavian-American cluster. Although the number of truly Scandinavian-American institutions was waning by 1890, within the Yankee-dominated field of politics the label "Scandinavian" survived. It was oftentimes bolstered by vote-grabbing Scandinavian-American politicians intent on making their appeal as ethnically inclusive as possible, yet it also remained open to assault on the basis of inter-Scandinavian jealousies, as would become clear in 1905, when Norway broke its union with Sweden. In Wisconsin, we should note, to be a Scandinavian American often seemed almost synonymous with being a Norwegian American, a perspective that informs the present study, even though an attempt has been made to keep the viewpoint comparative, the sources permitting.

The main focus of the present book is on political leadership. Many other studies dealing with the combination of ethnicity and politics have centered primarily on the voting behavior of the grass roots. Such works tended to emphasize the ethnocultural orientation of the ordinary late nineteenth-century Midwestern voter, his propensity to vote on the basis of his ethnic, particularly his religious, sensibilities.[9] This book does not challenge the basic proposition that many Scandinavian-American rank-and-file voters, particularly among Norwegian and Swedish Americans, were informed by a religious pietism that tended to place them solidly within the ranks of the Republican Party, which in the late nineteenth century they were liable to view as the party of temperance, rural Protestant virtues, and the Union, whereas oftentimes they saw the Democrats as the party of rum, Romanism, and rebellion.

By shifting the focus upward from the grass roots to the leadership, however, a different yet complementary story unfolds. This is a tale of the construction of a secular ethnic identity shorn of explicit reference to religiously divisive issues, an ethnicity based on *national* or sometimes even *pan-Scandinavian* attachments. Notwithstanding that it originated in processes of ethnic labeling evolving in the Yankee-dominated surroundings, a sense of collective identity was developed actively by Scandinavian-American leaders endeavoring to claim for themselves and the whole group that they represented a recognized place in American public life. They tended to gloss over internal differences within the group based on regionally or even parochially defined religious and cultural value systems.[10]

The very vagueness of this type of ethnic identity constituted one of its strengths. It seems often not to have been felt necessary to discuss exactly what it might entail politically to be a Norwegian American, a Swedish American, a Danish American, or simply a Scandinavian American. Sometimes, at least, labels sufficed. The emphasis was on the ethnic *connection*, on the manner in which common national or Scandinavian origins in and of themselves justified collective political action toward getting the right men elected to office. This convenient elusiveness functioned as a means of defusing the explosive ethnocultural energies radiating from the grass roots, energies igniting debates over for instance temperance and the use of the English language in the public schools. To be sure, some cynical leaders were willing to invest politically in those volatile issues, a notorious example being Milwaukee's Democratic boss E. C. Wall, who in 1892 argued that "prejudice is a far more potent factor than argument, and I hate to have prejudice work against us; I prefer to use my efforts to have prejudice work against the other side."[11] Many other politicians, however, including several Scandinavian Americans, drew back from a too divisive and dangerous politics of prejudice. To them, appeals to a vague, secular identity based on common national or simply Scandinavian attachments constituted a means of calming ethnic passions. Suffice it to get men of the right national background elected to office—ideally, that in itself would signify an ethnic victory.[12] In practice, however, the temperance issue proved especially difficult to avoid.

Considering Wisconsin progressivism from this perspective, we shall be investigating one of the great reform movements of twentieth-century America, a movement that unfolded in a state that from the 1870s through the early 1890s generally had been spared much, if not all, of the political turbulence caused farther west by agrarian, inflation-minded, anti-corporate Grangers, Greenbackers, and Populists who yearned for an age of supposedly greater political virtue in "the only country in the world that began with perfection and aspired to progress."[13] Despite the fact that by early 1890 Wisconsin still shone as the "conservative jewel of the Mid-west," from 1891 the state Republican party found itself enmeshed in a factional struggle that pitted Robert M. La Follette and his political allies against the conservative establishment of the party.[14] In late 1896 the battle expanded to become an ideological struggle over the concept of reform.

When in 1900 La Follette finally won the governorship after having signed a short-lived truce with his conservative foes, he and his allies began the dramatic struggle to turn Wisconsin into America's "laboratory of reform."[15] Over the following years, not only were the basic political rules of the state changed through the passage of such measures as the mandatory, statewide direct primary, a civil service law, and a corrupt-practices act, but Wisconsin also expanded the traditional limits of its legislative domain. A number of laws were enacted that gave the state new regulatory functions over growing corporate power. The 1903 act to tax the railroad companies on the basis of an evaluation of their physical property, rather than on the basis of the old license fees, was only the beginning. More consequential and far-reaching was the establishment two years later of a railroad commission to influence the rate-setting policies of the railroad companies, even though the commission's powers fell short of what some reformers envisioned.[16] Moreover, statutes were enacted that gave the state new social responsibilities. The 1911 legislature, radicalized by the growth of Milwaukee's Social Democratic movement and urged on by the energetic Republican Governor Francis E. McGovern (1866–1946), passed America's first graduated income tax and set up a Workmen's Compensation Board to aid laborers injured at work. An Industrial Commission was also established to determine safety codes covering each industry, and a number of conservation measures were enacted. Arguably, no other state legislature passed more progressive measures in one session than did Wisconsin's in 1911. Frederick Jackson Turner, the famous historian who himself had grown up in late-frontier Wisconsin, was roused by the state's "great step forward," and Theodore Roosevelt lauded Wisconsin for her "sane radicalism." Two other progressives each wrote their enthusiastic account of the Wisconsin Idea.[17]

What exactly characterized the progressive movement? The progressive era has been interpreted in so many ways that one scholar has gone so far as to write an obituary for the movement.[18] Most historians, even revisionists who viewed the progressive era as a triumph of conservatism or a bureaucratic search for order rather than as a period dominated first of all by political reform, agree that the Midwestern variety of the movement was generally more radical and reform-oriented than the federal version associated with Presidents Theodore Roosevelt and Woodrow Wilson.[19] In Wisconsin, the growth of progressivism was closely associated with the movement of the concept of reform from its conventional position on the fringes of Wisconsin's political universe to its center.[20] In that state, moreover, the political climate was highly charged during the progressive years from 1896 to 1914. Wisconsin progressivism was born in conflict and raised in a climate of public agitation over the rise of corporate power in America, and if the legislative fruits were hardly all that the most radical reformers asked for, the progressives nevertheless succeeded in earning the wrath and opposition of various corporate interests.

Above all, Wisconsin progressivism represented a new, mass-based mode of practicing politics and a new vocabulary that challenged the politics of tradition.[21] Its mass character was revealed not only in the direct rhetorical appeals to "the people" in their ongoing fight against the "interests," but also in the attempt to turn some types of large-scale organizations, private or semiprivate in nature, into public utilities—say, the railroad companies or the political parties. The new political language of the movement not only moved the concept of reform to center stage but also associated progress with activist statesmanship. Moreover, while elevating such concepts as "non-partisan principles," "individual merit," and "issues" to prominent positions, progressivism laid siege to various older assumptions. Among these was the idea that blind partisan loyalty was basically good; the belief that claims to political recognition on the basis of geography were just; the understanding that politicians might be entitled to political advancement due to their personal histories, in terms, for example, of bravery in the Civil War, rather than on account of their political views; and the whole notion that hard labor for the political party should routinely translate into patronage rewards. "Nationality" was another concept under attack, and we shall study the political consequences of that challenge, analyzing as we do so the actual change in political rhetoric that resulted and probing into underlying relations of power and economic interest.

An additional feature of Wisconsin progressivism, as of progressivism generally, was that it represented a conglomeration of diverse forces that, for a number of years, at least, cooperated sufficiently to enact several reform measures. The Wisconsin movement always thrived on the commitment to perceived common political goals of many interest groups. One of the most striking features of the movement, noted by several observers both then and later, was the degree to which it received support from Scandinavian Americans.[22]

Why was this so? A large part of the answer may be found by studying the *connections* that some Scandinavian-American politicians made with Robert M. La Follette's insurgent movement within the Republican Party in the early 1890s, even before La Follette emerged as the leader of a reform coalition. In La Follette the Scandinavian-American element found a politician who was ready to listen to the steadily rising demand that they be treated as the equals of the Yankees, rather than as members of an ethnic group occupying a niche within the political system. These Scandinavian-American calls for equality were always ambiguous, to be sure, for in theory, at least, American egalitarianism required of the Scandinavian-American politicians that they on their part renounce political support from their own ethnic institutions, such as the churches, the secular associations, and the press. In fact, the progressive attack on the "nationality factor" in politics seemed to demand as much. In practice, however, La Follette at least to a certain extent proved willing to accept compromises that made it possible for Scandinavian-American politicians to make use of their ethnic connections while muting explicit appeals to Old World origins.

Despite the importance of *connections*, the argument will also be made that some Scandinavian-American leaders, particularly within the press, attempted to align the vague concept of Scandinavian-American identity, open as it was to numerous interpretations, with certain *values*. What emerged was never a totally coherent or fixed picture. Events and ideas unfolded continuously on both sides of the ocean. Moreover, in Wisconsin, "Scandinavian-American" political identity often referred to things peculiarly Norwegian-American.

Despite its slippery character, however, at bottom this discussion was informed by the goal of keeping the Scandinavian Americans in line politically. Prior to the 1893–1897 economic depression, the Scandinavian-

American political case was frequently made in vague rhetorical flourishes, oftentimes revolving around broad ethnocultural symbols aiming at retaining the Scandinavian Americans within the Republican fold. With the Republican ascendancy that resulted from the depression, however, the nexus of political debate moved to internal Republican matters. In the ensuing battles over progressivism, the argument was increasingly being heard that Scandinavian-American identity had special progressive connotations. Ethnocultural energies emanating from the grass roots were now being rechanneled into a movement that represented powerful moral yet altogether secular positions. As it turned out, a group of Scandinavian-American legislators mainly from the rural western part of Wisconsin actually did support various progressive issues, at least for a while. Nevertheless, the link between avowed Scandinavian-American identity on the one hand and progressivism on the other was easily strained. As convincingly as the Scandinavian-American progressive case was argued by the ethnic press as it discussed the political battles in the Midwest in terms that brought to mind the struggles for democratic reform back in Scandinavia, that case remained open to doubt. Whenever Scandinavian Americans had to *choose* between progressivism and ethnic affiliations, as was the case in the gubernatorial struggle in Wisconsin in 1906, many of them opted for tradition, for the simple argument that blood was thicker than water, and that "nationality" counted for more than progressive values did.

The present book is a case study that investigates the role of Scandinavian Americans in Wisconsin politics. Indeed, in the discussion of specific factional battles and reform crusades, the Scandinavian Americans are definitely the main actors, and Wisconsin certainly sets the stage. In some important respects, however, the work moves beyond the Scandinavian Americans and beyond Wisconsin. To illuminate the situation of Wisconsin's *Scandinavian Americans*, it has been necessary to make a full-blown investigation of general political developments in Wisconsin between 1890 and 1914. For this reason I have included a short collective biography of all Wisconsin's elected state and federal officials in those years, close-ups on Robert M. La Follette and his conservative opponents, and probings into the nature of progressivism. Although the focus is on *Wisconsin's* Scandinavian Americans as far as institutional developments are concerned, I hope also to enlarge the received midwestern picture of the role played by churches, mutual-aid societies, the temperance movement, and the press in Scandinavian-American life. The ethnicity in view here, while investigated from a Scandinavian-American Wisconsin perspective, ought ideally also to have relevance for a general understanding of the role played by Old World national attachments in Midwestern politics.

ORGANIZATION OF THE BOOK

The present work divides into three parts. In part one, "Structures: The Scandinavian Americans and the Politics of Tradition," the main focus is structural, special attention being devoted to the institutions that provided the framework for nurturing sentiments both of Scandinavian-American identity and of common Scandinavian-American political destiny. Whereas chapter 1, "Entering Wisconsin's Ethnic Patchwork Quilt," presents the ethnic landscape of that state and provides a brief discussion of the concepts of nationalism and Scandinavian-American ethnic identity, chapters 2 through 4 center on the role of various ethnic institutions and their leaders both in nurturing sentiments of ethnic pride and in meddling in politics. Chapter 2, "Pastors and Politics," focuses on the church, the most powerful ethnic institution among the Scandinavian Americans, and chapter 3, "Secular Societies," on mutual-aid societies and temperance associations. Chapter 4, "The Press," investigates the role of Scandinavian-language newspapers not only in fostering feelings of ethnic pride but also in promoting the candidacies of Scandinavian-American leaders for political office. Finally, chapter 5, "Scandinavian Americans Enter Politics," analyzes the entry of Scandinavian Americans into Wisconsin politics, from the local to the federal level. That chapter also provides a brief collective biography of all Wisconsin's elected state and federal officials from 1891 to 1914 in an attempt to investigate the changing ethnic profile of the political actors, with a special focus on the state's politicians of Scandinavian background.

John Higham has pointed out that the study of ethnicity, and of social history generally, bears in it the risk of emphasizing structures at the expense of dynamics, resulting in a "motionless" history.[23] Whereas part one does indeed concentrate on structures, on the rules of the political game, part two, "Dynamics: The Progressive Assault on Tradition," introduces a dynamic historical element, Wisconsin's progressive movement. Chapter 6, "The Transformation of Politics in Wisconsin," introduces a full-blown "American" perspective and discusses the growth of Wisconsin progressivism in the 1890s, with a particular focus on the movement's break with tradition in terms of political style. In chapter 7, "Battles against Tradition," while the "American" perspective is retained, two political campaigns in which Scandinavian-American politicians played a central role are investigated: first, Norwegian-born Nils P. Haugen's vain attempt to win the Republican gubernatorial nomination in 1894 and, second, the parallel 1906 struggle between Norwegian-born James Ole Davidson (1854–1922) and Irvine Luther Lenroot (1869–1949), a second-generation Swedish American, just one year after Norway broke her union with Sweden. Those two campaigns are compared with a view to studying how, with the rise of progressivism, the political language changed, and what repercussions this transformation had for the nationality consideration in politics and for underlying structures of economic interest and power.

Whereas the first and second parts of the book concentrate first of all on political *connections*, part three, "Values: A Set of Scandinavian-American Political Principles?" constitutes an effort to investigate possible political principles associated with being Scandinavian-American. The backdrop of that analysis is that many Scandinavian Americans, especially among those of Norwegian and Swedish background, supported the Republican Party, and that several of them demonstrated a special affinity for progressivism. This distinction between connections and values mirrors the sharp division that some sociologists in their study of ethnic groups establish between structural patterns of social interaction on the one hand and cultural values on the other.[24] This partition also coincides nicely with the two main functions of the political party: first, to foster connections, to organize alliances of politicians and voters sufficiently strong to win elections; and, second, to provide, or at least reflect, values—to define and carry through a policy supposedly in the interest of the constituency.

In chapter 8, "Scandinavian-American Identity and Political Values," reader letters to the Scandinavian-American press are analyzed for commonly expressed political sentiments, and the manner in which the Scandinavian-American progressive case was made in the ethnic press is investigated. Finally, a limited investigation of roll calls in the Wisconsin Assembly addresses the problem of whether or not a possible Scandinavian-American progressive outlook also translated into actual legislative muscle.

PART ONE

Structures:
The Scandinavian Americans and
the Politics of Tradition

CHAPTER ONE

Entering Wisconsin's
Ethnic Patchwork Quilt

JOURNEY TO AMERICA

On Thursday, 5 April 1888, Kristoffer O. Skauge (1861–1896) from Børse-skogn in Southern Trøndelag boarded the steamship *Hero* in Trondheim, Norway's second-largest port of departure.[1] The *Hero* was headed for Hull on England's east coast, where many passengers, including Skauge, were planning to take the train to Liverpool, the largest port of departure in Europe, and there sail for America. Skauge's departure from Norway was not without drama, as he noted in his diary. One spectator wanted to jump on board the *Hero* to bid a passenger a last farewell but fell into the water instead. Fortunately, a brave person resolutely jumped into that deep, chilly bath and saved him. The waters of Trondheim's harbor were known to be dangerous. Just eight years earlier, a bridge crammed with a large crowd of spectators had given way, and some two hundred people had fallen into the water.[2] Drama aside, Skauge noted with satisfaction in his diary that the weather was good and that the Trondheim fjord looked re-markably beautiful from the perspective of the ship. His binoculars now truly proved their worth.

After stops at Christiansund and Ålesund, the *Hero* headed into the North Sea, where the weather quickly turned rough. Skauge, a native of a mountainous district in inner Southern Trøndelag, jotted down in his di-ary, "I began to feel queasy, exactly the same feeling as after I have been drinking." Except for bouts of seasickness, however, the voyage to Hull went well, and Skauge, like so many other migrants heading for America,

15

quickly proceeded to Liverpool where on April 18 he boarded the *Adriatic*, a White Star liner that since its maiden voyage in 1872 had brought thousands of immigrants to New York.[3] Sailing south along Ireland's east coast, Skauge enjoyed the sight of the emerald plains stretching down to the sea, and the experience put him in a historical mood: this was the country "where Magnus Barefoot slaughtered the Irishmen like cattle."[4] During a stop at *Kvinstauvn* (Queenstown) on Ireland's southeastern coast, "an awful lot of Irishmen came on board, a terribly impoverished people to look at." When the ship finally headed into the Atlantic Ocean a bad storm soon loomed up. The Irish women were hit particularly hard by seasickness; they "lay stretched out in the cabins and especially on deck in a state of near-unconsciousness and just vomited green bile." On the whole, however, the voyage to New York actually went well. Skauge belonged to the approximately three-quarters of all migrants going to America during the century of mass migrations who were fortunate enough to travel by steam, and eleven days after leaving Liverpool the *Adriatic* reached New York.[5]

Kristoffer Skauge was just one out of some fifty million Europeans, including more than two million registered Scandinavians (749,089 Norwegians, 1,016,659 Swedes, and 299,997 Danes) who sought economic opportunity in the New World during the era of mass migrations, the century between the end of the Napoleonic Wars (1815) and the onset of World War I. By far the majority of the emigrant Scandinavians (97.8 percent) headed for the USA.[6] Skauge himself left at a time when emigration from Scandinavia was booming. According to the official Scandinavian statistics, only in 1882 and 1887 did more Scandinavians go to the USA than in 1888 when Skauge left. He was thus a part of the second of three major waves of emigration from Scandinavia, and the third of four from Europe generally, to the New World (fig. 1.1, Appendix I).

We know very little about Skauge's Norwegian background, only that he was born on the farm of Skauge on 19 May 1861 and was almost twenty-seven years old when he journeyed to America. It is fair to assume that he left for economic reasons, as did most Scandinavians voyaging to America. Some, of course, left Scandinavia for religious and political reasons. Religious revivals in the Scandinavian countries in the nineteenth century produced both martyrs escaping prosecution and zealous converts crossing the Atlantic in search of Zion. When the sloop *Restauration* voyaged from Norway to America in 1825 and inaugurated the era of Norwegian group migration, Quakers and apparently also Haugeans, followers of the Norwegian pietistic lay preacher Hans Nielsen Hauge (1771–1824), figured prominently among the forty-five passengers.[7] Similarly, one of the earliest and most notorious examples of Swedish group migration consisted of the exodus in 1846–1848 of the prophet Erik Jansson (1808–1850) and some fifteen hundred of his followers from Hälsingland to Bishop Hill in Henry County, Illinois.[8] Baptists and Mormons played an important part in early Danish migration to America, not only because of their high public visibility as dissenters but also, at least as far as the latter group was concerned, because of their impressive numbers.[9]

Politics brought others to America. The nineteenth century witnessed a fight by the bourgeoisie and peasants and later also by rural and especially urban laborers for basic political rights. Unless we include young men escaping military service in this category, however, politically motivated migration was numerically less significant than that resulting from religious zeal.[10] Some colorful radicals, such as the Danish Louis Pio (1841–1894) and the Norwegian Marcus Thrane (1817–1890), both having served jail sentences for their views, departed from Scandinavia, but in the last analysis few individuals actually left the Scandinavian countries and settled in the USA for political reasons.[11]

Even though most Scandinavian immigrants did not venture to America for religious or political reasons, they may, of course, still have brought with them inspiration from the religious and political ferment at home; moreover, many Scandinavian migrants undoubtedly considered American religious and political liberty, together with the generally egalitarian spirit of Midwestern life, an extra bonus, as several contemporary sources suggest.[12] Yet material benefits were the great magnet.

Most emigrants from Denmark, Norway, and Sweden belonged, as did undoubtedly Kristoffer Skauge, to a broad stratum of the Scandinavian "working people": small peasants and cotters, and especially the unmarried, unestablished adult children of peasants and cotters, who together with an increasing number of people born into the status usually worked as rural laborers and servants, fishermen, artisans, skilled and unskilled urban laborers, and servants. Economic considerations usually played a determining role in the decision by these people to emigrate.

Among the Danes, only a few farmers and a relatively few cotters emigrated. The rural exodus consisted mainly of people from the landless strata of society. Among the urban emigrants, the lower strata of society likewise predominated, particularly unskilled laborers and servants, but also many artisans and apprentices. As far as Swedish emigration is concerned, presumably one in four emigrants was a farmer or a cotter. Some Swedish farmers, however, possessed holdings so small that they would have passed for cotters in Denmark.[13] Among the Swedes, moreover, an even larger proportion of the emigrants consisted of the unestablished adult children of farmers and cotters. Since Swedish society, like the Norwegian, was less urbanized than the Danish, relatively more rural people generally participated in the exodus (even though larger percentages of those Swedes dwelling in cities actually left).[14] As far as the Norwegian emigrants are concerned, one estimate has it that nine-tenths of them belonged to the lower, but not the very lowest, rungs of society. In Norway, the children of cotters and landless rural laborers and artisans formed the backbone of migration to America, although more peasants than cotters left. Besides masses of unskilled laborers, many artisans and people employed in the shipping industry also emigrated.[15]

Even though each individual and family opting for America undoubtedly took numerous pros and cons into consideration before making the decision to leave, the aggregate of the migrant stream was influenced above all by one factor: the perceived gap in economic opportunity between Scandinavia and America. In the course of the era of mass migrations perceptions of America and of its possibilities changed, as the world kept on shrinking in size. After midcentury, Scandinavia was increasingly integrated into an evolving capitalist world order—economic contacts between individual countries grew rapidly as trade barriers were lowered, and domestic economies entered a dramatic and erratic process of modernization in both the countryside and the cities.[16] With the conversion of ocean traffic from sail to steam, moreover, large trans-Atlantic shipping companies swiftly monopolized passenger transportation to America, employing countless local agents in the process whose function it was to spread information about and sell tickets to the New World.[17] American railroad companies intent on selling the land that they had received as grants from the federal government to finance their building activities engaged in the same effort.[18] In order to lure European immigrants, some American states created immigration bureaus, and with a similar end in mind the federal government dispatched consuls to Europe.[19]

From 1866, trans-Atlantic cables enabled European news services to report instantly about happenings in America, and as the century entered its last decades, dramatically increasing numbers of people read those papers in Scandinavia.[20] Stories about the opportunities of America arrived in Europe in the form of letters from the earliest settlers. Books and various immigrant guides soon supplemented letters and often used a language as subjective as that of the letter writers.[21] Moreover, Scandinavians returning home from America on a visit created local sensations, arousing additional interest in the New World. Finally, as Scandinavians began to establish themselves in America, some of them sent back not only letters but also money and even prepaid tickets in order that they might be reunited with their loved ones in the New World. Furthermore, the presence of friends and family in America made that country a much less strange place to go to for would-be immigrants.[22] Indeed, when colonies of Scandinavians became established in sections of the Middle West, they tended to lend the migration process momentum by drawing over friends and relatives from the Old World.[23]

If much of the information about America that gradually circulated in Scandinavia was rosy, it did not obstruct interested Scandinavians from getting a fairly accurate idea of economic possibilities in the New World. During the American Civil War and again during every major economic downturn (i.e., the depressions of 1873–1879 and 1893–1897, the milder recession of 1883–1885, and the panic of 1907), the number of Scandinavian emigrants to America dropped dramatically. During the depression of 1893–1897, one Norwegian American returning to Norway after a thirty-year absence reported to a newspaper how difficult it was to convince his fellow Norwegians that American conditions really were not all that bad: they felt convinced they knew better![24] Another Norwegian, a critic of emigration, to be sure, even complained, "It is remarkable how little people know about their own country. Those in Gudbrandsdalen and Valdres as a rule know extremely little about conditions in Smaalenene and Jarlsberg. No, they are much better acquainted with conditions in Dakota and Minnesota."[25]

Of course, the shrinking of the world did not happen overnight, and perceptions of America as a means to escape economic want or fulfill social ambition did not spread to all districts of the Scandinavian countries. Whereas some communities developed strong emigration traditions, with many coming down with the "America fever," other communities, sometimes even in the same neighborhood and with a similar socioeconomic profile, remained strangely immune to the movement.[26] It may be that the local leaders were hostile to emigration, perhaps the area lacked ambitious upstarts to lead the way, or possibly the local folks were impressed by sinister stories of shipwrecks, deadly epidemics, and murderous Indians, especially after the Sioux War of 1862 in Minnesota. Nevertheless, emigration fever spread to ever larger areas in network-like patterns, as long as economic conditions sustained the movement. The gradual dissolution of old, vertically oriented social loyalties and the slow development of new, horizontally oriented ties—as seen in the religious awakenings in the early nineteenth century and later in the temperance, cooperative, and labor movements—probably only added momentum to the migration drive.[27]

If not all individuals, households, and communities were ready to acknowledge the possible benefits of emigrating to America, the information stream about the New World was sufficiently powerful to convince many individuals, households, and even whole communities to leave. The actual gap between economic opportunity in Scandinavia and America was, in any case, very real. Even though Thomas Jefferson had been overly optimistic in predicting in 1801 that America's seemingly endless tracts of untilled land would last the nation "to the thousandth and thousandth generation," until about 1890 the USA did beckon with masses of cheap and, with the passage of the 1862 Homestead Act, even free land.[28] Further, during the era of mass migrations, American wages, economic downturns aside, remained significantly higher than those in Scandinavia.[29]

The gradual transformation of economic opportunity associated with the closing of the American frontier and the continued expansion of the labor market presaged a certain change in the composition of the emigrant population. During the early years of emigration, when cheap or free land was still easily attainable, many whole families, the indispensable social unit for any farming venture, migrated to the New World.[30] This process was complemented, moreover, by the generally severe economic conditions in Scandinavia at the time. If powerful economic persuasion was needed to send off whole families to the New World, such arguments were provided not only by the profusion of cheap land in America but also by the overcrowding of particularly the Norwegian and Swedish countrysides in the decades straddling midcentury.

In Norway and Sweden, many a young son of a farmer or a cotter now had to face at least the possibility of sinking down into a status of permanent landlessness.[31] In Denmark, conditions were not quite as severe. First, around midcentury Denmark had the most advanced economy of the Scandinavian countries and also by far the best agricultural soil. Second, during the first half of the nineteenth century its demographic growth was less dramatic and more even than that of either Norway or Sweden, even as the Danish population, like the Norwegian and Swedish, indeed, the European, more than doubled in the nineteenth century.[32] Whereas during these decades many Norwegians and Swedes began to till marginal soils, the Danes expanded their agricultural areas only later in the century. The tendency to divide farms into smaller units reached frightening dimensions particularly in Sweden around midcentury, but in Denmark the parallel movement came later and with less force.[33] In Denmark, economic development never lagged as far behind demographic growth as in Norway and Sweden, and in Denmark the emigration fever thus never attained the same proportions as in Norway and Sweden.[34] In the 1860s and again in the 1880s, moreover, Denmark did not witness agricultural crises as grueling as those that swept Norway and particularly Sweden; during the years 1867–1868 the latter nation endured its last famine.[35]

Later in the century, when wages, together with dreams of upward economic mobility, became the main attractions of the New World, single young people, especially males such as Kristoffer Skauge, dominated the migrant population.[36] Again, economic development in Scandinavia complemented this tendency. The last three decades of the nineteenth century witnessed spectacular economic expansion in all three Scandinavian countries, as the domestic economies entered a phase of accelerating modernization. Indeed, between 1870 and 1913, Sweden boasted Europe's highest rate of growth of output per capita, Denmark came in second, whereas Norway was to be found somewhat further down the list, on a par with France. Each country witnessed a shift in agricultural emphasis from grain to animal production, as tough foreign competition drove down grain prices, and as especially England offered a bountiful outlet for dairy products and bacon. Denmark led the way, its farmer class, if not its cotters and rural laborers, growing both in self-confidence and political ambition with the flourishing of the cooperative movement in the 1880s.[37]

Yet even this domestic growth did not match American expansion. Those were the years when American coal and steel production surpassed that of England, the former world leader; the period in which John D. Rockefeller, Andrew Carnegie, Cornelius Vanderbilt, and John Pierpont Morgan founded private industrial and financial empires on a scale unheard of before in the history of mankind. America emerged in this era as the economic locomotive of the world.[38] Above all, American wages remained higher than Scandinavian and hence served as a powerful attractor for would-be migrants. Scandinavian economic growth, in contrast, was not sufficiently powerful to arrest the emigration movement. Norway and Sweden did not have employment for all the young people entering the labor market in the late 1870s, and when their economies stalled temporarily in the 1880s, at the same time that the American economy flourished, emigration truly soared.[39]

Even so, for the emigrant leaving after, say, the mid-1870s, the aspect of opportunity and adventure probably loomed larger than for his or her Scandinavian predecessors in the 1860s and early 1870s. Kristoffer Skauge could only pity the Irish people boarding the *Adriatic* in Queenstown. *They* looked poverty-stricken indeed (and yet even the numerous Irish who fled to America in the wake of the potato blight were not among Ireland's very poorest individuals).[40] In Scandinavia, by the late 1870s economic conditions had improved to the point where nobody was compelled to eat bread made of bark flour, and with the world shrinking in size, the possibility of returning to Scandinavia after some years of employment in the New World labor market seemed more realistic than it had earlier.[41] Thus many youths, their economic and social ambitions only whetted by erratic economic growth at home, opted for America. Among them was Kristoffer Skauge.

ENTERING WISCONSIN

In the late afternoon of 27 April 1888, the *Adriatic* finally entered New York's harbor, and the next morning, on a day so warm "that it rarely gets that hot in Norway," Kristoffer Skauge and his fellow passengers trans-

ferred to a smaller steamboat and sailed to Castle Garden, until 1892 the final checkpoint in New York. The American metropolis overwhelmed and
exhilarated Skauge: "I have never lived through a day like this before, there
was simply too much for my eyes to watch . . . my eyes could hardly stand
watching this magnificent sight, and my hand tires from describing it." If
New York City jolted Skauge with a culture shock, however, he eased the
impact, as did numerous other Scandinavian immigrants, simply by leaving the city as quickly as possible and heading for the Midwest.

For the next couple of days Skauge's diary radiates an air of excite-
ment over the new country and its possibilities. He rode through upstate
New York with "all kinds of trees, all kinds of agriculture on both sides of
the railroad" and passed Niagara Falls, "which a man once traversed on a
line." He boarded a train in Chicago with "wagons so nicely equipped that
we could only admire them." Skauge was exuberant over having landed
in the New World. His tone is quite different from that of a migrant *returning* to Norway in 1897: "The Niagara Falls were not as large as I had
expected. . . . Along the railroad on which we traveled to New York the
land looked very bad for farming."[42]

Skauge did not travel to America on his own. He was accompanied
by several men from his home district in Norway. He lent two of them five
kroner in Liverpool and was still keeping tabs on their debts upon arrival in
the Midwest. He evidently expected to see them again. Skauge, like so
many of his fellow immigrants, was part of a pattern of chain migration.
This is the more significant as Skauge was not destined to become a farmer
and did not remain long at his first destination in the Middle West.

This pattern of "loose" chain migration was strong among Scandinavian immigrants, even after the possibilities of acquiring cheap or free land
evaporated in the United States during the 1880s, as it had generally somewhat earlier in Wisconsin. Judging by their settlement patterns, the migration of Danes was relatively loosely organized. Danish immigration began
late, and thus complicated the process of establishing near-homogeneous
ethnic enclaves on the dwindling Midwestern land base. Denmark with its
open, flat landscape and advanced infrastructure was also a more integrated society in the late nineteenth century than either Sweden or Norway
and arguably less open to single-stream migrations from comparatively
isolated localities. Yet even among those 12,534 Danes who between 1868

and 1903 stated their intention of traveling to Wisconsin, 32.1 percent told the Danish police that they were heading for one and the same area, the city of Racine. Although Danes named more than three hundred Wisconsin localities in all, 79.3 percent of them stated that they were heading for just twenty-four places.[43]

Among Norwegians and Swedes, on the other hand, the chains across the Atlantic Ocean were sometimes more tightly knit. Whole subcommunities sometimes moved from one area in the Old World to one or a couple of destinations in the New.[44] Peer O. Strømme (1856–1921), a second-generation Norwegian-American newspaper editor and writer, reminisced that when in his late boyhood he finally left the rural Winchester settlement in Winnebago County, Wisconsin, to travel to Luther College in Decorah, Iowa, he heard the Sogn dialect for the first time in his life and wondered whether this was really Norwegian, for in Winchester, after all, he heard only the vernacular of Telemark.[45] Tight chain migration also caused another second-generation Norwegian American to pronounce, "I am a Norwegian, and a Sogning, at that, but I have never seen Norway."[46]

At last Skauge reached his destination—Norway, Illinois![47] He only remained in that little rural hamlet southwest of Chicago for three months. Later he literally worked his way up into southern Wisconsin where by 1892 we find him laboring as a blacksmith in Strum, Unity Township, Trempealeau County. He was, of course, following in the footsteps of countless other Scandinavian immigrants. According to the 1890 census, fully seventy-nine percent of the Union's 1,568,446 inhabitants of Scandinavian parentage lived in the Midwest, the band of twelve states stretching from North Dakota to Michigan in the north and from Kansas to Ohio in the south.[48] As many as eighty-eight percent of all Norwegian Americans flocked to that region, along with seventy percent of the Swedish Americans and sixty-eight percent of the Danish Americans, but with sizeable presences of the Norwegian element also in the Pacific Northwest, of the Swedish in New England and Pennsylvania, of the Danish among Utah's Mormons as well as in California, and of all three groups in New York.[49]

By moving to Wisconsin Skauge furthermore joined the 188,753 people of Scandinavian parentage who in 1890 made up 10.9 percent of a state population comprising 1,686,880 individuals. The peopling of Wisconsin had been swift. The 1830 census counted only 3,635 individuals in the Wisconsin Territory but by 1850, two years after statehood, the population had increased nearly a hundredfold, to 305,391 individuals. Thirty years later, the million mark was passed, and by 1900 the population stood at 2,069,042. Over the following two decades it would grow by another half million. Many different ethnic groups participated in the colonization of Wisconsin. By 1890 fully 73.7 percent of the state's inhabitants were of foreign parentage. The largest group consisted of the 626,030 German Americans, comprising 37.1 percent of the population and dominating especially several eastern counties, including Milwaukee, the state's only metropolitan area. The state also included numerous people of Irish and British background, as well as a rapidly increasing number of Polish immigrants.[50]

Wisconsin early became a magnet for Scandinavians. In 1850, nearly fifty percent of America's Scandinavian immigrants lived there, and even in 1890 only Minnesota and Illinois counted a larger Scandinavian contingent. Despite a few Danish and Swedish fur traders who had come in the first three decades of the century, Scandinavian mass movement into the Wisconsin Territory only truly began with the arrival at Jefferson Prairie, Rock County, of Norwegians from the Fox River Valley settlement in northern Illinois in 1838. The following year, others began entering via the Great Lakes and established the Muskego colony in Waukesha County, soon to house the first consecrated Norwegian-American church (1845).[51]

Until 1850, when land could still be acquired in the fertile prairies in the south of the state, Wisconsin remained the favorite target of Norwegian immigrants. By midcentury, 68.2 percent of all Norwegian Americans lived in that state. After 1850, with the lands to the south largely settled, an ever growing share of Norwegian immigrants ventured further west, especially to Minnesota and Iowa.[52] Through the remainder of the century, however, Norwegian immigrants often headed to Wisconsin, settling along the Mississippi in a movement away from the rich southern prairie, destined to become the heartland of the state's famed dairying industry, and into the woods of the northern three-fifths of the state. By century's end this conjunction of resources and people had temporarily turned Wisconsin into the leading lumbering state in the nation.[53] By 1890, Wisconsin's 130,737 Norwegian Americans constituted the state's second-largest population group of foreign parentage, making up 7.8 percent of the population.

By 1900 the Norwegian Americans were America's most rural ethnic group.[54] Nearby cities like Chicago and Minneapolis-St. Paul boasted sizeable Norwegian-American populations, and within the state of Wisconsin some smaller cities, particularly Stoughton in Dane County; Eau Claire, a western lumbering town; and La Crosse, a sawmilling and transportation center on the Mississippi, contained large percentages of Norwegian Americans.[55] Nevertheless, by 1905 77.5 percent of Wisconsin's Norwegian-American family heads lived in townships and villages, with especially large contingents in several west-central counties, particularly Kristoffer Skauge's Trempealeau (nearly fifty percent Norwegian-American), but also Vernon and Dane counties where many Norwegian Americans found a lucrative niche in tobacco farming (fig. 1.2, Appendix I).[56] Norwegian Americans often lived in tight-knit ethnic enclaves, the most famous of which was the prosperous Koshkonong settlement in Dane County, with several offshoots to the west. In townships such as Pleasant Springs and Christiana in Dane County, Pigeon and Unity in Trempealeau, and Scandinavia in Waupaca, more than eighty percent of the family heads were of Norwegian parentage, and in Westby and Coon townships, both in Vernon County, more than ninety percent had been born of Norwegian parents.[57] Most Norwegian Americans, however, lived in ethnically more mixed environments. By 1905 only 29.2 percent of all Wisconsin's family heads of Norwegian parentage lived in areas that were more than fifty percent Norwegian-American.[58]

Danish and Swedish immigrants were latecomers to Wisconsin and never caught up numerically with their Norwegian counterparts. Still, by 1890 Wisconsin's 29,993 Swedish Americans comprised the state's sixth-largest ethnic group, outnumbered only by the German, Norwegian, Irish, English, and Canadian elements, whereas the 23,882 Danish Americans occupied eighth place, just behind the Bohemian Americans.[59] Swedish Americans were particularly slow in finding their way to Wisconsin. They made an early start with the founding in 1841 of the ill-fated Nya Upsala, or Pine Lake, settlement in Waukesha County by the Swedish student and later Episcopalian minister, Gustaf Unonius.[60] Yet overall the Swedish immigrants were latecomers to Wisconsin, which explains why many of them had to make do with some of the state's least fertile soil.

In Wisconsin, the Swedish Americans were almost as rural as their Norwegian-American counterparts. In the United States as a whole, the

Swedish element was somewhat more urban, with particularly sizeable, and growing, colonies in Chicago and the Twin Cities, but by 1900 the Swedish Americans were the ethnic group with the fourth-largest share of farmers among their male breadwinners.[61] By 1905 they were Wisconsin's second-most rural element, with 72.7 percent of the family heads living in the countryside, despite sizeable presences in such urban centers as Ashland, Superior, and Marinette.[62] Many Swedish Americans settled in the far north of the state, on the fringes of a belt of Swedish-American settlements stretching into Minnesota. On the Wisconsin side, some attempted to scrape out an existence on farms literally carved out of the woods or planted on the cutover waste that remained when the lumberjacks, themselves often Scandinavian-American, left.[63] By 1905 thinly populated Burnett County, which in 1900 claimed the lowest average farm real estate values in the state, boasted a 42.1 percent Swedish-American presence, and many fellow ethnics also flocked to neighboring Polk, Barron, and Douglas counties, as well as to Pepin and Pierce counties further to the south and Price and Marinette counties to the northeast. Some Swedish Americans lived in tightly knit ethnic enclaves, such as Stockholm in Pepin County and Trade Lake in Burnett County. Still, just 14.9 percent of Wisconsin's Swedish-American family heads lived in areas that were more than fifty percent Swedish-American.[64]

Overall, Danish immigrants arrived somewhat earlier in Wisconsin than the Swedes, and as late as 1880 outnumbered the latter. A few of the Danish pioneers even succeeded in settling in the fertile southern region. In 1843 some of them established the earliest Danish rural colony in America, alongside Nya Upsala.[65] Most Danish immigrants, however, arrived after 1860, when the prime southern land had been taken. This, of course, limited their chances of participating in Wisconsin's southern dairying boom, despite Denmark's growing reputation from 1880 on as a nation of cooperative dairy farmers. In Wisconsin, the dairying industry was first organized by Yankees from New York.[66] Even though Danish Americans dominated several city wards in Racine just a couple of miles south of Milwaukee in Wisconsin's southeastern industrial corner, they remained Wisconsin's third-most rural ethnic group, with 63.7 percent of the family heads by 1905 living in townships and villages. At a national level, the Danish Americans trailed only the Norwegian Americans in terms of their share of farmers among male breadwinners.[67] Besides a fairly heavy presence in Polk County to the northwest, many Danish Americans lived in the central east, in counties such as Waupaca, Brown, Oconto, and Winnebago. Some Danish Americans also lived in ethnic enclaves, notably in Luck Township at the core of the West Denmark settlement, Polk County, a colony deliberately established in a remote forest location in 1869 to ensure Danish control, but also at Withee in Clark County and New Denmark in Brown County.[68] Overall, however, only 6.5 percent of Wisconsin's Danish-American family heads lived in areas that were more than fifty percent Danish-American, a much smaller share than among the Norwegian and Swedish Americans.[69]

Wisconsin's Scandinavian Americans shared certain common characteristics. Together, they constituted the state's three most rural ethnic groups, and despite their presence in some urban settings, only few of them lived in the state's single metropolitan area, Milwaukee.[70] Moreover, even though Norwegian Americans, in part undoubtedly owing to their greater numbers and early arrival, were most prone to cluster together in tight-knit ethnic enclaves, in their settlement patterns all three ethnic groups proved less clannish than their German-American and Polish-American neighbors yet considerably more so than their English-American and Irish-American counterparts.[71] Once settled in an enclave, the members of the ethnic group in question tended to remain there for a long time.[72]

In other respects, Wisconsin's Scandinavian Americans differed from each other. Thus, only few settlements in the state were truly pan-Scandinavian in a manner to match Swenoda in neighboring Minnesota, whose eccentric name was an abbreviated compound of "Swedish," "Norwegian," and "Danish." Two of Wisconsin's best bids for pan-Scandinavianism were Garfield in Polk County and Baronette in Washburn.[73] From some of these not too common "mixed" Scandinavian settlements came reports of language compromises between for instance Norwegian-speaking and Swedish-speaking spouses. Usually, however, Scandinavian-American enclaves were based on common national attachments, although within such a community, *dialects* might still clash.[74] Yet other Scandinavian Americans were willing to settle in ethnically much more diverse communities. Reminiscing about his boyhood in Pierce County, Nils P. Haugen, the former Republican congressman, wrote that in a neighboring tight-knit enclave the Norwegian-American children had difficulty learning English, yet in his home community, with the presence of Yankees and Irishmen: "The melting pot was doing its work."[75] In the long run, even in these enclaves pressure from the Anglo-American language community proved inexorable, American words usually first entering into the areas of business, communication, transportation, and politics, and only at a much slower rate into the spheres of the home and religion.[76]

Kristoffer Skauge's further life in Wisconsin illustrates the ease with which at least some immigrants from the Old World might adapt to life in an ethnic subcommunity in the New. Judging his social life from his diary alone, one might get the impression that Skauge was in Norway, for all names mentioned sound Norwegian. Strum, the little hamlet that Skauge finally settled in, lay in Wisconsin's "Norwegian" region, in northern Trempealeau County. This settlement on the Buffalo (or "Beef") River dated back only to 1885, noted *Arbeideren*, a small newspaper coming out of Eau Claire. By the following year, Strum consisted of just two streets, yet already boasted two grocery stores, two shoemakers, two carpenters, one steam-powered feed mill, a blacksmith, a church, and a schoolhouse.[77] In the 1890s, the railroads also reached Strum.[78] By the turn of the century, Strum proper was inhabited by some 150 individuals, eighty-five per-cent of them of Norwegian background, with the larger share of them coming from the Oslo (Kristiania) diocese. By then the area boasted three Norwegian-American Lutheran churches, two belonging to the United Norwegian Church and one to the older Norwegian Synod, along with twenty business enterprises, including three blacksmith's shops, two gen-eral stores, two shoemakers, a drugstore, a butcher's shop, and a painter's shop, all operated by Norwegian Americans.[79]

We do not know why Skauge chose finally to settle in Strum. All we know from his diary is that one Sivert Rekstad helped him build his home. Rekstad had earlier offered Skauge board and also lent him money. Rek-stad appears to have been a community leader, for later he sat on the board of trustees of the St. Pauli congregation of the United Norwegian Church.[80] Skauge seems to have settled down well in Strum, quickly becoming so-cially active and marrying. On 14 April 1896, however, only eight years after his arrival in New York, the little Norwegian-American paper *Reform* of Eau Claire reported that Skauge had died after suffering a devastating bout of pneumonia. "His funeral proved that he had many friends," wrote a correspondent. "I do not think that I am being untruthful when I state that this was the largest assemblage of people that ever gathered at a funeral in Strum. He leaves a young wife behind who feels the loss very heavily."[81]

From his beginnings as a day laborer in northern Illinois, Skauge quickly succeeded in joining the little Norwegian-American world in northern Trempealeau County, establishing himself as a blacksmith, marrying, and participating actively in Strum's social life. He accomplished all this within a social world made up largely of people of his own national background, even if most of the individuals came from another region of Norway than he had. The only indication in Skauge's diary that he actually was also part of a larger social world in America appeared in the form of a single laconic note: "Wraamands Textbook in English. B. Anundsen, Decorah, Iowa." Even that book had been produced in one of America's Norwegian centers by one of the most successful Norwegian-American newspaper publishers, Brynild Anundsen.

ETHNICITY WITH A NATIONAL TWIST

Despite powerful parochial and regional attachments, many Scandinavians traveled to America with at least vague ideas about national or even Scandinavian identity, and such notions increased decade by decade. Indeed, when Kristoffer Skauge sighted Ireland, a perverse sense of national pride had inspired him to imagine Magnus Barefoot slaughtering the Irishmen like cattle. Even a certain sense of Scandinavianness was revealed when at Castle Garden he saw five steamships "with passengers from Scandinavia and other countries."[82]

In the second half of the nineteenth century, nationalism was on the rise in Scandinavia, as in much of Europe. Its impact on ordinary working people is hard to measure, yet should neither be exaggerated nor ignored. Three main sources fed Scandinavian nationalist sentiments. First, internal improvements brought people closer together. On the one hand, improved means of transportation and communication not only opened up the avenues by which the Old and New Worlds were being woven together into an Atlantic whole, but also contributed to the integration of regions within each country. By 1900, Denmark boasted a fully developed railroad system, with Sweden and Norway trailing somewhat behind.[83] On the other hand, the enhancement of the public school systems of Denmark, Norway, and Sweden both contributed to ensuring the Scandinavian peoples some of the highest literacy rates in the world and worked towards establishing more homogeneous linguistic cultures in each nation. Even the Norwegian *Landsmål* movement, pioneered by urban elite groups, aimed at creating a whole out of vernacular diversity by placing a new tongue developed out of western rural dialects on an equal footing with the official Dano-Norwegian, and thus, ideally, imbuing the farmer class with national sentiments.[84] Towards the end of the century, furthermore, feelings of unity were catalyzed by the vastly increased number and circulation of newspapers.[85]

Second, foreign policy added notably to the growth of nationalism in each Scandinavian country. Just prior to the onset of mass migration from Denmark, Danish soldiers twice confronted Prussian armies over the duchies of Slesvig and Holsten, first in the Three Years' War (1848–1850) and then in the War of 1864, when the Danish monarchy lost control of those duchies. Norwegian foreign political experiences were equally conducive to the rise of nationalism. In 1814, as a consequence of the Napoleonic Wars, Norway was forced to substitute its union with Denmark, which had lasted since 1380, for a new union with Sweden. Even though the practical terms of the new partnership were far more liberal for Norway, since Sweden did not meddle with Norway's internal affairs, whereas Denmark had imposed upon Norway a class of Danish-speaking state officials including the clergy, it became increasingly clear as the nineteenth century progressed just how sensitive Norwegians were, especially those belonging to the emerging liberal Left party (*Venstre*), to any political demands from Sweden. In 1892, a crisis between Norway and Sweden loomed when the Norwegian Parliament decided to establish an independent Norwegian consular service, a decision promptly vetoed by the Swedish-Norwegian king. By 1905, the relations between the two countries had deteriorated to the breaking point, and Norway left the union without bloodshed.[86] The union crisis also influenced the buildup of patriotism in Sweden, but since the strongest proponents of retaining the union were the conservatives, and since they were on the defensive, this nationalism tended to have a more conservative and subdued tenor.[87]

Third, within each Scandinavian country dramatically increasing grassroots activism contributed to enhanced feelings of national unity among many people. That activism had its roots in the same economic and demographic growth that was detaching masses of people from traditional life patterns in the countryside and propelling them to the cities and to the New World. The awakening of the masses began early in the nineteenth century, first of all with widespread, but sometimes regionally based, religious revivals, but popular activism soon branched out into other fields as well: the temperance and prohibition movements, especially powerful in Norway and Sweden; the cooperative movement, growing astonishingly in Denmark in the 1880s, but never matched by Norway or Sweden; and the labor movement.[88] Folk high schools in Denmark and Norway, finally, not only wallowed in national romanticism but also contributed to forming a vision of the peasant as the backbone of society, not at all unlike the myth of the American farmer.[89]

Participation in these movements taught many people valuable first lessons in democracy and added extra momentum to the mounting calls for democratic reform. In the 1860s and 1870s, due to age, income, and property requirements, only an estimated 52.4 percent of Danish males above the age of twenty could vote in parliamentary elections, and then only for the lower house, *Folketinget*, along with just 38.1 percent of their Norwegian and, after the introduction of a bicameral *Riksdag* in 1866, a bare 20.4 percent of their Swedish brethren. Women, of course, were denied suffrage.[90] Yet the fight for democratic reform, along with the growth of mass political parties in Denmark during the 1870s, in Norway in the early 1880s, and in Sweden in the late 1880s, involved steadily growing numbers of people in the national political conflicts. In Denmark this strife escalated dramatically when the nationalist-militarist Right party (*Højre*) under the leadership of J. B. S. Estrup established a semi-dictatorship lasting until 1901. At that point, cabinet responsibility triumphed and the liberal Left majority (*Venstre*) took over the reins of government.

During the middle decades of the nineteenth century even feelings of a common *Scandinavian* destiny sometimes surfaced. In the 1840s, a political "Scandinavianism" developed among students in the Scandinavian countries and even gained favor with the Danish and Swedish monarchs, actually leading to the mistaken impression that Sweden might aid Denmark against Prussia. Generally, however, it did not reach down into the broader layers of the population. After Denmark's defeat by Prussia in 1864, the concept was left in tatters.[91]

If many Scandinavians traveled to America with vague nationalist sentiments, the American environment catalyzed thinking in rough ethnic categories. Skauge might view himself first of all as a Børseskogning or perhaps a Trønder, yet to most Americans of non-Scandinavian origins he was at most a Norwegian American and often simply a *Scandinavian* American. Take the case of a Wisconsin politico reporting to Norwegian-American Andrew H. Dahl (1859–1928), a would-be Republican gubernatorial candidate: "I also went to see Alderman Eric Erickson. . . . He is a power in Racine among the laboring men, especially the Swedes & Danes. . . . He said 'Dahl is a Swede,' and I said 'You bet,' but I happened to think later maybe you were a 'Norsk.' They all look alike to me anyway."[92] When V. C. S. Topsøe, a Danish traveling writer and journalist, was granted an interview with President Grant around 1870, he noticed that the president, like so many other Americans, did not distinguish between the three Scandinavian nationalities.[93] Likewise, when Henrik Cavling, another Danish reporter, spoke with President Cleveland a quarter of a century later, the president made some polite remarks about the Scandinavians upon hearing that Cavling was Danish.[94]

With ascription thus sometimes compelling Scandinavian Americans to think in rough, "national" ethnic terms by force of the American surroundings, ethnic animosity sometimes had the same effect.[95] Marshall M. Strong, one of Wisconsin's founding fathers, hardly meant to be polite when around midcentury he implied that he would rather vote for an African American than a Norwegian American. In 1847, moreover, the Norwegian-Swedish consul general to America reported home that some Yankees spoke derogatorily of the ignorant "Norwegian Indians."[96] On the other hand, when half a century later a Norwegian-American pastor who had been invited to speak in Boston begged to differ when his host remarked that Scandinavians, Poles, and Italians were "undesirable immigrants," the surprised host exclaimed, "Why, Mr. Bergesen, I thought you were Norwegian."[97] As Pastor Bergesen commented with smug satisfaction, "He thought that . . . Scandinavians were a separate nation, something like the Poles."

As this little episode in fact illustrates, the amount of adversity suffered by Scandinavian Americans should not be exaggerated. The Scandinavian Americans, after all, had the good fortune of sharing their skin complexion, as well as their basic religious outlook (Protestant, hence non-Catholic, non-Jewish), with Yankee "Americans." Unlike the Irish, for example, they were typically identified with rural virtues rather than urban vices. In 1850, another consul general reported to the Swedish government that "in general, the Swedish immigrants, as well as the Norwegians, stand higher in the estimation of the Americans than several other nations."[98] Perhaps President Grant was not simply dealing in platitudes when he told the above-named Danish journalist that the Scandinavians figured among the best citizens of the Union.[99] At least prior to the outbreak of World War I, whenever the public atmosphere soured ethnically, the Scandinavian Americans found themselves placed in a relatively safe zone, not too far removed from that of the Yankees themselves.[100]

Actually, Scandinavian Americans might themselves display hostility toward other groups, particularly the Irish Catholics. Kristoffer Skauge, it is true, could only pity the poor, bedraggled Irish boarding the *Adriatic* at Queenstown. Another Scandinavian immigrant there was more hostile: "These foul, short-tempered Irish with their whisky and superstitions are a daily source of arguments. Nobody knows when open warfare will begin."[101] By the 1890s, the nativist, anti-Catholic American Protective Association boasted a Norwegian-American branch in Wisconsin.[102] "For the sake of God, our homes and our wonderful country," wrote one Norwegian-American supporter in 1894, "you must vote with us in the spring election in order to sweep the Roman power out of our city."[103] In the same vein, one Danish-American commentator decried the recent immigration of the "scum and dregs of the expanding population of the Catholic church" who now supposedly were threatening American democracy, and a Swedish-American censured Democratic President Cleveland for "protecting Catholic propaganda in this country with his fat fist."[104]

An 1891 editorial in the Norwegian-American *Skandinaven* of Chicago summed up the ethnic self-understanding of many Scandinavian Americans in concise terms: "We all tend to make a model of ourselves and to pass judgment over all those seemingly not created in our own image. From their own experience the Scandinavians in this country are well acquainted with this. You probably do not have to journey far to find a Norwegian who considers himself fully the equal of the Yankee, somewhat better than the German, and vastly superior to the Irishman. To compare him with a Pole, a Bohemian, or an Italian he would consider outrageous."[105] If the editorial was hardly liberal in its further suggestion that African Americans be deported to Africa, its author did diagnose precisely the way many Scandinavian Americans viewed themselves: as rather closely affiliated with the Yankees and people of British stock, not too far removed from the often Lutheran Germans, and vastly superior to everyone else.

Many Scandinavian immigrants traveling to America did carry with them certain ideas about national identity, yet the confrontation with the ethnically diverse New World environment was crucial. There, processes of ascription, and to a limited extent adversity, catalyzed thinking in rough, "national" ethnic terms. To the degree, however, that ascription and adversity might in fact be viewed as ethnically oppressive tagging devices, signaling the otherness of Scandinavian Americans in a Yankee-dominated America, many Scandinavian-American leaders would have flinched at the suggestion that their conceptions of identity were the outcome of ill-defined Old World memories in combination with powerful processes of ethnic labeling beyond their control. Surely, the kind of assertive ethnicity based on Old World national attachments that by 1890 had come into full flower among Norwegian Americans, Swedish Americans, and Danish Americans, was something much more positive and willed than this![106]

Did not the Scandinavian-American churches, split into myriad different denominations, reveal something about Scandinavian-American accomplishment in the New World? Or what about the many temperance and prohibition organizations, the mutual-aid associations, and the Scandinavian-American press, the second-largest foreign-language press in America, second only to the German-American press?[107] Did not their very existence project Scandinavian-American greatness? To erase any lingering doubts, such assertions were soon backed by books celebrating the feats of Norwegian Americans, Swedish Americans, Danish Americans, or simply Scandinavian Americans.[108] As Waldemar Ager (1869–1941), a nationalistically minded Norwegian-American prohibitionist, insisted in 1905, it was essential to *create* a Norwegian-American identity in the New World: "It is necessary for us to try to create something ourselves. An immigrant heritage which only exists in its ability to continue to nurture itself on Norwegian culture is unthinkable. . . . In some ways, we are more Norwegian here than they are in Norway."[109] In a similar vein, J. A. Enander (1842–1910), a prominent Swedish-American editor, proclaimed, "It is not the cause of Sweden but of Swedish America I am fighting for."[110]

By the 1890s, Scandinavian-American leaders were actively nurturing a fledgling, nationally focused ethnicity by staging Norwegian-American, Swedish-American, Danish-American, and occasionally even Scandinavian-American festivals, although by now the latter were declining. Come the Seventeenth of May, and Norwegian Americans in both rural and urban environments would be found celebrating the anniversary of their 1814 constitution.[111] In a similar spirit, Norwegian Americans organized a Leif Ericson day in commemoration of the Viking discovery of *Vinland* in the year 1000, a celebration that was pushed especially vigorously by Rasmus B. Anderson (1846–1936) of the University of Wisconsin, who in 1874 published *America Not Discovered by Columbus*.[112] Reports of Danish Americans celebrating the Danish Constitution Day (5 June) in both the countryside and the city were likewise heard.[113] The Swedish Americans, with weaker constitutional traditions, held various festivals honoring their forefathers, not least Gustavus II Adolph.[114]

The strength of this type of ethnicity with a "national" twist was indicated by the celebration at the 1893 World's Columbian Exposition in Chicago of May 17 as Norway's Day, June 5 as Denmark's Day, and July 20 as Sweden's Day.[115] Sometimes actual *Scandinavian*-American celebrations also took place. Outside the strictly political sphere, however, due first of all to rising immigrant numbers that enabled nationally defined communities to thrive, after about 1890 pan-Scandinavianism was waning, after its first bloom in the early years of settlement.[116] Still, some pan-Scandinavian celebrations persisted. Beginning in 1892, Det Nordvestlige Skandinaviske Sangerforbund (The Northwestern Scandinavian Singing League), an umbrella organization for many local singing associations, held regular festivals commemorating the rich Danish, Norwegian, and Swedish song heritage.[117] As late as 1911, some cranks were even toying with the idea of creating a new state, New Scandia, out of the northern parts of Minnesota and Wisconsin, as well as Michigan's northern peninsula.[118]

These various ethnic festivals paid homage to both the motherland and the adopted fatherland. Invariably, the participants would celebrate the old country along with the United States, singing the anthems and waving the flags of both nations. The Scandinavian and American parts were seen as simply matching each other, adding up to a complementary identity that ideally would help secure the Scandinavian Americans a legitimate place in the New World alongside other ethnic groups, with each group joining together in the mosaic called the American people. An editorial in the Norwegian-language *Amerika* gave voice to such thoughts: "Be a loyal citizen of the United States, be a true American, but do not forget that you can only be so when you are faithful to yourself and your Norwegian heritage. The term 'Norwegian-American' conveys the understanding that the Norwegian is only a true American when at the same time he is a true Norwegian."[119] Only during World War I, when particularly the German Americans were accused of dividing their loyalties between the Old World and the New, would this vision truly be challenged.

This celebration of identity based on national attachments took place in an environment crisscrossed by numerous ethnic counterpressures. On the one hand, integrative forces kept on growing, as the expanding and consolidating railroads, Wisconsin's third economic pillar besides the dairying and lumbering industries, reached ever deeper into every nook and cranny of the state after the Civil War, particularly during the 1880s and 1890s. In this manner the townships, villages, and cities were linked into a common market that spelled the doom of the isolated "island community." At the same time, modern American tools and utensils entered the ethnic household and workplace, sometimes challenging old cultural habits. Furthermore, the second generation of immigrants, usually mastering the English language to perfection, came to maturity.[120] On the other hand, ethnic diversity was maintained by the continuing influx of immigrants: the newcomers not only kept alive the language from the Old World but contributed to the picture of ethnic confusion and profusion by carrying with them ideas from their home country and visions of the New

World that might well conflict with those of the pioneers who had left Scandinavia decades earlier. How much besides national origins, for instance, did the Norwegian greenhorn of 1860 have in common with the newcomer of 1910, who, one observer insisted, had been brought up with socialism and nurtured with the Norwegian language question?[121] As early as 1894 one Norwegian immigrant suggested that the "Germans, Scandinavians, and Polanders, who have come in later, with all their virtues, brought along some customs and habits which had better have been left behind."[122] Similar observations were made among Swedish Americans.[123] Despite these cross-pressures and the generally tenuous nature of a nationalistically inspired ethnicity in the quintessentially "American" field of politics, appeals to national background would continue to be made time and again.

Chapter Two

Pastors and Politics

The Church and Old World National Attachments

In the late nineteenth century, the church was the most formidable ethnic institution in the Upper Midwest. From the early institutional beginnings in the 1840s and up through the remainder of the century, hundreds of Scandinavian-American churches representing a wide array of denominations sprouted all over the region, contributing their significant part to turning the landscape into a patchwork quilt of ethnicities. Besides offering the communicants spiritual guidance every Sunday, usually in the mother tongue, the Scandinavian-American church was the focus of a wide range of social activities, fulfilling many an immigrant's need for a sense of community.[1]

In Strum, Pastor Carl Johan Helsem headed the congregation of the St. Pauli church, preaching every Sunday and presiding over other social events, for instance the 1893 Christmas party where, as one observer noted, he spoke "stirringly." Helsem's daughter, moreover, graced the local choir with her "clear and pure voice – some day she will be famous for her beautiful song."[2] Helsem also led Strum's youth club, an organization that aimed "to awaken the young people to everything that is true, just, pure, pious, and praiseworthy, and to oppose sin and vice."[3] In many other congregations scattered across the Midwest a women's club was likewise attached to the church, arranging picnics or bazaars to raise funds for the church, often for the purchase of a new organ, altar, pulpit, church bell, or even a new church structure; sometimes the youth club also chipped in.[4] Strum's temperance society aimed to protect each and every member of the community, not only the young people, from the baneful rule of King Alcohol. In Strum, the temperance society and the church entertained cordial relations, with Pastor Helsem actively supporting temperance legislation.[5] Generally speaking, the relationship between church and temperance club varied across the Midwest. This seems usually to have depended upon the synodical affiliation and personal convictions of the pastor and the moral fervor of the "drys."

If its strongly ethnic character marked the immigrant church as essentially American, so did its relationship to secular power: in the United States, unlike Scandinavia, the church and the state were separate institutions. The Scandinavian-American church was a voluntary and basically democratic organization that the individual might or might not choose to support. This made for an aggressive, competitive spirit among the American religious denominations, more so than among their Scandinavian counterparts. Nineteenth-century Scandinavia, to be sure, experienced religious ferment on a hitherto unprecedented scale, as antirationalist revivalism swept across many areas, some of it homegrown, some imported from the Anglo-American world. Indeed, with the awakening of so many earnest, fervent souls, from the day laborer and up, to their individual religious responsibilities, many a state pastor now had to face the fact that the era when he had been able to view his parishioners, literally, as his flock of sheep was drawing to a close.

Yet the fact remained that whereas in the Scandinavian countries the established churches dominated religion, no such institution existed in America. In Denmark and Norway, the state churches succeeded in keeping many fervent souls within their structures simply by relaxing doctrinal requirements. In Denmark, liberal-minded Grundtvigians as well as stern, pietistic Inner Missionaries thus found room within the state church, and in Norway the church comprehended both lay-oriented, pietistic Haugeans and confessionalist Johnsonians, although in both countries some people were nevertheless lured away from Lutheranism altogether and joined Baptist, Methodist, or Mormon congregations. The Swedish picture was more complicated, for there, owing perhaps to the extraordinary conservatism of the state-church leadership, a large proportion of the population opted for the doctrinally radical free-church Swedish Mission

Covenant or for one of the Anglo-American groups like the Baptists or Methodists.[6]

In America, the situation was fundamentally different. With no state to underwrite the authority of the church, and with proselytizers from several Anglo-American sects ever ready to lure Scandinavian-American Lutherans away from the old path of piety, doctrinal controversy might rapidly result in denominational fissure. At the local level, religious controversy seemed sometimes simply to reflect the clash of Old World regional customs, as people originating in different landscapes settled close to each other in the New World, only to realize how dissimilar they really were.[7] On rarer occasions, the novel environment might even make adversaries of former neighbors, one North Dakota farmer reporting how his fellow settlers, many of them baptized by the same pastor back in Norway, had divided between two Norwegian-American denominations.[8]

More generally, in the religiously competitive environment of America, Danish- and particularly Norwegian-American Lutheranism experienced several agonizing schisms, the Danish-American Lutheran church thus splitting into its Grundtvigian and Inner-Mission components in 1894, and Norwegian-American Lutheranism witnessing the creation of no less than fourteen separate synods down through the nineteenth and early twentieth centuries, even though by 1900 two branches clearly predominated numerically, the old doctrinally rigorous Norwegian Synod and the more recent middle-of-the-road creation, the United Church.[9] Swedish-American Lutheranism was spared much, if not all, of this turmoil, with the Augustana Synod clearly dominating the stage, arguably because much of the religious fighting had already taken place in Sweden.

If the primary ethnic strength of the Scandinavian-American church lay in fostering among the immigrants and their children a sense of community, and oftentimes also a feeling of continuity with some specific locality in the Old World, what part, if any, did the church play in nurturing pride in Old World national attachments? A cursory glance at the names of the major Scandinavian-American denominations suggests, of course, that the churches did focus on the national heritage, at least at a superficial level (fig. 2.1, Appendix I). Interestingly, whereas the smallest churches usually carried Scandinavian names, the somewhat larger ones tended to divide into their Swedish and Norwegian-Danish counterparts, and the very largest were defined along purely Old World national lines. Yet even some of the latter had only attained "national" independence after going through a phase of "international" cooperation necessitated by small numbers. Thus, between 1857 and 1883 the Norwegian Synod worked together with the German Missouri Synod, and from the Synod of Illinois, which originally contained Norwegian, Swedish, German, and Yankee elements, there emerged in 1860 the pan-Scandinavian-American Augustana Synod, which ten years later split into its Norwegian-Danish and Swedish counterparts. Prior to the latter event, T. N. Hasselquist (1816–1891), the Synod's Swedish-born president, had begun complaining about the intense nationalism of his Norwegian-American brethren. Conversely, six Norwegian-American congregations asking permission to remain within the Synod were turned down by their Swedish-American co-religionists.[10]

The fact that especially the Danish- and Norwegian-American denominations did not crystallize into truly "national" institutions, but splintered into smaller denominations using nationally inclusive names, might have indicated that no real effort was made to forge that sort of ethnic unity. Yet especially Norwegian Americans did often lament their lack of "national" cohesion. In practice, compromises were sometimes worked out. When, in the spring of 1897, bad weather prevented a funeral procession from reaching the church of the Norwegian Synod at Thor, Iowa, mourners were thus permitted to use the nearby edifice of the United Norwegian Church instead.[11] At Heron Lake in Jackson County, Minnesota, the congregations of Hauge's Synod and the United Norwegian Church actually shared the same church building.[12] Farther out west, in sparsely populated Idaho, members of the Norwegian Synod, Hauge's Synod, and the United Norwegian Church congregations reunited in a Lutheran free church congregation. It may have been that here the small number of communicants did not permit too much theological controversy.[13] More important, the United Norwegian Church, which was created in 1890 by the fusion of three church organizations, did on several occasions negotiate with its chief Norwegian-American rivals in an effort to foster that unity which finally came about in 1917, when the United Church merged with Hauge's Synod and the Norwegian Synod.[14] Attempts, on the other hand, to reunite the Grundtvigian Danish Church and the Inner-Mission United Danish Church foundered.[15]

Along with aspirations to national representation, some of the Scandinavian-American denominations that emulated most closely the state churches in the Old World, and aspired most strongly to national leadership in the New, early endeavored to cooperate with the state churches in Scandinavia in an effort to import much-needed, university-trained pastors. The Danish state church demonstrated by far the greatest willingness to help her independent daughter in America, the Danish Evangelical Lutheran Church and, as the membership figures clearly indicate, the latter was sorely in need of support. Prominent leaders within the Danish state church thus created a select committee, dominated by Grundtvigians, to promote Lutheranism among Danish Americans, and in 1872 initiated a special program for the education of America-bound pastors at the folk high school in Askov, a center of Danish nationalism.[16] Between 1872 and 1890, the committee dispatched thirty-seven pastors trained in Denmark, including six educated at the University of Copenhagen, an impressive figure when considering that until 1890 the Danish Church in America was represented by only fifty-seven pastors.[17] Relatively speaking, the Norwegian state church was more stingy: although by 1890 the Norwegian Synod included 694 pastors in its ranks, during the first half-century of Norwegian-American Lutheranism only some sixty-odd pastors journeyed from Norway to America.[18] The Swedish state church was more indifferent and at times perhaps even hostile to the spiritual needs of the emigrants.[19] Up to 1890, only eight Swedish-educated pastors ventured to the United States, not many when considering that by then 291 Swedish-American Lutheran pastors worked in America.[20] After 1890, however, the relationship between the Augustana Synod and the Swedish state church gradually improved.[21]

Another "national" aspect of the Scandinavian churches concerned their function as preservers of the Old World languages. Generally, the switch from a Scandinavian language to English progressed slowly in the Scandinavian-American churches, and American words rarely made their way into the Scandinavian-American religious vocabulary.[22] The speed of transition varied, however, from denomination to denomination, with nationalistically minded high-church elements generally caring more about language preservation than low-church pietists who at least in theory, but not always in practice, placed all the emphasis on pure faith.[23]

Moreover, whereas in Scandinavia the language of the pastor served frequently to create a certain distance between himself and his congregation because he preached in a tongue often quite different from the local vernacular (especially in Norway where the official Dano-Norwegian language was standard in the pulpit), in America that same circumstance could be turned into an advantage, enabling pastors to speak to regionally heterogeneous parishioners, or even to "international" Danish-Norwegian congregations. Several Danish-American pastors, for example, worked within Norwegian-American churches.[24] Numerous Norwegian-American leaders expressed worry at the mounting strength of the movement back in Norway to substitute the *Landsmål* dialect for the old, official Dano-Norwegian language.[25]

The important "national" function served by the Scandinavian immigrant churches is also suggested by the central role that pastors typically played whenever a celebration of the old country occurred. In Strum, Gjermund Hoyme (1847–1902), president of the United Norwegian Church, was invited to speak on the Seventeenth of May 1897, and at the celebration of Leif Ericson Day in Minneapolis in 1891, Pastor Melchior Falk Gjertsen (1847–1913), who had published a volume of songs from the homeland (*Hjemlandssange*), spoke proudly about the enormous triumphs that Scandinavians in general and Norwegians in particular were celebrating across the Midwest. The Norwegians, he was sure, were now in the process of outdistancing the Yankees.[26]

PASTORS ENTER THE POLITICAL FRAY

If the Scandinavian-American churches were strongly ethnic institutions with the potential, at least, for nurturing feelings of "national" pride, did they also play a role in politics? At grassroots level, the immigrant church, like the revivals and the budding associational life in Scandinavia, functioned to some extent as a school for democracy. For religious activities to take place locally, some kind of organization had to be effected to deal with the everyday problems of maintaining a church, and since the state remained uninvolved, members of the local congregation were obliged to act. Since the immigrant church was invariably the most important local social institution, networks of individuals belonging to the same congregation might conceivably also cooperate with each other in temporal matters, say, in politics.

Undoubtedly the pastor normally functioned as the local church authority, yet the Scandinavian-American balance struck between authority and freedom differed markedly from that of the Scandinavian countries.[27] Despite religious ferment in nineteenth-century Scandinavia, the state-church pastor there hardly confronted conditions as harsh as those that greeted some of his Scandinavian-American colleagues: immigrants bristling at the mere sight of clerical garb or other supposed symbols of the state church or a drunkard invading the premises of a pastor, reasoning that he had contributed to building the home. One notorious boozer was acquitted in court after disrupting a Sunday service. The defense argued that the Norwegian-American pastor, the parishioners, and in fact the Lutheran church constituted "a menace to our blessed freedom!"[28]

In no instance was a Scandinavian-American pastor actually compelled to fire a gun from his altar at an angry congregation or to seek police protection, as sometimes happened with his Polish Catholic clerical counterparts, if we are to believe the gleeful reports in the Scandinavian-American press.[29] Usually the disturbances that the Scandinavian-American pastor had to put up with during the Sunday service were more innocent: "conversation, laughter, stolen glances at other people's Sunday dress, and maybe also a little nap."[30]

Many pastors retained positions of natural local authority. One function of the schisms so common among Norwegian-American Lutherans, especially, was to create a better fit between the pastor and his communicants. Praise of the local minister was a recurrent feature in reader letters to *Skandinaven*, and reports of quintessentially American "surprise parties" appeared frequently.[31] Those were grand affairs in the lives of the pastor and his family, as well as of the congregation, exhibiting first of all a mutual warmth of feeling, yet also hinting subtly at the material dependence of the former on the latter.[32] The parties varied in size and splendor. On New Year's Day of 1896, the congregation at Wiota, Lafayette County, Wisconsin, surprised their pastor with a nice celebration, donating him money for new clerical garb.[33] More grandeur attached to a celebration in Fillmore County, Minnesota, when three congregations surprised the pastor and his wife on their fifteenth wedding anniversary. Some three or four hundred people turned up at the parsonage, presenting the couple with a buggy, six chairs, new carpets, new curtains, an escritoire, a rocking chair, plates, cloth, and bed linen; but then this minister had also fought Methodism successfully and kept the Norwegian Synod intact.[34] The exact price of the gift was often reported to the public. A Swedish-American minister in Marinette, Wisconsin, was given a clock worth thirty dollars, whereas his Norwegian-American colleague at Baldwin, St. Croix County, Wisconsin, received presents adding up to nearly one hundred dollars.[35]

While pastoral authority differed in Scandinavia and in America, most ministers retained leadership in day-to-day spiritual matters. Symptomatically, at the annual meetings of the Scandinavian-American ecclesiastical organizations, the lay delegates tended to remain silent.[36] The pastor, in fact, usually remained in control of his church and as a functionary called by his congregation he was often both well liked and respected. Whereas it is a well-known fact that Scandinavian male immigrants in America generally abandoned the Old World habit of doffing their hat when meeting prominent citizens in the street, at least most Swedish-American Lutherans kept up that custom whenever they came across their minister.[37] The Norwegian-American Peer O. Strømme summed up the position of the Scandinavian-American pastor in the United States: "The admiration with which so many of our people view their pastor *in spite of everything* is touching."[38]

Was the Scandinavian-American minister also influential in worldly matters, or, to be more specific, in politics?[39] The question is not easy to answer, because with the separation of church and state, for a minister to get too mixed up with temporal matters was not considered altogether proper and hence not something to be discussed openly. Lutheran pastors generally prided themselves on their ability to keep secular and religious matters apart—as opposed to the Catholics. One prominent Norwegian-American theologian, in fact, dismissed intimations to the contrary with incredulity: "Just the other day I was talking with a more than ordinarily well-informed American who fully believed that we Lutherans, as Lutherans, strive for political power, just like the Catholics."[40]

Not that Lutheran ministers never got openly involved in politics. Danish-born Claus Lauritz Clausen (1820–1892), from 1843 until his death in 1892 a pioneering clergyman among Norwegian Americans, was not only the founding editor of the Democratic *Emigranten*, but in 1856–1857 he also served as a member of the Iowa legislature.[41] In 1894, moreover, Pastor O. V. Holmgrain, a Swedish American, ran for the county treasurership in Ford County, Illinois. One of his supporters took pains to assure the voters that the minister would keep church and political matters strictly apart.[42] Generally speaking, however, pastors only rarely stepped directly into politics.[43] Tufve Nilsson Hasselquist, the towering figure within the Swedish Augustana Synod from 1860 on, learned early the risks of getting involved in politics. Even though in the words of one scholar the typical Augustana pastor was "ultra-conservative" and "an old-line Republican," in October 1890 Hasselquist and his colleague C. O. Olander came out openly for B. T. Cable, a *Democrat* running for Congress, because Cable and his father had donated money to Augustana College.[44] In the ensuing debate in the columns of the Republican *Hemlandet*, Hasselquist and Olander were accused of being politically corrupt and a disgrace to the Swedish Americans, with one commentator further querying, "Is it possible that our ministers are the Judas of our times?"[45] Most Scandinavian-American clergymen were more cautious. "This is about politics," wrote a Lutheran pastor to Norwegian-born Governor James O. Davidson of Wisconsin in 1908, "so I am writing you in Norwegian."[46]

Several Scandinavian-American synods attempted to solve the dilemma of aspiring to both religious purity and worldly ethnic leadership by supporting two papers, a purely religious one and a more secular one. Thus, in 1851, C. L. Clausen, A. C. Preus (1814–1878), and H. A. Stub (1822–1907) began publishing the religious *Maanedstidende for den norsk-evangelisk-lutherske Kirke i Amerika*, and, as noted, less than a year later Clausen became editor of the secular *Emigranten*.[47] In similar fashion, from 1851 the Norwegian Synod sponsored the churchly *Kirketidende* and in 1884 was involved in setting up the secular *Amerika*. From 1856 the Swedish Augustana Synod put out the synodical *Rätta Hemlandet*, in 1874 consolidated into *Augustana*, just one year after Hasselquist founded the Republican *Hemlandet*. The Danish Church was responsible both for the publication of the religious *Kirkelig Samler* (1872) and of the secular *Dannevirke* (1880), whereas the United Danish Church was involved both in printing the churchly *Dansk Luthersk Kirkeblad* (1877) and the more secular *Danskeren* (1892).[48] In 1891, on the other hand, the United Norwegian Church began publishing *Luthersk Kirkeblad*, in 1895 consolidated into *Lutheraneren*, but no secular paper. Likewise, the smaller Hauge's Synod and the Norwegian Free Church only published religious journals.[49]

Not many sources illuminate the role played by Scandinavian-American pastors in day-to-day politics, yet by piecing together the fragmentary evidence from Wisconsin for the whole period 1890–1914, a picture emerges of several Scandinavian-American Lutheran pastors becoming deeply involved in the political fray. In the primary campaign of 1914, Andrew H. Dahl, a prominent second-generation Norwegian-American Republican from Westby, Vernon County, who aspired to the governorship, received letters from three Norwegian-American pastors. "I have a large congregation here at Washburn and also preach to the people in different sections of the country," wrote one minister, "and I shall consider it my duty to speak a grand word for you, – a duty and a pleasure."[50] More craftily political in tone was a Norwegian-American Lutheran minister from Edgerton in Rock County who only offered help "with due allowance for changes of opinion which unforeseen events may force upon me."[51] A third minister, finally, assured Dahl, "I come in contact with many people, the whole field between Waupun and Fond du Lac including the smaller villages. And my word counts among our friends and neighbors."[52] Probably none of these three ministers intended to campaign for Dahl from the pulpit. More likely, they simply planned to use their prominent social position within their congregations to boost him. In 1906, one politico thus informed Norwegian-born James O. Davidson that he could expect help from the Lutheran clergy, but "that their efforts in your behalf will be of a strictly non-parochial nature – that is, they will simply exercise their rights as ordinary citizens."[53]

The three letters addressed to Dahl within eight days in 1914 suggest that the latter was making a conscious effort to enlist Norwegian-American Lutheran pastors in his cause. So did Nils P. Haugen, another would-be Norwegian-American Republican governor, when in 1894 he solicited Gjermund Hoyme, head of the United Norwegian Church, to sway Norwegian-American Hans B. Warner (1844–1896) to withdraw from the gubernatorial race.[54] Apparently Hoyme did not answer Haugen in writing, and Warner did in fact run for the governorship. As one Haugen supporter suggested, "it will be hard for him [Hoyme] to do anything for you while he is working for the Lord."[55] Overall, Haugen's strength among the Norwegian-American clergy appears to have been weak at best. One friend reported that he had done legwork for Haugen at the annual meeting of the United Norwegian Church in St. Paul, Minnesota, yet the list of supporters that he mailed Haugen contained only eleven names, with just one person recorded as a minister.[56]

Norwegian-born James O. Davidson pursued a more aggressive "Lutheran" strategy when in 1906 he ran successfully for the Republican nomination for governor. Sigurd Gryttenholm, himself a Norwegian-American politico, informed Davidson that Pastors R. Anderson of La Crosse and O. Gulbrandsen of Westby were offering their help: "With these two gentlemen I entered into a partnership for the purpose of enlisting every minister of the 'United Church' in Wisconsin in the service. They have promised to write each to those of their colleagues with whom they are best acquainted, to do what they can in their respective congregations. In this way a complete list of all the members of such church in Wisconsin can be obtained. But before this is started I wish to have a conference with you, as I want to direct the move personally so as not to break the unwritten law that the clergy should not take part in politics."[57]

Welcoming the clergy's support, Davidson noted approvingly, "I realize that they can do very much for my cause, if they enter into it in a judicious way. I know they are very influential with their congregations."[58] The exchange between Gryttenholm and Davidson not only illustrates the tightrope that Lutheran pastors had to walk when entering the political fray but also suggests that networks of pastors had to be won over denomination by denomination, for, as Gryttenholm further stated, "When you remember that one of your strongest opponents is an influential member of the other faction of the Norwegian church, you will understand the importance of having this work done in a way that will not encourage the enmity of his religious confreres."

Political efforts of this nature were not limited to politicians and ministers of Scandinavian origins. Sometimes Yankee politicians also attempted consciously to forge good relations with ministers of some particular ethnoreligious background. E. C. Wall, the chairman of the Wisconsin Democratic state central committee, played that game cunningly. In 1890, Wisconsin was shaken to its political foundations by the

Bennett Law controversy. One year earlier, a Republican-dominated state legislature had passed a law that sought to extend a measure of state control over private and parochial schools by stipulating that their pupils be instructed in the English language in the fields of reading, writing, arithmetic, and American history for a minimum of twelve weeks a year. The law, which was introduced by Michael Bennett, himself a Catholic, hardly caused a stir at its passage, but months later brought down upon the Republican Party the wrath of a rarely united German Lutheran and German Catholic clergy, and also caused some controversy among Scandinavian Americans. Since the latter, unlike the German Americans, did not boast a very strongly developed system of parochial schools, their anger remained within narrower bounds.[59]

In his successful efforts to make the Bennett Law the central issue of the state campaign of 1890, Wall deviously exploited the anger of the German-American clergy. As he later explained: "It is important for political success to overcome prejudice with prejudice."[60] Wall not only launched a campaign to enroll the German Lutheran clergy of the state under the Democratic banner, but he even succeeded in winning over the leadership of the Norwegian Synod: "There are two factions amongst the Norwegians that have bitter enmity one towards the other. Bishop Preus [president of the Norwegian Synod] is beloved and adored by those of his synod and he and all his followers are abhorred by the other synod. It was amongst the followers of Bishop Preus that we made the break; he advised them openly to espouse the Democratic cause."[61]

There was substance to Wall's assertion, for whereas during its annual meeting the high-church Norwegian Synod passed a resolution censuring the Bennett Law, Gjermund Hoyme, the president of the middle-of-the-road United Norwegian Church, made speeches in favor of the measure.[62] The attitude of the Norwegian-American low-church elements towards the law is unclear, yet the Norwegian-American paper *Skandinaven* of Chicago, which originally identified with low-church attitudes, came out strongly in favor of the Bennett Law, as did the Prohibition paper *Reform*.[63] Among Danish Americans apparently a rather similar split occurred: Frederik Lange Grundtvig, the relatively high-church Grundtvigian leader, openly condemned the Bennett Law, whereas P. S. Vig, a prominent representative of the more pietistic Inner Mission, at one point prior to 1890 stated, "To keep the children born in this country from coming into contact with its language and life is a violation of nature that will take its revenge in the long run."[64] Finally, the Swedish Augustana Synod, like its Norwegian- and Danish-American high-church counterparts, came out in opposition to the law, while the position of Swedish-American low-church elements remains unclear.[65]

Interesting as these splits along denominational lines are, they do not always reflect a corresponding general division in political values at the elite level between culturally defensive, ritualistically oriented high-church elements and aggressively reformist, pietistically inclined low-church elements.[66] The Bennett Law campaign of 1890 definitely agrees with a ritualist-pietist logic, since high-church synods went on a determined cultural defensive, notwithstanding that *Amerika,* the paper closely affiliated with the Norwegian Synod, actually *defended* the Bennett Law, and that President Preus had to countenance his sharp anti-Bennett Law resolution being tabled by the Synod in favor of a milder one.[67]

In the gubernatorial campaigns of 1894 and 1906, however, the combinations between Scandinavian-American clergy and politicians were arguably of a more pragmatic character. They imply the existence of personal alliances between a handful of politicians and a network of pastors. Some ministers definitely weighed personal connections above denominational loyalties. "When you need *me, command me* at any time," wrote a Methodist minister to Davidson in 1907. "Don't for a moment think that I am a friend of McGillivray. He is a member of my church, but that *don't count. I have private means.* I have stood by *you.*"[68] Davidson himself, incidentally, had a special inclination for visiting churches during political campaigns, irrespective of denomination. "I have found that 'Yim' Davidson has a strong leaning to church sociables," wrote one observer, "as a means of promoting his candidacy as I have several times noticed him at social gatherings of the Episcopal Church in company with Houser, Frear and other politicians, and I have an idea he likes them better than county fairs."[69]

In fact, had the Lutheran pastors supported Scandinavian-American politicians for purely denominational reasons, they could hardly have found a less supportive lot to back. In their personal attitudes, a striking proportion of Scandinavian-American politicians were less than enthusiastic about Scandinavian-American Lutheranism. Knute Nelson

(1843–1923) of Minnesota, America's first Scandinavian-born governor and U.S. senator, apparently despised the Norwegian-American Lutheran clergy, both for humiliations he suffered during his Wisconsin childhood, and because he believed the clergy were lukewarm in their attitude towards the Civil War. In his youth, Nelson began attending meetings of Norwegian Methodists, and when in 1868 he married Nicholina Jacobson, a justice of the peace administered the ceremony.[70] John Lind (1854–1930), likewise of Minnesota, the first Swedish-American governor, was also estranged from Swedish-American Lutheranism. Lind's parents were originally Lutherans but became Baptists as a result of the cruel behavior of a pastor upon the death of their unchristened baby. John Lind himself never affiliated with any church and actually had to fight public charges of being an atheist.[71]

Likewise, several of Wisconsin's leading Scandinavian-American politicians had a lax attitude towards the Lutheran church. Congressman Nils P. Haugen, Wisconsin's most prominent Scandinavian-American politician in the 1890s, supported his own congregation of the Norwegian Synod with small money donations now and then, and back in River Falls, Pierce County, Belle Haugen sometimes reported to her husband in Washington, D.C., about Pastor Blomholm's sermons.[72] Yet it was Congressman Haugen who in 1894 attempted to enlist Chairman Hoyme of the rival United Norwegian Church in his cause, and Belle Haugen actually flirted with Methodism: "Today as I said I went to the Methodist church and heard Bradford. I must say it was a treat in every sense of the word. . . . I could not but help think to myself, you certainly will not hear such a sermon this afternoon from Blomholm."[73] Even though Congressman Haugen revealed no Catholic inclinations, as a vote-grabbing politician he did not mind receiving the local support even of the *Catholic Sentinel* of Chippewa Falls: "You may think it a queer combination, but it is even thus," he wrote a friend.[74]

From a Lutheran point of view, matters were generally worse with James O. Davidson, Wisconsin's first Norwegian-American governor. In 1906, Davidson confessed to having broken his connection with the local Norwegian Lutheran congregation in Soldiers Grove, Crawford County.[75] Only to a Methodist minister and potential supporter did he reveal the full truth, however: "Myself and family affiliate with the Methodist church, although I was brought up and confirmed a Lutheran." Davidson added that maybe for ministers to interfere in politics was improper, yet "of all men, ministers should be interested in good government."[76]

During the campaign of 1906, James O. Davidson's most formidable Norwegian-American adversary was Herman Lewis Ekern (1872–1954), who backed Swedish-American Irvine L. Lenroot, La Follette's candidate for the governorship. Even though Ekern was brought up in a family that affiliated with the United Norwegian Church, he married a Norwegian-American Methodist, much to the chagrin of his mother: "Oh, Herman, dare I once again refer to the wound and the perpetual pain that continually afflicts me, for as long as Lily refuses to stand by all that she has learned in her childhood, as long as she will not let herself be baptized, she is nothing in my eyes."[77] Incidentally, Hans A. Anderson (1855–1939), Ekern's Methodist father-in-law, was elected district attorney of heavily Norwegian-American Trempealeau County with the help, as he himself recalled, of his countrymen, notwithstanding that he was viewed by them as "a reputed heretic and a possible infidel."[78] Even Ole A. Buslett (1855–1924), a religiously undogmatic and nationalistically inspired Norwegian-American poet from Northland in Waupaca County, was elected to the Wisconsin Assembly in 1908: "Now you need no longer be ashamed of your old, minister-like 'Free Thinker,'" Buslett wrote his wife. "Yesterday I had to promise Pastor Siljan to speak soon in the Men's Association, and every single minister in the Madison district has either visited me at my desk or sent me his greetings. . . . This is also funny – think of it, yes, who would have imagined that the ministers would be the 'people' who should agree *with* me."[79] Of those fifty-six seats in Wisconsin's one-hundred-man lower legislative chamber occupied by Scandinavian Americans with an identifiable religious affiliation between 1891 and 1914, eleven (19.6 percent) were taken by non-Lutherans, all Republicans (see Appendix II).

Patronage matters, the stuff of nineteenth-century practical politics, also sometimes attached to the wheelings and dealings of pastors and politicians. Often strictly local matters were involved. Thus, in August 1900, Pastor Carl Johan Helsem, the man who had buried Kristoffer Skauge four years earlier, petitioned Nils P. Haugen for help in the matter of a pension for a Strum inhabitant.[80] Was Helsem asking Haugen to return a little favor? In any case, in May Haugen had recommended Helsem as a possible campaign worker in the upcoming struggle to get Robert La Follette elected governor of Wisconsin.[81] Moreover, the abovementioned Methodist minister who had assured Governor Davidson of his support regardless of Davidson's religious views (obviously not realizing that Davidson was in fact a Methodist), asked the governor to write him a letter of recommendation, since "I am looking for a better appointment in my chosen field."[82] Finally, one German-American and two Swedish-American ministers, each involved in church-building ventures, intimated to Davidson that they would support him if he donated money for their churches.[83]

Occasionally ministers expected larger plums than help in local matters, but only rarely did their political strength match their ambitions. When in 1893 U.S. Senator William F. Vilas appointed Professor L. S. Reque of Luther College consul general at Rotterdam, he did so, it is true, only after H. A. Preus (1825–1894), president of the Norwegian Synod, had recommended him for the position, yet apparently the senator was favorably disposed towards Reque beforehand, referring to him in a couple of letters as a political asset.[84] Generally speaking, however, the influence of Lutheran pastors was limited. When one local West Denmark politico asked Nils P. Haugen about his chances of winning the position as U.S. minister to Denmark, Haugen answered, "You might with a lively hustle get it, but I think the chances 100 to 1 against it. The Lutheran ministers of northwestern Wisconsin combined would not tip the scales if there were one little politician on the other end."[85]

Some Scandinavian-American clergymen thus got deeply involved in politics, but their influence on elections, while generally sustaining a culture of Republicanism, was limited. One study of Norwegian-American voting behavior concludes that the circumstance of belonging to different Norwegian-American denominations had no measurable impact on election returns.[86] Among Swedish Americans, of course, the effects of political schisms along denominational lines were limited, since the Augustana Synod played so dominant a role. The case of the Danish Americans was more complex. They appear never to have united wholeheartedly behind the Republican Party and a possible political split between Grundtvigians and Inner Missionaries seems only to have occurred at a very late point in time in some of the (very few) Danish-American enclaves, around the outbreak of World War I.[87] In 1896, a frustrated E. C. Wall, whose Democratic Party had recently suffered a crushing defeat, acknowledged the limits of clerical support: "During the recent campaign there were a number of Lutheran clergymen who were quietly in correspondence with me, advising and aiding to the best of their ability in this campaign as friends of mine. It was not the Lutheran clergymen we lost; it was the rank and file that we lost in 1892 and 1894."[88] The grass roots did not always act as pastors and politicians expected.

This is not to suggest that especially various Norwegian and Swedish Lutheran denominations did not play an important role in fostering a moral atmosphere among their congregations that favored the Republican Party, nor that several Lutheran pastors did not become deeply involved in the temperance question. Yet when Scandinavian-American politicians cooperated with Scandinavian-American ministers, this did not necessarily happen on strictly denominational terms. Sometimes a network of pastors, working within a "national" framework, jumped onto the bandwagon of a politician more for partisan reasons than because of theological considerations. Of course, as far as the politician was concerned, any additional vote regardless of its religious baggage was welcome. Ministers must have reasoned that favors might some day be returned, either personally or to their congregations. In their practical support of specific Scandinavian-American politicians, these men of the cloth by 1890 had abandoned pan-Scandinavianism and begun to nurture a form of nationally inspired ethnicity not based narrowly on theology.

CHAPTER THREE

Secular Societies

ASSOCIATIONAL LIFE IN SCANDINAVIA AND AMERICA

"Our town of Grantsburg looks like the traditional railroad station," reported a correspondent from Burnett County, Wisconsin, to *Skandinaven* in 1892. "It has four grocery stores, one iron store, two blacksmith shops, two hotels, five churches, two livery stables, two saloons and attorney's offices. Besides that we have two secret societies. And you want to know whether we have religion. Yes, we have plenty of it; there is everything here that you could name, right from the United Church to the most extreme 'dists' and 'tists'; Catholics, Norwegians, and Swedes and everything else."[1] Three years later, another correspondent described social life in Hayward, Sawyer County: "We have a large multitude of associations. I shall first mention the religious: Congregationalists, Scandinavian Lutherans with Pastor Nord from Rice Lake as minister, Episcopalians, and Swedish Methodists. Then we have three or four women's associations, among which the Lutheran Women's Association takes first place. Two Goodtemplar lodges, one Scandinavian Knights of Pythias, G.A.R., S. of V., and the Independent Scandinavian Workingmen's Association, and many others."[2] Similar reports came out of Strum where Kristoffer Skauge had settled in the early 1890s. In addition to the Lutheran congregation, a temperance society, and two youth clubs, by 1899 Strum also boasted a local chapter of Klippen (the Rock), the Independent Scandinavian Workingmen's Association.[3]

While information of this type reaffirms the centrality of the church to the everyday lives of many Scandinavian Americans, it nevertheless suggests that by the 1890s other social institutions were also available.[4] By then a host of secular societies, frequently organized along ethnic lines, sprouted all over the Midwest. These included debating clubs, literary societies, choirs and orchestras, sporting associations, mutual-aid fraternities, and a throng of temperance and prohibition organizations. As with the churches, typically the earliest of the Scandinavian-American secular associations made broad pan-Scandinavian-American appeals, only later diversifying along Old World nationality lines. After the turn of the century, various Norwegian-American and Swedish-American societies cropped up that based their existence wholly on *regional* roots.[5] Even though some of these organizations dated back to the 1850s, the take-off phase occurred in the 1880s and 1890s. By the end of the latter decade, Scandinavian-American secular societies could be counted by the hundreds. In one 1898 estimate, Swedish-American secular organizations alone amounted to more than one thousand.[6] No doubt the range of associational possibilities was most diverse in those metropolitan areas with large concentrations of Scandinavian Americans, yet such societies also budded in a number of towns and rural hamlets.

Scandinavian-American societies of all sorts triggered political activism. In 1890, the Students' Quartet of Augsburg Seminary campaigned for temperance reform among Norwegian Americans, and in 1906, the Norwegian-dominated National Skiing Association aided Norwegian-born James O. Davidson in his successful bid for the Wisconsin governorship.[7] By their sheer size and strength, however, two types of organizations stand out and command special attention: the mutual-aid associations, which combined a variety of social functions with the provision of basic insurance, and the temperance societies.

Organizations of these types were not necessarily foreign to Scandinavians migrating to the United States in the second half of the nineteenth century, for in those years each of the Scandinavian countries witnessed the flowering of a welter of secular activities. If the revivals paved the way, they later simply constituted one part of a wide range of popular movements that in their totality signified a break with the form of society typified by absolutism and the state church.[8] Denmark, Norway, and Sweden thus saw the growth of various kinds of mutual-aid associations, typically relating to illness and fire insurance and sometimes dovetailing with the emergence of cooperative ventures, and each country became a battle-ground for fights over temperance. Anglo-American organizations as well as home-grown associations scored major successes, especially in Norway and Sweden.[9] America simply set a new stage for movements that were already under way in Scandinavia, even if the temperance crusade had originated in the New World. The novel setting had significant effects. In the Scandinavian countries, one social function of the movements was to align people in an increasingly individualized world with a new sense of belonging in the face of the dissolution of old, community-based hierarchical loyalties. There emerged in time new, horizontal, geographically sweeping attachments, as new nationwide classes began to emerge out of the old local communities.[10] In the Midwest, in many respects a more egalitarian, democratic setting, the multicultural environment gave a special ethnic and national twist to this urge for community, and that, in turn, had political repercussions.

MUTUAL-AID SOCIETIES: THE INDEPENDENT SCANDINAVIAN WORKINGMEN'S ASSOCIATION

The mutual-aid society was a popular institution in the turn-of-the-century Midwest. First, by combining a bold financial strategy of keeping reserves low with a plan of attracting young, hence generally healthy, settlers, it offered lower assessment rates than the traditional stock insurance company. Second, it provided its members with an array of social activities. In 1911, no fewer than 256,718 fraternal membership certificates, amounting to an aggregate value of more than 322,000,000 dollars, were reportedly held in Wisconsin.[11] Most of the fraternities had headquarters outside Wisconsin, but according to one 1906 report at least seventeen originated in the state, ranging in size from 500 to nearly 15,000 members. Several of the associations were organized along ethnic lines, including the Bohemian Roman Catholic Union, the German-American Order of Hermann's Sons, and the Polish Association of America, all centered in Milwaukee. Another such body was the Independent Scandinavian Workingmen's Association (ISWA), which had its head office in Eau Claire.[12] Most of these fraternities were all-male in membership, but after the turn of the century some female orders appeared, including the Scandinavian Sisters, literally the ISWA's sister organization.[13]

At a national level, several Scandinavian-American mutual-aid associations were larger than the ISWA, which by 1912 claimed 4,826 members in ninety-six lodges (sixty in Wisconsin). Two years earlier, the Sons of Norway, founded in Minneapolis in 1895, boasted 8,000 members and about 100 lodges, but mostly to the west of Wisconsin.[14] As early as 1907 the Danish Brotherhood claimed 17,173 members in 255 lodges nationwide. This made it larger than the two most important Norwegian-American mutual-aid associations combined. In Wisconsin, however, the official membership of the Danish Brotherhood in 1907 stood at only 1,574 (fifteen lodges).[15] The national membership figures of the largest Swedish-American insurance fraternities were equally impressive. By 1910, the Independent Order of Svithiod counted 7,642 members, and four years later the Vasa Order of America boasted fully 35,374 members. In view of overall Swedish-American settlement patterns, probably only few of these members lived in Wisconsin.[16]

By the first decade of the twentieth century the ISWA clearly figured as Wisconsin's largest Scandinavian-American insurance fraternity, even though the Danish Brotherhood also made its presence felt, especially in Racine.[17] When *Superior Tidende* editor Henry P. Peterson was elected as secretary of a newly formed lodge in Superior, his weekly functioned for a short while (1898–1901) as the ISWA's official mouthpiece.[18] In 1900, however, the circulation of the paper amounted to just 2,700.[19]

The ISWA was established in early 1893 when the Eau Claire lodge of the Chicago-based Scandinavian Workingmen's Association cut loose from the mother organization and formed its own *Independent* Scandinavian Workingmen's Association.[20] The Eau Claire leaders could hardly have found a more inappropriate moment to form an organization based on a dues-paying membership. During the depression years 1893–1897 only six new lodges were added to the ISWA. With prosperity returning, however, the association truly expanded. By 1900 it boasted thirty-five lodges with 2,075 members. The largest lodge by far was the Eau Claire mother lodge with 438 members, followed by the Superior lodge with 172 members. The rural lodges were smaller, varying in size from 27 members in Bloomer, Chippewa County, to 135 in Hayward, Sawyer County. Of these thirty-five lodges, thirty-two were located in Wisconsin, most of them to the north; twelve were situated in cities, twenty in rural areas.[21]

The organization called itself "Scandinavian," even though Norwegian Americans clearly predominated. The ISWA did, however, include some Swedish Americans, and for several years one Danish immigrant, Peter J. Smith (1867–1947) of Eau Claire, was Grand Lodge Secretary, at one point even advancing to the presidency.[22]

Generally speaking, the Scandinavian-American fraternities had frosty relations with the church.[23] First, as secret orders they were suspected of practicing improper rituals. The Danish Church, the Norwegian Synod, the United Norwegian Church, and the Augustana Synod, in fact, all passed resolutions condemning secret societies.[24] To counter criticism from the church, Grand Lodge Organizer F. A. Scawie of the ISWA emphasized that religious ceremonies were actually excluded by his organization.[25] Second, mutual-aid fraternities were generally believed to condone immoral excesses, including drinking, dancing, card-playing, and other supposed vices.[26] Again, the ISWA worked to ward off such suspicions. In 1901 it excluded saloon owners and bartenders from membership after "an animated debate."[27] Third, the mutual-aid societies constituted a secular threat to the Lutheran churches, offering their members alternative social activities on a weekly or semiweekly basis and providing them with other leaders.[28] Judging by available membership figures, among Danish Americans, if hardly at all among Swedish Americans, and definitely not among Norwegian Americans, the largest fraternity actually represented a greater share of adult males than the largest religious body.[29] Still, the claim by one observer that for each church communicant ten fraternity members could be found was vastly exaggerated. Another came closer to the truth when he contended that the losses for the Lutheran churches would be devastating if they decided to expel the members of the secret orders.[30] It could hardly have been reassuring to the Lutheran clergy when one commentator remarked that the secret lodges "in no way intend to challenge the first rank of the church. The two can coexist side by side." No more comforting can have been ISWA Grand Lodge Organizer Scawie's dismissal of "the fallacious assumption that the lodge can take the place of the church."[31] Some enemies of the fraternities felt certain that the latter were stealing members from the Lutheran church. There were simply too many temptations in "this land of freedom."[32] Therein lay the crux of the matter: in the free American environment the Lutheran clergy could really do nothing to counter the secret orders. They could only watch in bitter resignation as some of their members defied warnings and turned to the fraternities not only for insurance but also for social activities and leadership. After the turn of the century, some church leaders acknowledged this situation and began looking for a practical working relationship with the secret societies.[33]

In one respect, as one observer noted acidly, the fraternal orders seemed better poised to represent Scandinavian America than the churches: "The members behave in a brotherly manner towards each other and do not always bicker and fight."[34] The leaders of the ISWA definitely hoped to play a major part in sponsoring a secular Scandinavian-American identity. This was to be a truly pan-Scandinavian-American venture. According to Grand Lodge Organizer F. A. Scawie, the ISWA aimed "to function as a connecting link between the three elements of the Scandinavian people; to maintain the sentiments of nationality by arranging lectures on Nordic literature and history; to labor for the preservation of the Scandinavian languages; to provide its members with a life insurance. . . . We Scandinavians are often divided in religious, political, and other matters. Here is a platform upon which we can unite."[35] In practice, however, the numerical superiority of the Norwegian Americans was sometimes telling.

Judging by their names, the early ISWA lodges were organized on a truly pan-Scandinavian basis. Thus, the first lodge was named "the North" (*Norden*) and the second "the Triplet" (*Trillingen*), in a reference to the unity of the three nations. Later, with particularly the numbers of Norwegian-American members increasing, selectivity on a national basis sometimes crept in. It is not likely that many Swedish Americans joined lodge No. 21, "Tordenskjold," named after the eighteenth-century Norwegian-Danish war hero who fought the Swedes in the Great Nordic War.[36]

The ISWA also arranged a number of celebrations, some genuinely Scandinavian-American. In September 1897, the association helped organize "Fraternal Day" in Chippewa Falls, where fraternities of different national backgrounds planned to march together. "Here is an occasion for us Scandinavians to represent our nationality," insisted one enthusiast. "Let us make sure that at least two hundred of our members unite under our beautiful banner so that we can show the Yankees [*Jænkierne*] and the Germans what the I.S.W.A. stands for."[37] The Yankees did not always get the message. In May 1886, shortly after the tragic labor riots at the Chicago Haymarket and in Milwaukee, the Scandinavian Workingmen's Association of Chicago arranged a *Syttende Mai* parade in Eau Claire. Some spectators thought that the marchers were on strike.[38]

The annual meeting of the ISWA was a huge social event. According to *Superior Tidende*, no fewer than 8,000 visitors attended the 1901 convention in Superior, many of them arriving on special trains. That year, Norwegian-American ex-Congressman Nils P. Haugen was the keynote speaker, and five years later Norwegian-born Governor James O. Davidson, himself apparently a member, attended the convention.[39] At the 1899 convention, Norwegian-American Professor Rasmus B. Anderson lectured on "The Heritage of Our Forefathers," and the Saturday parade, estimated to include some 800 participants, featured a horse-drawn float resembling a Viking ship with a full crew of Vikings, followed by a band, and behind them Eau Claire's mayor and the officials of the Grand Lodge, all in wagons, and then finally the marching delegates.[40]

Promotion of ethnic pride was a legitimate preoccupation. Tampering with politics was quite another matter, especially if, under the veil of pan-Scandinavian-American harmony, leaders within the ISWA tended to invite *Norwegian*-American keynote speakers and to support *Norwegian* Americans for political office. The official policy of the ISWA was to stay aloof from politics. In 1899, editor Henry P. Peterson dared any reader of *Superior Tidende* to find "one word in any of our rituals or rules that refers to religion or politics, and I will pay him twenty-five dollars in cash!"[41] In practice, the temptation to meddle with politics was hard to resist. During the gubernatorial campaign of 1906, Peterson wrote James O. Davidson, "I know that hundreds of our boys in the I.S.W.A. and outside will celebrate the day, when it [the first name on the state ticket] shall read J. O. Davidson, Governor."[42]

This was not empty talk. In the same letter Peterson informed Davidson that he was running for the presidency of the ISWA with a view to boosting Davidson's chances at the governorship.[43] As it turned out, Peterson did not win the presidency of the ISWA, but in 1905 he was elected to the group's board of directors. Stating that for reasons of confidentiality he would henceforth write in the Norwegian language, Peterson reported to Davidson, "I accepted the appointment . . . as much in order to be able to come into contact with our Scandinavian reform friends all over the state as for any other reason. During the past month I have given lectures in Rhinelander, Black River Falls, and Scandinavia. *Everywhere* I find that they are taking a lively interest in your political future."[44] After that point, something went wrong, and Peterson evidently switched horses. In March 1906, he wrote U.S. Senator La Follette, who supported Swedish-American Irvine L. Lenroot for the governorship rather than Davidson, that the ISWA could be made to work for "the cause." The secretive Peterson added, "I wish you could read Norwegian."[45] By June 1906, a Davidson ally was warning that Peterson, under the pseudonym of O. B. Server, had begun writing articles against Davidson in *Superior Tidende*. Peterson admitted this when confronted with it by Davidson himself. Peterson now argued that he could not support a gubernatorial candidate who, or so he insisted, was being backed by the conservative, anti-reform faction within the Republican Party.[46] Having thus shifted from a Norwegian-American to a Swedish-American candidate, Peterson apparently lost influence within the ISWA. The organization, in fact, invited Davidson to attend its 1906 convention.

Henry P. Peterson was not the only person using his leadership within the ISWA for political ends. In the summer of 1902, John L. Erickson, editor of *Superior Tidende* since late 1901, wrote two editorials boosting T. M. Thorson, a Republican of Superior, for state senator.[47] Thorson, who in previous campaigns had supported Nils P. Haugen for Congress (1890) and Robert M. La Follette for governor (1896), sat on the judicial committee of the ISWA's Grand Lodge.[48] Two weeks after the second editorial in his favor, Thorson was promoted to the ISWA board of directors. He never made it to the state senate, however.[49] The evidence in the case of Thorson is, of course, circumstantial, as it is with Norwegian-born Nels Nelson, who became Grand Lodge President in 1899 and mayor of Washburn in 1900.[50]

Julius Howland of Chippewa Falls, another Norwegian American, would have had more difficulty proving his innocence. In 1906, Howland, then county treasurer of Chippewa County and ISWA board member, ran as a Republican candidate for the state treasurership in the primary-election campaign.[51] Apparently hoping to win political prestige, he worked hard to persuade a hesitant Governor Davidson to attend the annual ISWA convention at Chippewa Falls.[52] When Howland further suggested that Davidson be the private guest of the archconservative Congressman John J. Jenkins, however, Davidson backed down.[53] After receiving a joint letter from Howland and Peter J. Smith, the Danish-born Grand Lodge Secretary, Davidson decided to come to Chippewa Falls after all. Howland's and Smith's argument that "you cannot miss the opportunity of meeting practically all the northern Wisconsin representatives" may have persuaded him.[54] Yet Davidson refused to accept the hospitality of Congressman Jenkins, who felt snubbed.[55]

In his own campaign for the state treasurership, Howland went one step farther. He used his position within the ISWA to pose as the spokesman for the small mutual-aid fraternities. "At the risk of making myself obnoxious to certain interests," he stated, "I cannot refrain from saying that I am deeply interested in the subject of fraternal insurance, believing it to be the greatest boon to the people of limited means of this day and generation, that class which someone has called the 'Common People.'" He thus pledged to fight for the fraternal insurance organizations against what he considered the encroachment of the powerful old-line insurance companies, "which have and which even now are wielding such influence in the administration of government affairs."[56]

Howland neither won the Republican nomination for the state treasurership in 1906 nor in 1910, when he ran again. During the latter campaign, he and Peter J. Smith, now president of the ISWA, as well as Charles Barker, a conservative Republican, went on a two-day road trip through northern Wisconsin in Barker's automobile. *Skandinaven* of Chicago, which sided with the progressive faction within the Republican Party, uttered the hope that Howland's claim that Smith was simply taking a vacation was correct, for "Smith heads a nonpolitical association, and he would not only be abusing his position but hurting the association if he took a prominent part in political campaigns."[57]

Patronage played a role in these processes. Several ISWA leaders did in fact receive political plums. The appointment of Peter J. Smith to the assistant postmastership in Eau Claire in early 1907 was not likely occasioned by his work for Davidson in the campaign of 1906.[58] On the other hand, when Smith years later was appointed a member of the State Normal School Board, the president of the renamed Scandinavian-American Fraternity planned officially to thank Governor John J. Blaine for the appointment on behalf of the fraternity.[59] Moreover, when Henry P. Peterson applied for a position as assistant labor commissioner in 1905, one of his active supporters was Peter J. Smith.[60] Furthermore, when Nels Nelson, the former president of the ISWA and mayor of Washburn, applied successfully for the postmastership of Washburn, he received recommendations from both Smith and Peterson.[61]

Whereas the ISWA indulged in loudly celebrating a secular version of Scandinavian-American identity, emphasizing worldly unity over religious strife and even underscoring pan-Scandinavian roots, in politics the fraternity spoke with a softer yet firmer voice. The picture emerges of several ISWA leaders using their positions within the organization for distinctly political ends. Despite its professed pan-Scandinavian-American orientation, moreover, the ISWA tended to gravitate first of all towards politicians of Norwegian background. Some of the latter appreciated the efforts of the leaders within the ISWA. In 1906, Governor Davidson commended Peter J. Smith for his talent for gathering intelligence "by reason of your connection with the workingmen's society, and your keen sense of ascertaining things."[62] In 1914, moreover, when Norwegian-American Andrew H. Dahl ran for the governorship, he asked Smith to endorse his candidacy "among your large circle of friends," adding, "there are few people in the state whose personal influence would be of more help to my candidacy than that of Mr. Smith of Eau Claire."[63] Politicians, of course, were good at distributing words of praise openhandedly, yet undoubtedly both they and the leaders within the ISWA understood the worth of sharing each other's ethnically based networks. In all probability they were thus participating in a game of politics that extended well beyond both the Scandinavian-American group and the borders of Wisconsin. The influence of the fraternities was dangerous to ignore.

THE TEMPERANCE AND PROHIBITION MOVEMENTS

"I began to feel queasy, exactly the same feeling as after I have been drinking."[64] Thus Kristoffer Skauge described his rough voyage across the North Sea in 1888. Eight years later, however, his obituary stated that over the

past four years he had been a "good and active member" of Strum's temperance society.[65] Skauge, like so many other Norwegian and Swedish
Americans, if not quite as many Danish Americans, had joined the temperance movement, one of the powerful moral forces in turn-of-the-
century U.S. politics. In fact, even the settlement itself appears to have
been named after a temperance activist, one Louis Strum of Eau Claire,
who incidentally was a personal friend of Pastor Carl Johan Helsem.[66]

In those years, mention of temperance societies was a recurring feature in reader letters to the Scandinavian-American press, and almost invariably the writer signaled a moral stand. "We have three ministers and
no attorney, two churches and no saloon, a large temperance club and no
blind pig [a place that sells intoxicants illegally], one Farmers' Alliance and
very few Democrats, five shops, one drug store, one hardware store, one
furniture store, a creamery, a lumberyard, a doctor, a dentist, and much
more, so I think that this town may be called exemplary, even though we
do not live in a prohibition state," philosophized one *Skandinaven* correspondent in 1890.[67] In fact, more than one in ten of 2,234 reader letters to
the Norwegian-American *Skandinaven* and the Swedish-American *Hemlandet* sampled by the present author for the period 1890–1910 focused
on alcohol, ranging from passionate discussions of prohibition to literally dry remarks about the local saloon, in a broad presentation of the
community.[68]

The case of Stoughton, the little mainly Norwegian-American city in
the vicinity of Madison, Wisconsin, illustrates just how the temperance issue might ignite Scandinavian-American minds. In the municipal election
of 1890, the city voted to ban the saloon. The temperance forces were jubi-
lant. One reporter noted: "At 9:30 in the evening, all the church bells began
tolling, virtually vying to announce this almost incredible piece of news."[69]
The following spring, however, the wets emerged victorious: "After the
proclamation of victory, as a sign of their pleasure and satisfaction, the
Stoughton music corps played in the streets."[70] Church bells versus marching brass bands, or, as another commentator put it, the "church people"
versus the "saloon element": inviting as such dualisms are, they actually
disguise as much as they reveal, for Scandinavian-American attitudes on
alcohol were spread over a wide spectrum.[71]

In Wisconsin, an 1889 local-option law set the rules of the game.[72]

A town could vote to ban the saloon from its own boundaries, nothing more than that, and even in that event blind pigs might maintain a shady existence within the town limits, or a new saloon open on the township border.[73] In the state legislature futile attempts were made to replace the local-option law with county option, and to introduce the Swedish Gothenburg system, which would have allowed one local authority to monopolize the sale of liquor. However, all such schemes were anathema to Wisconsin's large German-American element, as well as to the Pabst and Schlitz breweries that by the turn of the century were in the process of turning Milwaukee into the beer capital of the world.[74] Those corporations, identified as the "liquor interest," actively supported such anti-temperance organizations as the Anti-Prohibition League and the Liberty League, as well as the German-American Alliance.[75]

The earliest Scandinavian-American temperance association was organized by Norwegian Americans at Muskego in Waukesha County in 1848, and three years later nine more were in existence, most of them calling themselves "Scandinavian." During the Civil War era, however, the majority of these early societies foundered, "until the event of [the] Women's Crusade in the late 1870s again awakened the public conscience."[76] From that point, the movement spread rapidly, indeed often serving as "an entrée for women into political activism."[77] Not only did the Wisconsin Prohibition Party occasionally, if not consistently, insert women's suffrage planks into its platform, but *Reform*, the little Norwegian-language prohibition weekly coming out of Eau Claire, supported the same reform.[78]

Scandinavian-American temperance and total-abstinence societies divided into two main groups, the first associated closely with the church, the second with older American organizations. Among the Norwegian Americans, church-related temperance clubs ran into the hundreds nationally, and they were also important among Swedish Americans.[79] Waldemar Ager, the editor of *Reform*, noted, however, that Danish Americans generally were less active. Omaha, Nebraska, actually housed a Danish-American anti-prohibition league.[80]

The official attitude of various Scandinavian-American Lutheran church bodies confirms this impression of a certain division between Norwegian and Swedish Americans on the one hand and Danish Americans on the other, even though not all the Norwegian-American churches took the staunch stand of the Swedish Augustana Synod, which as early as 1890 came out strongly in favor of prohibition.[81] Within the doctrinally rigorous Norwegian Synod, some ministers, like Pastor Adolph Bredesen of Stoughton, were strong prohibitionists. Others, however, supported the temperate consumption of alcohol and were critical, for instance, of the efforts by the Women's Christian Temperance Union to ban wine from holy communion. Generally, *Reform* attacked the Synod for not advocating total prohibition.[82] Overall, the middle-of-the-road United Norwegian Church took a tougher stand on alcohol, with President Hoyme speaking up and pamphleteering against the saloon.[83] Among the Methodists and Baptists, Scandinavian-American members followed the pioneering prohibitionist prescriptions. Waldemar Ager, the leading Norwegian-American prohibitionist, was a Methodist, and examples of active cooperation between Norwegian-American Lutheran and Methodist prohibitionists exist.[84] The low-church Norwegian-American Haugeans, furthermore, condemned the consumption of alcohol, yet were critical of the temperance movement, dismissing it as too secular. Even the Haugeans, however, harbored individual sinners. In Cambridge, Dane County, one inn was known simply as the "Haugean saloon."[85]

While support for some form of temperance legislation was sufficiently widespread among Norwegian and Swedish Americans to make alcohol a hotly disputed topic in church circles, the Danish-American ecclesiastical bodies paid less attention to the issue. The histories of the Danish-American churches, written by prominent contemporary clerics, simply ignored the topic.[86] In everyday life, however, personal abstinence was undoubtedly a stronger force among Inner-Mission "Gloomy" or "Holy Danes" than among the Grundtvigian "Happy Danes." Arguably, by stifling the growth of the Baptists and Methodists, the success of Grundtvigianism in Denmark hurt the temperance cause.[87] While both the Norwegian- and Swedish-American press included prohibition and temperance papers like *Reform*, *Afholdsbasunen*, and *Svenska Amerikanska Posten*, the Danish-American papers did not.[88]

Various umbrella organizations enabled several of the Scandinavian-American church-related temperance groups to cooperate with each other in various states. The Minnesota Total-Abstinence Society, formed in

1885, led the way and by 1914 comprised 125 clubs with about eight thousand largely Norwegian-American members. In 1888, a corresponding Wisconsin association was founded, which soon joined forces with temperance groups in South Dakota. By 1905, the resulting merger (the National Abstinence Union) boasted some four to five thousand members.[89] The Anti-Saloon League, established in 1893 by the reformist Catholic Archbishop John Ireland, was a truly interdenominational undertaking. The Wisconsin chapter, whose slogan was "Unity, Perseverance, Victory. Ballots Are Our Bullets. The Saloon Must Go," included Catholic, Baptist, Methodist, Presbyterian, and Norwegian Lutheran clerics.[90]

Besides the church-related temperance associations, a number of secular American organizations played a vital role in the growth of the temperance movement. Chief among these were the International Order of Good Templars, founded in 1851, with Methodist roots, and the Women's Christian Temperance Union, established in 1874.[91] Beginning with Swedish immigrants in Chicago in 1866, the IOGT quickly founded its own Scandinavian-American lodges. "Skandinaven," the first "Norwegian" IOGT lodge in the world, was established in 1874.[92] In 1883, however, many Norwegian- and Swedish-American IOGT lodges broke with the mother organization and instead joined the new Templar Order (*Templar Orden*), a Scandinavian-American organization. A renewed drive by the IOGT in the late 1880s and early 1890s resulted in the establishment of several novel Scandinavian-American IOGT lodges in the Midwest, in Minnesota alone more than one hundred.[93] Likewise, the WCTU had a significant presence in the Midwest and included some Scandinavian-American chapters.[94]

In Wisconsin, the western city of Eau Claire was a hotbed of Scandinavian-American temperance activities. It not only housed the National Abstinence Union, but *Reform* was also published there, first under the energetic editorship of Ole Broder Olson from 1889 to 1903, then of Waldemar Ager until his death in 1941, when the paper folded. Eau Claire also housed the largest lodge of the Independent Scandinavian Workingmen's Association and, as it turned out, the two organizations developed good relations with each other. Ager joined the ISWA and helped to establish a new monthly journal for the ISWA as a substitute for *Superior Tidende*.[95] Conversely, by 1924 Danish-born Peter J. Smith not only served as ISWA Grand Lodge Secretary but also as director and vice-president of "Fremad," *Reform's* publishing company.[96] Ten years earlier, Smith, traditionally a Republican, had already asked Danish-born State Treasurer Henry Johnson (1854–1941), "Who shall I vote for for Governor? I believe I must vote for the Prohibition candidate."[97]

Despite the flourishing of this organizationally diverse temperance movement, it hardly reached out to all Norwegian and Swedish Americans, not to mention the Danish Americans. In heavily Norwegian-American Stoughton, after all, the victorious saloon people had marched in the streets in 1891. When Knut Hamsun, the Norwegian author, visited Stoughton in 1883, he commented, "All they know how to do down there is to drink. That is the worst pigsty I have yet seen. The worst places in Norway are better than Stoughton. . . . It is not a shame to drink in Stoughton, it is fun."[98] Studies of voting patterns among Norwegian Americans on local or county option suggest similar diversity.[99]

Likewise, the Scandinavian-American press represented a wide range of opinions on temperance. At one end of the scale stood the dry papers, whereas a middling course was pursued by for instance *Skandinaven*, which opposed rabid prohibitionism but in several editorials supported the Swedish Gothenburg system and by 1910 even agitated for county option.[100] *Reform* often scolded its much larger rival for printing liquor ads.[101] *Svenska Amerikanaren*, by 1900 the largest Swedish-American paper, stood on the other flank.[102] In 1890, an editorial in that paper trumpeted, "And finally a couple of words to our temperance friends! If you are truly thirsty and no water is available, then a glass of lager really does taste good."[103] Sophus Neble (1862–1931), editor of *Den Danske Pioneer*, by far the most popular Danish-American paper, actually ventured to suggest that the grueling crisis that Kansas went through in the mid-1890s should be ascribed to the fact that the state was dry. The gubernatorial candidate of Wisconsin's Prohibition party, on the other hand, blamed the 1890s recession on liquor.[104]

Frequently, however, the drys had a moral edge over the wets. Peer O. Strømme, the Norwegian-American editor and author, cited an episode when one young fellow ethnic only dared to admit that he was running a saloon upon being questioned closely by Strømme. "But dear friend," commented Strømme, "you have just admitted that you are ashamed of your job."[105] Likewise, the editor of the Norwegian-American *Superior Tidende* felt compelled to counter complaints that the participants in an 1898 Norwegian-American singing festival were "beer guzzlers" with the assertion that Superior's citizens had never seen "a more respectable or well-behaved group of visitors," notwithstanding that the latter drank.[106] Danish-American editors could afford to be more lax in their temperance attitudes. The editor of *Folkets Avis* had no scruples about informing his readers that at a recent Danish-American affair in Racine, people had been very merry, "But then, again, refreshments of all sorts were served."[107] That same year, *Folkets Avis* reported that at a carnival in Racine, which involved several Danish-American associations, things really got out of hand: "No serious damage was done, anyway, even if now and then a spectator got a rotten fruit flung in his face, and if he complained, well, maybe he had his hat crushed. But this was simply part of the carnival fun, and everyone had to put up with it. If someone did not like it, he might as well have stayed at home."[108]

In the interplay between the temperance movement and the emergence of Scandinavian-American identities, two sides of the crusade against alcohol were particularly important. First, the temperance issue could be employed to distinguish between Scandinavian Americans (especially Norwegian and Swedish Americans), along with Yankees, on the one hand, and German and Irish Americans on the other. From the town of Nelson in Buffalo County, Wisconsin, one reporter noted that "the Norwegians and the Americans voted against license and the Germans, taken as a whole, in its favor."[109] From Cashton, Monroe County, a Norwegian-American Lutheran pastor similarly wrote, "It is almost hopeless to take up the work against drinking here, especially because so large a proportion of the population in and around the town are German or Irish Catholics. Yet I, for one, am not going to give up."[110]

The fight against drinking often took on religious overtones, with attention frequently focused on the attitudes of the clergy. During a prohibition riot in Omaha, Nebraska, reported *Reform*, one rotten egg missed its target, a Swedish pastor, and hit a German saloon guest instead.[111] At a German-American drinking celebration, on the other hand, "in the midst of this torrent of beer and screaming and squalling, the German minister walked around smiling jovially."[112] For Scandinavian-American temperance people, this was the crux of the matter. It might be conceded that many Scandinavian Americans did indeed drink too much and that more temperance work was required, but could anyone seriously imagine a Scandinavian-American *minister* gladly participating in a drinking festival? Who other than Catholic priests and, sadly, German Lutheran pastors, would sink so low? No mere coincidence that the 1894 convention of the Wisconsin Prohibition Party took place in Liberty Hall, Milwaukee, the headquarters of the anti-Catholic American Protective Association![113]

Besides separating Scandinavian Americans from other ethnic groups like the German and Irish Americans, the temperance movement served a second ethnic function: temperance activists nurtured their own networks of communication across the Atlantic Ocean. Thus, *Reform* sometimes reported about temperance meetings in Norway and Denmark.[114] Indeed, the Eau Claire weekly cooperated with *Orkdølen*, a like-minded paper in Norway. The editor of the American paper at one point in the mid-1890s actually traveled to Orkdalen to participate in a temperance conference there.[115] Occasionally, *Reform* also printed reader letters purportedly written in Norway.[116] In the summer of 1889, moreover, *Reform* reported that P. Sunde, a disciple of Norwegian temperance pioneer Asbjørn Kloster (1823–1876), was on his way to America.[117] Tallak Ellingson, another follower of Kloster, established a Norwegian-American total-abstinence society in Chicago in 1874.[118] When temperance organizations in Scandinavia proposed to make June 16 a pan-Scandinavian temperance day, *Reform* suggested that Scandinavian Americans duplicate their effort.[119]

In Waldemar Ager of Eau Claire, Norwegian, if not Scandinavian, America found a spokesperson who combined a strong commitment to temperance with a powerful ethnic appeal. Ager, the editor of *Reform*, was active in temperance circles on both sides of the Atlantic. He was an occasional writer in *Menneskevennen*, the organ of the Norwegian Total-Abstinence Society, and he wrote the keynote article in the 1903 *Almanac of the Abstinence Friends*, published in Oslo. In 1912, moreover, he kept up a correspondence with the Norwegian editor of *Goodtemplarbladet*.[120] Ager's interest in the temperance issue was highlighted by several of the novels he wrote, including *Paa Drikkeondets Konto* (*To Be Charged to the*

Evil of Drinking, 1894) and *Afholdssmuler fra Bokhylden* (*Temperance Crumbs from the Bookshelf,* 1901).[121]

At the same time Ager emerged as one of the leading Norwegian-American nationalists.[122] He visited Norway in 1914 to take part in the centennial celebration of the Norwegian constitution, and arranged a Norwegian exhibition in Eau Claire the same year. He also raised a subscription for a statue of Norwegian-American Civil War hero Hans Christian Heg, which to this day stands on the lawn in front of Madison's capitol building. For a number of years he was also secretary of Det Norske Selskab (The Norwegian Association). In 1923, King Olaf V of Norway knighted Ager, and sixteen years later he received the St. Olaf Medal.[123] In Ager the temperance movement and the celebrators of Norwegian-American identity had a unifying figure, even though not all temperance people were as ethnically minded as Ager and not all ethnic activists as temperance-minded as he.[124] Among Swedish Americans, not to speak of Danish Americans, no equally powerful exponent of temperance and of ethnic pride emerged.

Politically, Scandinavian-American temperance reformers could choose between throwing their strength behind the Prohibition Party or attempting to win a hearing in one of the two major parties. In Wisconsin, the Prohibition Party played no significant role, while in Minnesota Kittel Halvorson of this party was elected to the House of Representatives.[125] Between 1890 and 1912, the Wisconsin party's share of the gubernatorial vote hovered between a low of 1.8 percent in 1896 and highs of 3.6 percent in 1890 and 1892, and no Prohibitionist was elected to the state legislature.[126] Scandinavian Americans did not play too impressive a role within the leadership of the party. Between 1890 and 1914, it is true, almost every Wisconsin Prohibition state ticket included one person with a Scandinavian-sounding name, but none of these candidates made it to the head of the ticket. Ole Broder Olson came closest when in 1894 he was nominated for the lieutenant governorship. Fourteen years later, Waldemar Ager was nominated for the state treasurership.[127] During the same years, the Republican Party definitely offered Scandinavian Americans better terms, placing at least one Scandinavian American, almost invariably of Norwegian background, on each state ticket, and Norwegian-born James O. Davidson was elected governor in 1906 and 1908.[128] Even so, the Prohibition Party was the focus of much animated Scandinavian-American debate, and when Ole Broder Olson made his 1894 bid for the lieutenant governorship, he ran well ahead of the rest of the ticket, a feat not repeated by Waldemar Ager in 1908.[129]

The Prohibition Party suffered precisely from being a *political* party. For a number of pastors and lay people, to agitate against the (unrestrained) consumption of alcohol was one thing; for a political party to focus exclusively on this issue quite another. The Prohibitionists generally hoped to enlist Scandinavian-American ministers in their cause, and *Reform* always found occasion to celebrate whenever a Scandinavian-American ecclesiastical body passed a strongly worded resolution against the liquor traffic. Yet while many Lutheran pastors did support temperance efforts of some kind, only a few identified openly with the Prohibition Party and some expressed hostility towards it. In one instance, a Prohibition lecturer planning to speak in the Norwegian Lutheran church in Bennett Valley, Trempealeau County, was threatened with imprisonment.[130] Generally the pastors preferred not to participate in the work of the Prohibition Party. One minister within the United Norwegian Church excused himself with the familiar maxim that the clergy ought to stay out of politics.[131] To no avail might the editor of *Reform* carp, "Keep politics out of our churches! We are tired of hearing that argument. Do our ministers never consider that they through their *silence* help promote one type of politics – saloon politics?"[132] Better for temperance-minded pastors to work quietly through the Republican Party.

With no election victories in sight, the Prohibition Party had no direct influence on the patronage policy of the major parties. Why squander a postmastership on non-Republicans? asked Congressman Nils P. Haugen. "I understand that Mr. Green is a Prohibitionist and would prefer to recommend some straight Republican."[133] Nevertheless, the appointment by President Harrison in 1889 of Østen Monson, a Norwegian-American former saloon keeper, to the position of deputy collector of internal revenue in Eau Claire caused bitterness in Prohibitionist circles. "It is said that this appointment was made in appreciation of the Republican Scandinavians!" observed *Reform*. "Are Eau Claire's Scandinavian Republicans . . . really happy to learn that their party press tells not only themselves but the whole world that the President has appointed a former saloon keeper in order to show appreciation for their loyalty to the party?"[134]

Contributing to the weakness of the Prohibition Party was the circumstance that the two major parties traditionally had clear positions on the temperance issue. At least until the mid-1890s, northern Democrats were considered "wet," and this caused uneasiness among some Norwegian Americans flirting with the Democratic Party. Two cases in point were Professor Rasmus B. Anderson, and John A. Johnson, a prominent Madison machine manufacturer, who both were active within the Democratic Party in the late 1880s. "I hardly think either you or I will feel like making a permanent home in the democratic party," ventured Johnson, "unless its standard is raised very much. . . . But the liquor interest has it in its grasp, the leaders rally to that interest, and are both unwilling and unable to shake it off."[135] Soon after, in fact, Johnson ran as the Prohibition candidate for the mayoralty of Madison.[136]

Wisconsin Democratic Chairman E. C. Wall in Milwaukee was deeply aware of the general association of his party with rum and Romanism. He suggested that "the German Lutherans have been kept from us for years because we were called the Catholic-whiskey party."[137] This problem Wall hoped to right, not by changing the party's general pro-liquor stance but by arguing that its stand was taken in the interest of "individual liberty." Therefore, the Democratic Party should make sure not to support the Anti-Prohibition Society of Milwaukee, which, declared Wall, was "simply an organization acting now for the benefit of whiskey and saloon men." One year later, Wall found further cause for worry, for the Milwaukee Democratic municipal ticket was "loaded down with Catholics, Irish and saloon keepers. This does not please the Lutheran and independent voter."[138]

With the nomination by the Democratic Party of William Jennings Bryan for the presidency in 1896, it is true, the identification of the Democrats with pro-liquor attitudes weakened, because Bryan, as one historian writes, "excited the pietistic longings of pietistic Midwestern farmers."[139] If a note of uncertainty could already be detected in *Reform*'s cocksure 1896 assertion, "The Democratic Party is today what it has always been, a whisky-stinking, saloon-drooling party," two years later the paper surrendered and expressed genuine surprise and pleasure at the party's nomination of Norwegian-American Peer O. Strømme for the Wisconsin state treasurership, since he was renowned for his temperance views.[140] Nevertheless, unlike the Republicans, the Democrats did not include a temperance plank in their 1896 national platform, nor do they in fact appear to have attracted additional Scandinavian-American votes that year.[141]

While the Democrats traditionally were identified with pro-liquor attitudes and "individual liberty," the Republicans were usually associated with notions of state control and temperance, and a widely held opinion was that at least Norwegian- and Swedish-American Republicans could be tempted to vote with the Prohibitionists.[142] The association of the GOP with temperance views was sufficiently powerful for *Reform* actually to blacklist those Wisconsin Republicans who supported pro-liquor legislation in the House of Representatives. It was not necessary to blacklist Democrats. After all, they were Democrats.[143] Yet between 1891 and 1914, the Wisconsin Republican Party was also sufficiently tolerant to allow five of its seats in the Wisconsin Assembly to be occupied by brewers and saloonkeepers, with three of those seats in fact being taken by two Danish-born members.[144] Indeed, since the state both housed such large contingents of German Americans and was the home of a formidable brewing industry, the liquor question remained a dangerous issue for any Republican state politician. It was thought safer to leave the temperance issue out of state and federal politics. As Congressman Nils P. Haugen suggested in 1892, "good Republicans will agree to fight the battle upon national issues and let the people of the localities take care of the liquor traffic as heretofore."[145] Sixteen years later, a Milwaukee politician similarly expressed concern over "the attempt on the part of the large corporations working through the liquor interest to put the Republican party in the false position of standing for Prohibition or anything allied to Prohibition in Wisconsin."[146]

Haugen, who did not subscribe to *Reform*, and who occasionally enjoyed a glass of port in the company of Robert M. La Follette, might insist that it was dangerous to inject the alcohol issue into state politics, but in practice Scandinavian-American politicians found the issue hard to eschew completely.[147] Thus, in the gubernatorial primaries of 1906, the temperance issue came to play a certain, if somewhat bizarre, role in the contest between Norwegian-born James O. Davidson and Swedish-American Irvine L. Lenroot.[148] *Reform*, explained ISWA Grand Lodge Secretary Peter J. Smith to Davidson, would be of only limited value, for although editor Ager promised to do all that he could for Davidson, "he is

[a] prohibitionist and [his] paper is also a prohibition paper and for that reason he cannot do so much as if it was a republican paper, but it is worth a whole lot to have his good will and I have given him a little item, which will come out tomorrow."[149] If Davidson was known for his temperance record, however, the German-language *Die Germania* of Milwaukee presumed that Lenroot held even drier views, a circumstance that was brought to Davidson's attention.[150] Less than two months earlier, a Superior judge had worried that Lenroot might indeed be in trouble, for "*the liquor interest will oppose him* while we have no assurance that offsetting strength can be secured from the saints. The latter may not be aroused, the former never sleep."[151]

The Davidson forces did their part to ensure that the "liquor interest" would not fall asleep. Just prior to the primary election, O. G. Munson, Davidson's private secretary, sent a letter to E. L. Tracy of the *Milwaukee Free Press*, detailing Lenroot's record in the Wisconsin Assembly on temperance-related roll calls.[152] Thus, not only did the Davidson forces endeavor to get their candidate a friendly hearing with the dominant Norwegian-American temperance forces in Wisconsin, but they also did their bit to assure negative attention in German-American-dominated Milwaukee to Lenroot's dry stance. The alcohol aspect of the 1906 campaign hardly explains Davidson's ultimate victory, but it does demonstrate how Davidson's political allies schemingly turned the temperance question to his advantage.

If the primary-election campaign of 1906 illustrated the problems that a temperance-minded politician risked running into, the 1908 contest between Herman L. Ekern, Speaker of the Assembly, and Albert T. Twesme (1879–1949), a fellow ethnic from Trempealeau County, demonstrates how the temperance forces might organize. In 1906, Ekern lost much support among Wisconsin's Norwegian-American contingent when he supported Swedish-American Lenroot rather than Norwegian-born Davidson in the gubernatorial primaries. In 1908, this circumstance was used by his more conservative enemies within the GOP to boost Twesme for Ekern's seat in the assembly.[153] Ekern excelled in two fields of legislation, insurance, an area in which he was one of the state's leading experts, and temperance.[154] He was not a believer in total prohibition and in 1907 even opposed a county-option measure, but he was very intent on introducing the Swedish Gothenburg system to Wisconsin. To that end he made connections with politicians as far away as Massachusetts, South Dakota, and Georgia. He exchanged letters with Lutheran and Methodist ministers, as well as with Catholic Archbishop Messmer of Milwaukee, and issued a circular.[155] Even though Ekern considered the bill that he introduced to the Wisconsin Assembly in 1905, and again in 1907, "a very moderate measure," it was defeated because, asserted Ekern, "The large brewers became very active in opposition."[156]

In the battle between Ekern and Twesme, the temperance issue quickly took center stage. Several observers reported that the "saloon element" and the "brewers" were aiding Twesme, and Ekern noted that both the "liquor element" and the insurance companies were actively opposing himself.[157] The campaign soon turned ugly. In late August, one correspondent informed Speaker Ekern, "Your 'friends' are telling the temperance people that you placed brewers on the temperance committees and telling liquor men that you favor county option. Got you both ways. Looks a little as if the liquor question will be in politics whether we will or not."[158] Ekern, however, was not without his own resources. Reverend J. I. Seder of the nondenominational Wisconsin Anti-Saloon League informed Ekern that, assuming that he would support county option in the next legislature, the League would again support him, as it had in the past. Seder added, "I am thinking of writing a letter to all the preachers in the county."[159] Four days later, Seder sent Ekern a list of twenty-two ministers in Trempealeau County (including Pastor Carl Johan Helsem of Strum), explaining that he had written letters to all the clergy in the county save Catholics and German Lutherans.[160] Thus, German Americans, both Catholics and Lutherans, were counted out, whereas in this legislative field Norwegian-American pastors were approached on an interdenominational basis, even though in theory some Lutheran church bodies were more adamant about temperance reform than others.

How much support Ekern in fact received from the Lutheran pastorate is difficult to ascertain, because, as one Norwegian Synod pastor noted, "We are working in the quiet as well as we can and hope for victory."[161] In late August, even though Ekern thought the outlook good, on primary election day he was in fact beaten by Twesme.[162] To both Robert M. La

Follette and Irvine L. Lenroot, Ekern emphasized the role played by "the brewers" and the insurance companies in bringing about his defeat.[163]

The issue of county option finally came to the fore as a state issue in the election campaign of 1910. Understandably, this worried Irvine L. Lenroot, who now from his position as member of Congress found the prominence of the issue in Wisconsin "very alarming." His greatest fear was that the alcohol question would hurt Francis E. McGovern, the pro-liquor, progressive Milwaukee Republican candidate for governor. If "McGovern fails to take any stand upon the question of County Option, or rather if he fails to take the stand that was suggested last September in Milwaukee, I do not believe that when the votes are counted, that he will know he was running." Personally, Lenroot proposed to contact the national leadership of the Anti-Saloon League and solicit their support for McGovern.[164] Other observers similarly feared that county option, backed by the Scandinavian-American Lutheran pastorate, would split the ranks of the progressive reformers.[165] In fact, in Waushara County a pamphlet was circulated that distinguished between those progressives in favor of and those opposed to county option.[166] *Skandinaven* quickly came out openly for county option: "That this is a good, a just, and a beneficial reform that demands the support of the voters, has been proven adequately. . . . The Scandinavians have carried this issue forward in the Northwest."[167] As a direct consequence, *Skandinaven* supported McGovern's pro-county-option rival, Captain William M. Lewis of Racine. *Reform* urged its Republican readers to do the same.[168]

In the end, McGovern survived the liquor dispute of 1910, won the governorship, and inaugurated the most intensive period of progressive reform legislation in Wisconsin history. On the other hand, in the same year county option played a central role in frustrating Norwegian-American Ole A. Buslett's efforts to win a seat in the Wisconsin Senate. During the campaign, Buslett, the nationalistically inspired poet and politician, had to defend himself in *Skandinaven* against charges that he opposed county option in the 1909 Assembly. "Those people who have lied to the Norwegians about my voting against county option have also lied to the Germans, who constitute the main part of my Assembly district, and have said that I favored county option!"[169] Apparently Buslett had now forgotten how, back in 1895, his own little Stoughton-based paper *Norman-*

nen had trumpeted, "After county option has existed for a number of years, not one single mother's soul of all these women will dare to admit that she had agitated for county option."[170] In the election of 1910, Buslett went down to defeat. In his own view, "Money and treachery did it."[171]

Republican-minded Scandinavian-American temperance forces certainly made themselves felt in patronage politics. In 1892, Robert M. La Follette suggested that the employee at the post office in Edmund, Iowa County, not be removed from his position, for "he is a sound republican and a strong temperance man and lives in a temperance community."[172] The fate of Østen Monson, the former saloonkeeper in Eau Claire who to the consternation of *Reform* had been awarded a federal position by President Harrison, illustrates the difference between the limited influence that *Reform* as the organ of the Prohibitionists wielded and the authority held by temperance activists friendly to the GOP. In 1892, Congressman Nils P. Haugen recommended that Monson be retained in office for another term: "The fact was that I went down to Eau Claire and looked the ground over very carefully and interviewed the Norwegian clergymen there, before we dared to ask his appointment, as he had formerly been in the saloon business. If Mr. Hoyme [president of the United Norwegian Church] had not expressed himself as perfectly satisfied with him, he would not have been appointed."[173] Even though the patronage strength of the Norwegian Lutheran clergy was limited, those ministers friendly to the Republican Party had more of a power of veto than the Prohibitionists.

The temperance issue clearly played an important part in activating many Wisconsin Scandinavian Americans ethnically and politically, especially those of Norwegian and Swedish background. In this case, however, leading Scandinavian-American Republicans had cause for concern. Here was an issue that simply could not be "secularized," and yet the grass roots, sometimes still operating on a pan-Scandinavian basis, along with numerous members of the clergy, demanded action. To be sure, the members of the Prohibition Party could legitimately be written off as reformist cranks, but teetotalers within the GOP warranted a respectful hearing. The dangers that the temperance issue posed were illustrated by the fates of Irvine L. Lenroot in 1906, of Herman L. Ekern in 1908, and of O. A. Buslett in 1910, even though alcohol was hardly solely responsible for Lenroot's defeat in 1906, nor for Ekern's in 1908. Scandinavian-American temperance forces would sometimes, it is true, provide support for a favored politician, but that assistance had to be offered in a very quiet way, so as not to provoke the hostility of other ethnic groups or economic interests in the state, and occasionally the aid was not very efficient. Although the temperance issue was hard to ignore, the growth of a new type of "progressive" politics centering on forward-looking social and economic issues introduced a new political vocabulary. For a number of years, temperance would be relegated to second place.

CHAPTER FOUR

The Press

THE SCANDINAVIAN-AMERICAN PRESS

Even though Strum did not boast its own Norwegian-language newspaper, its inhabitants nevertheless belonged to the world of the Scandinavian-language press. On 24 February 1897, a letter written by Sivert Rekstad, the man who five years earlier had helped Kristoffer Skauge build a home in Strum, appeared in *Skandinaven* of Chicago. The letter invited a man with "capital, insight, and entrepreneurial pluck," to come to Strum and build a flour and feed mill on the Beef River.[1] In 1908, moreover, Pastor Carl Johan Helsem, who in 1896 had laid Kristoffer Skauge to rest, informed Wisconsin Assembly Speaker Herman L. Ekern that he was presently in Chicago discussing Trempealeau County politics with editor Nicolai Andreas Grevstad (1851–1940) of *Skandinaven*.[2] Even a hamlet like Strum was not beyond the reach of the Scandinavian-American press.

Being an editor of one of the many small Scandinavian-American weeklies serving one or two localities could be a nerve-racking business. Not long after his 1892 purchase of *Posten* of Superior, Wisconsin, the Norwegian-American writer and ex-minister Peer O. Strømme complained, "My buying this paper was a foolhardy business anyhow, and I was swindled badly out of my little money last fall, so that I am simply fighting from day to day against actual want."[3] Of course, establishing a *Democratic* weekly among Superior's Norwegian-American population might have been considered reckless and, generally speaking, Strømme was not good at making ends meet. Indeed, by 1918, at age sixty-two, he was begging Waldemar Ager of *Reform* for a job, for otherwise "I will journey up into the woods and earn my living with an ax or a saw or find work in a saw mill."[4] Even after *Posten* folded in 1893 and was succeeded by the Republican *Superior Tidende*, the problems of publishing a Norwegian-language paper in Superior persisted. In 1905, editor John L. Erickson wrote that he had recently been "under treatment for a severe case of nerv-ous prostration, a result of over-work, worry and anxiety for the paper."[5] Even some of the larger Scandinavian-language newspapers, most of them published in Minneapolis or Chicago, experienced problems. In 1890, Peer O. Strømme, at this point almost solely in charge of *Norden*, a Norwegian-language Chicago daily with an estimated circulation of more than fourteen thousand, suffered a nervous breakdown. One year later, I. T. Relling, the owner of the paper, took an overdose of morphine in a Chi-cago hotel room because he believed his paper was in severe economic trouble.[6]

Overwrought editorial nerves readily reflected worrisome statistics. Of the eighty-three Scandinavian-language publications listed by *N. W. Ayer & Son's American Newspaper Annual* in 1889, only thirty-three were listed also in 1900 and 1910, although by the latter year the total number of Scandinavian-language publications had grown to 129. Of twenty-eight Scandinavian-language newspapers and journals published in Wisconsin between 1891 and 1913, only three were listed in each edition of the bien-nial *Blue Book of Wisconsin* (fig. 4.1, Appendix I).[7] To many a local editor fighting day-to-day want and cutthroat competition, it can only have been cold comfort to realize that among America's foreign-language newspa-pers the Scandinavian-American press was exceeded in total size only by the German-American.[8]

Usually, the larger publications were more secure than the small ones. The editors of papers like the Norwegian-language *Skandinaven* of Chicago with an estimated circulation in 1900 of more than 44,000; the Swedish-language *Svenska Amerikanaren*, likewise of Chicago and with a circulation of more than 38,000; or the Danish-language *Den Danske Pio-neer* of Omaha, Nebraska, with a circulation of more than 25,000, wielded real influence and power (fig. 4.2, Appendix I). This was the case even when the new, sensationalist "yellow journalism" entered the stage in the 1890s. To be sure, the largest Scandinavian-language papers could hardly match the circulation figures of, for example, Joseph Pulitzer's New York

World, which by the late 1890s regularly passed the million-issue mark. On the other hand, the semiweekly *Skandinaven* boasted a circulation in 1900 that almost equaled that of the Sunday edition of the *New York Times* (ca. 50,000), and that in fact was twice the size of that of Wisconsin's two largest English-language dailies, the *Milwaukee Journal* (ca. 22,500) and the *Milwaukee Sentinel* (ca. 20,000).[9]

The Scandinavian-American newspapers came in many different sizes and shapes, but a number of common features predominated. Most were issued as weeklies, even if a very notable exception was the largest paper of them all, *Skandinaven* of Chicago, which in 1898 changed from a weekly into a semiweekly, and which already in 1870 was supplemented by a daily bearing the same name.[10] Most newspapers, moreover, were published in an eight-page format. A few sheets that were either very local in orientation or that represented marginal groups were in the smaller format of four pages. Through the 1890s, on the other hand, *Skandinaven* boasted sixteen pages.[11] The papers also varied in size over time. In 1891, *Norden* of Chicago expanded from eight to twelve pages, the following year to sixteen pages, and in early 1893 to twenty-four pages. By 1894, with America trapped in a devastating depression, the paper returned to its eight-page format.[12]

Notwithstanding this variation in size, as a minimum almost all papers featured four basic types of information: general American news; information from one or more of the Scandinavian countries; editorials and other debating matter, often including reader letters; and news from the local area. Most papers also made room for one or more serialized novels. Some of these were translated from English and others were written by Scandinavian or Scandinavian-American authors. The largest papers, finally, featured pages dealing with farming matters, with legal advice, and with reports from some of the Midwestern state legislatures.

As long as the immigrant stream from the Scandinavian countries persisted, a reading public was readily at hand. Not only were literacy rates exceptionally high among Scandinavians, but each new wave of immigrants included an ever growing proportion with experience reading newspapers in the homelands. In the closing decades of the nineteenth century, in the Scandinavian countries newspaper publishing experienced tremendous expansion and technical refinement.[13] While in Scandinavia growth tended to trigger a diversification of newspapers along party lines with an emphasis on class differences, in America the pattern was different. A certain branching out of papers along party lines also took place, to be sure, and this even included the emergence of a little chorus of Scandinavian-American sheets trumpeting the opinions of Socialists, Populists, and Prohibitionists.[14] Yet America's two major political parties themselves did not represent social classes to the same degree as did their Scandinavian counterparts. Instead of class, the Scandinavian-American press tended to concentrate on ethnicity, which hardly precluded strong political activism. Indeed, no other Scandinavian-American institution made such a clear, strong, and outspoken link between ethnicity and politics as did the Scandinavian-American press.

THE ETHNIC AND POLITICAL OUTLOOK OF THE SCANDINAVIAN-AMERICAN PRESS

Ethnicity with a focus on national background played a key role in the project of maintaining a Scandinavian-language press in the United States. One important function of that press, after all, was to keep the reader informed about news in the old country. *Den Danske Pioneer* of Omaha, Nebraska, and *Danskeren* of Neenah, Wisconsin, even dedicated a special column to reporting from Southern Jutland, the area conquered by Germany since 1864.[15] Moreover, the titles of several of the papers, and the languages of almost all of them, reflected their national background. Again, as in the case of the churches, a certain tendency to begin with a pan-Scandinavian whole, followed by crystallization along Old World nationality lines could be detected. Thus, *Skandinavia*, the first Scandinavian-language paper to appear in America, coming out of New York City in a spurt of eight issues in 1847, carried columns in both Norwegian-Danish and Swedish.[16] Another early paper of that sort was *Skandinaven*, likewise of New York City, which under the editorship of Swedish-American Gustaf Öbom lasted from 1851 to 1853.[17] The separation along lines of European nationality proceeded rapidly, however. In 1847, *Nordlyset*, the first truly Norwegian-American newspaper, saw the light of day, and eight years later *Hemlandet*, the first regular Swedish-American paper, began to appear.[18] Thus, by 1894 Norwegian-born Congressman Nils P. Haugen of Wisconsin could easily state, "The Swedes and

Norwegians do not read the same papers."[19] The first truly Danish-American paper appears to have been *Fremad* of Chicago, launched in 1868; some Norwegian-Danish ventures, however, had Danish-born editors.[20] The connection between the Danish and Norwegian Americans never faded entirely, however. One reason was the extremely close link between the written Norwegian and Danish languages. "I am writing you in Danish, since the journal I read . . . was Danish or Norwegian," one Danish immigrant wrote to Wisconsin's Norwegian-born governor in 1906.[21] Most Norwegian-language papers reported news from Denmark and even printed an occasional letter to the editor from a Danish-American reader.

In the late 1880s and early 1890s, a determined effort to turn the national tide and publish a pan-Scandinavian-American paper was attempted in Minnesota by Norwegian-born Luth Jaeger and Colonel Hans Mattson, his Swedish-born father-in-law.[22] This was to be a paper truly for *Scandinavian* Americans. "The existing Scand. Am. papers are confined to one nationality only, or at best, in a few instances to two (Norwegians and Danes)," wrote Jaeger. "Our paper would seek and find readers among people hailing from either of the Scandinavian countries."[23] One advantage of this approach, he added, would be the larger advertising patronage that would accrue when all three groups were involved. In 1888, Jaeger attempted to interest Rasmus B. Anderson, then American ambassador to Denmark, in the project, asking him to investigate Scandinavian wire services and to suggest good Danish papers to subscribe to.[24]

The paper was also to be a paper truly for Scandinavian *Americans*. It would be published in the English language. "I can see one great advantage in having an English paper," wrote Nils P. Haugen several years later to Nicolai A. Grevstad in another connection. "The charge of running the nationality issue could not be made against it and it would ally the adopted citizen more closely to his native brother, – a consummation devoutly to be wished."[25] Jaeger's newspaper became a reality in 1889 when he and Mattson each invested 1,000 dollars in the venture. It appeared as the *North*. An advertisement stated that since it was published in the English language, especially the children of immigrants would derive pleasure from this paper. The advertisement continued, "On the one hand, it reflects the intellect of the immigrant, and advocates uncompromisingly his rights. On the other, it is the spokesman of an Americanization which aims to fuse all the different races and nations inhabiting our country into one great American nation."[26] The *North* was an economic failure,[27] but managed to hang on until the depression year of 1893 when it finally drew its last breath.[28] "Hereafter I expect to leave newspapers severely alone at least until the debts incurred by me in this unfortunate *The North* venture have been paid," Jaeger concluded in early 1894.[29] The pan-Scandinavian idea ultimately succumbed to the national trend.

In the field of politics, Scandinavian-American papers sometimes played an impressive role. Most of the twenty-eight Scandinavian-American publications printed in Wisconsin between 1890 and 1913, however, had scant political influence. Discounting four religious or literary publications, as well as eight "independent" newspapers (with no bonds to any political party), only sixteen papers were directly involved in politics, with the Republican Party dominating (fig. 4.1, Appendix I). Whereas the roles played by *Superior Tidende* as the organ of the ISWA and *Reform* of Eau Claire as the mouthpiece of Norwegian-American temperance forces have been discussed in earlier chapters, four more of these sixteen "political" newspapers merit brief mention due to their longevity. Each carried on for more than a decade.

Svenska Amerikanska Tribunen was a joint venture of publishers in Superior, Wisconsin, and Ironwood, Michigan. The paper, according to editor N. L. Bendz in 1890, had "a large circulation throughout the state." Indeed, if Congressman Nils P. Haugen would only "feel like contributing something towards the expense, I should be able to still farther increase it, and you could be assured that your interests should not be neglected."[30] Three years later, Haugen in fact recommended the paper to a Wisconsin railroad agent, adding that he himself subscribed to it. In 1895, however, upon retiring from Congress, Haugen dropped his subscription.[31] Generally speaking, *Tribunen* played only a modest part in politics. In 1906 the paper published a couple of items in favor of Swedish-American Republican Irvine L. Lenroot's nomination for the governorship.[32] On the eve of the primary elections, however, *Tribunen* also printed a short article praising Lenroot's Norwegian-American rival, James O. Davidson, adding that this was a "political ad." The Lenroot pieces also appeared to be advertisements.[33] After the election, the paper's interest in Wisconsin politics faded immediately. Davidson's victory was mentioned only in a one-sentence item in small print in a column dedicated to mixed news.[34]

Lumber-manufacturing Marinette in Wisconsin's northeastern corner was the only city in the state to host two Swedish-language newspapers. *Förposten* was a Republican paper that in the early 1890s under the editorship of James M. Enström sometimes made calls for greater Swedish-American involvement in politics.[35] By 1900, however, when Gustav L. Forsen was editor, the paper abandoned almost all interest in state politics.[36] *Marinette Tribunen*, which had a clear temperance profile, was somewhat more active. In the early 1900s, the paper supported the La Follette wing of Wisconsin's Republican Party. Throughout August 1906, however, it remained silent on Lenroot's gubernatorial candidacy. On August 31 the paper carried ads for various local political candidates, complete with their photos, but still remained silent on gubernatorial matters. A completely identical front page, not only with the same photos of local politicians but with the same text, word for word, was printed by *Förposten* on that date.[37] In connection with the 1910 primaries, the editor of *Marinette Tribunen* offered Herman L. Ekern a write-up, at the favorable rate of five dollars, that would back Ekern for the state insurance commissionership.[38]

For a number of years, one significant Norwegian-American Republican paper was in fact published in Wisconsin. This was *Amerika*, the weekly founded by leaders within the Norwegian Synod in 1884. In 1896, *Amerika* moved from Chicago to Madison, and two years later Professor Rasmus B. Anderson became its proprietor.[39] This became one of the most important Norwegian-American papers. In 1895, it gobbled up Ole A. Buslett's little *Normannen* in Stoughton, and two years later it swallowed *Norden*. For the next twenty years or so Anderson and *Amerika* became almost synonymous.[40] Anderson might have turned *Amerika* into a truly impressive Norwegian-American newspaper. From his position as one of the strongest spokesmen for Norwegian America, that was almost to be expected. During his 1869–1883 professorship, after all, Anderson had introduced Scandinavian studies at the University of Wisconsin, if only with moderate success. In 1874, moreover, he wrote *America Not Discovered by Columbus*, calling for the celebration of Leif Ericson as American's true discoverer. Between 1885 and 1889 Anderson made the personal acquaintance of such prominent Scandinavian intellectuals as Georg Brandes,

August Strindberg, Henrik Ibsen, and Bjørnstjerne Bjørnson. Indeed, he organized Bjørnson's lecture tour of the Midwest in 1881. By 1892, Anderson dreamed of becoming vice-president of the United States.[41]

Yet Anderson did not manage to turn *Amerika* into the leading paper among the Norwegian Americans. In fact, *Amerika* never reached a circulation of ten thousand.[42] During his years as editor, the always short-tempered, bombastic, and outspoken Anderson turned inward ethnically. He aimed most of his fire at internal Norwegian-American cultural rather than political matters. He devoted endless space to condemning patent-medicine ads in rival Norwegian-American publications. He decried Norway's modern literature. In matters of religion, his independent stance infuriated President Koren of the Norwegian Synod (Anderson's own church) to the point of his canceling his newspaper subscription in 1910.[43] In politics, Anderson, who had been appointed minister to Denmark by Democratic President Cleveland, returned to the Republican fold in 1894. Yet he found his place with the conservative, anti-La Follette wing of the party, apparently bearing a permanent grudge against La Follette, who during his student days at the University of Wisconsin had initiated a movement to remove Anderson from his position as a university librarian.[44] During the campaign of 1900, when La Follette ran for the Wisconsin governorship, Anderson unleashed a couple of editorials criticizing La Follette vehemently, but ending on the sarcastic note, "Vote for La Follette."[45] Due to his strong stance against La Follette, Anderson had difficulty expanding *Amerika's* reading circle. As one conservative Republican politician noted in 1901, not many copies of the paper circulated in heavily Norwegian-American Trempealeau County.[46] In his autobiography Anderson himself concluded, "Politically I was friendless among the Norwegians because I was a stalwart republican while they were nearly all enthusiastic admirers and supporters of La Follette."[47]

On the national scene, a similar Republican affiliation predominated among the Scandinavian-language publications. Of 103 Scandinavian-language publications listed with circulation figures in *Ayer's Directory* in 1900, forty-two were politically oriented, and of those all but four were Republican (fig. 4.3, Appendix I).[48] Comparing the information for that year with that for 1889 and 1910, it appears that in the latter two years, besides another twenty-nine Scandinavian-language papers sympathizing with the

Republican Party, an additional five papers supported the Democratic Party, five advocated the Socialist cause, three agitated for temperance reform, and one championed the Populist cause. Of these non-Republican papers, none, however, had a circulation above 4,000.[49] Nevertheless, by the early 1890s some Scandinavian-American editors were beginning to worry about the growing strength of populism, as well as the emergence of a number of Democratic papers.[50] In 1890, in fact, the usually staunchly Republican *Skandinaven* of Chicago sympathized strongly with the Farmers' Alliances and actually supported the Minnesota Alliance candidate for the governorship.[51] A similar loosening of Swedish-American Republican loyalties also took place.[52] At the other end of the chronological scale, by 1910 the existence of six Scandinavian-language Socialist publications, up from just one in 1900 (and none in 1889), pointed to the presence of a small but vocal minority of Scandinavian-American Socialists. Thus, the Republican Party clearly dominated the Scandinavian-language press, but not to the exclusion of other parties.

The largest and most influential Scandinavian-American newspapers were printed outside Wisconsin. Of the twenty-six Scandinavian-language publications that in 1900 boasted a circulation of at least ten thousand, twenty-two came out of Chicago or Minneapolis (fig. 4.2, Appendix I). Several of these large papers were nonpolitical, and only nine of them openly affiliated with a political party. Evidently, a large audience existed for papers not dealing in political controversy. By 1900 the neutral *Decorah-Posten*, published by Brynild Anundsen, and immensely popular for its serialized novels by H. A. Foss, was the largest Norwegian-language *weekly* in the world.[53] Among the large "political" papers, the Republican Party dominated overwhelmingly. Only the Danish-language *Den Danske Pioneer* was anything other than Republican. It was "Independent Democrat," and displayed Democratic sympathies without direct involvement in party politics.

Most of these sizeable Scandinavian-American papers, especially the Swedish- and Danish-American, dealt only perfunctorily with Wisconsin politics. Such papers as *Svenska Amerikanaren*, the largest Swedish-American paper in 1900, and *Svenska Amerikanska Posten*, Swan Johan Turnblad's influential paper, covered affairs in Wisconsin only sporadically. Notwithstanding his Swedish-American background, neither paper mentioned Irvine L. Lenroot's 1906 gubernatorial campaign.[54] The only major Swedish-American paper of any consequence to Wisconsin politics was the Republican *Hemlandet*, the secular organ of the Augustana Synod.[55] It supported Norwegian-born Nils P. Haugen's 1890 congressional campaign editorially, if not his 1894 bid for the governorship, and in 1900 it covered La Follette's gubernatorial struggle, complete with a photo of the Republican nominee.[56] When Irvine L. Lenroot battled against James O. Davidson in the Republican primaries of 1906, *Hemlandet* mentioned Davidson's victory, yet the paper made no reference to the national background of either candidate, nor did it support any of them editorially.[57]

Only one Danish-American paper found a place among the largest Scandinavian-American publications. This was Sophus Neble's *Den Danske Pioneer*, published in Omaha, Nebraska. The tenor of the *Pioneer* was always more radical than that of the larger Norwegian- and Swedish-American papers. After the 1886 riots at the Chicago Haymarket that left seven policemen dead, the bulk of the Norwegian-American press condemned the anarchists who were eventually arrested and executed, whereas the *Pioneer* expressed sympathy for them and reported their execution in excruciating detail.[58] Due to its free criticism of the Danish government and the royal family, the *Pioneer* was actually banned in Denmark between 1886 and 1898. In 1899, during the Great Lockout, a major labor conflict in Danish history, the paper reportedly collected more than 9,000 dollars in funds for the Danish workers.[59]

The radicalism of the *Pioneer* stemmed in part from Neble's left-of-center Danish political sympathies and from his periodic cooperation with Paul Geleff, the Danish Socialist émigré who occasionally wrote articles for the *Pioneer* and apparently even toyed with plans of taking over the paper.[60] The radicalism of the *Pioneer* in the early 1890s also reflected the mood of Nebraska populism. As *Norden* noted dryly in 1893, even though the *Pioneer* had recently opened an office in Chicago, its temper was still all Omaha.[61] Indeed, the general attitude of the *Pioneer* was too westerly to deal in any great detail with Wisconsin affairs. When Nils P. Haugen was not nominated by the Republican Party for the governorship in 1894, the *Pioneer* did note that the winner, William H. Upham, sympathized with the American Protective Association and was a "lumber capitalist."[62] The Republican state convention that two years later rejected Robert M. La

Follette for the governorship was not mentioned, however, nor was his dramatic 1901 fight for the direct primary.[63] At any rate, Wisconsin did not figure among the states discussed regularly in the weekly column, "Domestic News."

Despite the evident popularity of the *Pioneer*, Danish Americans did have other alternatives. They could read not only a number of small Danish-American Republican papers but also the Norwegian-American press which, after all, was written in Dano-Norwegian, and usually reported about life in Denmark. Among the largest Norwegian-American newspapers, two remained politically neutral, *Decorah-Posten* and *Minneapolis Tidende*.[64] Both papers usually abstained from editorializing, even if in 1906 the former did venture to suggest that James O. Davidson won the Republican nomination for the governorship "in spite of inexplicable resistance from La Follette."[65] Generally, however, that paper remained a yardstick of political neutrality, prompting U.S. Senator Knute Nelson in 1912 to criticize another Norwegian-language publication for recently having become "entirely colorless and almost as blank as the Decorah Posten."[66]

One major Norwegian-American newspaper did get deeply involved both in Wisconsin and American politics, more than any other Scandinavian-American paper. This was *Skandinaven* of Chicago, started in 1866 by John Anderson (1836–1910) and Knud Langeland (1813–1888). Anderson became the sole proprietor in 1878.[67] As far as Wisconsin politics was concerned, there was *Skandinaven* and there were all the other Scandinavian-American newspapers. There was Nicolai A. Grevstad, editor of *Skandinaven* in 1892–1911 and again in 1930–1940, and there were all the other Scandinavian-American editors.[68] Originally, the paper was identified with the Norwegian-American low-church element, not least due to its spirited defense of the public school system in the post-Civil War years.[69] By the 1890s, however, its appeal was broad, and even though it faithfully covered the proceedings of each Norwegian-American ecclesiastical body's annual meeting, it openly stated its refusal to get mixed up in religious controversy.[70]

Notwithstanding its 1890 flirtation with populism, *Skandinaven* was generally a solidly Republican paper. As such it made its influence felt all over the Midwest. John Anderson, the proprietor, was known both for his personal energy and for the great demands that he placed upon his staff.[71]

By 1892, editor Peter Hendrickson would have no more of it. "I could not endure the overwork and the disagreeable associations in 'Skandinaven.' Mr. A. [Anderson] is sinking deeper and deeper in whiskey and is getting more greedy and arbitrary. I could not stand it any longer."[72] With Hendrickson's exit, room was made for Nicolai A. Grevstad, the most influential editor in the history of Norwegian America. Born in 1851 of cotter background, he worked himself up in the expansive Norway of the late nineteenth century, graduating in law in 1878. His flair for writing soon took him out of the legal business and placed him in the editor's chair of *Dagbladet* of Oslo, a paper that under his editorship strongly supported Johan Sverdrup and his emerging liberal Left party (*Venstre*) in the fight to make parliament the principal state power in Norway.[73] Due to his eager backing of Sverdrup, however, Grevstad was ousted as editor in 1883 and later that same year sailed for America, immediately finding a job as co-editor of *Nordvesten* of St. Paul. In 1886, however, Prime Minister Sverdrup recalled Grevstad to Norway, hoping to see him head a new liberal newspaper. When that venture did not materialize, Grevstad quickly returned to America and found work, first as chief editorial writer for the *Minneapolis Tribune*, then as editor of the *Minneapolis Times*. *Skandinaven* marveled at Grevstad's impressive mastery of the English language.[74]

As a writer with the *Minneapolis Tribune*, Grevstad was early attracted to Wisconsin politics and offered a grateful Congressman Nils P. Haugen his support in the columns of the *Tribune*.[75] Grevstad also expressed interest in a couple of newspaper ventures in the booming city of Superior, including *Posten*, the paper that was soon to cause Peer Strømme such headaches. In the end, however, Grevstad determined not to leave Minnesota, among other things because he believed he might win a Republican seat in the Minnesota Senate.[76] Even though Grevstad ultimately moved to Chicago, he did maintain a strong commitment to Wisconsin affairs. In 1895, Nils P. Haugen thus suggested that Grevstad join the Wisconsin delegation heading for the national convention of Republican clubs in Cleveland, Ohio: "You have nothing in common with the Illinois delegation anyway, and we will adopt you."[77]

By November of 1890, Grevstad, for the past several months editor of the *Minneapolis Tribune*, decided to leave that paper because it had recently fallen into Democratic hands.[78] After an attempt by himself and a number of other prominent Minneapolis Norwegian Americans to launch a new Republican paper failed in early 1892, and with Hendrickson leaving *Skandinaven*, Grevstad took over the editorship of the latter paper.[79] *Skandinaven* thus entered its golden age. Grevstad quickly gained a controlling position on the paper's staff. By 1896 he and Nils P. Haugen were seriously discussing the possibility of buying out John Anderson. This would keep *Skandinaven* from succumbing to conservative forces within the GOP. Under present circumstances, Grevstad noted, Anderson was already "getting nervous" about his editor's pronounced support for Wisconsin's insurgent Republican faction under Robert M. La Follette. "He is irritated every time I mention Wisconsin politics."[80] Even though the idea of Grevstad's takeover found a favorable hearing with prominent members of the emerging progressive faction within Wisconsin's Republican Party, the money was never raised. John Anderson, who had seemed interested in selling, remained in economic control of *Skandinaven*.[81] Even so, Grevstad continued to dominate the paper. In 1911, President Taft referred to the editor as "the most influential person among his people in the country."[82]

During Grevstad's editorship, both friends and enemies of *Skandinaven* acknowledged its strength and influence. As one conservative Republican state senator from Trempealeau County suggested, the paper was the "political Bible" of the Scandinavian Americans, with "its teachings," as another Trempealeau politico added, "taken as the gospel truth."[83] As James O. Davidson, the 1906 Republican nominee for the governorship, suggested, "The man who underestimates the influence of Skandinaven in Wisconsin among our countrymen is not wise."[84] The little *Normannen* of Stoughton even printed a poem scolding *Skandinaven* for its powers of persuasion.[85] Henry P. Peterson of *Superior Tidende* might in 1903 advise Governor La Follette that in Wisconsin, "outside of the Chicago organ [*Skandinaven*] there are three Norwegian papers with more or less influence and circulation," naming Rasmus B. Anderson's anti-La Follette *Amerika* in Madison, Waldemar Ager's prohibitionist *Reform* of Eau Claire, and *Superior Tidende*; and he might further claim falsely that *Skandinaven* was being influenced by La Follette's enemies. He could not, however, convince La Follette of the advisability of shifting priorities in order to help *Superior Tidende* expand its circulation.[86] Since Nils P. Haugen and Grevstad were close friends politically, it comes as no surprise that the former, who in 1890 stated that he read most Scandinavian-American papers, advertised the latter as "by far the best Scandinavian writer."[87] More noteworthy is the displeasure that Rasmus B. Anderson expressed with Knute Nelson, Minnesota's Norwegian-born U.S. senator. "When Knute Nelson gives campaign speeches for the Norwegians, he usually uses the occasion to recommend 'Skandinaven' to his listeners."[88]

THE SCANDINAVIAN-AMERICAN PRESS AND
POLITICAL PATRONAGE

With the emergence of yellow journalism in the decades straddling 1900, the political parties lost much of their hold on the press, because the new mass-circulating papers depended first of all on large-scale advertising for their survival.[89] Among several immigrant papers, however, political independence remained a mirage. Early in the twentieth century, the Polish-American editor Louis Hammerling organized the American Association of Foreign-Language Newspapers, one of whose main functions was to distribute advertising contracts to the immigrant press of eastern European background in return for political support.[90] Among the Scandinavian-American press of the Midwest, it is true, several "independent" publications survived in good health without political funding. Still, the temptation to receive money from the war chests of the political parties proved hard to resist. The staunch political independence of the *North*, of Minneapolis, insisted Democratic-leaning editor Luth Jaeger, was earning the paper a splendid reputation but no money. The owners were now discussing whether the paper "should not in due time take a political stand in favor of some party. Col. M. [Hans Mattson] naturally would prefer to see it Republican, my views go in a different direction."[91]

In Wisconsin, the editors of some of the small Scandinavian-language papers did now and again contact politicians in hopes of soliciting funds. "If you have a cut we will use that, or else write what you want, and we will translate it to Swedish. Our price is 75 cts. per inch each insertion."[92] The larger Scandinavian-American papers could make much greater demands of the politicians. In Wisconsin, *Skandinaven* was of course in a category all by itself. Not only did the editor as a matter of course expect prominent Scandinavian-American politicians to secure funds for the paper from the national leadership of the Republican Party, but also asked individual leaders to perform actual newspaper work. In Wisconsin several politicians thus willingly became correspondents for the newspaper. In 1895, Hans Borchsenius, a Danish-born politician and Civil War veteran, and A. R. Hall, a full-blooded Yankee and pioneer progressive reformer, agreed to send the paper weekly reports from the Wisconsin legislature. In 1909, Norwegian-American Ole A. Buslett, a Republican member of the assembly, performed the same function and apparently received money for his effort.[93] When Norwegian-American Assemblyman Herman L. Ekern began writing a weekly column on legal matters in *Skandinaven* in 1905, on the other hand, he did so free of charge since, as editor Grevstad explained, "the incidental advertising is worth more than cash."[94] By May 1906, when *Skandinaven*'s campaign for James O. Davidson was warming up, Ekern, who did not support Davidson, at first decided to quit his job with *Skandinaven*, citing intense work pressure in his legislative committee.[95] In July, however, he changed his mind, noting that by staying on at *Skandinaven* he might be able to induce the paper to print articles in support of his gubernatorial favorite, Swedish-American Irvine L. Lenroot.[96] As it turned out, Ekern's decision to remain with *Skandinaven* had no impact on the paper's editorial policy. In fact, his connection with Lenroot's cause only worked as a boomerang against himself politically, so that by August he was complaining, "notwithstanding the fact that I have answered much of their legal correspondence for some time without any pay, they have ignored even those [items submitted by political friends] in my behalf."[97] Not only could the editor of *Skandinaven* successfully ask politicians to perform work voluntarily, but in a narrow factional sense he could also retain his paper's independence. When, on the other hand, the much smaller *Superior Tidende* announced in 1895 that Nils P. Haugen was going to be a correspondent for that paper, he was quick to deny that statement.[98]

In the early 1890s, Haugen was instrumental in securing *Skandinaven* political favors. During those years, the general standpoint of the Norwegian-American press caused worry among Republicans. Not only did the Democrats as well as the Populists score several electoral victories in the Midwest, with the Democrats winning in Wisconsin in 1890 and 1892, but a number of Norwegian-language papers began coming out for the Democratic Party. As early as 1888, Rasmus B. Anderson informed

U.S. Senator William F. Vilas that *Norden* had gone Democratic, and three years later Nicolai Grevstad worried that this paper would swallow *Amerika*.[99] In 1892, Grevstad and other prominent Minnesota Norwegian Americans issued a call for a new, strong Republican paper and discussed the present miserable conditions. In Wisconsin, for instance, "there is one Prohibition paper of general circulation [*Reform* of Eau Claire], one Democratic paper of general circulation in the northern part of the state [*Posten* of Superior], one Democratic paper in the southern part of the state [*Normannen* of Stoughton], and one small Republican paper of only a limited circulation in La Crosse [*Varden*]."[100] One year later, on the other hand, the mood among Norwegian-American Democrats remained buoyant. "A few years ago, we had no Norwegian democratic paper in the country – today we have half a dozen."[101]

According to Haugen it was precisely these Democratic gains that in 1892 caused *Skandinaven* to employ Nicolai A. Grevstad as editor, in direct cooperation with the Republican Party, which was planning to distribute free copies of the paper to large numbers of voters in the upcoming presidential campaign.[102] Haugen himself, running for reelection to Congress, played a pivotal role in the latter move. As he informed John Anderson of *Skandinaven*, Haugen and Swedish-American John Lind of Minnesota had secured the pledge from a member of the Republican national committee that the GOP would distribute 30,000 copies of the paper on a regular basis during the campaign. To the same end Haugen contacted large numbers of post office employees in Wisconsin, asking them to furnish him with the names of all Norwegian Americans and Danish Americans in their postal district.[103] The Republican Party thus provided 2,460 Wisconsin households with *Skandinaven* during the 1892 campaign.[104] Haugen hoped that upward of 1,000 copies of the Swedish-language *Hemlandet* would be distributed in Wisconsin's northwestern corner, just as it had been distributed by the Republican Party in Minnesota, Michigan, and Massachusetts. Yet, as he noted, "Our Com. [committee] has no money."[105] Finally, Haugen investigated the possibility of subsidizing two Swedish-American Wisconsin Republican locals, *Ashland Bladet* and *Svenska Amerikanska Tribunen*.[106]

In the momentous presidential campaign four years later, a similar scenario was enacted. On 21 October 1896, Nicolai Grevstad thus in-

formed Haugen that the Republican national committee had placed an order for 25,000 copies of *Skandinaven,* with some 5,000 to be distributed in
Wisconsin.[107] That same day, an editorial in *Hemlandet* boasted that the
previous issue of that paper had been published in 100,000 copies, but the
editorial did not state how this had happened.[108] In its October issues, even
the little *Förposten* of Marinette, Wisconsin, announced that it was now
being distributed without charge.[109] Perhaps *Den danske Pioneer* was not all
wrong in accusing sixty-five Scandinavian-American newspapers of having been "bought" by Republican chairman Mark Hanna's national committee.[110]

Grevstad's personal importance to the Republican Party was acknowledged in the summer of 1911, when President William Howard Taft
appointed him American minister to Paraguay and Uruguay. Grevstad
thus left *Skandinaven* after more than twenty years of service.[111] Twenty-
two years earlier Johan Enander, editor of *Hemlandet*, had similarly been
offered the position of minister to Denmark, much to the disgust of Peter
Hendrickson of *Skandinaven*.[112] The largest Scandinavian-language newspapers and their editors were clearly forces to be reckoned with when matters of patronage came up for consideration.

THE NATIONALITY MODE OF DISCUSSING POLITICS

No other Scandinavian-American institution made so clear and outspoken
a link between ethnicity and politics as did the press. To church leaders,
the open link between those two factors always remained problematic due
to the so clearly formulated separation of the state and the church. Likewise, whereas the leaders of the mutual-aid fraternities might easily celebrate ethnic origins, again, a too obvious involvement in politics was
embarrassing. To many Prohibitionists, finally, the blend of ethnicity and
politics was definitely attractive, yet their political influence was limited.
The press remained the Scandinavian-American institution that most
openly and powerfully combined the two. When this happened, ethnicity
was invariably presented in terms of Old World nationality.

Come election time, arguments stressing the importance of national
attachments would invariably appear in the editorials of the most politicized papers. Such loyalties were frequently presented with a thin veneer of
pan-Scandinavianism.[113] The smaller Wisconsin papers would participate

in the chorus: "The reason for our backward place is largely our own," complained the Swedish-language *Förposten* in 1892. "Look at the Irish, the Germans, and other nations, how eagerly, unanimously, and aggressively they act on the political stage, winning one government office for themselves after another."[114] In 1914, at the other end of the chronological scale, *Superior Tidende* expressed frustration at the political humility of Norwegian Americans in Superior.[115] When on occasion *Svenska Amerikanska Tribunen* meddled in politics, it typically did so also by emphasizing national background: "He [Irvine L. Lenroot] is an honor to the Swedish name and is a man of honest political convictions."[116] In 1896, even the otherwise politically colorless Danish-American *Folkets Avis* urged its readers to support Peter Bering Nelson for the district attorneyship of Racine County. The paper explicitly mentioned his Danish background, and six years later it championed him for the mayoralty of Racine, arguing that he "has never forgotten that he is Danish."[117]

The larger Scandinavian-American newspapers likewise tended to discuss electoral politics in this "national" mode. In 1890, *Svenska Amerikanaren* thus complained about Swedish Americans being neglected by the American political system.[118] Eight years later, *Hemlandet* wailed that whenever a Swedish American ran for office, he risked being opposed with the words, "He is a Swede."[119] In 1912 that same paper asserted that every Swedish American supporting John Lind for governor of Minnesota was acting like a conscientious man of honor.[120] In a similar vein, in 1894 *Den danske Pioneer* urged its Colorado readers to vote for Danish-American H. W. Baerresen of Denver for the state legislature on the Populist-Democratic fusion ticket.[121] As far as the leading Norwegian-American papers were concerned, in 1894 *Norden* wished "all our countrymen who thus attempt to raise up our nationality good luck, irrespective of what political party they belong to," and *Amerika*, not yet Rasmus B. Anderson's paper, made a distinction between Nils P. Haugen and the "anti-Norwegian" Republican candidates for the governorship.[122] Four years earlier, *Skandinaven* had lamented that Haugen was the *only* Norwegian-American member of Congress and had hypothetically conjured up the sinister scenario of "Scandinavian voters" supporting "strangers" rather than "men of their own flesh and blood."[123] In 1914, the same paper urged its readers to vote for all eight Scandinavian-American members of Congress.[124]

The above examples illustrate a mode of discussion that permeated the editorials of the politicized Scandinavian-American newspapers from 1890 to 1914, even though an impressionistic observation would be that the mode was more pervasive in the former year than the latter. This nationalist argument was so persistent that even when it was put under logical strain, it was sometimes given a bizarre twist rather than being dropped. Why not for instance argue that *two* Norwegian Americans ought to appear on the Minnesota state ticket and on the Wisconsin state ticket in 1892, since in each case one of them could easily pass for an "American"?[125] Or why not urge that the Scandinavian Americans support a German American for office in Douglas County, Wisconsin, since "the Germans and the Scandinavians have always been good friends in this nation"?[126] Six years later, Peer O. Strømme, the Norwegian-American Democrat who had penned those words, was nominated for state treasurer in Wisconsin, an action that immediately prompted *Skandinaven* to argue that his nomination was a ploy by the Democrats "to capture the Scandinavian vote," adding with malice that "Strømme was supported by German delegates."[127]

Why not, finally, take exactly this type of criticism one step further and contend that some Scandinavian-American politicians simply were unworthy representatives of their Old World nationality? In 1892, *Svenska Amerikanaren* expressed the hope that no Swedish American in Illinois would vote for Henry L. Hertz, the Danish-American Republican candidate for state treasurer: "We hold nothing against Hertz on account of his being Danish. Far from it! . . . But whenever possible, he has always exploited the political influence that he, being a very 'smart' politician, has won over the years to work against the Swedes and thereupon ingratiate himself with the Irish."[128] National identity might even be employed to contend against a type of politics based on class by arguing that the Scandinavian-American group ought to be recognized fully by the advancement of Nils P. Haugen to the governor's chair. As *Skandinaven* asserted in 1894, "This will be an honor to the whole nation; it will lift the whole nation, and it will help everyone within the nation to elevate his position within society, whether he be a day laborer, a businessman, or something else."[129]

As far as *Skandinaven*, the most important of the Scandinavian-American papers, was concerned, the typical mode of discussing electoral politics was not only "national" but also explicitly nonreligious. *Skandi-naven* did occasionally display the anti-Catholicism so characteristic of the Scandinavian-language press in the decades straddling 1900.[130] At the same time, however, the paper made a conscious effort to minimize Norwegian-American religious schism, so as not to threaten ethnic unity. It explicitly urged the clergy not to bring up such matters in the large political journals and cautioned readers against listening too much to theologians eager to fight.[131] In 1897, *Skandinaven* refused to print one particular letter to the editor, arguing that it might trigger a religious dispute.[132]

In all its cutthroat growth and diversity, the Scandinavian-American press played an important role in the emergence of distinct Scandinavian-American identities in the New World. This was in some contrast to emerging class identities in Europe. The Scandinavian-American press played a crucial role in introducing the question of nationality into midwestern politics. Unlike some of the other Scandinavian-American institutions, the press did not have to be cautious and secretive about its general interest in the "nationality issue" and its application to politics, and the leading editors could count on receiving active assistance from the political leaders and parties much more so than could Lutheran pastors, mutual-aid fraternity leaders, and temperance people. To be sure, the economic side to this relationship between the press and the politicians was toned down by the interested parties, if not by the opposition papers, but the direct link between national background and politics was made very explicit. In *Skandinaven*, the most important Scandinavian-language newspaper in Wisconsin, whenever political topics were discussed, religious issues, anti-Catholic slurs aside, were correspondingly muted.

The national argument, however, never stood on its own. First, as will become clear, it was often presented in conjunction with statements that highlighted the party, locality, and personality of the candidate, with vague value judgments sometimes being added. Second, Wisconsin's progressive leadership would at least attempt to challenge this mode of political argument and introduce a new type of politics that focused on social and economic issues rather than on retrospective symbols.

CHAPTER FIVE

Scandinavian Americans
Enter Politics

LOCAL POLITICS: THE POINT OF ENTRY

In Kristoffer Skauge's Strum, politics were central to the life of the community and often caused local strife. At some point during the first Democratic administration of Grover Cleveland (1885–1889), Strum's post office was renamed Tilden. Even though this move apparently was unrelated to the death in 1886 of former Democratic presidential candidate Samuel J. Tilden, upon returning to power the Republicans promptly changed the name back to Strum again.[1] Strife over the post office continued when two rivals, each belonging to their own Norwegian-American denomination (in Haugen's emphatic opinion, a circumstance "of no relevance to the case"), vied for the postmastership. The matter was settled only after six weeks of bickering. At one point Ole Nysven, the ultimate winner, even accused Haugen of having forwarded their mutual correspondence to the rival candidate. The congressman proclaimed his own innocence by promptly returning all these letters to Nysven.[2]

Scandinavian Americans had their earliest say in politics at the local level. Immigrants did not, of course, turn to politics as their first priority upon their arrival in America. Most of them went through a period of adaptation, finding work, establishing a home, learning the English language, and forging social and religious ties with the local community before getting actively involved in politics.[3] The early Scandinavian immigrants were arguably slower to acclimatize politically than the later arrivals, simply because the latter found more ethnic institutions to fall back upon in the

102

New World for help and guidance, and typically also had undergone more substantial political education in Scandinavia. American legislation certainly inspired political participation by the male immigrants. The federal Naturalization Act of 1801 granted newcomers citizenship only five years after filing application, but in Wisconsin, like in so many other midwestern states, citizenship was not a precondition for suffrage. Male aliens stating their intention to become citizens could vote after just one year's residence in the state.[4] Scandinavian immigrants were usually eager to apply for citizenship. By 1890, despite the surge in immigration in the 1880s, only 11.1 percent of the Norwegian immigrants, 13.7 percent of the Danish, and 14.5 percent of the Swedish were aliens. These numbers were typical for western European immigrants and lower than those for eastern European newcomers.[5]

Merle Curti's classic account of frontier life in Trempealeau County illustrates the manner in which Scandinavian Americans might enter local politics.[6] In the 1860s, one decade after the first Norwegian-American settlements in the county were established, the first Norwegian-born officials were elected to town office. In 1871, by which point the Norwegian-American population element nearly matched the Yankee, the first Norwegian-born town chairman was elected, and five years later seven of the county's fifteen townships had Norwegian-American chairmen, and the Republican Party's county slate contained its first Norwegian-American name.

In local affairs, ethnicity easily became an issue. In 1878, with the Norwegian Americans emerging as the largest population group within the county, one K. K. Hagestad, upon failing to win the Republican nomination for sheriff, ran as an independent, openly flaunting his Norwegian background and complaining that the GOP was cheating the Norwegian immigrants: he won the election. That same year, the Norwegian Americans captured all offices in the town of Pigeon. On election day, many Yankees stayed at home in prescient resignation. By 1880, it is true, the town government again included some Yankees.[7]

During the 1890s and into the early twentieth century, the ethnic factor remained important in Trempealeau County politics. Thus, the nationality argument reverberated in several reader letters to *Skandinaven*. In 1910, for instance, one correspondent recommended ex-sheriff Hagestad for a seat in the Wisconsin Assembly, employing ethnic arguments.[8] Hardly surprising, in other localities with many Scandinavian Americans the nationality factor also figured prominently. From Castle Rock in Grant County, Wisconsin, came a plea to support Republican Thomas Peterson for sheriff, for any other behavior by the Norwegian Americans would be shameful.[9] In Polk County further to the north, West Denmark locals warmly endorsed M. C. Peterson, the founder of their colony, for county judge, commending his Danish background.[10] In Rock Island in neighboring Illinois, readers of *Hemlandet* were advised to support Swedish-American Charles R. Swanson for county clerk.[11] Usually requests of this kind were strictly "national"; only on rarer occasions were pan-Scandinavian-American appeals made, as when in one case a Norwegian-American correspondent to *Skandinaven* insisted that "we Norwegians" ought to support Danish-American candidates for office in Turner County, South Dakota, since the Danish Americans had so often supported the Norwegian Americans.[12]

Again, as when the nationality argument was advanced in newspaper editorials, reader letters sometimes gave this line of reasoning a strange twist, attesting to its pervasiveness in political debate. From Stoughton in Dane County, Wisconsin, one correspondent thus promoted the Democratic Mr. Ladd, a Norwegian by birth, for county treasurer, explicitly disavowing that this was on account of his national background, but rather because he was an old settler and a fair and honest man.[13] Another Stoughton correspondent warned against supporting Danish-born Christ. A. Hanson for county treasurer. "He is Danish, but he would like to be – German."[14]

The argument from nationality rarely stood on its own, however. In local and county politics, three other factors were equally important and typically went hand in hand with considerations of nationality, both among immigrants and Yankees. First, the party of any political candidate was crucial. The party, after all, represented a certain set of values, a particular moral outlook, that pertained both to community matters and to national affairs. In the arguments temperance and local taxes jostled with currency and tariff issues.[15] Second, the candidate's place of residence was important, because with regard to the pork barrel and patronage a candidate from the locality might easily prove more valuable than someone from the neighboring community. Third, the candidate's personality in

terms of his local standing, authority, and political experience was critical.[16] Between 1890 and 1914, these factors all remained important in local
politics, even as the progressive movement undertook to challenge them.
The ranking of the four elements varied from case to case. The party label
was usually, yet not always, taken for granted, but "nationality," locality, or
personality might all take second place.

In 1897, one Norwegian-American correspondent from Allamakee
County in Iowa presented the national argument in this broader context.
"We do not have much to complain about in this county, as far as offices are
concerned, for not a few of them are occupied by Scandinavians. We have
the county auditor and the clerk, as well as the supervisor, so we are really
very well represented. This autumn we also have a Scandinavian on the ticket,
and we expect to get the kind of person who has character and who can also
accomplish something, and who is sufficiently well-educated to be able to
write a document without misspelling every word or so. Such a person [with
no writing skills] would be of no honor to the Scandinavian people. Neither
would I consider anyone fit for office who could not make his neighbors vote
for him. Nor do we need the kind of person who thinks only of his own interests. But what we need is an honest and clever man for the job who is and
will continue to be an honor to the Scandinavian people."[17]

For leaders, the charm of this type of reasoning was that arguments
were reduced to mere labels. In the above case, there was no need even to
bring up the obvious fact that the candidate in question must be a Republican, nor to explain why Scandinavian Americans, in fact, ought to win office, not to speak of what it actually meant to be a Scandinavian American.
Nor was there need to clarify why local popularity or personality traits
were so vital to politics. In this instance, indeed, there is no mention
whatsoever of political issues. In other letters, discussion of values and issues would appear alongside arguments for party-nationality-locality-
personality, yet this is frequently in a very vague (and secular) form, relating, for instance, to the candidate's sympathy for "the people" or to the
corrupt ways of the powerful opponent. With labels, politicians could
communicate with their voters in a manner that diminished the threat
of conflict. Why run the risk of elucidating the meaning of being
Scandinavian-American politically if this entailed bringing up the explosive temperance question or moving into the minefield of Lutheran dis-

putes? Some people occasionally overstepped these boundaries and ventured an actual explanation of Scandinavian-American political identity, beyond the application of an ill-defined Republican tag. Even in these cases, however, ethnoreligious considerations, as we shall see, would not stand on their own but would be supplemented by influential "secular" arguments.[18]

SCANDINAVIAN-AMERICAN POLITICAL CLUBS

In the closing decades of the nineteenth century and the first decades of the twentieth, besides politics-as-usual three other types of ethnically structured political activism sprouted at the local level. This occurred first within the framework of Republican and Democratic clubs; second, especially after the turn of the century, among trade unions and left-wing parties; and third, among farmers.

In years of presidential elections, the Republican and Democratic national parties organized clubs to boost local enthusiasm for their presidential candidate. The clubs often sponsored prominent guest speakers and staged colorful parades. By 1892, the National Republican League, founded four years earlier in Iowa, reported a membership of two million organized into 20,000 Republican clubs.[19] Some of these clubs, if only a minority, were organized along ethnic lines. A main function of the "Scandinavian" clubs was to educate Scandinavian immigrants on American political issues. As one organizer of a Scandinavian-American Democratic club in Michigan wrote in 1892, "We are sadly in need of a Scandinavian speaker here, as [a] good many of our nationality are not sufficiently advanced in the English language to fully get the idea of the political questions when so addressed."[20] In those decades, the activities of Scandinavian-American clubs were reported not only from such population centers as New York, Chicago, and Minneapolis but also from much smaller localities.[21]

Wisconsin also boasted its share of Scandinavian-American clubs. In 1892, to ensure a strong voter turnout, *Skandinaven* urged its Wisconsin readers to form their own Republican clubs. In the fall of 1892, Congressman Nils P. Haugen discussed the tariff and silver questions at a Scandinavian-American club meeting in Deer Park, St. Croix County, and from Marinette, *Hemlandet* reported about a torch parade arranged by the local Scandinavian-American Republican club with hundreds of march-ers.[22] Fourteen years later, when James O. Davidson ran for the governor-ship in Wisconsin, a number of Davidson-Connor clubs arose in various localities.[23] Generally speaking, these clubs were not intended to be Scandinavian-American, but in some localities they in effect became Norwegian-American. "Everything up here are [sic] looking good," wrote one Davidson supporter, "and a few of us are commencing to organize Davidson and Connor clubs. I think we will have a Scandinavian club, a young men's club and also one that any nationality may belong to."[24]

Most of the clubs in Wisconsin were Republican. In 1852, before the outbreak of the Civil War and the general alignment of Scandinavian-American voters and institutions with the Republican Party, a "Scandi-navian Democratic Club" existed in Madison.[25] In the early 1890s, moreo-ver, with the memories of the Civil War wearing thinner, with some Scandinavian Americans further out west joining the Populist Party, with the Republican Party in Wisconsin suffering on account of the McKinley tariff and the Bennett English-language school law, Wisconsin Democrats began once again to dream of Scandinavian-American Democratic clubs. In fact, state chairman E. C. Wall recommended that U.S. Senator William F. Vilas employ Peer O. Strømme as a writer, speaker, and club organizer: "He understands the Norwegian people perfectly."[26] Even though Wall in-deed created a "Norwegian" bureau in 1892, it is doubtful that any Scandi-navian Democratic club actually came into being.[27] In Muskegon in neighboring Michigan, at least one such club did surface.[28] However, with the onset of the depression in 1893, only months after Democratic Grover Cleveland was sworn in as president, all talk of organizing Scandinavian-American Democratic clubs in Wisconsin ceased.

The existence of Scandinavian-American Republican clubs did not in itself necessarily imply strong ethnic unity. Editor Grevstad of *Skandi-naven* could only utter his misgivings when Ole A. Buslett, the editor of the little *Normannen* in Stoughton, organized a Scandinavian Republican club, for Buslett had opposed Nils P. Haugen's candidacy for the Wiscon-sin governorship in 1894.[29] Furthermore, Scandinavian-American political leaders had varying opinions of just how prominent a part ethnic consid-erations ought to play in American politics. As should become clear shortly, some oriented themselves inward toward their own ethnic group for their primary political strength; others, including several of the most successful politicians, took a fuller view of the situation and reasoned that their European nationality might indeed sometimes work to their advantage, but that they had also to acknowledge their wider role in an *American* political system. This latter acceptance of the complementarity of Scandinavian-American identity was lauded by *Skandinaven*, which in 1894 scolded one Scandinavian-American club in Pensacola, Florida, that had prohibited the use of the English language. "Let the cultus of offensive clannishness be left to the Spaniards and Italians. . . . If the Norsemen in Pensacola really are guilty of such un-American thought and action as charged, let the thing die now and bury it deep."[30]

LABOR RADICALISM

In the cities, another type of Scandinavian-American activism centered on the organization of labor. The earliest such activities dated back to Chicago in the 1860s and 1870s when some tailors, painters, shoemakers, carpenters, joiners, and apparently also machinists and blacksmiths, began organizing along Scandinavian-American lines. Most of these ethnic locals were subdivisions of larger "American" trade unions, several of them united within the National Labor Union, a non-Socialist umbrella organization founded in 1866. In the late 1870s, however, the Scandinavian-American locals foundered due, first, to the recession in 1873–1879, and, second, to the ill-fated attempt by the National Labor Union to launch its own political party.[31]

No signs indicate that these early Scandinavian-American associations cooperated in any organized fashion with the small group of Scandinavian-born Socialist intellectuals who resided in Chicago during those same years, a group that included such prominent émigrés as Louis Pio and Marcus Thrane.[32] From the 1880s, however, with the arrival of many "new," single, urbanized, predominantly male Scandinavian immigrants to metropolises like Chicago, Minneapolis-St. Paul, and New York City, leftist activities increased. In 1883, Scandinavian-American typographers in Chicago thus established their own union, and ten years later it split along Old World nationality lines, Swedish Americans on the one hand and Danish and Norwegian Americans on the other each going their separate ways.[33] In 1890, a Scandinavian-American local within the International Brotherhood of Painters, Decorators, and Paperhangers of America likewise surfaced in Chicago and by 1909 in fact was the largest painters' local in the world. The sources remain silent on the question of whether the appearance in 1906 of another such local, this one largely Swedish-American, signaled one more division between Swedish Americans on the one hand and Danish and Norwegian Americans on the other.[34] By 1914, ethnically based trade-union activities were taking place among Scandinavian-American painters, typographers, and shoemakers in Chicago and among bricklayers, bakers, painters, and decorators in New York City. In Minneapolis, on the other hand, Norwegian-American trade unions for bakers and typographers had by now gone out of existence.[35] Many other Scandinavian Americans joined "American" trade unions.[36]

At the national level, local Scandinavian-American departments also emerged in America's two Socialist parties, Daniel De Leon's tiny, New York-based Socialist Labor Party, formed in 1877, and Eugene V. Debs's much more influential Socialist Party of America with headquarters in Chicago, a party known between 1897 and 1901 as the Social Democratic Party (a label that Wisconsin's state party retained).[37] Over the years, the former party received support from *Den nye Tid*, the paper that Louis Pio and Marcus Thrane had each worked for during the late 1870s. The party itself published both the Swedish-language *Arbetaren*, launched in 1894, and the Norwegian-Danish-language *Arbejderen*, established two years later. In the closing decades of the nineteenth century, with the formation of Skandinaviska Socialistiska Förbundet (The Scandinavian Socialistic Federation), connections among the Scandinavian-American party members were formalized.[38]

In the early twentieth century, Scandinavian-American branches of Eugene V. Debs's larger Socialist Party also appeared. In 1904, the Norwegian-dominated Skandinavisk Socialist Forening for Chicago med Omegn (Scandinavian Socialist Association for Chicago and Its Vicinity) emerged, and three years later Danish immigrants in the same city organized Socialistforeningen Karl Marx (The Socialist Association Karl Marx), a club that seven years later merged with the Norwegian-American association. In 1908, the Swedish-dominated Lake View Skandinaviska Socialistklubb (The Lake View Scandinavian Socialist Club) formed in Chicago,

whereas Minneapolis saw the appearance of the short-lived Den Skandinaviske Socialistforening (The Scandinavian Socialist Association).[39]

Countering the usual Scandinavian-American trend towards crystallization along lines of nationality, in 1910 the Scandinavian-American
Debs Socialists inaugurated an era of cooperation when Skandinaviska So-
cialistförbundet i Amerika (The Scandinavian Socialist Federation of
America) was founded.[40] The Scandinavian-American branches of Debs's
Socialist Party likewise boasted their own organs, Svenska Socialisten, established in 1905, and the Norwegian-Danish Social-Demokraten, started
in 1911.[41] Four other Scandinavian-American papers with Socialist sympathies retained a profile independent of the two Socialist parties.[42]

Generally speaking, the American trade-union movement was not
organically connected with any one political party. Samuel Gompers, head
of the American Federation of Labor established in 1886, rejected cooperation with third-party movements and attempted instead to cooperate with
America's two main political parties on a pragmatic case-by-case basis
through "pressure-group unionism."[43] One study of activities among the
Scandinavian-American members of the International Brotherhood of
Painters demonstrates, however, that a few years prior to the outbreak of
World War I the two Scandinavian-American locals in Chicago deviated
from Gompers's line and began supporting Eugene V. Debs's Socialist
Party.[44]

Even though Wisconsin boasted one of the strongest labor movements in the United States, evidence of labor activities among the state's
Scandinavian Americans is scanty. In 1893, the Wisconsin State Federation
of Labor (WSFL) emerged as a branch of Gompers's nationwide organization, and seven years later Wisconsin's Social Democrats captured the state
chapter. They remained in control for the next thirty-five years.[45] By 1910,
Milwaukee was emerging as one of the strongest Socialist centers in America. It elected Emil Seidel as mayor and put his colleague Victor Berger in
the U.S. House of Representatives as the first Socialist ever elected to that
body.[46] Yet Wisconsin's labor movement and the Social Democratic party,
strong as they proved to be in combination, concentrated all their power
in the state's only metropolitan area, Milwaukee. Even there the organization remained largely a German-American undertaking for dues-paying,
skilled laborers, modeled after the Social Democratic party in Germany,

and usually devoting only scant attention to Milwaukee's growing group of Polish-born unskilled workers.[47] One Danish American, it is true, rose within the ranks of both the Social Democratic Party and the WSFL. In 1900, Frederick Brockhausen, born and raised in Fredericia, Denmark, played a central role in the Social Democratic takeover of the WSFL. He became the latter body's secretary-treasurer and between 1905 and 1912 was a member of Wisconsin's Assembly.[48]

No evidence survives to indicate that Brockhausen engaged in activities among Milwaukee's few Scandinavian Americans. Indeed, the Scandinavian Americans of Wisconsin's southeastern industrialized corner appear to have engaged in only very limited trade-union and Socialist activities. Prior to 1910, to be sure, the city of Kenosha boasted a Norwegian-Danish-American Socialist club, and at the founding meeting of the Scandinavian Socialist Federation of America, Norwegian- and Danish-American delegates from Milwaukee, Kenosha, and Racine participated.[49] By 1914, however, the latter organization included only three Scandinavian-American locals in Wisconsin, one in Racine and two in Kenosha, and together they totaled just forty-nine members in good standing.[50]

Wisconsin's large lumbering industry, which as late as 1897 employed nearly one-fourth of the state's manufacturing work force, was even less affected by unionism and almost completely avoided socialism.[51] In the logging camps trade unions were exceedingly difficult to organize, simply because the labor force was largely migratory. In the sawmill cities, on the other hand, some organization did take place.[52] To be sure, Marcus Thrane's presence in Eau Claire in the twilight of his life did not leave much of an imprint. Until his death in 1890, the tired, old rebel who now lived on the top floor of his son's house limited his labor activism to flying the anarchists' black flag each November 11 in commemoration of the men executed in the wake of the Haymarket riots in Chicago.[53] Until 1886, however, Eau Claire did boast an organization called the Scandia Trade Union.[54] La Crosse, moreover, housed a Norwegian-American labor association which in 1890 invited Viggo Ullman, president of the Norwegian parliament and member of *Venstre*, Norway's liberal party, to speak.[55] Whether these two labor clubs were really trade unions or simply mutual-aid fraternities remains unclear, however. As *Skandinaven* pointed out, the two types of organizations were difficult to distinguish from each other.[56]

In Superior in Wisconsin's northwestern corner, finally, *Superior Tidende* announced in late 1898 that the editor had become aware of the recent interest in "the study of social questions by our people and other nationalities."[57] Proclaiming that the paper was planning to publish a series of articles on these issues, it further stated that a Scandinavian-American club had been formed at Superior's steel works a short time ago with such matters in mind, and the *Tidende* suggested that others follow their example. Three years later, the same paper reported sympathetically about the ongoing national steel strike.[58] By 1914, as it turned out, Superior boasted the largest Wisconsin chapter of the Scandinavian Socialist Federation of America, with seventy members in good standing. Another thirty-eight belonged to locals in Green Bay and Ashland.[59] In comparison with the strength of the mainly German-American Socialists in Milwaukee, however, those figures were not very impressive. The difference between the political affiliation of trade-union people inside and outside Milwaukee was captured by one Superior unionist in 1906. "In Milwaukee most of the union men belong to the social Dem. party while in Superior most of the labor union men are republicans."[60]

FARMER RADICALISM AND COOPERATION

Traditionally, farmer radicalism beyond the pale of the Republican Party flourished in states to the west and south of Wisconsin. The Populist Party of the late 1880s and early 1890s had its strength in newly settled wheat-growing areas in Kansas and Nebraska, as well as in some states in Dixie. The People's Party also gained a foothold among some Scandinavian Americans living to the west of Wisconsin. In Minnesota, Haldor E. Boen, a Norwegian-born Populist, was thus elected to Congress in 1892, apparently receiving the support of many Norwegian-American voters, and in Nebraska, Sophus Neble's *Den danske Pioneer* supported the Populist cause for a time.[61] After the turn of the century, the American Society of Equity, founded in Indianapolis in 1902, likewise gained a hearing in the grain and tobacco belts in the West. Like the Populist movement, the Society of Equity supported cooperative farming, and in Minnesota and North Dakota it met with considerable success.[62]

To the degree that both populism and the Society of Equity espoused cooperative principles, one might have expected these movements to have prospered among Wisconsin's Scandinavian-American farmers. Generally speaking, however, this did not happen, notwithstanding that Wisconsin by 1911 boasted a quite sizeable cooperative movement, comprising 244 of the state's 1,784 cheese factories and 347 of its 1,000 creameries.[63] Cooperation bloomed particularly in Dodge and Green counties in the agricultural heartland to the south, areas without many Scandinavian Americans.[64] Even though heavily Scandinavian-American Polk County to the northwest was not part of Wisconsin's prime dairying region, several cooperative ventures were also established there.[65] Many of the Polk County dairies were founded by Danish immigrants, and occasionally the Scandinavian-language press also mentioned cooperative ventures in other distinctly Scandinavian-American localities.[66] In Minnesota, asserted *Skandinaven*, the cooperative creameries "are to a large extent offshoots of the Danish cooperative dairies."[67] In Wisconsin, however, at least some of the Danish-American farmers received instruction in modern dairying techniques from an expert of Yankee background, Professor William A. Henry of the University of Wisconsin.[68]

The success of the cooperative movement in Wisconsin, both among its Scandinavian and non-Scandinavian elements, should not be exaggerated. In 1912, the State Board of Public Affairs concluded its investigation of Wisconsin's cooperative movement with the remark that in the future the state ought to help advance cooperation: "Failures in the past in no wise argue against this proposition."[69] When years later Frederic C. Howe, a prominent progressive reformer, wrote a glowing book about the cooperative movement, he turned not to the farmers of the Midwest but to Denmark, whose cooperative movement also impressed Robert M. La Follette when he visited the country in 1923.[70]

Despite its cooperative experiments, Wisconsin never hosted a strong Populist movement. In Wisconsin, the People's Party remained largely an urban working-class movement restricted to Milwaukee, with a very limited appeal among Scandinavian-American farmers.[71] In 1890, to be sure, James Larsen, a Danish-American fish dealer and boatbuilder from Menekaunee, was elected to the Wisconsin Assembly as the only representative of the Union Labor Party, a temporary substitute for the Wisconsin People's Party.[72] In 1892, furthermore, P. L. Scritsmeier, a Danish-born Populist, ran for a seat in Congress from the tenth district of

Wisconsin, but was soundly defeated by Nils P. Haugen, his Norwegian-born Republican rival.[73] That year, moreover, some Norwegian immigrants in a few newly settled poor rural areas apparently supported the People's Party.[74] Indications of more widespread support for populism among Wisconsin's Scandinavian Americans are lacking, however.

The American Society of Equity met with somewhat greater success in Wisconsin. The first local chapter was established in 1903, and in 1906 a state branch was founded. By the following year, the state organization boasted slightly more than 10,000 members, as it still did by 1911.[75] In 1907, however, Governor Davidson had to admit that he hardly knew what the movement stood for.[76] Even so, the Society of Equity had some appeal among the state's Scandinavian-American farmers. In 1908, in fact, Garret M. Walrod, editor of the newly started *Wisconsin Equity News*, claimed that the Wisconsin organization comprised "maybe three thousand members who are Norwegian."[77] That figure is open to doubt, since it was printed in an ad, but Walrod's sixteen-page biweekly publication nevertheless soon included a six-column Norwegian-language section, as well as one in German.[78] Moreover, in the summer of 1909, Rasmus B. Anderson's *Amerika* of Madison became the official Norwegian-language organ of the organization and remained so until August 1910.[79] During that period, each issue of *Amerika* contained one page with Equity news.

Prior to World War I, the Society of Equity did not play a very prominent political role in Wisconsin, either generally or among the Scandinavian Americans. In 1908, an Equity picnic in Trempealeau County proved fateful to Speaker Herman L. Ekern's vain attempt to be reelected to the assembly, but that was due simply to the presence on that occasion of a Republican politician criticizing Ekern.[80] Prior to World War I, Wisconsin did not witness an election of politicians to the state legislature on the basis of their affiliation with the Equity movement, as neighboring Minnesota did.[81]

Generally speaking, the Wisconsin branch of the Equity movement was dwarfed by another farm organization, the Wisconsin Dairymen's Association, whose most prominent leader, William Dempster Hoard (1836–1918), was Republican governor of Wisconsin in 1889–1891. By 1894, Hoard was urging the dairymen to enter politics in large numbers, and at about the same time Robert M. La Follette, who had earned Hoard's friendship in the late 1880s by campaigning actively in Congress against the production of synthetic butter, began to cooperate with the latter in a teamwork that lasted into the early twentieth century.[82] The Wisconsin Dairymen's Association had no Scandinavian-American subsidiaries. Hoard himself was a strong Americanizer who by stubbornly agitating for the Bennett English-language school law in 1890 was instrumental in bringing about Republican defeat. On one occasion, Hoard was asked to consider the possibility of helping a Danish immigrant find a position as a butter maker. His answer to the request was candid: "There will be no difficulty whatever in securing a place for him simply by advertising in Hoard's Dairyman, if he is a competent butter maker from a Danish standpoint, as all butter makers from that country are highly esteemed on account of their acquirements, but not being able to speak English makes it very difficult to find a place for him."[83]

EARLY SCANDINAVIAN-AMERICAN PARTICIPATION IN STATE POLITICS

It was not fortuitous that James Denoon Reymert (1821–1896) of Muskego, Wisconsin, became the first Scandinavian American in the United States to gain any kind of political prominence beyond the county level. Although he was born and raised in Farsund, Norway, his mother was Scottish by birth. Before setting sail for America in 1842, he worked for some years in Scotland, first for a commercial house in Leith, then in an attorney's office in Edinburgh. Reymert had thus mastered the English language before setting foot on American soil. Traveling to Wisconsin, in 1847 he became America's first Norwegian-American editor when he started publishing *Nordlyset*. The following year, he was a member of Wisconsin's constitutional convention and was also elected to the state assembly, a feat repeated in 1856. In 1853, furthermore, he won access to the state senate. For a number of years he was Norwegian-Swedish vice-consul to the western states. He was on at least one occasion a presidential elector, and in 1860 stood as an unsuccessful Democratic candidate for Congress.[84]

During the 1850s and early 1860s, signs of mounting political interest among Scandinavian Americans appeared. In Wisconsin, a couple of Scandinavian Americans besides Reymert thus rose to a certain level of prominence.[85] In 1852, Hans Christian Heg, a Free Soiler who during the Civil War would command the Fifteenth Wisconsin Regiment, was defeated in an assembly race. Five years later, however, the Danish-American Peter C. Lütken of Racine County won election to the assembly, as did in 1860 Norwegian-born Knud Langeland, cofounder of *Skandinaven*. Seven years later, Knute Nelson of Dane County, the future U.S. Senator from Minnesota, was also elected to that body.[86] Whereas very little is known about the career of Lütken, the three legislators of Norwegian background all later rose to prominence. The growing political importance of Wisconsin's Norwegian-American element was signified in 1859 when Norwegian-born leaders appeared on the state tickets of both the major parties, Henry C. Fleck of Dodge County for the Democrats and Hans Christian Heg of Racine County for the Republicans. The ethnic character of this selection was suggested both by the fact that the two candidates were nominated for the same office, and by the circumstance that the position in question, the state prison commissionership, figured at the very bottom of the state ticket, a logical starting point for an ethnic group only beginning to rise politically. Indeed, at the Republican state convention that year, a point was made of Heg's Norwegian background, the delegates being reminded that the nominee was the son of Even Heg, the renowned Norwegian pioneer and Free Soiler.[87] In the ensuing political battle, Heg defeated Fleck, thus becoming the first Scandinavian American in the United States elected to state office.[88]

The Civil War only strengthened the position of the Scandinavian Americans, because the war, besides producing countless anonymous Scandinavian-American heroes, elevated Swedish-born John Ericsson, the engineer who designed the ironclad *Monitor*, to nationwide fame, and made a martyr out of Hans Christian Heg, the commander of the Fifteenth Wisconsin, who fell at Chickamauga. In the closing decades of the nineteenth century, Civil War symbolism played an overwhelming role in midwestern politics, and war veterans were immensely popular. Hans B. Warner, a Norwegian-American secretary of state in Wisconsin in 1878–1882, lost a forefinger in battle; his successor, German-born Ernst G. Timme, lost a hand; Warner's superior, Governor Lucius B. Fairchild, lost an arm.[89]

SCANDINAVIAN AMERICANS IN THE
WISCONSIN ASSEMBLY, 1891 TO 1914

From the end of the Civil War and until 1894, Wisconsin was, in effect, a Republican-dominated state in which the GOP won every gubernatorial election save those in 1873 and 1890–1892. The Democratic vote, on the other hand, never dropped below forty percent of the two-party total and usually hovered around 46–47 percent.[90] With the onset of the 1893–1897 depression, however, the political situation changed markedly. The Republicans monopolized the governorship until 1932, when another depression finally toppled them from power. Between 1890 and 1912, the widening gap between the Republican and Democratic parties was reflected in the elections to Wisconsin's lower house, the one-hundred-member assembly. Whereas the Democrats won legislative majorities in the elections of 1890 and 1892, from 1894 through 1912 they attained more than thirty seats in only one election, that of 1912, when they received thirty-five; at the other extreme, they won just eight seats in 1896. Conversely, from 1894 through 1912 the Republicans scored one victory after another, their share of seats dropping as low as fifty-nine only in 1910 and 1912 and peaking at ninety in 1896.[91] Thus, from 1894, intra-party fights within the GOP were of greater significance to the future of Wisconsin than the battle between the Republicans and the Democrats.

The membership of the assembly reflected Wisconsin's ethnic and religious diversity. Of all the 1,204 seats available in Wisconsin's lower house in 1891–1914, 25.6 percent were taken by immigrants, and countless others by second-generation ethnics. Of 392 seats occupied by *American*-born assemblymen whose second-generation roots could be traced, only 48.3 percent belonged to individuals of American parentage, whereas German Americans took 20.2 percent, British Americans 12.6 percent, Irish Americans 8.4 percent, Scandinavian Americans 6.7 percent, and others 3.7 percent.[92] Moreover, among 379 seats taken by members whose religious affiliation could be identified, 21.6 percent were occupied by Catholics, 21.4 by Lutherans, 12.7 percent by Congregationalists, 11.4 percent by Methodists, 10.3 percent by Presbyterians, 6.3 percent by Episcopalians, 4.0 percent by Baptists, and 12.4 percent by other groups.[93] The connection between ethnocultural background and party affiliation was reflected in the fact that of the major religious groups, only among the

Catholics did the Democrats boast a majority, taking 72.0 percent of all identifiable "Catholic" seats; in fact, all recognizable Polish Catholics were Democrats, as were 75.0 percent of all discernible Irish Catholics. Among traceable Lutherans, on the other hand, Republicans boasted 77.8 percent of the seats, among Scandinavian-American Lutherans indeed 97.8 percent.

Overall, the Scandinavian-American presence in the assembly was quite marked (fig. 5.1.a, Appendix I). From 1891 through 1914, Scandinavian immigrants made up 5.4 percent of the membership of the assembly while comprising 5.1 percent of the 1900 state population; together, first- and second-generation Scandinavian Americans constituted 10.4 percent of the assembly membership in 1891–1914 and 11.2 percent of Wisconsin's 1900 population. As might be expected, over time the ratio of second-generation to first-generation Scandinavian-American assemblymen increased as more and more children of immigrants came of age (fig. 5.1.b, Appendix I). Moreover, over the years, the Scandinavian Americans' share of seats in the assembly generally grew, especially after 1900, the year that Robert M. La Follette was elected governor.

Despite partisan and religious diversity, the assemblymen born in Scandinavia and occupying sixty-five legislative seats in 1891–1914 shared at least two traits with their other immigrant colleagues who occupied another 243 seats. Those traits set both groups off from their native-born counterparts in the remaining 896 seats (fig. 5.2.a, Appendix I). First, the immigrant assemblymen included fewer professionals within their ranks than did their native-born counterparts, i.e., fewer attorneys, educators, newspaper editors, and physicians.[94] Whereas almost one in three native-born assemblyman was a professional, only about one in ten immigrant members belonged to that category.[95] In fact, of the just five assembly seats taken by Scandinavian-born professionals, three were occupied by individuals who had arrived in Wisconsin as children. Slightly more than half of Wisconsin's Scandinavian-born assemblymen, on the other hand, were rural businessmen and farmers, most of them undoubtedly individuals with a record of personal success and leadership in the local community.[96] The Scandinavian-American members included only one laborer in their midst, the Danish-born Social Democratic cigar maker Frederick Brockhausen.

A second common characteristic of immigrant politicians was that they were older than their native-born colleagues. In this case, a sharp age differential existed between the political parties: whereas seventeen of the Democratic Party's seats in the assembly and six of the Social Democrats' were taken by individuals aged twenty-six to thirty-six, the youngest Republican immigrant member of the assembly was thirty-seven years old.[97] More generally, the average Scandinavian-born assemblyman was five years older than his native-born counterpart, whereas the average immigrant politician of another ethnic background was six years older. In a third respect, the Scandinavian-born assemblymen actually differed markedly from other immigrant politicians. Whereas only one in three Scandinavian-born politicians lived in urban areas, more than half of their other immigrant colleagues did so. The American-born members occupied a middle position in this respect.[98]

Thus, the Scandinavian-born assemblymen, like their immigrant colleagues of other national backgrounds, tended to be older and less well educated than their native-born counterparts, and most of the Scandinavian-born members, furthermore, lived outside the cities. Only a small minority of immigrant assemblymen belonged to the one group within the assembly that undoubtedly constituted its politically most dynamic element: the young, urban professionals.[99] Only one Scandinavian-born individual, Kapp E. Rasmussen, a lawyer from the tiny city of Rice Lake in Barron County, who entered the assembly in 1899 at the age of thirty-nine, approximated the young, urban professional type. He was only five years old, however, when he left Denmark for America.[100] With so few professionals among the Scandinavian-born politicians, some kind of immigrant logic definitely attached to the sarcastic suggestion by *Reform* in 1895 that attorneys be denied access to the legislature; that what the state needed was "Fewer attorneys, more men."[101] From this perspective, Norwegian-born Assemblyman Ole A. Buslett's denunciation of lawyer-politicians hypocritically demanding "reform" also makes sense, as does the complaint by one Swedish American that America was becoming a nation dominated by attorneys who only wrote laws to help the rich people.[102]

Second-generation immigrant assemblymen conformed much more closely to "native" patterns than did their immigrant forebears (fig. 5.2.b, Appendix I). First, among the 392 American-born assemblymen in 1891–1914 whose parents' nativity may be ascertained, a slightly larger proportion of the "Scandinavians" were professionals than was the case among their "native" colleagues, and assemblymen with other ethnic roots boasted only a slightly smaller share. Second, on average, second-generation immigrant politicians, including those of Scandinavian background, were markedly younger than their "native" counterparts. In a third respect, however, the "Scandinavians" deviated both from their "native" colleagues and from other second-generation ethnics. Only one in five second-generation Scandinavian-American assemblymen lived in the cities. Thus, the group of American-born politicians of Scandinavian parentage did indeed include a sizeable portion of young professionals, but less than one-quarter of them lived in the cities.[103]

Even though the Scandinavian-American assemblymen were a fairly diverse lot, in one basic respect most of them were alike: they were Republicans. Of the 125 assembly seats held by Scandinavian Americans in 1891–1914, 88.0 percent belonged to Republicans (fig. 5.3, Appendix I). This included all seats occupied by identifiable Swedish Americans, as well as 95.5 percent of the seats held by identifiable Norwegian Americans; among the Danish Americans, "only" 78.8 percent of the seats belonged to Republicans, but even though the non-Republicans occupied seven seats, just three individuals were actually involved: Frederick Brockhausen, the Social Democrat, was elected to the assembly four times, whereas James Larsen, who figured as a Union Laborite in 1891–1892 and as an independent in 1913–1914, was elected twice. Only one Danish-American member of the assembly was in fact a Democrat.

The distribution of seats in the assembly among people of Danish, Norwegian, and Swedish ancestry is surprising: thirty-two seats were held by Norwegian-born, thirty-one by Danish-born, and only two by Swedish-born legislators.[104] Thus, the Norwegian immigrants, who in 1900 comprised 3.0 percent of Wisconsin's population, accounted for 2.7 percent of the seats in the assembly; the Danish immigrants, who in 1900 constituted just 0.8 percent of the state population, occupied fully 2.6 percent of the seats in the lower house, whereas the Swedish immigrants, who in 1900 accounted for 1.3 percent of the state population, controlled only 0.2 percent of the seats in the assembly. By including the forty seats occupied by second-generation Scandinavian Americans whose national origins may be pinpointed, this distribution changes somewhat.[105] Then Norwegian-American superiority becomes clear, since they controlled thirty-five of these additional seats, whereas the Swedish Americans occupied three, the Danish Americans two.

Why this marked underrepresentation of Swedish-American politicians and overrepresentation of Danish-American? To the extent that "national" factors accounted for these differences, some suggestions occur. With regard to Swedish Americans, the picture of relative political passivity holds true outside Wisconsin, as several researchers have noted. In neighboring Minnesota, Norwegian Americans completely outnumbered Swedish Americans in county politics and also surpassed them in the state house of representatives, and as far as Swedish settlers in Worcester, Massachusetts, are concerned, two Swedish scholars noted, "Our general impression is that the Swedes were active everywhere else but in politics."[106] Arguably, the small number of state legislators of Swedish background in Wisconsin may be ascribed in part to two general conditions. First, the development of modern political institutions took place at a slower pace in Sweden than in Denmark and Norway. Whereas the Norwegian parliamentary system dated from 1814 and that of Denmark from 1849, Sweden did not adopt a modern system until 1866. Until the early twentieth century, restrictions in male suffrage based upon age as well as income and status requirements also clearly disadvantaged Swedes, and the political parties that today still dominate the political stage in each of the Scandinavian countries likewise were slower to develop in Sweden than in Denmark and Norway.[107] Thus, overall, Swedes came to America with lower levels of democratic experience than their Danish and Norwegian counterparts. Second, the process of migration itself tended to sharpen Norwegian-Swedish political differences. Norwegian mass migration to America began somewhat earlier than Swedish, and this not only had repercussions for the timing of the growth of ethnic institutions like the church and the press but arguably also for political mobilization.

These general differences between Norwegian and Swedish immigrants may indicate why Norwegian Americans overall were better represented in American politics than Swedish Americans, but they hardly explain fully the particularly sharp contrast in Wisconsin. In that state, two factors exacerbated the contrasts. First, the matter of timing was especially acute in Wisconsin. In America at large, Swedish immigration caught up with Norwegian in the late 1860s, but that never happened in Wisconsin.

Whereas the largest Norwegian-American expansion in Wisconsin took place in the 1860s, the largest Swedish-American population growth occurred as late as the 1880s, and it was always overshadowed by immigration to other states. Only after 1880 did the number of Swedish immigrants in Wisconsin exceed that even of the Danish.[108]

Another factor specific to Wisconsin was geographical. The Swedish-American settlements in northwestern Wisconsin lay on the eastern fringe of what was becoming the largest area of concentrated Swedish migration to America, the region in Minnesota between the St. Croix and the Mississippi rivers.[109] To the degree that Swedish Americans in northwestern Wisconsin felt that they were a part of this "Swedish America," they looked westward rather than toward their Norwegian-American, German-American, and Yankee neighbors in Wisconsin.[110] Conceivably for the same reason, the Swedish-American press usually did not expend very much political energy on the Swedish Americans in Wisconsin. For Swedish-American would-be politicians hoping to enter Wisconsin politics on ethnic terms, the lack of strong press support was problematic.

The overrepresentation of Danish Americans in the Wisconsin Assembly is as remarkable as is the lack of Swedish Americans. During the legislative sessions of 1891 through 1913, thirty-one seats were occupied by Danish immigrants, and at least another two by second-generation Danish Americans. To the degree that the strong Danish-American presence in the assembly indicated a high level of political activism among Danish Americans, it is tempting to view this as a result, first, of the comparatively high levels of democratic experience in Denmark among Danish immigrants and, second, of Norwegian-Danish institutional cooperation, which tended to outlast the Norwegian-Swedish collaboration.

Neighboring Minnesota deviated substantially from the Wisconsin pattern, for in that state the Danish Americans did not figure very prominently in county and state politics.[111] According to a report by the Danish journalist Henrik Cavling, Governor Knute Nelson even joked about the shyness of the Danish Americans, as well as the Swedish Americans, ascribing their caution to stiffer courtly traditions in Europe: "When a Dane steps into my office, he bows and says, 'Sorry to disturb you, Mr. Governor!' When a Swede comes in, he stays by the door and out of sheer politeness forgets his mission. A Norwegian, on the other hand, kicks open the door and says, 'Hello, Knute!' And then, maybe, he spits on the floor and puts up his feet on the table and speaks to me as the man whom I must thank for my dignity would speak. He is almost more American than the American."[112]

Knute Nelson's remarks notwithstanding, at least three phenomena specific to Wisconsin account for the large share of Danish Americans in the assembly. First, whereas at the national level the time factor worked against the Danish immigrants, since they generally arrived in America later than their Norwegian and Swedish counterparts, in Wisconsin the Danish immigrants made their presence felt, if not before the Norwegian, then at least before the Swedish. Second, Danish Americans were arguably elected to the assembly less on the basis of their ethnicity than were their Norwegian- and Swedish-American colleagues. An analysis of the percentage of Scandinavian-American voters in each specific assembly district in 1890–1912 supports this argument. Whereas 69.7 percent of the assembly seats occupied by first- and second-generation Danish Americans represented constituencies less than twenty percent Scandinavian-American, only 38.8 percent of the Norwegian-American seats and no Swedish-American seats did so.[113] More generally, of course, the share of Danish-American family heads living in ethnic enclaves was smaller than that of Swedish and particularly Norwegian Americans in Wisconsin.[114] This suggests that a larger share of Danish-American legislators entered state politics in spite of their ethnicity, rather than in large measure due to it. Third, whereas the Danish-American legislators held thirty-three identifiable assembly seats, due to patterns of election and reelection those seats represented only nineteen individuals, the average term of office thus amounting to 3.5 years; the sixty-seven identifiable seats belonging to Norwegian Americans, on the other hand, were taken by fifty individual legislators, the average term thus amounting to only 2.7 years. Danish-American representation in the assembly was thus enhanced by virtue of the simple fact that a larger share of Danish-American legislators were reelected to office than was the case with the Norwegian Americans. National background in itself hardly accounted for that circumstance.

ASSEMBLY POLITICS AND THE NATIONALITY ARGUMENT

From a policy perspective, assembly politics differed markedly from
county politics, since the former focused on the state, the latter on the
county. From an electoral point of view, however, the difference was less
dramatic. After all, the number of assembly districts (100) was larger than
the number of counties (seventy-one), so that, on an average, the assembly
district was actually smaller than the county, even though some thinly
populated assembly districts comprised several counties. It is hardly surprising, then, that the type of arguments employed in county electoral
politics might also be found in assembly politics. The matrix of party, nationality, locality, and personality, so typical of electoral politics in the
county, was also at work in assembly election campaigns.

One communication to *Skandinaven* from Grant Township in Dunn
County in the central western section of Wisconsin illustrates this point.[115]
The letter was written in support of Ole G. Kinney, a second-generation
Norwegian-American Republican would-be assemblyman from Colfax, a
village to the northeast of Menomonie, the county seat. In a historical review of all assemblymen from Dunn County, 1863–1890, the correspondent summarized: "First, no Scandinavians; second, no members, either,
from the Scandinavian settlements; third, half of all members from Menomonie City; the rest, excepting three, from the few towns south of Menomonie; fourth, the majority have been such men who had an office, were
attorneys, and so forth." The correspondent proceeded to recommend
Kinney to the voters: "That this gentleman is a man with a broad education
who possesses both theoretical and practical skills, and who with the greatest of ease can write and speak the language of the nation, that he has a rare
eye for many things and has talent and strength so that he can fill his seat as
a member of the assembly with ease; that he is all in all a respectable man
through whom both we and other nationalities surely will achieve our
goals I shall not mention here[!], for Mr. O. G. Kinney is as well-known as
he is generally well-liked and respected for what he really is: *the man.*" This
letter well combined the four elements of the argumentative matrix, adding a touch of lingering distrust of the assembly's professionals. The letter
did not, however, land Kinney the coveted seat in the assembly, which
went instead to A. R. Hall, who thus launched his career as Wisconsin's

pioneering progressive reformer. Only when Hall retired in 1902 was Kinney finally elected.

Whereas the letter about Kinney clearly illustrates the importance of all four elements of the argumentative matrix at the assembly level, a communication at the other end of the chronological scale, written to *Skandinaven* in 1914, while taking the Republican Party for granted, emphasized mainly nationality and personality, adding some doses of temperance as well as a touch of anti-Catholicism[116]: "This year, T. T. Sime, a good Norwegian from Gays Mills, is a candidate for the assembly for Crawford County, and in all respects a better man for this office would probably be hard to find. . . . Sime is no money man but a doughty, hospitable farmer who by his own hard work has earned a living for himself and his family. . . . Is it not about time that we should unite and send a Norwegian to Madison, a man who would look after the interests of the common man and at the same time be a worthy representative of our Norwegians in the county? We can rest assured that Sime will not vote in the interest of either the breweries or Columbus Day."[117]

Other letters promoting Scandinavian-American candidates to the Wisconsin Assembly employed the national argument in a more bizarre and strained manner, and once again attest to its strength as a mode of reasoning. In one case the Scandinavian-American argument was inverted by pointing to the defects of a Democrat from Dane County who not only, it was emphasized, was a Scot by birth, but whose personal qualities conspired against reelection: "He is the kind of man who supports people that he does not know, but who does not care about his own neighbors."[118] In Trempealeau County, insisted another letter writer, many Norwegian Americans were supporting J. B. Beach, the *Yankee* editor of the Whitehall *Times-Banner*, for the assembly—first, because he was a good and honest man, and second, because he was a friend of Iver Pederson, a Norwegian American.[119] A third correspondent inverted considerations about the connection between party affiliation and national background. L. L. Løberg of Portage County ought to be elected to the assembly, suggested the writer, first, because he was a Norwegian American, and second, because even though he was running on the Democratic ticket, "Everybody who knows Mr. Løberg, after all, is aware of the fact that he is no Democrat."[120]

The importance of representation along lines of nationality was emphasized also by correspondents discussing the actual ethnic composition of the assembly after the election. In 1895, one Norwegian-born politico thus noted that the new assembly only included four Scandinavian-born members, but added that no other ethnic group boasted as many patronage jobs in the capitol building as the Scandinavian Americans, who now occupied fifteen positions.[121] "This is quite a remarkable list," commented the writer, "in a state where the Scandinavians have practically never had any other position on the state ticket than on its tail end." Indeed, from a Scandinavian-American perspective the situation now looked much better than back in 1891 when, as another commentator then noted, the assembly claimed only three Scandinavian Americans, and when all but one Scandinavian-American patronage applicant "had to put up with being pushed aside by Irishmen, Germans, and Poles."[122]

As a rule, *Skandinaven* and other large Scandinavian-language newspapers devoted little space to assembly-level electoral politics, and then usually only in the shape of reader letters. Under normal circumstances, assembly elections were simply considered too insignificant to merit attention from the largest papers.[123] Somewhat more room was allotted the assembly races in locally oriented newspapers. In 1896, *Superior Tidende* thus gave would-be assemblyman Simon Thoreson front-page coverage, and occasionally Rasmus B. Anderson's *Amerika* discussed candidates that Dane County Norwegian Americans ought to support, just as *Förposten* now and again recommended a politician to its Swedish-American readers in Marinette County.[124]

As in county campaigns, "national" reasoning in assembly-level electoral politics frequently went hand in hand with arguments focusing on the candidate's party affiliation, place of residence, and personality. Moreover, when this type of argumentation was employed, it was usually the candidate's national background that received most emphasis. A factor conspicuous largely by its absence was religion, aside from an occasional anti-Catholic slur.

UP THE POLITICAL LADDER

Whereas between 1891 and 1914 the Wisconsin Assembly boasted its fair share of Scandinavian-American politicians, the state senate, the thirty-three-man upper house, did not contain one single legislator born in Scandinavia and only three second-generation Scandinavian Americans. Generally speaking, whereas immigrants of all national backgrounds made up 25.6 percent of the Wisconsin Assembly (and 24.9 percent of the population in 1900), their share in the senate amounted to just 14.9 percent.

Why this marked underrepresentation of Scandinavian Americans and other immigrant groups in the state senate? Three factors were of particular importance. First, no simple organic connection existed between being a member of the assembly and of the senate. Of all the 198 seats up for grabs in the senate from 1890 through 1912, only 32.5 percent went to previous members of the assembly. The rest went to other politicians who simply began their career in state politics at a different entry level. Something rather similar was true of the ninety-one elective positions to state office and the 125 Wisconsin seats in the U.S. House of Representatives available between 1890 and 1912: not more than 50.5 percent and 40.8 percent, respectively, were awarded former members of either the assembly or the state senate. With regard to the election of U.S. senators (until 1913 the task of the state legislature), six of the eight races benefited former assemblymen or state senators.

Second, the composition of the state senate by job categories and by place of residence was markedly different from that of the assembly and apparently handicapped Scandinavian immigrants. In the higher reaches of the political system, professionals dominated more markedly than in the assembly and comprised nearly fifty percent of the senate membership (fig. 5.4.a, Appendix I). Farther up the political ladder, that same tendency was even more pronounced, so that among state officers and the Wisconsin delegation in Congress more than fifty percent of all positions were taken by professionals. In those upper echelons, moreover, the representation of farmers, rural businessmen, artisans, and laborers dropped correspondingly. More generally, in this upward move, city dwellers tended clearly to outdistance rurals (fig. 5.4.b, Appendix I).

Overall, a significantly smaller share of the foreign-born politicians who moved beyond the assembly level were professionals than was the case among their native-born counterparts. Whereas 51.4 percent of all "native" seats in the state senate belonged to professionals (71.1 percent of those professionals living in the cities), for immigrant politicians the corresponding figure was considerably lower, just 32.1 percent (with 66.7 percent of those professionals dwelling in urban areas). Among state officers and members of Congress the discrepancy between native-born and foreign-born politicians was equally marked.[125]

Whereas the state senate contained no politicians born in the Scandinavian countries, thirteen elective seats in the state administration and in Congress were occupied by politicians born in Scandinavia. Again, only a small fraction (15.4 percent) belonged to professionals. Indeed, the two seats in question both went to one and the same individual, the Norwegian-born attorney and Republican Congressman Nils P. Haugen of rural River Falls in Pierce County. Haugen, on the other hand, turned out to be one of the most important Scandinavian-American leaders in the history of Wisconsin. In neighboring Minnesota, three prominent Scandinavian-American politicians likewise launching congressional careers were also attorneys: Norwegian-born Knute Nelson, as well as Swedish-born John Lind and Charles A. Lindberg Sr. Like Haugen, these Minnesota politicians all immigrated to America as infants.[126]

Again, as was also the case among assemblymen, second-generation Scandinavian-American politicians fit the native political profile much better than that of their immigrant peers, for of the sixteen seats taken by second-generation Scandinavian Americans above the assembly level, eleven (68.8 percent) were occupied by professionals (81.8 percent of those professionals living in urban areas).

The third factor explaining the relative absence of Scandinavian Americans in the state senate was that the nationality argument seemed particularly ill suited for senate politics. The shift from assembly to senate politics marked a change from local to regional, if not statewide, politics, since the average senatorial district was three times as large as the typical assembly district. In senatorial politics, the national argument tended to lose strength, simply because local numerical ethnic superiority tended to be diluted within the larger district. Not surprisingly, therefore, senators representing English-speaking cultures were strongly overrepresented among immigrant senators. While people of British, Canadian, and Irish birth constituted just 16.2 percent of Wisconsin's foreign-born population, representatives of those groups occupied fully 64.4 percent of the seats taken by immigrants in the senate.[127] In all likelihood, these figures reflect the weaker position of the national argument in senatorial politics.

Presumably, a larger share of British and Canadian Americans, if not of Irish-American Catholics, were in a position to enter politics on nonethnic terms than was the case with politicians from non-English-speaking cultures.[128] This latter expectation is borne out by a 1906 complaint to *Skandinaven* that Congressman John J. Jenkins of Chippewa County, born in England, was considered more American than Ole G. Kinney, his second-generation Norwegian-American rival, born in Wisconsin.[129] With the same Jenkins in mind, Congressman Haugen had argued fourteen years earlier, "I claim to be as good an American as anybody, and as between Mr. Jenkins, born in England, and myself, born in Norway, it would seem that the native American ought not to have much preference on the basis of nationality."[130]

One further explanation supports the hypothesis that the national argument was particularly weak at the senatorial level. Elections to the senate, like those to the assembly, were usually not considered sufficiently prestigious to reach the headlines of the large Scandinavian-American newspapers, even though, again, reader letters supporting individual candidates were printed now and again.[131] Thus, the would-be Scandinavian-American state senator found himself in the position, first, of typically not being able to rely on strong local ethnic support due to the unwieldy size of his district and, second, of aspiring to a political office that was not of sufficiently high status to merit much attention from the largest Scandinavian-American newspapers.

The situation was otherwise with state administrations and federal politics. Especially in the selection of state officials, Scandinavian immigrant leaders were well represented. Of the ninety-one positions available on the state tickets, 1890–1912 (offices ranging from state insurance commissioner up to governor), twenty-two were taken by immigrants generally, *half* of whom were Scandinavians by birth. Only the election of 1910 saw no Scandinavian immigrant represented on the state ticket, and that year Andrew H. Dahl, a second-generation Norwegian American, was elected state treasurer. As a matter of fact, besides the eleven Scandinavian immigrants elected to state office, four second-generation Scandinavian Americans experienced similar success. Thus, fifteen out of a total of ninety-one positions on the state ticket (16.5 percent) were filled by Scandinavian Americans.

In this elevated political arena, it is true, national arguments along *lo-*

cal ethnic lines were diluted still further, but here demands for *symbolic* ethnic representation, along with calls for a fair regional distribution of offices, became powerful, backed as they were at this high level by the Scandinavian-American press. Within the Republican Party of Wisconsin a tradition was instituted of granting the Scandinavian Americans a position on each state ticket, another going to the German-American element. By the 1890s, this tradition was firmly entrenched, and by then it regularly happened that a Scandinavian American entered the Democratic slate. This tradition faded in 1906, when the old system of nominating party candidates through the caucus and convention system was succeeded by the direct primary.[132]

Until that point, as Nils P. Haugen later observed, "It had become a matter of political policy to recognize different nationalities in making up the state ticket."[133] Sewell A. Peterson, the Norwegian-born Republican candidate for the state treasurership in 1894, illustrated the system of ethnic checks and balances: "I might stand some show for Treasurer in case a German was nominated for Governor, Lieutenant Governor or Secretary, but if not, the Germans will undoubtedly claim the Treasurer's office, and the Norwegians would have to yield."[134] When Norwegian-born James O. Davidson ran for the nomination for the state treasurership in 1898, he argued in a quite similar vein: "While I do not believe in making nationality a point, that question does and will enter in the making up of the state ticket, and if our people are given the usual representation I shall be proud of being their choice. I became a candidate for the office of state treasurer because it seemed to me that our people ought to hold the high position they have now attained."[135] As *Skandinaven* reported, a general understanding formed that year that a Scandinavian American was to have the treasurership. Davidson in fact only won the nomination after defeating three other Norwegian-American candidates for that same office.[136]

No similar Republican "Scandinavian" tradition was established with regard to Congress. In practice, however, a number of Scandinavian Americans did win access to that body. In 1888, Nils P. Haugen became the first from Wisconsin to do so, retaining his seat there until 1895. He was only the third Scandinavian-born politician in the United States to attain that honor—Knute Nelson of Minnesota, elected in 1882, was the first, and Swedish-American John Lind, likewise of Minnesota and elected four years later, was the second.[137] Yet once having been elected to Congress, in his reelection campaigns Haugen could count on strong support from several leading Norwegian-American newspapers, especially *Skandinaven*. Not only did these papers time and again remind their readers of his Norwegian background, but Haugen's congressional speeches were quoted and commented upon with much enthusiasm and at great length.[138] Three second-generation Scandinavian Americans from Wisconsin, Herman Bjørn Dahle (1855–1920) and John Mandt Nelson, both of Norwegian background, as well as Irvine L. Lenroot, of Swedish parentage, later won seats in the House of Representatives. Lenroot later won election to the U.S. Senate.[139]

In many ways, the arguments employed to support political candidates at the state and federal levels resembled those articulated in county and assembly electoral politics. Here as well, the matrix of party, nationality, locality, and personality played a prominent role, especially in the 1890s, but this pattern weakened somewhat after the turn of the century. At these higher levels of power, however, the nationality issue was typically employed with greater caution, since a too strong emphasis on ethnicity might backfire among other ethnic groups. Thus, in the Scandinavian-American press the nationality issue was frequently presented in a subdued manner, and the *complementarity* of Scandinavian-American identity, the American side to it, was emphasized strongly as was the adversity that Scandinavian-American politicians supposedly faced from the host society.

A letter to *Fædrelandet og Emigranten* in favor of Nils P. Haugen's 1890 reelection to Congress illustrates how the argumentative matrix of party, nationality, locality, and personality was applied at the federal level, and how the argument from nationality might be modified: "We do not recommend his reelection because he was born in Norway – far from it. We recommend him because his outstanding position has not made him either conceited or arrogant; yet we recommend him first of all because he has represented his district with an astuteness that matches that of any of his predecessors."[140] Even so, the same letter writers cried, "shame on the Scandinavian voter who will not with all his might support his reelection," and warned Scandinavian Americans against giving in to Yankee nativism. On a similar note of caution, *Skandinaven*, making full use of the complementarity of Scandinavian-American identity, queried, "Why must one immediately hear, when somebody of Nordic ancestry is mentioned as an aspirant for office, 'Oh, he is a foreigner!' If he is a good and enlightened citizen, American-minded body and soul, then in Wisconsin he is as much a 'foreigner' and as much an American whether his parents migrated to the state from New England or from Norway." Yet again this caution in applying the nationality argument simply functioned as a preface to its full-blown use: "In spite of all this, the nationality issue has entered politics, and it is not within our power to remove it. We may blame whomever we like for this state of affairs, but we must accept it as an accomplished fact."[141] The editorial ended on the note that the Norwegian Americans deserved a position not far from the top of the Republican state ticket, and that Nils P. Haugen should get all the support possible in his fight for reelection to Congress against a "Yankee money man." In 1894, when Haugen ran for the Republican gubernatorial nomination, the same newspaper even asserted that Norwegian Americans opposing Haugen were mere tools in the hands of the powerful former railroad attorney and present U.S. Senator, John C. Spooner (1843–1919), "in this unfair and un-American war waged upon a man whose only flaw is that he is a Norwegian and a clever and honest man."[142]

PATRONAGE POLITICS

In his guide to Danish emigrants heading for America, Christian B. Nielsen, former justice of the peace in Omaha, Nebraska, recommended that newcomers apply for government work: "First, it usually means steady employment for many months at a time, and there is no deduction in the salary for rainy days or when for other reasons there is no work to do. Next, it is rarely as hard as working for private people, since the supervisor usually has a relaxed attitude. Third, the monthly pay is good, and food is included, and the worker even receives clothing at the government's cost price, and, finally, the 'money' is always safe, and the worker can deposit it as long as he likes and thus more easily save up a sum than if he carries the money in his pocket."[143] From the time that Nielsen wrote his book in the late 1860s up to the turn of the century, American government employment, whether at the local, state, or federal level, formed part of a complex patronage system that doled out jobs on a strictly *quid pro quo* basis. In most cases the individual on the receiving end "earned" the position through work for a politician. In the cities, it is true, many immigrants fresh off the boat got jobs as laborers constructing city streets, bridges, buildings, and the like, but were then expected to pay back the favor later through labor for the local "machine."[144]

The patronage system constituted one of the foundations of the American political order, especially in the closing decades of the nineteenth century. While the ideological commitments of the Civil War era were wearing thin, the organizational basis of the political parties grew stronger. Those were the years when according to the British observer James Bryce the most cohesive force in American politics was "the desire for office and for office as a means of gain"; the years when, in one scholar's words, the parties "were based on patronage, not principle; they divided over spoils, not issues."[145] In the expanding federal and state governments, as well as in the fast-growing urban areas, whenever the vote had been counted, thousands of jobs came up for grabs, and at this point the loyal party activists began their scramble for rewards. The patronage principle was indeed so deeply ingrained in the party system that it, together with nominations and elections, constituted the most important means of defining intra-party political relationships.[146]

By the turn of the century, it is true, the patronage system came under moral and legislative siege. At a federal level, the Pendleton Act of 1883 was slowly doing its work, the share of federal employees appointed on the basis of civil service examinations growing from about ten percent in 1883 to some fifty percent by 1900.[147] In Wisconsin, moreover, a 1905 civil service law recommended by Governor La Follette proved very efficient in strengthening the merit principle.[148]

Prior to 1905, however, Wisconsin boasted a fully developed patronage system, with the members of Congress controlling more than five thousand federal government positions and the state administration a couple of hundred.[149] Indeed, in 1899 the conservative Elisha W. Keyes (1828–1910), former chairman of the Republican state central committee, noted caustically, "Even at this day and age of the world of pure politics, of reform methods, of legislative honesty, the influence of patronage is tremendous."[150] Two years later, ex-Governor William Dempster Hoard complained to Governor-elect Robert M. La Follette, "The average politician has no *patriotism*. With him the object and purpose of politics is to afford him an office."[151]

In local patronage politics, the party-nationality-locality-personality matrix worked as effectively as in electoral politics. The party label of an appointee was almost invariably taken for granted. Nils P. Haugen at one point argued sarcastically that the Democratic administration would invariably "prefer a drunken Democrat to a sober Republican every time."[152] The place of residence of a patronage applicant could also be of some consequence, Haugen thus recommending one Mr. Bouch to "a small position" with the comment, "I think on the whole that the local effect in your county would be good."[153] When Governor La Follette received patronage applications, his staff sorted them by noting in the top right corner of the letter the county of the applicant.[154] In matters of patronage, finally, the personal qualifications of the aspirant were extremely important, but more often in terms of a strong political record, Civil War bravery, and the like than actual merit. Job seekers would invariably endeavor to prove their indispensability in past political campaigns. "It was through my efforts," averred J. P. Peterson of West Denmark, Polk County, "that N. P. Haugen was nominated for Congress in 1887. In 1897 I did what I could to aid ex-Governor Hoard in his efforts to secure a place in President McKinley's cabinet; and so on."[155] Some positions were also set aside for war veterans.[156]

Among Scandinavian Americans applying for local patronage jobs up to and including the level of postmaster, the national argument tended to play a very important part. A. A. Johnson of Superior thus believed that he ought to be appointed oil inspector, for "the Norwegians of Wisconsin must have something," and one Danish American argued that he deserved a position as mailing clerk or janitor, for "I find that there ought to be a Dane in one of the departments, especially because most Danes in Visconsin [*sic*] are Republicans."[157] Congressman Haugen summed up the arguments of the party-nationality-locality-personality matrix nicely: "I have two appointments at my disposal in the Census Bureau ... and I would like to put at least one of them in Dunn. One is as Abstractor of Recorded Indebtedness, and needs a man familiar with county records, or a young attorney, who can visit the different county seats. ... Naturally I would like some one who is friendly and discreet, and withal a *strong partisan* and who would be able to give a pretty fair and unbiased opinion as to the *out-*

look. How would J. C. Ticknor fill the bill? If not he, is there any Scandinavian in your county who would do?"[158]

Going beyond the level of postmaster, the nationality argument also sometimes retained its importance. It thus seems highly probable that Democratic U.S. Senator William F. Vilas secured Rasmus B. Anderson the appointment as minister to Denmark in 1885 on account of Anderson's prominence as a spokesman for the Norwegian Americans, just as President Taft for similar reasons made Nicolai A. Grevstad, the editor of *Skandinaven*, minister to Paraguay and Uruguay.[159]

In the case of F. A. Husher, the former editor of *Fædrelandet og Emigranten*, Congressman Haugen definitely employed the nationality argument when recommending him to President Benjamin Harrison in 1889: "Having been intimately acquainted with the political, social and business standing of Hon. F. A. Husher of Minneapolis, Minnesota, for the last twenty years, and enjoying special knowledge of his value as a republican worker for the fact that we are both Norwegians by birth, I feel that I can unhesitatingly recommend him to the favorable consideration of a republican administration. He has ever since he came to this country been engaged in active newspaper work, conducting and editing one of the leading, – for a long while *the* leading, – Norwegian newspaper in the country, and has had no small share in making our adopted citizens of Scandinavian birth almost solidly republican. He has been an active worker in our campaigns both as a writer and speaker, being unquestionably the best Norwegian and Danish campaign speaker we have."[160]

In another instance, Haugen indicated just how embarrassingly little actual merit meant according to the rules of the patronage system. Recommending Hans Borchsenius, a Danish-American Wisconsin politician, to the U.S. Secretary of the Treasury, Haugen argued, "He is a Dane by birth and is well educated. Served as Adjutant of the 15th Wisconsin Regiment during the war. He is well known to the Scandinavians of the state, and has stumped the state in many campaigns speaking in English or Danish. I know of no appointment above postmaster held by any Scandinavians in Wisconsin under this administration." And then only as an afterthought: "But Mr. B– should be appointed on merit, I know. Still in future campaigns recognition of an important element in the party without detriment to the service ought not to be lost sight of."[161]

With Congressman Haugen, sometimes a certain note of embarrassment with the workings of the patronage system crept into his letters, as when in 1890 he warned, "Patronage is a stumbling block and a curse to the party in power always."[162] At times, moreover, he would strike a self-defensive pose, arguing that in patronage matters, "The question of nationality is sometimes forced to the front in spite of us."[163] To the publisher of the little *Augusta Eagle* he further insisted, "As the charge has been made that my recommendations have favored the Scandinavians, I have divided the appointees into two classes – 'Scandinavians' and Americans. The former consist of Norwegians, Swedes and Danes. The latter principally of Americans, – a few Germans, Welsh etc." Listing all his appointments, Haugen concluded, "there are *eight* more Scandinavian postmasters under the republicans than under the democrats, I think their vote warrants a much larger increase and am inclined to look around for a good Scandinavian at Eau Claire."[164]

Indeed, as the 1880s turned to the 1890s not only were mounting expressions of genuine disgust with the traditional workings of the patronage system beginning to enter into Haugen's correspondence, but Haugen was in fact taking decisive steps to move beyond "politics as usual," beyond a type of politics defined largely by party, nationality, locality, and personality. To be sure, he would never cut loose from his Scandinavian-American electoral base, but he would consciously attempt to broaden and diversify his political appeal. This happened at the same time that his political friendship with Robert M. La Follette began to warm.

LOOKING INWARD, LOOKING OUTWARD

Even though the national argument generally played a significant role in Wisconsin politics in the decades straddling 1900 and was a factor that most first- and second-generation Scandinavian-American politicians found impossible to ignore, they did nevertheless have an arsenal of strategies at their disposal. Some politicians preferred to look inward to the ethnic community for almost all their political strength, whereas others took a fuller view of the situation and stressed heavily the American dimension to what they considered their complementary Scandinavian and American identities.

On 17 May 1909, Ole A. Buslett, Norwegian-born merchant, poet, and journalist, and presently member of the Wisconsin Assembly from Waupaca County, was invited by the Speaker to address the assembly in celebration of Norway's national holiday, *Syttende Mai*. In his speech, Buslett gave an enthusiastic description of how the Norwegian constitution came into being on the Seventeenth of May 1814.[165] He also used his oration to attack one of the recent fruits of Wisconsin progressivism, the growth of government by commission, at the same time that he gave his speech a slight anti-Catholic tilt: "Stop your creations of government by the few, your commissions and your inquisitions! Stop repeating the history of the Roman republic and the Spanish hades of the middle ages, or I will be after you! The blood of that old man Rollo of Normandy is just as red and full of the germs of freedom for soul and body on the American soil as it was when it fought for the Magna Charta, and the 17th of May!" In his address, finally, Buslett emphasized his complementary identity, singing his praise for both Norway and the United States.

Even though Buslett thus definitely paid his respects to his adopted fatherland, he was as inwardly oriented toward his own ethnic group as it was possible to be. The assemblyman's letters to his wife Anlaug in the rural hamlet of Northland, Waupaca County, indeed illustrate his full participation in Norwegian-American life in Madison. In January 1909, shortly after arriving in the state capital, he reported having visited the literary society Ygdrasil, where he met Nils P. Haugen as well as Professor Julius E. Olson of the University of Wisconsin, both of whom he was soon seeing privately, along with Peer O. Strømme.[166] In February, Waldemar Ager, the editor of *Reform*, invited Buslett to Eau Claire for a meeting of Det Norske Selskab (The Norwegian Association).[167] In March, Buslett was scheduled to speak before the Madison lodge of the Sons of Norway, and that summer Buslett attempted to organize a lodge in Northland.[168] That same year, Buslett arranged for Halvdan Koht, the distinguished Norwegian historian who had recently been granted a scholarship by the Norwegian Parliament to undertake research at the University of Wisconsin, to give a speech in the assembly chamber. "On Friday evening Koht from the University of Kristiania will be here," Buslett enthused, "and on that occasion the assembly chamber will undoubtedly be full of Norwegians – for once, and then we will be speaking Norwegian."[169]

Overall, it is true, Buslett did not keep up very close relations with his fellow Norwegian-American assemblymen. Even though those members sometimes participated in joint activities at, for example, the Old Settlers' club, or held a celebration together with their Swedish- and Danish-American colleagues, for instance at Keeley's Assembly Hall, and despite the fact that at least one former Norwegian-American assemblyman congratulated Buslett on his critical attitude towards Robert M. La Follette, the representative from Waupaca County did not express much enthusiasm for his fellow Scandinavian-American colleagues. "Of the fifteen Scandinavians here in the assembly I am the only one who is invited to participate in all kinds of arrangements," he wrote his wife in May.[170] "What the others think about this is of no consequence; they have not, after all, used the pen and the book in the manner that I have. They seem to possess money, yet still they cannot *buy* what I am being *given*. So much for poverty – and for poetry!" The very fact that Buslett was reflecting on the doings of his fellow Scandinavian-American colleagues in the assembly is, however, significant.

When Buslett wrote reports to *Skandinaven* about Wisconsin politics, they oozed with Norwegian-American emotions. In a 1901 communication to *Skandinaven* he insisted that nine-tenths of Wisconsin's Scandinavian-American population supported the hotly debated direct-primary bill that Governor La Follette was staking his political career on and scolded Danish-born Assemblyman Andrew Jensen for not falling into line.[171] Eight years later, Assemblyman Buslett, by now a sworn enemy of La Follette, again employed ethnic appeals in one of his so typical rhetorical flourishes: "And for this man I have for years worn down my shoes, used my time and my hard-earned money, my mouth and my pen, but he has never shown me any kind of gratitude, and as for the Norwegian people of the state who have elevated him to his current position, he has simply spit in their face! – figuratively speaking – by opposing us when we demanded a thing or two of him."[172] One year later, when Buslett ran in vain for the state senate, he told the readers of *Skandinaven*, "Verily, I am not only an American; wherever I walk or stand, old Vikings follow me."[173]

Scandinavian-American politicians might also attempt to employ a strongly ethnic strategy even at the federal level. In early 1888, Rasmus B. Anderson, the former U.S. minister to Denmark, began dreaming of becoming Democratic presidential candidate Grover Cleveland's running mate.[174] Two years later, his dream had been publicized sufficiently to merit negative comment in the Norwegian-American Republican paper *Fædrelandet og Emigranten*.[175] At that point in time Anderson was the most prominent champion of Norwegian-American identity in the United States. In the spring of 1891, Peer O. Strømme began tickling Anderson's vice-presidential ambitions. "I want to write an article for one or more of our Norwegian papers, suggesting that we Scandinavian American Democrats unite in working for your nomination for the vice presidency next year. We now ought to have an opportunity, which comes only once in a lifetime. . . . Now, I would like to take the lead in this movement, but I do not want to do it without your consent, which you might give me, in confidence, of course. Then I want to be a delegate to the National Democratic Convention next year and there make the speech of my life, nominating you for the vice presidency."[176]

Probably no one besides possibly Anderson himself really believed that his vice-presidential dream would come true.[177] "I notice that our people are always inclined to laugh at the idea of any of us looking for any place of importance," Strømme wrote Anderson in June. "When I have hinted that I would like to go to Chile or Peru for instance as minister, everybody considers it a huge joke. However, I am in earnest."[178] Yet earnest as Strømme sounded, he later admitted that he had his own ulterior motives. He wanted to win back his position as editor of *Norden*, which he had given up in 1890 upon his nervous breakdown and subsequent journey to Norway. He believed that by promoting Anderson for the vice presidency, the latter might use his influence with Paul O. Stensland, the present owner of *Norden*, in Strømme's behalf.[179] Strømme's plan worked. In early June 1891, he told Anderson that his article would be published in *Norden* this week, adding shrewdly, "I suppose you know that 'Norden' under Mr. Sorensen's editorship is not likely to say much in favor of you, but Mr. Stensland is in sympathy with my idea, and he is, as you know, the owner of the paper."[180] More than that, apparently Strømme also persuaded Anderson to purchase a one-year subscription to two hundred copies of the paper.[181] In early July, Strømme reported to Anderson that he was now editor of *Norden* once again and thanked Anderson for his hand in the matter, adding, "When I take charge of the work, I shall not let the grass grow under my feet, and I shall not allow your 'boom' to grow cold."[182]

That boom never developed much strength, however. In late June, to be sure, Professor L. S. Reque of Luther College in Decorah, Iowa, a Democrat, did congratulate Anderson on the flattering attention that he was receiving in the press, adding, "I hope you will give me a fat good job in '93."[183] Moreover, a couple of prominent Minnesota Norwegian Americans put in some fieldwork for Anderson. At the Democratic national convention in the summer of 1892, however, Anderson failed even to win a complimentary vote.[184] Indeed, as the Republican *Skandinaven* commented gleefully, none of the English-language Democratic papers had mentioned his candidacy. "He ought to get himself a better manager another time."[185]

Anderson's bid for the vice presidency was clearly "national." Thus, one argument in his favor stated, "Professor Anderson has a world wide reputation, being known as the foremost Scandinavian in America. The Democratic lines need to be strengthened, especially in the Northwest where the Scandinavians form a large and ever increasing element."[186] Anderson himself, who by early January 1892 realized fully that he would not win the vice presidency, similarly insisted to Ole A. Buslett, "I am not seeking the office of vice-president nor any other office, but if I can contribute something to eradicating the cotter spirit so prevalent among the Scandinavians in this country, I would be justly proud."[187]

The examples of Ole A. Buslett, Rasmus B. Anderson, and Peer O. Strømme suggest that some politicians definitely attempted to win political power by making strong appeals to their fellow Norwegian Americans on ethnic grounds. They tended primarily to look inward to their own ethnic community in their quest for political strength. Other possibilities, however, also lay open to Scandinavian-American politicians. At the county and assembly level it might even transpire that a Scandinavian American won political prominence irrespective of his national origins, as the case of the Danish-born Social Democrat Frederick Brockhausen suggested. At the state or federal level, however, the nationality issue was impossible to avoid, yet it might still be handled in much subtler ways than those exemplified by Rasmus B. Anderson and Strømme, as later chapters will demonstrate.

One example can suffice for the moment. In 1896, Mark Hanna, the national chairman of the Republican Party, wired Nils P. Haugen, requesting him to make a couple of speeches for William McKinley in the state of

Washington, pointing out how essential it was to have a "Scandinavian speaker" tour that state.[188] Haugen, who was a *first*-generation Norwegian immigrant, replied, "I do not know from your dispatch whether you expect me to talk in any other language than English or not. The fact is that I have not for ten years made a political speech in any other language than English, and prefer not to."[189] During that same campaign, however, *Superior Tidende* reported that Rasmus B. Anderson, who was a *second*-generation Norwegian immigrant, and who by now had returned to the Republican fold, had agreed to give a number of addresses in the Norwegian language.[190] Thus, in some cases, a second-generation immigrant politician might attempt to make more capital of his ethnicity than his first-generation immigrant counterpart.

Our investigation of the entry of Scandinavian Americans into American politics indicates that whenever a political campaign turned ethnic, as happened frequently when a politician of non-English-speaking roots was involved, the arguments employed centered overwhelmingly on *national background* and only sometimes, and thus secondarily and in a very rough sense, on religion. This was the case both at the local, county, and assembly levels, where the nationality consideration frequently revolved around the numerical strength of one or more ethnic groups in the legislative district, and at the state and federal levels, where the natural dilution of the national argument was prevented through a line of reasoning that emphasized the hostility of the surrounding society to the just demands by the group for recognition, and that simultaneously underscored the "American" qualities of the candidate. At these higher levels of power even the second-generation Scandinavian-American politician, whose biographical profile typically matched that of his "native" counterpart well, could not completely avoid the stigma of being classified as a foreigner rather than an "American." Still, even in the upper reaches of the political system Scandinavian-American politicians had a number of different electoral strategies at their disposal, ranging from blind acceptance of the rules of the political game at the one extreme to Nils P. Haugen's frustration over the nationality issue at the other. In 1894, when he was approached by an enthusiastic member of a newly established Scandinavian-American Republican club, a clearly annoyed Haugen wrote, "I believe it would be better to melt the question of nationality into one pot of loyal Americanism and present only one common front to the enemy. Those who are new in the country would be benefited by the introduction to purely American surroundings, and they are the ones who need Americanizing the most."[191]

PART TWO

Dynamics:
The Progressive Assault
on Tradition

CHAPTER SIX

The Transformation of Politics in Wisconsin

DELEGATED AUTHORITY VS. MASS APPEAL

On 27 May 1900, just eleven days after Robert M. La Follette officially entered the primary race for the Wisconsin governorship, he received a report from Nils P. Haugen discussing the outlook in Trempealeau County. Listing dozens of people, Haugen named five individuals from Strum whom La Follette ought to contact, among them Pastor Carl Johan Helsem, the man who four years earlier had buried Kristoffer Skauge, and Sivert Rekstad, the person who had helped build Skauge's home. Over the next couple of years, indeed, the latter would figure in several poll lists relating to election campaigns.[1] Therein lay one key to La Follette's political success: he was building a grassroots organization within the Republican Party that reached literally into every nook and cranny in the state and not just to the usual leaders in the county seats. As La Follette had already said to Haugen back in 1894, when the latter made an ill-fated bid for the governorship, "*We* want *not county* bosses but men in townships. . . . Remember, the more names the better."[2]

La Follette's insurgent Republican coalition, formed in the early 1890s and functioning as a *reform* movement from 1896, powered the earthquake that prior to the outbreak of World War I reshaped Wisconsin's political landscape. Wisconsin progressivism represented the dynamics of the era. Scandinavian-American institutions, on the other hand, formed part of an old and largely fixed structure. Despite much internal cutthroat competition, as well as growth associated with the continued influx of immigrants, the Scandinavian-American churches, the secular societies, and the press retained a stable presence. Those institutions were only shaken later, with the aggressive calls for "one-hundred percent Americanism" during World War I, as well as with the drying up of the immigrant stream during the 1920s. The dynamics of Wisconsin progressivism did, however, have an impact on Scandinavian-American involvement in politics. In fact, the progressives aimed at nothing less than the creation of a new political order that had among its many goals the eradication of the ethnic factor from politics. Despite that circumstance and to some extent *due* to it, many Scandinavian Americans were attracted to progressivism.

What later flowered into the progressive movement of Wisconsin had its first beginnings on 17 September 1891 in the parlor on the second floor of the Plankinton House in Milwaukee, when Robert M. La Follette, the thirty-six-year-old Madison attorney and ex-Congressman, had a stormy encounter with U.S. Senator Philetus Sawyer (1816–1900), an old lumber baron from Oshkosh, one of the lumber-manufacturing centers of the Old Northwest. Afterward, La Follette would always insist that Sawyer attempted to bribe him at the Plankinton. The crux of the matter was that Judge Robert G. Siebecker, La Follette's brother-in-law, was presiding over lawsuits filed by the recently installed Democratic administration against former Republican state treasurers. Sawyer, La Follette claimed, offered him money to influence Siebecker to vote "right" in these cases. "If you struck me in the face you would not insult me as you insult me now," a shocked La Follette purportedly responded, leaving the Plankinton in a rage, never to speak with Sawyer again.[3]

It is clear, however, that matters of patronage were also involved in the confrontation: La Follette was furious with Sawyer because earlier in 1891 the latter, along with U.S. Senator John C. Spooner, had been instrumental in having Frank Oakley, a Dane County politician, appointed U.S. marshal "in spite of the protest of La Follette, whom Oakly [*sic*] and Phil and Roger Spooner openly opposed at the last election."[4] As Sawyer confided to a friend shortly after the sensational clash, "Mr La Follette was very much offended at the appointment of Col. Oakly [*sic*] U.S. Marshall, and out of patience with me because I would not have him summarily dismissed but never supposed that he would allow this little difference to get the better of his judgment."[5] In early October, weeks before the La

Follette-Sawyer clash made headlines in the Wisconsin press, Senator Spooner actually conferred with La Follette, trying to explain, as the latter recalled, "that it was not his purpose and had never been his intention to ram Oakley down my throat here."[6] After the break had become known to the public, however, a revengeful Sawyer saw to it that the appointment of Oakley, which had been temporary at first, was made permanent.[7]

The confrontation at the Plankinton House resulted in a complete and public break between La Follette and the older leadership of the Republican Party. In hindsight, La Follette's clash with Sawyer came to represent not only a fight over moral and political values but also a battle over novel, aggressive methods of handling party organization. Both new approaches were functions, to some extent, of the dramatic economic expansion that American society was undergoing in the closing decades of the nineteenth century, a growth that gradually wove Wisconsin's multitude of small, inward-looking, parochial "island communities" into a complex whole.[8] Sawyer and La Follette each attempted to bring a measure of uniformity to Wisconsin's multifaceted political landscape, characterized as it was by several party strongholds babbling each in its political tongue, representing each its ethnic and religious constellation, embodying each its specific economic setting, and all making demands upon the leadership of the party on the basis, frequently, of party, nationality, locality, and personality.

Philetus Sawyer and his political associates came closest to practicing "traditional" politics. During the 1880s, Sawyer together with John C. Spooner, a corporate attorney of Madison, and Henry C. Payne (1843–1904), a public utilities and finance magnate of Milwaukee, formed a triumvirate that dominated the Republican Party of Wisconsin until 1900. All three men represented the corporate growth that so characterized America in the post-Civil War decades. Sawyer, who was no speaker and never felt secure with a pen in his hand, had made a successful career for himself in Wisconsin's booming lumbering business.[9] Indeed, his wealth, along with his shrewd knowledge of human nature, were his main assets when in 1881 he won entry to the U.S. Senate, then renowned as a "rich men's club." He remained a senator for twelve years, always displaying a keen interest in pork-barrel politics and personal matters and never becoming identified in public with any great issue.

John C. Spooner was a specialist in the railroad business and in the 1880s he together with Sawyer made a fortune by meddling with government land grants for railroads, most notably in the so-called "Omaha land grant case."[10] Like Sawyer, Spooner's political career propelled him to the U.S. Senate, first in 1885, then again in 1897. Like Sawyer, Spooner was usually not identified with grand moral issues but with day-to-day politicking in the company of lobbyists and power mongers. In 1907, one year after La Follette had entered the U.S. Senate, Spooner decided to retire from politics and to return fully to the corporate world that he had never entirely left, this time settling in New York City.[11] Henry C. Payne, the third member of the Wisconsin triumvirate, was a public utilities magnate from Milwaukee who never held a major elected position in his life. His lobbying on behalf of the Chicago meat-packing industry in the 1880s and for his own public utility interests in Milwaukee in the 1890s earned him a reputation for greed and corruption that climaxed during the Milwaukee street-railway strike of 1896 when, in the estimate of one historian, he became Wisconsin's most hated man.[12] Nevertheless, from 1880 until his death in 1904, he remained a member of the Republican national committee.

During the 1890s, among La Follette's inner circle, complaints about the wealth of all three members of the triumvirate were expressed frequently. Shortly after the Plankinton House incident, William T. La Follette, Robert's brother, thus referred to Sawyer as "the old cuss" who "made his immense fortune by bribery and fraud."[13] Five years later, ex-Congressman Nils P. Haugen complained about the money and the railroad passes that Sawyer and Spooner had at their disposal, and La Follette himself stated, "The trouble is, we poor fellows who have to earn a living can only occasionally take a hand in politics. They keep at it all the while."[14] Assemblyman A. R. Hall used even stronger words: "No state in the Union is more completely under the control of corporate power than Wisconsin."[15] This was hyperbole, to be sure, for even though Wisconsin was definitely beginning to feel the mixed blessings of large-scale industrialism, some of the states further east were even more exposed. In Wisconsin, men of lesser means but greater political talent seemed always to be on hand to challenge the wealthiest politicians.[16]

Sawyer and his political allies embraced the political system of Wisconsin largely as they found it. They accepted, first, the political party as an extra-constitutional organization more private than public in nature. These were organizations, moreover, that based their existence upon principles of strictly delegated authority, as practiced through the caucus and convention system.[17] Second, they were well satisfied with the traditional political geography of Wisconsin, characterized as it was by numerous Republican strongholds. Yet the business activities of Sawyer and his allies continued to expand. Sawyer acquired varied interests not only in many different parts of Wisconsin but also in neighboring and distant states, as well as in at least one foreign country.[18] Conversely, in connection with the dramatic economic expansion, the spoils of office in terms of government subsidies and contracts also kept increasing.[19] Thus, with the growth in the scope and integration of their several business activities on the one hand and in the value of political office on the other, the interest of Sawyer and his allies in controlling the majority party of the state intensified. Sawyer's combination of a local point of view with an urge for greater overall control was reflected in the fact that during his years in the U.S. Senate he set a record of reporting more than two thousand bills, almost all dealing with specific local matters.[20]

The fear that the Republican Party of Wisconsin was becoming dominated by corporate interests seemed to be justified when in 1901 Charles F. Pfister, a Milwaukee tannery magnate and business partner of Henry C. Payne, bought the *Milwaukee Sentinel,* Wisconsin's most widely circulating daily. Payne and Spooner were both deeply involved in the purchase, and indeed, at Payne's urging, Spooner wrote the first anonymous editorial after the takeover, pledging the paper not to "attack individuals unjustly because connected with corporate interests," nor to "attack corporate interests because of any dislike of individuals connected with them."[21] In sum, Sawyer and his political allies, viewing politics as a sound investment object to protect their expanding economic interests, let their capital work for them to assure a degree of direction and organization in the *existing* framework of politics never seen before. These individuals constituted a threat to parochialism above all because they were ready to embrace it with their influence and economic might.

After his break with Sawyer, Robert M. La Follette came to personify a challenge to traditional politics. During the depressed and turbulent mid-1890s, he built a faction consisting of several friends and "out" politicians, as well as a few reformers. In Madison, his closest political companions were his wife Belle Case La Follette (1859–1931) and his three law partners, Samuel Albert Harper (1853–1898), Gilbert Ernstein Roe (1865–1929), and Alfred G. Zimmerman (1862–1935), as well as George Edwin Bryant (1832–1907), a Civil War colonel popular among the veteran element within the GOP. Outside Madison, La Follette found a political ally in ex-Governor William Dempster Hoard of Jefferson County in south-central Wisconsin, a leader within the powerful Wisconsin Dairymen's Association, as well as in Norwegian-born Congressman Nils P. Haugen of Pierce County in the rural west-central section of the state, and in Assemblyman Albert R. Hall (1842–1905) of neighboring Dunn County, arguably Wisconsin's first progressive reformer, and incidentally the nephew of Oliver Hudson Kelley, founder of the Granger movement.[22] In 1896, La Follette emerged clearly as the leader of his faction when he made his first unsuccessful bid for the Republican gubernatorial nomination. In the fall of that year, moreover, he began the process of broadening his political appeal by announcing plans to agitate not only against the old "machine" element within the party but also for positive political reform, first of all the direct primary.[23]

In the following years, the La Follette faction strengthened its appeal by cooperating with various reform elements in Milwaukee: in 1897 with the Municipal League, a nonpartisan city movement founded four years earlier, and in 1898 with the Republican Club of Milwaukee County, an organization led by a group of young attorneys who aimed to rid the city of what they saw as its corrupt, bipartisan coalition working in the interest of powerful public utilities magnates.[24] Besides his Milwaukee allies, from 1899 La Follette could count on the cooperation of a number of Republican leaders disenchanted by the election in the Wisconsin legislature of Joseph V. Quarles to the U.S. senatorship. Chief among these men figured seventy-year-old, Canadian-born Isaac Stephenson (1829–1918) of Marinette, Wisconsin's wealthiest lumberman-politician, and Joseph W. Babcock (1850–1909) of Necedah, Juneau County, another lumber baron and member of Congress since 1893.[25] Whereas by 1901 Babcock had already drifted back to the conservative faction within the Republican Party, Stephenson clung to La Follette right until 1908–1909, when their ways finally parted due to a squabble over Senator Stephenson's right to run for reelection.[26]

If Sawyer, Spooner, and Payne hoped to transcend the traditional boundaries of parochial politics by tightening their grip over the existing party machinery, La Follette and his allies wanted to change the whole concept of the political party by turning it into a public utility rather than a semiprivate organization, by taking it out of the hands of what they dubbed "the interests" and supposedly restoring it to "the people."[27] Turning the political party into a public utility could be done, the reformers insisted, by introducing the statewide, mandatory direct primary that would abolish the caucus and convention system, based as it was upon the principle of delegated authority, and turn the nomination process into a general election within the party. For the same reason, La Follette's conservative opponents feared the measure. "I believe the primary election bill, if passed as proposed, will break the party to pieces," wrote Senator Spooner to Henry C. Payne in early February 1901.[28]

La Follette and his allies wanted to get into closer touch with the broad element of the party, to communicate not only with the local party leaders in the counties and cities but also with the grass roots in the townships and villages. This was to be done, first, by way of La Follette's eminent oratorical skills, which he had first demonstrated in 1879 when he won an interstate speaking contest.[29] La Follette was always an enthusiastic speaker, eager to reach out to as many voters as possible, from his Dane County horse-and-buggy days back in the early 1880s to his 1900 whistle-stop campaign for the governorship, when within twenty-three days he reportedly traveled 6,433 miles by rail, making 208 speeches to almost 200,000 people in sixty-one of Wisconsin's seventy-one counties; from his pioneering use of an automobile in the 1902 campaign to his statement to a crowd of spectators two years later that "if airships were available, I'd use them also."[30] The continuing transportation and communications revolution fit La Follette's purposes perfectly.

Second, La Follette was equally enthusiastic about the possibilities of the press. In 1897, he cooperated with the Municipal League of Milwaukee in publishing a newspaper supplement propagating the direct primary and a corrupt-practices bill, a supplement that purportedly was published in some 400,000 copies. That same year, he also took over the *Old Dane*, a little Dane County paper, and in characteristically ambitious fashion renamed it *The State*.[31] From 1901, moreover, with the aid of Isaac Stephenson, La Follette gained control of a daily paper with ambitions of being truly statewide, the *Milwaukee Free Press*, in which "Uncle Ike" reportedly invested $183,000.[32] Undeniably, its circulation never matched that of the *Milwaukee Sentinel*, but Stephenson's break with La Follette in 1908–1909 still constituted a blow.[33] From that point, La Follette had to make do with publishing his own little *La Follette's Magazine*.[34]

Third, and perhaps most important, was the actual organizing work: making poll lists, writing letters, pamphleteering, and "hustling." To a large extent, these activities aimed at the general Republican electorate rather than merely the local party chieftains. In effect, La Follette and his closest allies proposed to circumvent the old party machinery by building their own statewide network of clubs within the GOP. By 1894 Samuel A. Harper, La Follette's closest friend and former law partner, figured as the president of the Wisconsin Republican League and remained in that position until his sudden death in 1898, when La Follette apparently lost interest in the venture.[35] Nevertheless, La Follette's own poll lists of potential and actual supporters all over the state kept growing. By 1904, they contained "a splendid militant force of some 1,500 or more; then a list of 10,000 unquestioned supporters, and finally a large list of 100,000 or more voters to whom reasonable appeal for aid could be made." The state had never witnessed anything like it before.[36] Truly, La Follette was in the process of establishing direct, personal relations with voters all over the state, an approach to politics eventually institutionalized by the enactment of the direct primary.

Sawyer, Spooner, and Payne hoped to tighten the reins on the existing Republican Party machinery of Wisconsin, whereas La Follette and his allies endeavored to change that machinery by circumventing, to a certain extent, the traditional local leaders and appealing directly to the grass roots of the party. As La Follette stated in characteristically proud and self-righteous fashion in 1900, whereas "we depend upon the rank and file of the party for our chief strength . . . they have only to satisfy the few in each county who manage the politics of the county in order to continue control."[37]

TRADITION UNDER SIEGE

Through a number of political events, some antedating Wisconsin progressivism, the traditional way of arguing electoral politics, so often centering on the concepts of party, nationality, locality, and personality was put under siege. First, the concept of the political party underwent fundamental change. Important in this respect was the voter realignment that in connection with the 1893–1897 depression took place in Wisconsin and throughout the Midwest in the elections of 1894 and 1896. This downturn weakened the Democratic Party and virtually turned Wisconsin into a one-party state. La Follette only worsened matters for the Democrats by diverting all media attention to the dramatic battle over progressive reform unfolding within the GOP.[38]

A number of reforms likewise laid siege to traditional notions of partisanship. As noted previously, federal and state civil-service reform aimed at heightening governmental efficiency by pulling the teeth of the patronage system.[39] Moreover, in 1896 La Follette began planning his fight for the direct primary, the battle to transform the political party into a public utility by making the nomination process a general election within the party.[40] By opting for "open" primaries, La Follette threw his political support behind a proposal that jeopardized the very concept of party membership. The open primary allowed any voter to participate in the nomination process of whichever party he chose, irrespective of his actual party preferences. As future experience was to show, for tactical reasons it would often happen that party activists participated in the primaries of the opposing party.[41] Opening up the primary not only constituted a huge step towards turning the political party into a public utility; it also dealt a shattering blow to the time-honored concept of party loyalty. Notions of blind partisanship now came under sharp attack from progressives, demanding that the voters reflect on the actual issues that the parties represented. "The corruption of this country is rooted in loyalty to party," noted Lincoln Steffens, the muckraking journalist, in 1904, "and the blind partisan who boasts of his blindness is kissing the rod that smites, the toe that kicks, the hand that betrays him and his country."[42]

With the flowering of progressivism, consideration of nationality was likewise put under siege. Whereas the established Republican triumvirate never openly questioned the policy of recognizing some groups of supporters on the basis of their Old World national attachments, La Follette and his allies, on the other hand, were Americanizers in the sense that they generally attempted to avoid ethnic issues, even as they oftentimes combined that approach with doses of quiet affirmative action in behalf of the Scandinavian-American population element. This policy ran the risk of becoming ethnically more offensive than that of the Old Guard, it is true, for the concept of Americanization always remained ill defined, spanning a spectrum of positions running all the way from acceptance of all ethnic groups on a more or less equal footing at the one extreme to blind insistence on conformity to Anglo-American patterns at the other.[43] To the degree that La Follette and Haugen sympathized with the assimilationist approach to politics, they represented the tolerant end of the spectrum.

For years, however, both Haugen and La Follette suffered for their support of Governor Hoard's ill-fated pet issue, the Bennett Law, the ethnically offensive English-language school law that played so formidable a role in the Republican cataclysm of 1890. Belle La Follette always insisted, correctly, that the attacks by the German-American press upon her husband for nativism were wholly unfair. She herself was of German descent, was born and raised in a German-dominated county, and wrote and spoke German. Moreover, a tutor gave Fola, their daughter, instruction in the German language six days a week.[44] Robert La Follette himself was also always annoyed with ethnic issues and maintained that whereas nativists accused him of being a Catholic, Catholics blamed him of being a nativist.[45]

John C. Spooner, Philetus Sawyer, and Henry C. Payne, on the other hand, remained extremely skeptical of the Bennett Law.[46] Spooner was especially disgusted with Governor Hoard's nativism: "A more pestilent, pig-headed, ignorant and offensive political boss, I have never known, . . . and the damned squint he would take into his eye when he spoke about a German, was enough to make a man mad. . . . A man who is as narrow and bigoted and suspicious as he is, cannot be honest at heart. I do not blame the Germans for not being willing to trust him."[47]

Political developments during the progressive era illustrate even more vividly how the traditional ethnic consideration, just like the understanding of party, gradually came under fire. Again, the all-important event was the virtual transformation of Wisconsin into a one-party state in the mid-1890s. Some political observers were quick to perceive the change. In 1896, Samuel A. Harper thus predicted that the Republican Party would be strengthened in the upcoming election, because Norwegian Americans would continue to vote Republican, as they had done all along, whereas

German Americans would switch from the Democrats to the GOP in large numbers.[48] Assemblyman A. R. Hall, moreover, noted that a "loosening up of party ties" was taking place, so that henceforth the religious and geographical background of the political candidate would mean less.[49] Other observers suggested that in the future the outcome of the Republican nomination process would be more important than the general election.[50] Indeed, in 1896 Robert M. La Follette became interested in direct primaries that would virtually turn the nomination process into a general election within each political party. Could the national argument, which always remained more strongly attached to party labels than to factionalism, survive this shift in political emphasis?

At least one aim of the direct primary was to eliminate the nationality as well as the locality consideration from politics. To be sure, that was never the central issue, for the main debate revolved around whether the direct primary would drive out corporate power from politics or simply represented populism at its worst.[51] Nevertheless, both nationality and locality entered the heated discussion. In early 1901, when the newly elected Governor La Follette made primary-election reform his top legislative priority, at one hearing a leading proponent of the direct primary thus suggested, "Men ought not to be nominated for office simply because they live in some particular corner of the state or the country, or because they or their ancestors were born in some foreign land." Another added that he did not "recognize a man fit to run for office as a German, Norwegian, Irish or Scandinavian, but only as an American," and a third asserted, "The day is not far distant when men for public office will be chosen by the people of this great commonwealth, not because they are located in the northeast or the southwest corner of a particular town, not because they are Irish, German, Spaniards, English, or Americans by birth, but because they are able, efficient, and honest men." An opponent of the direct primary, on the other hand, insisted: "The provisions of the bill make it impossible to consider location or nationality in the nomination of tickets."[52]

As the above examples suggest, ethnic reasoning often went hand in hand with arguments revolving around the political candidate's place of residence. Indeed, under the caucus and convention system, politicians often thought in terms of territories. As one would-be gubernatorial candidate wrote hopefully of a political rival in 1896, "I presume he will not care to make any contest with me for these northwestern delegates as I shall not intend to interfere with his territory."[53] Localities were in fact typically expected to support their own "favorite son": "Of course if you have a candidate all I shall expect is [for you] to have a friendly feeling towards me as long as he is in the race with a hope of securing substantial aid if he should drop out."[54] Again, La Follette opposed such geographical considerations: "I have never asked support for local reasons. It is of no significance where a man eats or sleeps."[55] With the direct primary, which forced the candidate for state office to communicate with the electorate of the whole state, rather than simply to mobilize local support and then hope for the best at the state convention, the locality factor was weakened considerably. In addition, civil-service reform, by lowering the political stakes, further impaired the efficiency of making political claims on the basis of locality and national background.

Finally, the idea of choosing a man for office largely because of his personal qualities, in terms of his being a good neighbor, a brave Civil War veteran, a loyal partisan, a man of great *past* accomplishment, was challenged by the notion that the man should represent, first of all, certain political issues. During the 1870s and 1880s, the great moral questions of the Civil War era had gradually been supplanted by much more down-to-earth debates over the size of the tariff and currency matters. Although the Republican Party was traditionally associated with the protective tariff, in practical politics party lines often blurred. Prior to 1896, something similar was the case when talk turned to the monetization of silver. In the presidential campaign of that year this issue truly divided the parties, with the Democrats coming out in favor of "free silver" and the Republicans supporting the gold standard. Moreover, to the degree that the rather colorless presidents of that era might have entertained grand legislative visions, they were blocked in all such ambitions by the near-balance of power between the major parties in Congress. In 1879, Woodrow Wilson caught the temper of Gilded Age politics in eight words: "No leaders, no principles; no principles, no parties."[56]

Overall, neither Philetus Sawyer, John C. Spooner, nor Henry C. Payne were identified with popular issues. As diligent as Sawyer was in promoting bills relating to pension matters, land grants, and the pork barrel, he never sponsored any grand, national issue.[57] Nor, as a general rule, did Spooner. The two main exceptions proving that rule were, first, a 1901 act establishing civil government in the Philippines; second, the famous 1902 Spooner Act that laid the foundations for the construction of the Panama Canal.[58] Henry C. Payne, finally, became identified with just two issues: synthetic butter, for which he lobbied in behalf of the Chicago meat-packing industry, and tax privileges for the street railway and lighting companies operating under his and Democratic boss Edward C. Wall's executive leadership.[59] Those issues earned him the contempt of many people living in Wisconsin's dairying districts, as well as in Milwaukee.

From the fringes of the world of politics, from marginalized leaders typically representing agriculturally depressed areas in the far West and in the South, there gradually rose a chorus of voices insisting on reinvigorating politics, on reshaping politics in radical fashion, on reintroducing the political issue in the form of meaningful, righteous, and necessary political reform. Already in the wake of the 1873 recession, the agrarian Granger movement, founded in 1867 to educate farmers and forward their interests, had become increasingly politicized. During the late 1880s and early 1890s, moreover, with the deepening of an agricultural crisis, in the north especially among cereal producers farther west than Wisconsin, the Populist movement grew powerful and became politicized. Demands were now heard for reforms to regulate the railroad companies; to aid the cooperative marketing of agricultural products; to ensure that the voice of "the people" be heard through such direct-democracy devices as the initiative, referendum, and recall; and to inflate the money supply through the free coinage of silver.[60]

The Populists made a strong point of insisting that they, unlike the two major parties, represented true, pure reform, as their 1892 national platform, attacking the two major parties, made clear: "Neither do they now promise us any substantial reform. They have agreed together to ignore in the coming campaign every issue but one. They propose to drown the outcries of a plundered people with the uproar of a sham battle over the tariff."[61] The depression of 1893 seemed only to lend substance to this complaint by the People's Party, for the two major parties simply blamed each other for the crisis and pointed to traditional tariff and currency measures to combat it.[62] In Wisconsin, even though the Populist movement never grew strong, it still helped color people's perception of reform, giving that concept a radical twist. Indeed, this association with radicalism helps explain why La Follette did not emerge as a reformer until late 1896, five years after he began his insurgent revolt against the established leadership of the Republican Party. For a long time, La Follette simply remained too steeped in tradition to give serious thought to reform. In 1892, pondering Populist success, he commented, "We are in no danger of such anarchistic repudiation as appears to threaten Kansas, Nebraska and some of the other more western states."[63] In fact, as late as July 1896, La Follette gave more attention to national politics than to state reform. "I think the best way to prepare one's self for the stump is to get the best speeches made in Congress on the issues likely [to] arise, more especially the tariff and money questions."[64]

By the time that La Follette converted to reform, it is true, the concept was in the process of moving closer to mainstream politics. Especially at the municipal level, reform was becoming increasingly accepted. When the Milwaukee Municipal League was founded in February 1893, the *Milwaukee Sentinel* trumpeted, "the cause of municipal reform is moving."[65] In the ensuing years of economic depression, the League grew somewhat in strength, and similar city movements surfaced inside and outside of Wisconsin. The Milwaukee League never gained sufficient vigor, however, truly to sustain progressivism.[66] First, the activities of the League remained largely restricted to municipal politics, even though the League did make one departure into state politics in 1895–1897 by sponsoring a corrupt-practices bill that two reformers within the emergent La Follette faction, A. R. Hall and Nils P. Haugen, actually had been discussing since late 1892.[67] As noted, by 1897 the La Follette faction and the League in fact cooperated on this measure. Generally speaking, however, the step from municipal to state politics was large, and the League soon returned to municipal matters and left state politics to La Follette.[68]

Second, the Municipal League of Milwaukee was always hampered considerably both by its declared nonpartisanship and, paradoxically, by League President John A. Butler's open affiliation with the Democratic Party. "I have also preached Mr. Cleveland's doctrine vigorously and openly in connection with the Municipal League of this city," Butler confided to U.S. Senator William F. Vilas in the spring of 1893.[69] But then again, Butler may still have been dreaming of receiving that coveted consulship in Europe, preferably Dresden, that he had written Vilas about earlier.[70] By the late 1890s, the Republican Club of Milwaukee County, led by the young, energetic attorney Francis E. McGovern and his allies, had clearly taken over the reform initiative from the League. McGovern thus began the dizzying ascent that in 1911 would land him in the governor's chair. Moreover, after the turn of the century another powerful reform impulse emanated from Milwaukee in the shape of Victor Berger and Emil Seidel's Social Democratic Party. Thus, in the history of Wisconsin progressivism, the Municipal League of Milwaukee simply faded from view. As one La Follette supporter pointed out in 1901, "Sporadic movements of reform in municipalities gleam like comets and are about as lasting. The permanent renovation of city governments will be accomplished when party organizations are renovated."[71]

Third, even though it is correct that the Municipal League of Wisconsin gained strength during the depression, and notwithstanding that La Follette emerged as a reformer only in late 1896, shortly before the coming of better times, at the state level progressivism only began its real expansion after the turn of the century, long after the return of prosperity. Only in 1903, two years after the La Follettes had moved into the governor's mansion, did the progressives begin truly to enact their reform program, and only in 1911 did Wisconsin progressivism develop fully.[72] The main political result of the depression was indirect. It brought about a voter realignment that strengthened the Republican Party immensely and stifled stale debate between the two major parties, at least temporarily. This inaugurated an era characterized by more meaningful and soul-searching intra-party discussions focusing on actual reform.

By the time that La Follette came out for political reform, that very concept was striking an increasingly responsive chord among a growing number of people in Wisconsin, but in state politics many individuals nevertheless viewed reform as an assault on the normal, an anomaly of paradigmatic proportions to be equated with "freak, populistic measures" and "populistic fireworks."[73] A. R. Hall, already in 1891 a reform zealot in the assembly, was viewed by conservatives as a crank, indeed, as "the crank of the cranks," just as La Follette's 1901 reform crusade caused one Old Guard Republican to comment, "The party just now is in the condition of the fellow who, not knowing what to do with himself, planted a louse in his pelt."[74] Likewise, when in 1903 one former progressive had second thoughts about reform, a conservative offered the opinion that this man had had "the film of populism removed from his eyes."[75] In 1899, finally, Elisha W. Keyes, an old Republican warhorse now in the pay of the Chicago and Northwestern Railway Company, contrasted the present "reform spasm" with what he considered "a normal condition." Eight years later, the same Keyes uttered the forlorn hope that now that La Follette had departed for the U.S. Senate, "The reform sentiment, once so rampant, is dead. . . . A reaction has fully set in. A normal condition is at hand."[76]

With the enemies of La Follette viewing him as "a wild-eyed reformer" and "a modern reform gladiator," La Follette and his allies, on their part, were also well aware of the depths of the political change that was taking place.[77] As early as 1896, La Follette was telling supporters that "the old order of things must go down," and one ally expressed the hope, "Give us a new deal of new men, but men somewhat experienced in public affairs and men who will carry out some plans of needed reform."[78] In 1902, when Governor La Follette ran for reelection on a reform platform, he took a broader view of the situation. "The question of primary elections is not one of partisan politics," he announced in Milwaukee. "It is a question of citizenship. It is a question of patriotism. It is a part of a progressive movement."[79]

While fighting an ever expanding battle for political and economic reform, La Follette consciously and successfully harnessed his issues to his impressive, statewide, grassroots-based organization and thus built the progressive movement of Wisconsin. Despite the fact that La Follette always used reform issues to create a climate of perceived danger and moral urgency, invariably aiming most of his rhetorical wrath at corporate power—despite the fact, in other words, that he generally did precious little to calm conservative worries about reform—La Follette's fight to substitute a new, issue-oriented type of politics for blind partisan loyalty was highly successful. In his view, the issues ought to define the party. "Political platforms must be upheld if political parties are to be maintained," he exclaimed in 1902.[80] Indeed, two years later he instituted his practice of invading the political territory of his enemies to explain to shocked audiences how local members of the legislature had betrayed the platform: "I tell you, when you see a band of men who are willing to bind themselves together to corrupt and defeat good legislation they ought to be tagged and marked for life."[81]

La Follette's conservative opponents were baffled by this new orientation towards issues and felt compelled to respond in kind. As one conservative politician noted despairingly, "The Stalwarts can not content themselves with obstructing the passage of La Follette measures, they must stand for something definite."[82] By 1910, the new emphasis on issues was clearly revealed in the Republican state platform. The 1894 platform had been a half-page document dealing mostly in generalities. By 1910, however, at the high point of Wisconsin progressivism, the platform amounted to a seven-page document crammed with plank after plank calling for specific legislation.[83]

At first sight, the proposition that Wisconsin progressivism represented an endeavor to replace political personality with issues might seem absurd, since Wisconsin progressivism, after all, became synonymous, largely, with La Folletteism. Even so, in public La Follette always insisted on being recognized not so much for his personal qualities as for the issues that he stood for. To the degree that traditional politicians were elected to office on the basis of their record of *past* accomplishments, he wished to be recognized above all for his willingness to fight *future* battles in the name of reform. Indeed, increasingly he came to view himself as a political prophet.[84] A political platform by George E. Beedle, Republican candidate for a seat in Congress in 1910, caught the way the person of La Follette was being identified with issues. Making no reference to party, nationality, locality, or personality, Beedle's personal platform read in its entire length, "I am now and always have been a staunch supporter of Robert M. La Follette and the progressive principles advocated by him. I am opposed to Cannon and Aldrich policies. I favor control of government by the people. I am opposed to control by or favor to special interests."[85]

The Wisconsin progressives thus made a conscious attempt to change the terms of political debate in Wisconsin. The concept of the political party underwent fundamental change, and the notion of giving special consideration to the nationality argument and to locality questions was put under siege. At the same time, the future-oriented political issue was pushed to the front at the expense of a politician's past accomplishments. As one close friend of La Follette noted years later, "The advent of

La Follette was to prove disruptive of practically all political parties in Wisconsin. Previous to his time the antagonisms were chiefly between the old parties and on national lines alone. Since then such animosities have been rather retrospective and fanciful and those entertaining them rightly classed as old-fashioned, whatever their party."[86] Moreover, as another observer noted in 1914, "It is not so important that nationality lines be observed as it once was under the convention system...because people nowadays are looking for right men."[87] In July 1906, La Follette himself summed up in precise terms how he believed politics had changed within recent years, referring as he did so to *all the four* elements of the traditional argumentative matrix: "In the last ten years great changes have taken place in this commonwealth. Principles have become more important than party names. Issues have towered above men. The nationality and the location of candidates have become less important than the character and ability of the individual."[88] To what extent, however, did the Wisconsin progressives in fact succeed in rooting out the consideration of nationality from politics?

CHAPTER SEVEN

Battles against Tradition

THE 1893 DEPRESSION

On 29 March 1893, *Skandinaven* featured a reader letter from an anony-mous "Farmerboy" from Kristoffer Skauge's Strum, prophesying the consequences of free trade now that a Democratic president, Grover Cleveland, had been inaugurated. "I think that we shall see that when 'free trade' is introduced, things will change considerably, especially for the working class that needs to work in order to survive. As a consequence of the imports, their wages will be reduced to next to nothing, because the American manufacturing companies cannot sell their goods as cheaply as for instance England. . . . The tariff is there to protect us, and I think that 'free trade' will be one of our biggest evils."[1] Many Republicans would have agreed with that analysis, and a very superficial glance at events in the late spring of 1893 only seemed to prove the "Farmerboy" right, even before the new Democratic administration had had a chance of developing its economic policy.

The economic downturn began with a stock market crash in early May, followed by a series of bank closures. By October, the president of the Northwestern National Bank of Superior was reporting, "Every banker I see grates his teeth when you mention the subject."[2] Indeed, America was plunging into the worst depression yet in its history. By the end of 1893, 500 banks had closed nationwide, and 16,000 business bankruptcies had occurred. By mid-1894, overall unemployment in America stood at three million.[3] The general feeling of hopelessness was captured by an editorial in *Den danske Pioneer*: "Even though this is the best time of the year, in

163

every city the laborers are drifting about without being able to find work. . . . And now, in addition to all this misery, come the stories from Nebraska, Iowa, Illinois, Kansas, Missouri, etc. about crop failures that will force thousands of farmers to leave their homes empty-handed, having lost everything."[4]

Wisconsin also suffered its share of misery, with nearly one-quarter of the state's 119 banks failing by the end of 1893 and several other businesses following suit. Observers estimated that in 1893–1894, some thirty-five to forty percent of Milwaukee's work force was unemployed, and the Milwaukee County board, copying Mayor Hazen Pingree's reform in Detroit, allowed poor people to cultivate potatoes on vacant parcels of land. Outside Milwaukee, several paper mills, the largest employers in the Fox and Wisconsin river valleys, closed down, and the construction industry entered a period of sharp decline.[5] Judging by the many reader letters in *Skandinaven*, some Wisconsin farmers also felt the pinch of hard times. These letters typically bore out the "Farmerboy's" analysis by decrying the low "Democratic prices."[6] Other letter writers granted, however, that agricultural conditions were even worse farther out west, and some suggested that the Wisconsin dairy farmers, especially, were sufficiently prosperous to withstand hard times.[7]

The depressed economy caused some political unrest in America. In the spring of 1894, Jacob S. Coxey's "army" of unemployed people thus marched from Massillon, Ohio, to Washington, D.C., and struck a new note in American politics by demanding federal relief. In the nation's capital, however, they were greeted by a large police force, and a riot ensued. The Coxeyites ought, perhaps, to have listened to President Grover Cleveland's 1893 inaugural address: "While the people should patriotically and cheerfully support their Government, its functions do not include the support of the people."[8] Furthermore, the spring and summer of 1894 witnessed not only a large coalminers' strike in the Midwest, but also the Pullman strike among railroad workers, a strike that involved some 260,000 laborers and sent Eugene V. Debs, cofounder of the American Railroad Union and later leader of the Socialist Party, to jail and propelled him to national prominence.[9]

In Wisconsin, the depression did not result in any dramatic labor or other grassroots upheaval in 1894. The Municipal League of Milwaukee, founded just months before the economic downturn, did not yet have much of an effect.[10] In Wisconsin, as in large sections of the Midwest, the Democratic Party bore the main brunt of grassroots frustration, losing massive numbers of voters in the elections of 1894 and 1896. In the former year, it is true, unrest also haunted the Republican Party: Congressman Nils P. Haugen made a vain attempt to win the Republican nomination for the governorship.

CONGRESSMAN NILS P. HAUGEN:
THE TRANSFORMATION OF AN ETHNIC POLITICIAN

By 1894, Nils Pederson Haugen was Wisconsin's most prominent politician of Scandinavian lineage. Born in 1849 in Modum, Norway, and coming to Wisconsin at the age of five in company with his parents and five sisters, he grew up on a farm in the Norwegian-dominated Rush River settlement in Pierce County in west-central Wisconsin. The Haugens kept in close touch with the Norwegian-American community. Nils's father, Peter, worked as a farmer and doubled as a blacksmith. He subscribed to several Norwegian-language papers, and the whole family participated in the activities of the local Norwegian Lutheran congregation. In 1869, at age twenty, Nils journeyed to Decorah, Iowa, to study at Luther College, an institution under the auspices of the Norwegian Synod. Soon realizing that he did not want to pursue a theological career, he left in late 1871 and enrolled as a law student at the University of Michigan, graduating in the spring of 1874. As an attorney Haugen thus belonged to that tiny group of immigrant politicians attaining professional status in America. He would always remain highly aware of his status as a professional.

Setting up a law practice at River Falls together with Charles Smith, a former county school superintendent, and C. R. Morse, editor of the *River Falls Journal*, and working on the side as a court reporter, Haugen quickly became involved in the world of politics. In 1878, he was elected to the assembly, and in 1880 he received the "Norwegian" nomination on the Republican state ticket, to the office of railroad commissioner. Subsequently winning that position in the general election and reelected three times, Haugen received a boost in 1887 when he was elected to fill the unexpired term of the deceased Congressman William T. Price.[11]

For years Haugen accepted the role of being a prominent Norwegian

American in the politics-as-usual of Wisconsin, and of arguing politics on ethnic terms. In January, 1886, Railroad Commissioner Haugen thus reported to Rasmus B. Anderson in Copenhagen that in the up-coming Republican state convention, "Of course there will be a Scandinavian for some position, but who and what will not be settled until determined by the convention."[12] Later that year, he wrote the editor of *Fædrelandet og Emigranten* a letter discussing the political strength of the Scandinavian-American element in Wisconsin.[13] Since the state boasted 40,000 Scandinavian-American voters, and suggesting that five-sixths of them voted Republican, Haugen concluded that the Scandinavian Americans comprised one-quarter of the total Republican column. "*With one-fourth* of the *Republican vote*, our representation in the state as far as state offices are concerned is only *one-eighth*, and our share of *appointments* is even smaller."

Haugen did not abandon his Scandinavian focus after he was elected to Congress. Indeed, one observer grumbled that Haugen owed his new position in the House of Representatives exclusively to his ethnic background: "What influence can such a man have in Congress, backed by such a vote? It will be absolutely nothing. He will be looked upon only as a Norwegian, squeezed in *only* as a Norwegian."[14] In practice, Haugen's special awareness of his ethnicity was reflected not only in his affinity for appointing postmasters of Scandinavian background but also in the reports that he sent Rasmus B. Anderson regarding the other Scandinavian-American members of Congress, Norwegian-born Knute Nelson and Swedish-born John Lind, both of Minnesota.[15]

Haugen never developed close ties with Knute Nelson, even if Haugen had characterized the Minnesota politician as "a level-headed, trustworthy man, a good type of our nationality" and later applauded his election to the U.S. Senate.[16] The truth was that Haugen and Nelson had wrangled with each other in Congress over a bridge-construction bill that would benefit Duluth, Minnesota, at the expense of neighboring Superior, Wisconsin.[17] Later, Haugen confided to Nicolai Grevstad of *Skandinaven*, "I cannot help but feel, and ought to tell you, that I am not the right person to go to N— for any purposes. You could probably get at him much better yourself."[18] Even so, the fact that Haugen several times reflected upon

Knute Nelson's career is significant in itself, as is the circumstance that he devoted a section of his memoirs to a discussion of him.[19]

Haugen became a closer friend politically and personally of John Lind, at least until 1896 when the latter broke with the Republican Party over the question of the free coinage of silver.[20] Before that point, they worked in tandem not only to secure Republican campaign funds for the leading Scandinavian-American papers but also for instance to establish a Scandinavian collection in the Library of Congress.[21] In 1893, furthermore, Haugen asked Lind his opinion on the question of the coinage of silver. On this occasion, Haugen made one of his increasingly rare switches to the Norwegian language, first asking Lind in English, "And how would you have voted, if here?" then adding in Norwegian, "Let this remain between you and me."[22] In 1894, finally, Lind wrote Haugen that had the latter only won the Republican gubernatorial nomination, he "should have been glad to have put in a couple of weeks in your state this fall." Privately, Lind not only introduced Haugen to a Wyoming land-speculation scheme but also suggested that the Haugens visit his own family in Minnesota.[23] By 1929, Haugen and Lind were still seeing each other occasionally.[24]

Even though during his years in Congress Haugen never let go of a Scandinavian focus, by the end of the 1880s and the beginning of the 1890s he was nevertheless attempting to broaden and diversify his popular appeal. True, his prestige as a representative of the Norwegian Americans only received an additional lift when Nicolai A. Grevstad began writing articles in his favor, first in the *Minneapolis Tribune*, later in *Skandinaven*.[25] Yet at the same time Haugen was moving markedly closer to a couple of Yankee politicians.

The most notable of these was Robert M. La Follette, incidentally a native of the Norwegian-dominated township of Primrose, Dane County, who could even speak a bit of Norwegian.[26] In 1885, at the age of twenty-nine, La Follette had entered the House of Representatives, and two years later, when Haugen was elected to that body, they occupied seats close to each other. La Follette and Haugen quickly established a working relationship with each other, the two in fact agreeing on most public questions and sometimes uniting in opposition to the old Republican guard, as when both of them refused to support a Nicaraguan Canal bill despite Senator Sawyer's urgings.[27] Besides cooperating with La Follette in patronage matters, by the summer of 1891 Haugen expressed the hope that La Follette might win the Republican nomination for the governorship.[28]

Another fact indicating that Haugen was broadening his political base is that from 1890 he became a friend of A. R. Hall, former Speaker of the Minnesota Assembly.[29] Hall lived in Dunn County, adjacent to Haugen's Pierce County, and Hall was elected to the Wisconsin Assembly that same year. Fighting to establish a railroad commission, and to abolish the practice by the railroad companies of distributing free passes to legislators, Hall quickly built a strong reputation as a reformer. By the end of 1892, he and Haugen were discussing political issues with each other on a regular basis. Haugen soon displayed a bent for political reform that almost matched Hall's zeal. Haugen suggested to Hall that a corrupt-practices bill along the lines of a British law be advanced in the Wisconsin legislature and at the same time urged La Follette to consult with Hall on the matter.[30]

In late 1893 and early 1894, Congressman Haugen's growing interest in reducing the influence of corporate power in politics was revealed in a heated exchange of letters with Roswell Miller, the president of the Chicago, Milwaukee, and St. Paul Railway Company, one of Wisconsin's two major railroad lines.[31] When Miller denounced the Interstate Commerce Act of 1887 for infringing on the rights of the railroad companies, Haugen answered that the railroads ought to be viewed as public utilities rather than private corporations. When Miller further suggested that the railroad companies would soon be obliged to "take vigorous measures to protect themselves" from hostile legislation, Haugen, reflecting on the Chicago Haymarket riot, warned Miller that "they have hanged anarchists in Chicago. I should be sorry to hear that you were strung up."

By the depression year of 1894, Congressman Nils P. Haugen of Pierce County stood out as Wisconsin's most formidable politician of Scandinavian-American background. This was not solely due to his ethnic support, which remained important, but also because he had entered into cooperation with various Yankee politicians who had ambitions to fundamentally change political conditions in the state. This would mean first of all cleaning out the old leadership of the party.

THE BATTLE OF 1894

Already in 1892, less than one year after the stormy encounter between U.S. Senator Sawyer and ex-Congressman La Follette at the Plankinton House, Haugen was approached by La Follette, who urged him to make a bid for the Republican gubernatorial nomination.[32] Haugen rejected the offer, but in the fall of 1893 renewed pressure was applied to make him run in 1894. Haugen once again turned down the proposal, arguing that the race for the governorship had become too expensive, and that Mayor John C. Koch of Milwaukee was the obvious candidate: "He is a German, and the Germans have been anxious for years to present a candidate to the republican convention."[33] As Haugen added with resignation, "Of course that fact alone amounts to nothing, but it is a factor to be taken into consideration in the matter of getting votes, when the candidate is otherwise acceptable."

Why should Haugen have considered relinquishing his seat in Congress for a highly uncertain bid for the governorship? The problem was that in the Tenth Congressional District, unlike many others, a tradition had been established that incumbents should withdraw after a few terms. In fact, Haugen's 1892 reelection to his fourth term had been precedent-breaking.[34] Even so, for a while Haugen, heeding La Follette's advice, let both options stay open. He was annoyed when the *Superior Wave* began boosting him for the governorship, realizing that the paper was simply attempting to sidetrack him from Congress, yet at the same time he began sending feelers out to La Follette about his gubernatorial prospects.[35] In mid-April 1894, however, only days after the editor of the *Milwaukee Sentinel* informed La Follette that his paper was not supporting Mayor Koch for the governorship, Haugen finally confided to Samuel A. Harper that he was going to try for the governorship.[36] One month later, Koch, now under fire for having bolted the Republican Party during the 1890 Bennett law controversy, withdrew from the contest.[37] Even though George C. Koeppen (1833–1897), editor of the influential *Die Germania* of Milwaukee, immediately began scouting around for a German-American substitute, Haugen used Koch's retreat as an opportunity to travel to Milwaukee and make his candidacy official.[38] *Skandinaven* turned matters upside down by declaring, "Mayor John C. Koch of Milwaukee withdrew the same day that Haugen announced his candidacy."[39]

In working for his candidacy, Haugen and his allies displayed a certain disposition, ambiguous, to be sure, to move beyond the traditional practice of politics as defined by the rules of the caucus and convention system, yet in the end they succumbed to those rules. Haugen and La Follette realized fully, of course, the former's strength among the Norwegian-American element.[40] Indeed, in promoting him for the governorship, one of Haugen's party workers even employed the traditional arguments of party, nationality, locality, and personality: "Haugen belongs to no clique, is strongly American in his feelings, is from the north and is of Scandinavian birth. He has never bolted his party, and has always voted right in Congress."[41]

In a circular that La Follette personally wrote for Haugen, on the other hand, traditionalism was utterly rejected: "Mr. Haugen is an independent, liberal minded man, and is not the candidate of any locality or interest, nationality or religion, person or machine."[42] Pointing to actual political-economic questions, La Follette continued, "I never knew him to dodge a vote or evade an issue, and at all times and under all circumstances he faithfully worked, spoke and voted in the interest of the people, as the dairymen, and tobacco and wool growers especially will remember." Haugen himself told Assemblyman Hall that under no circumstances did he intend his candidacy to be merely a "Tenth District matter or a Scandinavian matter."[43]

On 15 April 1894, one month before Haugen officially entered the race, La Follette outlined a purely "American" strategy, urging Haugen immediately to confer with the editorship of *Skandinaven* to ensure that his candidacy *not* be announced first by a Scandinavian-language paper.[44] Nine days later, Haugen himself illuminated the strategy fully to the editor of *Nordvesten*: "If I get into the field in earnest the movement will be from outside my own district to start with and will be backed by some of the best 'Americans' in the state. I have made this one of the conditions as the charge that it was a nationalistic boom, or a mere local boom, might be fatal."[45] True to this strategy, Haugen began sending La Follette lists of supporters, concentrating especially on those residing outside his present congressional district, yet being somewhat embarrassed by the meager result.[46] Haugen even kept his gubernatorial plans secret from most local supporters, a tactic shortly to cause him considerable embarrassment.[47]

The problem was that some of Haugen's Scandinavian-American allies, knowing precious little about his designs, were dreaming of getting a place for themselves on the Republican state ticket. The old unwritten rules of the game stipulated, after all, that only one Scandinavian American be nominated for state office. Haugen attempted to forestall such rival candidacies by asking Danish-born Soren Listoe of *Nordvesten*, and apparently also Nicolai Grevstad of *Skandinaven*, "not to say anything at present and not to commit yourself to any candidate for any minor position on the ticket."[48] Still, various Scandinavian-American candidates began to pop up. On February 16, Sewell A. Peterson, a Norwegian-born political ally from Rice Lake in Barron County, announced to Haugen that he was intending to run for the nomination for state treasurer. Peterson on his part expressed the hope that two other Norwegian-American rivals would stay out of the field, and that Haugen would use his influence with *Skandinaven* in Peterson's behalf.[49] At length, Haugen succeeded in working out an agreement with Peterson to the effect that Peterson support Haugen for the gubernatorial nomination, but in the event of Haugen's candidacy failing, the latter agreed to champion Peterson for the state treasurership.[50] Haugen likewise reached understandings with two other Scandinavian-American would-be candidates for positions on the state ticket, both of whom now pledged to support Haugen.[51]

Notwithstanding these arrangements, Haugen's troubles had only just begun. With Mayor Koch's withdrawal, the gubernatorial field was left wide open. At this point in time, it is true, Haugen thought that his own chances looked better than ever. Personal conferences with the editors of the *Milwaukee Sentinel* and *Die Germania* convinced him that both were friendly towards his candidacy, and he also had assurances that *Skandinaven* was ready not only to "strike immediately" but also to use its influence with the St. Paul *Pioneer Press* and the *Minneapolis Tribune*.[52] Traveling to Oshkosh at the suggestion of *Sentinel* editor Rublee, Haugen even saw Philetus Sawyer, who to Haugen's delight now finally seemed willing to let bygones be bygones and forget about the unfortunate clash with La Follette at the Plankinton House. "I would not do anything to hurt La Follette," Sawyer was reported to having stated. "On the contrary, I would do anything to help him."[53] During those days, finally, La Follette stepped up his mass-mailing campaign, informing Haugen that somewhere between 8,000 and 10,000 Haugen pamphlets were now circulating in Wisconsin.[54]

Other signs were more ominous. The same day that Koch withdrew from the race, Horace A. Taylor (1837–1910), editor of the *Wisconsin State Journal*, entered it, "with a smile on his face," reported one observer, "warm enough to melt a hardboiled egg."[55] Known widely as a political trickster with ties to the Old Guard, Haugen had long expected "Hod" Taylor's candidacy. "I am inclined to think that he will be a candidate for governor next year," Haugen wrote in October 1893. "He said he was not, which strengthens my suspicion."[56] With Taylor entering the race, strange things began to happen: one Scandinavian-American politician after another announced his candidacy for a position on the state ticket.

To be sure, the candidacy of Captain Ole Oleson of Oshkosh for the railroad commissionership was less than threatening, reasoned Haugen, for Winnebago County boasted only a few Scandinavian Americans.[57] Moreover, rumors that Norwegian-American John A. Johnson, the Madison machine manufacturer, wanted the lieutenant governorship hardly caused Haugen sleepless nights, for Johnson's past within both the Democratic and Prohibition parties did nothing to strengthen his Republican credentials.[58] Finally, Halle Steensland, a Norwegian-born businessman likewise of Madison, hoped for the nomination for the state treasurership. Even though one commentator observed that Steensland's announcement might well be part of a Taylor ploy, Haugen considered him a weak candidate.[59]

The candidacy of three other Norwegian Americans for state office was more critical. First, Mayor T. C. Lund of Norwegian-dominated Stoughton announced his candidacy for the position of secretary of state. This pained Haugen, for earlier Lund had pledged to support him. Even though Belle La Follette considered Lund the worst obstacle to success in Dane County, her husband in characteristically uncompromising fashion refused to negotiate with Lund beyond applying pressure to make him withdraw.[60] Norwegian-American Charles Lewiston of Hudson, St. Croix County, casting his eyes on the state treasurership, resided within the Tenth Congressional District and was thus a matter for Haugen, his former ally, to deal with. The fact that Lewiston lived in the same city that had fostered both Horace Taylor and John C. Spooner, along with Lewiston's refusal even to consider withdrawing from the race, soon convinced Haugen and his allies that Lewiston was cooperating actively with Taylor.[61]

A third Norwegian-American candidate, the most threatening to

Haugen of all, was Hans B. Warner, former secretary of state, and, like Haugen, a resident of Pierce County. Earlier, Warner had apparently pledged Haugen his support, but when Elisha W. Keyes urged Warner that he would be "the strongest and the best candidate," Warner willingly took the bait. Ever since 1881, after all, Warner had almost routinely made his bid for the gubernatorial nomination.[62] In reality, Keyes had no faith in Warner, soon complaining, "A lot of cheap and onerous men so far have forged to the front," and suggesting that the strongest gubernatorial candidate would be Congressman Joseph W. Babcock.[63] Probably Keyes simply viewed Warner in much the same manner that Haugen did, as the *typical immigrant politician*: "He was a good-natured and popular official, but with only a meager common-school education."[64]

Yet, even though Warner was no serious contender for the governorship, he was a powerful factor in Pierce County politics, a circumstance extremely disturbing to Haugen who thus risked losing his home county. "Yes! We are onto the whole racket," announced Warner to Keyes in late May. "I am in to *stay* and I told Mr. Haugen and La Follette so when they were here. I am going to bring the delegates from this county which will not sound well for a candidate [Haugen] without his own county."[65] The suspicion remained, moreover, that Warner, like Lund and Lewiston, was cooperating with Taylor, an old friend of Keyes. "Hod is doing the same thing with Warner in Pierce," Haugen suggested, "that he is with Lewiston in St. Croix."[66] Indeed, speculated Haugen, Warner was "undoubtedly encouraged to stay in the field by Taylor and Keyes of Madison who are after my scalp. Of course they are not for Warner – that is easily to be seen."[67]

Thus, Haugen and La Follette soon found themselves in a sea of trouble. Undoubtedly, they had known all along that no matter how vigorously they promoted Haugen as an "American" politician, no room would be left for another Scandinavian American on the state ticket. Had no other Scandinavian American risen to challenge Haugen, the ethnic issue might still have been laid to rest and other questions highlighted. As it was, with seven candidates of Scandinavian background in the field, that issue surged to the front. As Haugen noted in early June, "There is no doubt that Hod shows good generalship in getting so many Scandinavian candidates into the field; that is, it is good generalship if it is his object to defeat me. It is not if he desires to be nominated himself."[68]

What was Haugen to do? La Follette was not in doubt: "You must have [O. O.] Halls stir up the Norwegians in St. Croix to go and jump onto Lewiston. He must be so jumped on by his own countrymen as to get him out of the way. . . . Your friends in Pierce must simply squelch Warner."[69] Haugen, however, fearful that an open attack on his Scandinavian-American rivals would give the enemy occasion "to show that I was the candidate of a nationality and appealing to them to make it an issue on that basis," preferred to work quietly, having friends apply gentle pressure on Lewiston and Warner, at the same time that *Skandinaven, Nordvesten,* and *Amerika* opened their guns on the rival candidates.[70] In the end, however, nothing could be done to get Lewiston, Warner, and Lund off the track. In late June, a frustrated Haugen wrote Warner a thirteen-page open letter, calling the latter "the pliant tool in the hands of scheming men interested in defeating us both," and ridiculing his eternal bids for the governorship.[71] The editor of the *River Falls Journal* dared not publish it.[72]

In the ensuing primary campaign, La Follette captured Dane, the largest county within his old congressional district, for Haugen after losing in Madison (Taylor's home) and Stoughton (where Lund was mayor) but winning in the countryside. John Anderson, the owner of *Skandinaven*, turned up in Dane to participate in the field work.[73] Securing all thirteen Dane County delegates for Haugen constituted a bad blow to Taylor.[74] La Follette's further claim in his *Autobiography*, however, that he also carried the remaining four counties of his old congressional district in south-central Wisconsin is incorrect. At the state convention, only one of the twenty-three delegates from Grant, Green, Iowa, and La Fayette counties voted for Haugen on the first ballot (fig. 7.1, Appendix I).[75]

In Haugen's own congressional district to the northwest, the loss of Pierce, his home county, to Warner, was particularly devastating. Despite La Follette's entreaty to "keep in the saddle until dead sure of St. Croix. You must get it. It will knock out Hod's other eye," Haugen was defeated also in St. Croix.[76] In the remaining nine counties of his congressional district, however, Haugen secured all but one of the twenty-seven delegates on the first ballot.[77] Outside La Follette's old and Haugen's present congressional districts, Haugen gained the full support of an additional four counties, all of which lay within his old congressional district before it had been reapportioned. From other parts of Wisconsin, finally, Haugen secured another nine delegates but no whole county delegation.

Thus, when the Republican state convention convened in Milwaukee on July 25, Haugen and La Follette controlled sixty-five of the 345 delegates, an impressive figure but far short of the 173 votes required for victory. In all, ten candidates participated in the gubernatorial race. William H. Upham, a lumber manufacturer from Marshfield, Wood County, whom La Follette suspected of having been involved in some dirty pine land deals, led the gubernatorial fight from the first until the seventh and final ballot.[78] Haugen held down second place through the race and gradually increased his vote from sixty-five to ninety-nine, with his regional backing changing somewhat. Taylor started in the fifth place and ended in the fourth. Warner, finally, entered as number eight and dropped to the bottom of the list, with all his delegates deserting him for Haugen on the final ballot.

According to *Skandinaven*, of the 345 delegates participating in the Republican state convention, some forty-five were Scandinavian-American, the majority of them of Norwegian descent. Editor Grevstad was also present and conferred with Haugen in his hotel room shortly after Upham's nomination.[79] Haugen was not certain whether prior to the convention these delegates would meet in a separate caucus to unite on one candidate, as sometimes happened.[80] After the nomination of Upham, however, several of the Scandinavian-American delegates reportedly expressed anger with Lewiston and Captain Oleson for not at any point releasing "their" delegates for Haugen, and at Warner for only doing so when it was too late.[81] At that late point, the Scandinavian-American delegates did in fact convene to discuss the makeup of the remainder of the state ticket. There they decided to unite on two of Haugen's friends, Sewell A. Peterson for state treasurer and in the event of that failing, Halford Erickson, of Swedish background, for railroad commissioner. As it turned out, Peterson was in fact nominated for the state treasurership. According to one conservative observer, this move prevented a bolt by the Haugen-La Follette forces.[82]

Thus, ultimately, Haugen and La Follette's gubernatorial strategy failed. First, their bid for backing outside their local strongholds never really succeeded, even though their show of force in the northwestern and south-central sections of the state was quite impressive. Indeed, Haugen's forces became so locked in battle with Horace Taylor's that they neglected the contest with William H. Upham, even though Haugen viewed the latter as his most formidable opponent and thought that too much energy was being expended on the struggle in Dane County.[83] Second, Haugen's "American" strategy never worked according to plan. Several Scandinavian-American Republicans remained in the race to the bitter end. The *Madison Daily Democrat* even featured a couple of letters written under the pseudonym of Ole Olson, accusing Haugen of playing the Norwegian card: "Norvegans hav gud rite to dis kontry, better rite dan de Yankis. . . . Ei vant yob on kaptol meselv and ei tenk ei get von ef Nels Hogen be govner."[84] As it turned out, Rasmus B. Anderson composed these letters, and probably did so as much to spite the editorship of *Skandinaven* as to hurt Haugen, yet found that they "succeeded in making me very unpopular and aided in great measure the cause of La Follette."[85]

In the primary campaign of 1894 questions of nationality and locality played a prominent role. Yet these were not the only issues. In the first place, certain economic questions animated the campaign. Thus, La Follette pleaded with railroad workers to endorse Representative Haugen's record on railroad legislation.[86] Despite William Dempster Hoard's misgivings, La Follette also persuaded the Wisconsin Dairymen's Association to publish a circular urging that any state officer nominated "should be beyond suspicion in regard to their loyalty to the dairy interests."[87] Another pamphlet printed by the La Follette organization went out to Wisconsin's 2,500 cheese and butter-making factories in 50,000 copies, and a Haugen letter on dairying matters written at La Follette's request was published in the *Wisconsin Farmer*.[88] Interestingly, *Skandinaven* also published a couple of editorials emphasizing Haugen's warm feelings for the dairy farmer.[89]

Thus, the 1894 Republican primary campaign was not entirely devoid of economic issues, yet considering the depth of the ongoing economic crisis, as well as the Pullman railroad strike that summer, the relegation of economic concerns to second place is striking. The depression, however, was considered first of all a Democratic-Republican affair, not an intra-party matter. Moreover, as Belle La Follette noted correctly in her biography of her husband, the caucus and convention system was less than ideal for discussing state issues, simply because speaking campaigns were uncommon.[90] In 1894, the very idea of circulating dairy pamphlets actually worried Belle La Follette: "Do you think this sending of circulars savors too much of a campaign? This is the most I fear."[91] In fact, there are no indications that either La Follette or Haugen made one single speech in the 1894 primary campaign. Haugen, incidentally, was considered a weak orator. One hostile observer noted that Haugen was "utterly unable to speak, he completely broke down at Stoughton last fall."[92] In his autobiography, moreover, La Follette himself conceded that "I did not at that period [1894] put forward a broadly constructive policy. My correspondence of that time shows that appeal was made for support primarily with a view to overthrowing corrupt machine control."[93]

At a deeper level, however, economic factors were strongly involved in the 1894 battle, not directly related to the depression. The key issue was corporate power in American politics. This was the first organized political encounter between the forces of La Follette, representing a new, grassroots-oriented type of politics, and those of Sawyer, Payne, and Spooner, epitomizing the growth of corporate power. Haugen was strongly aware of this dimension to the struggle and he always felt convinced that the gubernatorial candidacies of William H. Upham and of Horace A. Taylor and Edward Scofield (1842–1925), a lumberman from Oconto, were engineered by the old Republican triumvirate.[94] Indeed, more than one month before the state convention Haugen predicted accurately that Taylor and Scofield's forces would eventually unite with Upham's and secure the latter's triumph.[95] Likewise, La Follette emphasized the close ties between especially Taylor and Spooner.[96]

Spooner was indeed extremely hostile to Haugen, characterizing him as "the candidate of a clique and faction as arbitrary, dishonorable and tyrannical as any which I have ever known in politics."[97] Moreover, apparently the ex-senator feared that the nomination of Haugen would ease La Follette's entry to the United States Senate at his own expense.[98] Accordingly, Spooner arranged meetings with both Horace Rublee of the *Milwaukee Sentinel* and George Koeppen of *Die Germania*.[99] Shortly afterward, Koeppen informed Haugen that due first of all to La Follette's strong support of the Bennett law, *Die Germania* would not support Haugen.[100] The editor was not being quite truthful, however, for as he stated to a conservative friend, at issue was no longer the Bennett law. The important point was that "Mr. La Follette alone is to [sic] much to bear."[101] In late June, editor Rublee likewise denied Haugen support, referring to La Follette's enmity with Sawyer and Spooner.[102]

Apparently, Spooner also had a hand in the strategy of forwarding multiple Scandinavian Americans for the Republican state ticket. Not only was he kept informed of Hans B. Warner's prospects in Pierce County, but he also invited Warner to St. Paul for a personal conference.[103] Spooner was equally active in Charles Lewiston's and Horace Taylor's fights in St. Croix County, keeping in touch, among others, with state senator William H. Phipps, a former land commissioner for one of Philetus Sawyer's railroad companies.[104] All in all, Spooner was pleased with the outcome of the state convention in Milwaukee: "I was very glad that Mr. Haugen was defeated, and think he owes me for a good deal of it."[105]

Spooner, however, was not present in Milwaukee at the Republican state convention. He had stolen off to his summer cottage in Nantucket in early July and remained there until the end of the month.[106] Sawyer, on the other hand, went to Milwaukee. The old lumber baron was instrumental in securing Upham's victory and, notwithstanding his previous friendly statements, in bringing about Haugen's defeat. As an ally confided to Spooner, "Mr. Sawyer got in his work very slyly, but very telling," convincing many Scofield delegates to support Upham, much to the anger of Scofield who felt double-crossed.[107] Scofield's support, noted another observer, was simply too narrow geographically.[108] Already in early June, Haugen became convinced that Sawyer was opposing his own candidacy.[109] Haugen thought that adjourning after the state convention's fifth ballot was a grave mistake. "It gave Sawyer an opportunity to work with the delegates during the night and in a manner which was very effective." After Upham's nomination, Sawyer reportedly twice told Haugen "that he had to down me on La Follette's account."[110]

Thus, Haugen's suspicion that the old Republican triumvirate was deeply involved in manipulating the nomination process was well founded.[111] He believed, moreover, that the battle had a deeper significance than the mere clash of personalities and factions. In his view, Upham was nominated with the help of the old Republican triumvirate because "he is just the kind of pliable fellow that they want. Then he lives on the line of the W.C. [Wisconsin Central] and has undoubtedly had discriminating rates like all the heavy lumbermen, and they will expect to control him for those reasons."[112] Haugen also felt convinced that in the final analysis Sawyer opposed him "not so much because of La Follette as because I could not be managed for the railroad interest."[113] In Haugen's view, at least, beneath the surface of political battle along ethnic lines, beneath even the contest between the two Republican factions, an economically rooted struggle for power was being fought. That struggle was not directly related to the depression of the 1890s, to be sure, but a group of insurgent politicians on the rise were expressing their deep apprehension about the growth of corporate power in American politics. In the following years, that struggle would be pushed to the front.

In the battle of 1894 Haugen, La Follette, and their allies made their first assault on the matrix of party, nationality, locality, and personality in politics. To be sure, the concept of party came out of the battle largely intact, in spite of some reports that local Republican politicians were "packing" the party caucuses with Democrats. The political issue, moreover, had not yet risen as a frontal challenge to the traditional concept of personality in politics.[114] On the other hand, Haugen and his allies, while always mindful of the support of the Scandinavian-American press, did attempt to contest the traditional place of nationality and locality in politics but they failed miserably. The Scandinavian-American issue backfired viciously on Haugen, and he was never able to convincingly overcome the regionally defined nature of his backing. The rules of the political game proved too strong, not least because beneath the surface of the battle an economically rooted struggle pitted La Follette and his allies against the old Republican triumvirate. In this context, each faction attempted to impose new forms of control over the Republican Party of Wisconsin.

INTERLUDE, 1894–1906

In the years between 1894 and 1906, Wisconsin experienced major political change. In the late summer of 1897, to begin with, the depression ended. As a result, La Follette, recently converted to reform, had to defend himself against charges that he was ignoring the coming of better times.[115] With the depression lifting, La Follette was free to define his own political issues. To be sure, in a world of urbanization, industrial expansion, and corporate growth, many a midwesterner was beginning to worry about the fate of old rural values and virtues rooted in the traditions of hard work and thrift, yet in Wisconsin the task of defining the specific issues was left largely to politicians, and La Follette proved a master. "One might even say that Mr. La Follette's function is to supply average men, who are discontented with corporations, with reasons for their discontent," suggested the *Milwaukee Sentinel* in 1897. Five years later, the *Milwaukee Journal* added, "We might very much like to hear him on some other subjects, but he chooses, not we."[116] Personally, La Follette cherished the idea that his mission was to educate the people of Wisconsin.[117]

In those years, the gallery of political actors also changed. For one thing, Hans B. Warner, recently appointed to the State Board of Control by a grateful Governor Upham, died in August 1896.[118] Haugen considered Warner "wholly unfit" for the position, for as the *typical immigrant politician* he was "just an innocent good fellow who will go around to the different institutions and have a good time."[119] Charles Lewiston likewise disappeared from the annals of Wisconsin history, but only after being appointed deputy labor statistician in early 1895, an act that *Skandinaven* denounced and that, as Haugen was told, amounted to "a slap right in your face."[120] T. C. Lund, on the other hand, was not rewarded for his more limited role in the 1894 contest, nor was he renominated for the Stoughton mayoralty.[121] By 1904, he had converted to La Follette's ranks and chaired the Roosevelt-La Follette club in Stoughton. When warned that he was losing friends on this account, Lund replied, "Am very sorry if such is the case, but with me it is a case of conviction."[122]

Warner, Lewiston, and Lund aside, the campaign of 1894 demonstrated that Wisconsin's Scandinavian Americans could expect more politically from La Follette and his forces than from the old Republican triumvirate. Spooner realized, "It would not do to leave the Scandinavian element of the party with only a commissionership" on the state ticket, and Haugen thought that the appointments of Warner and Lewiston represented the Old Guard's effort "to build up a Scandinavian party in the state with Warner and Lewiston as the leaders."[123] Nevertheless, by 1898 Haugen had reached the conclusion that Spooner was ignoring the Norwegian-American element, having use for them only when election time approached.[124] Even so, a few prominent Scandinavian Americans remained loyal to the old leadership, first of all Rasmus B. Anderson, but also Ander-

son's friend Ole A. Buslett. When in early August of 1894 Buslett took over
Normannen of Stoughton, he promptly began to attack Haugen.[125] John A.
Johnson, the Madison-based Norwegian-American machine manufacturer, on the other hand, attempted to steer a middle course between the
two Republican factions, an endeavor that La Follette and Haugen considered naive.[126]

Yet in the wake of the Haugen campaign, a significant group of Scandinavian Americans came over to La Follette. Sewell A. Peterson, elected
state treasurer in 1894 and 1896, belonged solidly to the insurgent faction,
as did James O. Davidson, Peterson's 1898 Norwegian-born successor. By
1906, La Follette was surrounded by a whole coterie of Scandinavian-
American politicians. Indeed, between 1890 and 1914, all the Wisconsin
Republicans of Scandinavian origins making it to top state or federal positions began as La Follette allies. Besides Haugen and Peterson, the group
included Herman Bjørn Dahle, a second-generation Norwegian-American
businessman of Mt. Horeb, Dane County, who was member of Congress,
1899–1903. When he fell out with La Follette in 1902, Dahle's political career swiftly came to an end.[127] John Mandt Nelson, a second-generation
Norwegian American, began his career in the law office of La Follette and
worked so vigorously for Haugen in 1894 that "Hod" Taylor's *Wisconsin
State Journal* made several blasts against him, infuriating Belle La Follette.[128]
In 1897, Nelson became editor of the *State*, the La Follette faction's Dane
County sheet, and in 1906 he was elected to Congress where with only one
interruption (1919–1921) he remained until 1933.[129] Andrew H. Dahl of
Westby, Vernon County, was another strong La Follette ally. After complet-
ing four terms in the assembly (1899–1907) he was elected state treasurer
and served in that capacity three times (1907–1913). When in 1914 Dahl
made a vain bid for the gubernatorial nomination, one of his campaign
speeches was printed full-length in *La Follette's Magazine*.[130]

Herman L. Ekern, a second-generation Norwegian American who
graduated from the University of Wisconsin law school in 1894 and later
that year was elected district attorney of Trempealeau County, was one of
La Follette's most trusted supporters. In 1902, he was elected to the assembly, campaigning vigorously for political reforms such as the direct primary and railroad taxation.[131] In 1907, he was elected Speaker, but the
following year went down to defeat in his battle for renomination to the

assembly. In 1910, Ekern won the state insurance commissionership (1911–1915) and many years later the attorney generalship (1923–1927), whereas his 1926 bid for the governorship failed. Two years previously, he had been one of the chief organizers of La Follette's presidential campaign.[132]

Besides James O. Davidson and Irvine L. Lenroot, one additional Scandinavian-American politician gained statewide prominence, Danish-born Henry Johnson, a farmer and lumberman from Suring, Oconto County, and member of the assembly (1903–1907). Johnson, whom Ekern described as "a jolly goodnatured little Dane," entertained especially good relations with Andrew H. Dahl.[133] When Dahl was elected state treasurer in 1906, he appointed Johnson assistant state treasurer, and in 1912, when Johnson was elected state treasurer, they simply swapped positions![134] By 1906, even some of La Follette's old Scandinavian-American enemies had come over to him, including Ole A. Buslett and even Peer O. Strømme, the erstwhile Democratic supporter of Rasmus B. Anderson for the vice presidency.[135] Anonymous letters to Skandinaven likewise sang Governor La Follette's praise for his generosity towards Norwegian Americans in patronage matters.[136]

Why this affinity among Scandinavian-American leaders for La Follette? While the fact that the latter willingly provided positions especially to Norwegian-American leaders is important, so is the fact that he otherwise paid scant attention to ethnic considerations, generally accepting Scandinavian-American leaders on equal terms, even though he was sufficiently pragmatic to acknowledge, of course, that the support of Skandinaven came in very handy, as did Scandinavian-American votes.[137] Yet La Follette's 1894 alliance with Nils P. Haugen was premised as much on his view of his former colleague in Congress as a political peer, a fellow attorney representing the young, dynamic element within the Republican Party, as upon Haugen's strength among Scandinavian Americans. Several of La Follette's closest Scandinavian-American allies, most of them second-generation immigrants, were likewise professionals on the rise. Even after Haugen broke with La Follette in 1917 due to the latter's resistance to American entry into World War I, he never accused La Follette of behaving in the manner of Spooner and "Hod" Taylor back in 1892, when Haugen campaigned for reelection to Congress: "Now, I want to give the devil his due. . . . I think Spooner and Hod Taylor want me nominated.

Not that they care for me. If that was all, they would be against me. But they are terribly afraid of the Scandinavians this fall, and think that my being on the ticket will help to keep them in line."[138] When writing his memoirs Haugen hoped to throw dirt on La Follette instead by proving that he had raised a double salary in 1905, when he was both governor and senator-elect. "I may be intruding on sacred soil," Haugen wrote Irvine Lenroot in late 1928, "but what is the use? You and I knew Bob better than anybody else, and let us have the truth." As it turned out, Lenroot reported that La Follette had in fact refused his senatorial wage.[139]

The most profound political change taking place between 1894 and 1906, a true groundswell, was the rise to power of the La Follette faction at the expense of the Old Guard. William H. Upham, the victor of 1894, enjoyed only one term as governor, for his name was blemished beyond repair when in 1895 he supported legislation to release the state treasurers and their bondsmen, including Philetus Sawyer, from further payments in the treasurer cases.[140] In 1896, Edward Scofield, the lumberman from Oconto, whom Haugen considered "the choice of bosses," won the governorship, defeating La Follette in the Republican race.[141] After another extremely bitter battle against Scofield in 1898, La Follette finally won the gubernatorial nomination of the Republican Party in 1900. He won, however, only after signing a truce with his conservative foes, who had been weakened by the death that spring of Sawyer.[142]

"Harmony" between the La Follette faction and the Old Guard ended abruptly in early 1901, when La Follette made clear that he was in earnest about reform. Copying the vocabulary of the Republican schism in Congress in the 1870s and 1880s, conservative "stalwarts" fought against "half-breed" reformers over such issues as the direct primary, taxation of railroad companies on an *ad valorem* basis and, later, the establishment of a railroad commission to regulate rates. This contest, which also involved the purchase by the conservatives of the *Milwaukee Sentinel* in 1901, came to a head in 1904, when the stalwarts, led by John C. Spooner, bolted the La Follette-controlled Republican convention in Madison and proceeded to nominate their own slate in the separate "Opera House convention." Even though the Republican national committee, which included Henry C. Payne, subsequently endorsed the bolters, the Wisconsin Supreme Court finally settled matters in favor of the La Follette faction. In 1907, with the stalwarts now utterly exhausted, Spooner threw in the towel and retired from the U.S. Senate, just one year after La Follette had entered that body.[143]

With La Follette's rise to power, the political temper of Wisconsin changed markedly. Several observers commented on the secretive ways of the new governor and on the air of suspicion pervading the capitol building.[144] More important, La Follette altered the nature of the governorship completely. Traditionally, the governors of Wisconsin had played only a limited role in the promotion of legislation, even though the assertion that customarily the governorship was "in the main a clerical position, by courtesy made ornamental" was exaggerated.[145] With the growth of reform sentiment in the legislative sessions of 1897 and 1899, however, the veto power of the governor had become increasingly important, as Elisha W. Keyes, then a lobbyist in the pay of the Chicago and Northwestern Railroad, was quick to acknowledge. "If it was not for grand Scofield, we should be in the soup. He is the pluckiest Governor we ever had. No mean bill can get past him."[146]

La Follette changed the governor's chair into a pulpit from which to preach reform. Not only was the very concept of reform novel in state politics, but the energetic manner in which he took over the legislative initiative from the legislature was equally precedent-breaking. The key reforms passed during his governorship were all personal causes: the direct primary law, passed in 1903 and endorsed by a popular referendum the following year; the *ad valorem* railroad tax statute, likewise enacted in 1903; and the railroad commission and civil service acts of 1905. These reforms were not only recommended by La Follette in his Governor's Message, delivered in person, but during the session itself he caused a sensation by issuing special messages insisting on the passage of specific bills, and in some cases he would use his veto power as a propaganda instrument to brand legislators who were openly breaking platform pledges.[147] In and out of election season, moreover, he went on lengthy speaking tours to advocate his pet measures. In 1904 he added a powerful novelty to his arsenal of rhetorical weapons by "invading" enemy territory and telling shocked audiences how their representative in the legislature had voted on specific reform proposals.[148] Indeed, La Follette was quicker than most leaders to dismiss political opponents as morally defective beings to be attacked from the stump rather than to be taken seriously in the conference room.

By 1906, not only had the political temper changed; so had Wisconsin's political rules. First, in September of that very year, the direct primary was going to be put to its first statewide test. Even though La Follette probably never stated, "Give us this law, and we can hold this state forever," as a hostile Haugen would claim years later, La Follette had great faith in the democratic promise of this measure.[149] Second, the Civil Service Law was now in operation. Even though it hardly rooted out all state-level patronage from politics, it proved quite an efficient instrument. After La Follette departed for a seat in the United States Senate in January, 1906, and left Lieutenant Governor James O. Davidson to fill the remainder of the gubernatorial term, the latter informed job aspirants that due to the new law he was unable to help anyone with patronage matters.[150]

One final event of significance to Wisconsin politics had taken place just one year earlier. On 7 June 1905, Norway declared its independence as a nation and severed its union with Sweden. Elisha W. Keyes viewed the Scandinavian situation as an opportunity to upset La Follette's political dominance, as he explained gleefully to the president of the Chicago and Northwestern Railroad Company: "The conflict between Norway and Sweden is likely to create quite a political revolution in this state, dividing those nationalities, one of which will not be of Half-breed predilections."[151] How Keyes must have smiled when he realized that the main battle in the Republican primaries of 1906 would be fought out between James O. Davidson, a Norwegian immigrant, and Irvine L. Lenroot, a second-generation Swedish American!

THE DAVIDSON-LENROOT CAMPAIGN OF 1906

In 1894 Nils P. Haugen lost both his seat in Congress and any hope of ever winning the governorship. Hans B. Warner's victory over Haugen in Pierce, his home county, was particularly mortifying. In south-central Wisconsin, moreover, Haugen's candidacy was heavily identified with La Follette: "He was the circus, you were the sideshow," Elisha W. Keyes informed Haugen in characteristically blunt style.[152] After 1894, Haugen resumed his River Falls law practice, no easy task with America still in the grip of a depression.[153] At the same time, Belle Haugen began worrying about her husband's lack of political ambition.[154] Indeed, by 1902 La Follette himself was complaining about Haugen's idleness in legislative matters.[155] Even so, one year earlier La Follette had been instrumental in securing Haugen a ten-year appointment to the Wisconsin Tax Commission, and in 1905 he recommended Haugen for the newly formed Railroad Commission, but had ultimately to yield to Senate hostility. Instead, Haugen remained on the Tax Commission until 1921.[156] All in all, by 1906, as Henry P. Peterson, the former editor of *Superior Tidende* sniggered, "The days are over when Nils Haugen etc. could sit on his broad ass and 'run' the rest of us across the entire state, and the time has also passed, thank God, when they could chase and chastise at their will those of us who hold the small ten-cent jobs."[157]

Actually, Peterson was writing these words to the man who now by all standards was Wisconsin's most powerful Scandinavian American, James O. Davidson (Jens Ole Davidson) of Soldiers Grove, Crawford County, who became governor of Wisconsin on 1 January 1906.[158] Born in 1854 in Aardal parish, Sogn, Davidson emigrated to America at the age of eighteen in company with several others from his home district.[159] Eventually settling in Soldiers Grove, he opened up a mercantile business there and became a neighbor and friend of Norwegian-born Atley Peterson, the local sawmill owner, banker, and postmaster. In 1887, the latter had succeeded Nils P. Haugen as railroad commissioner and in 1892 was also nominated for the state treasurership on the ill-fated Republican ticket. Probably with the aid of Peterson, Davidson soon launched his own political career. Starting out as village president in Soldiers Grove, 1888–1889, elected to the assembly in 1892, and twice reelected, he won the state treasurership in 1898, posing as the La Follette candidate on the Republican ticket.[160] Reelected to the treasurership in 1900, the year that La Follette finally won the governorship, Davidson was elected lieutenant governor two years later, repeating that feat in 1904. Thus, when in January 1906 La Follette determined to leave for the seat in the United States Senate that the Wisconsin legislature had bestowed upon him in early 1905, Davidson was appointed to fill the remainder of La Follette's third gubernatorial term.[161]

Even though Crawford was not one of Wisconsin's most "Norwegian" counties, it is inconceivable that the little village of Soldiers Grove could have elevated two Norwegian Americans to state office had those persons not been part of a Scandinavian-American network.[162] Davidson was clearly the "Scandinavian" candidate of the 1898 Republican state ticket.[163] Moreover, in matters of patronage, as Davidson freely admitted to a fellow national, "It has been my policy to stand by my countrymen, other things being equal."[164] Both Atley Peterson and James O. Davidson in fact possessed some of the traits of the typical immigrant politician. They were both self-made men, rural in outlook, and each had a limited educational background. In Nils Haugen's view, Atley Peterson had "pretty good business sense, but is ignorant as a horse when it comes to office work," and Governor Davidson was "the very personification of insignificance and nonentity."[165] Other observers agreed with the latter verdict. The former editor of *Superior Tidende* thus asked, "Are we Norsemen well served by one in the most important office in the state who has to rely on others for the least effort demanding clerical ability?"[166] La Follette himself wrote despairingly of "Jim's utter lack of qualification for the office."[167]

Indeed, Davidson was never part of La Follette's inner circle. To be sure, he early befriended A. R. Hall, the reform pioneer in the assembly, and, with the blessings of Hall and Haugen, Davidson even promoted measures to tax express and sleeping car companies.[168] Still, by late 1898 State Treasurer-elect Davidson's use of his patronage privilege was causing tension within the La Follette faction.[169] Governor La Follette in fact only rarely consulted with Davidson. During the legislative session of 1905, Davidson noted that he had not had a confidential talk with La Follette for the past two months.[170]

Davidson was appointed governor of Wisconsin when La Follette finally, after keeping his plans secret for almost a year, decided to leave Madison for the seat in the United States Senate granted him by the Wisconsin legislature in early 1905. An important reason for La Follette's procrastination was his desire to complete his legislative program and first of all to establish a railroad commission.[171] Moreover, La Follette seriously considered serving out his gubernatorial term and relinquishing his seat in the Senate to Isaac Stephenson, Wisconsin's wealthiest lumber baron. The fact was that Stephenson was so disgruntled with the outcome of the 1905 senatorial contest that he was threatening to leave La Follette's movement and take the *Milwaukee Free Press* with him. An additional advantage of remaining in Madison would be that Lieutenant Governor Davidson then would have no moral claim on the governorship.[172] Allegedly to improve the direct primary law and fix some details in connection with the railroad commission law, in December 1905 La Follette suddenly called an extra legislative session. It turned disastrous, however, because William Duncan Connor (1864–1944), another wealthy lumber baron feeling slighted, used all his energy to destroy the proposed reforms. Rumor even had it that he and La Follette nearly engaged in a fistfight.[173] The idea of promoting Stephenson to the senatorship now proved impossible to realize. According to Davidson, "The pressure was so strong among the members of the legislature that the Governor had no choice. Indeed, some of the members were exceedingly angry even at the suggestion that he would decline the Senatorship."[174]

Thus, on 1 January 1906, James O. Davidson was sworn in as governor of Wisconsin, and the day after, La Follette and his family left for Washington, D.C. If nothing else, La Follette had at least ensured that the amount of damage that Davidson might inflict would be limited, for legislative sessions were not held in even years, and all the important appointments had been made. The Civil Service Law was also now in effect.

Irvine Luther Lenroot of Superior, Douglas County, was La Follette's favorite gubernatorial candidate in 1906.[175] Born as the third son of Fredrika and Lars Lenroot (Linderoth) who both came to the United States from Sweden in the early 1850s, Irvine grew up in an English-speaking home, even though his father, a blacksmith also performing various odd jobs, was one of the chief organizers of the local Swedish Lutheran church. Notwithstanding that Lars Lenroot saw a future for Irvine in the lumber business, Fredrika insisted that her son be enrolled at the Parsons Business College in neighboring Duluth, Minnesota. Having completed his studies, in early 1889 Irvine Lenroot found employment as a stenographer with a prominent Superior law office. Four years later, he was appointed court reporter and simultaneously began studying law privately. The depressed times contributed to his decision not to enroll in the University of Wisconsin law school. In 1897, he was admitted to the bar.

In 1893, Lenroot became active in ward politics in the city of Superior, and the following year he was a campaign worker for Haugen. An energetic and ardent La Follette campaigner, in 1897 Lenroot became chairman of the Douglas County Republican committee and three years later was elected to the assembly. Lenroot displayed some interest in his Swedish background. He thus wrote highly of Halford Erickson, another Swedish-American La Follette ally in Superior, and in 1903 Lenroot gave an address at a dinner honoring the Scandinavian-American members of the state legislature.[176] Scandinavians, he asserted, were well poised to occupy middle ground, to save the country "on the one hand from becoming a Populistic and revolutionary government, and on the other hand, from being dominated in its policies by corporate influences." Even though Lenroot's speech was effusive in its praise for the Scandinavian Americans, it was presented in a mode quite different from the traditional one emphasizing the importance of party, nationality, locality, and personality. Instead, he employed the issue-oriented language of progressivism, outlining the role that the Scandinavian-American element ought to play in the ongoing battle against both revolution and corporate power. In fact, in a 1902 speech, Lenroot freely admitted that he had forgotten most of the childhood Swedish that he had mastered fifteen years earlier.[177]

In the 1901 legislative session, Lenroot certainly emerged as a strong progressive. He not only introduced stringent antitrust and anti-lobby bills but also played a forceful role in La Follette's fight for the direct primary and railroad taxation. Lenroot's fighting skills in the legislature in fact made him La Follette's favorite for the 1903 assembly speakership. Speaker Lenroot, on his part, not only presided over the tumultuous Republican state convention of 1904 but was also instrumental in securing the U.S. senatorship for La Follette in early 1905.[178]

From late 1905 and until September 1906, Lenroot and Davidson found themselves locked in battle over the Republican nomination for the governorship. Originally, Davidson, realizing his own limitations, seriously contemplated not running.[179] By the summer of 1905, however, with incoming reports suggesting his popularity in Wisconsin, "Yim" Davidson was beginning to feel an itch for the governorship.[180] For now, though, he proposed to remain silent. How could he possibly do otherwise without appearing disloyal to Governor La Follette, as long as nobody yet knew whether the latter was planning to take his seat in the Senate or serve out his term as governor?[181]

Speaker Lenroot had to be persuaded to run for the governorship. Like Haugen in 1894, he had originally had his eyes set on a seat in Congress. Still, one observer thought that Lenroot could be persuaded through a letter-writing campaign: "He is a pretty wise old trout, but we may land him if the flies are alluring enough."[182] By late October 1905, Lenroot had taken the bait and announced his candidacy.[183] Davidson, still compelled to remain silent, felt hurt and angered. He now confided to close friends that he would make a bid for the governorship in 1906 even if La Follette decided to serve his full gubernatorial term.[184] Allies of La Follette only added insult to perceived injustice when in early 1906 they began advising Davidson to run for Congress, much like opponents of Congressman Haugen had suggested in 1894 that he run for the governorship! By this point, however, Davidson had long since determined to enter the gubernatorial race and he could do so with a strengthened hand. On 1 January 1906, after all, he had become governor of Wisconsin.[185]

The 1906 Republican gubernatorial battle differed markedly from that in 1894, because the contest was now conducted under the auspices of La Follette's much-heralded direct primary rather than under the rules of the old caucus and convention system. Shouldn't this inaugurate a new age with political arguments based upon nonpartisan principles rather than blind partisanship, upon merit rather than nationality and locality, upon issues rather than persons? Shouldn't this, in turn, easily secure Lenroot the gubernatorial nomination?

Judging the 1906 campaign by 1894 standards, much had indeed changed in the intervening years. Thus, whereas political issues had played only a limited role in 1894, by 1906 the campaign rhetoric centered strongly on political and economic questions. Indeed, now there was a campaign rhetoric to consider, not only in circular letters, pamphlets, and newspaper items, as in 1894, but also in speeches. Whereas oratory had played no part in the primary campaign of 1894, in 1906 both Davidson and Lenroot went on the stump.[186] Issue-oriented speaking tours now became a central and natural part of the nomination process. "I care not what the papers say, – it matters not what the politicians say, GO TO THE PEOPLE, the masses," urged La Follette to Lenroot. "Irvine, the cheapest campaign you can make, the most effective one, the one which will bring results quickest, is a speaking campaign."[187] Heeding La Follette's advice, Lenroot took to the campaign trail and expanded his speaking activities dramatically. In late May, *Skandinaven* reported that Lenroot was planning to speak in all counties in Wisconsin save Crawford (Davidson's home county).[188] In no way, however, did Governor Davidson fall behind Lenroot. On September 1, the same day that Lenroot informed his wife that he was going to set a record of speaking in five places, Davidson's campaign manager reported that over the past three or four weeks the governor had spoken three to six times a day.[189] This was the more impressive because Davidson, quite unlike Lenroot, was no born orator, a fact he freely admitted.[190] Davidson, moreover, enlisted a whole array of speakers to aid him, even though none of them, of course, had anything like the stature of Lenroot's partner on the stump, Senator La Follette.[191]

The speaking activities of both Davidson and Lenroot focused heavily on political reform. Again, this ought to have been to Lenroot's advantage, for he was clearly the most zealous crusader of the two. Davidson, it is true, boasted a rather impressive reform record reaching back to his cooperation with A. R. Hall in the 1890s. Yet by 1905–1906, he had very little new to offer. A central part of his campaign strategy in fact consisted in highlighting his old friendship with the deceased Hall. In this connection, little did it matter, as one Lenroot supporter informed Davidson, that Hall had spoken admiringly of Lenroot on his death bed![192] Davidson's main issue was a reform to set a maximum flat rate of two cents a mile on first-class railroads, a proposal opposed by some progressives on the grounds that the newly established railroad commission ought to regulate the rates.[193] Generally, however, Davidson focused more on his own personality and on his past personal accomplishments as a reformer than on future issues. Moreover, his plea for a good working relationship between the legislators and the governor could easily be heard as an implicit criticism of "Fighting Bob's" battling style.[194] Davidson pledged to give the state a good "business administration."[195]

"I am aware of the fact that there have been times in the history of this state when it has been urged that the executive office required a 'business' man who could give the state a 'business administration.' Whatever may be said upon this question by others, I need only say that the troubles which bear so heavily upon the people at the present time arise from the fact that for years every state and the nation as well has given government over to 'business interests.'"[196] With this opening blast in Milwaukee in the summer of 1906, La Follette entered Lenroot's campaign. Lenroot's own speeches wholly matched La Follette's aggressive style and emphasized the need for continued struggle rather than harmony to accomplish further reform: "Is there a man so blind today, who believes that equal taxation of railroads, and control over transportation rates, would have come, if Senator La Follette . . . had not fought for it as he did?" Lenroot asked in Milwaukee.[197] He also called for an income tax, state regulation of life insurance companies and of the issue of stocks and bonds, a law to protect railway employees and the traveling public, and a statute enabling the voters to recall public officials if the need arose.

In the rhetoric of 1906, unlike that of 1894, economically oriented, anticorporate reform issues played a major role. This is the more noteworthy when considering that in 1894 America was gripped by depression, whereas in 1906 the economy was booming. Despite the dawning of better times, in other words, La Follette and his allies had succeeded in actually reforming the language of politics. In so doing they had enhanced its responsiveness to social and economic issues. Ought this not give Lenroot a clear advantage, even as the Davidson forces were winning some political capital by citing Lenroot's 1905 support of a piece of antilabor legislation subsequently vetoed by Governor La Follette?[198] According to the black-and-white logic of La Follette's Milwaukee speech, implying that Davidson was in fact the tool of the stalwarts, reformers ought to support Lenroot, and this should ensure victory.

In the confusing world of Wisconsin politics, however, Davidson clearly held the upper hand. As one commentator noted correctly, many people simply felt that Davidson through his past record and present incumbency was entitled to the governorship.[199] Others expressed their disgust at La Follette's bossism in interfering with the governorship, a charge that La Follette answered in his Milwaukee speech by arguing that the direct primary allowed a free and open exchange of opinion by everybody, including himself.[200] As it was, several friends of La Follette lined up with Davidson, including ex-Governor Hoard; John M. Nelson, former editor of the *State*; General George E. Bryant, La Follette's "political godfather"; and A. G. Zimmerman, his former law partner.[201] Even more important, Isaac Stephenson, still bitter over the outcome of the 1905 senatorial contest and miffed at not having been consulted on Lenroot's candidacy, refused to come out openly for Lenroot, and his *Milwaukee Free Press* showed no enthusiasm either.[202] Of equal significance, *Die Germania* quickly determined not to support Lenroot.[203]

Furthermore, as La Follette implied, a large share of stalwarts actually supported Davidson. Of course, the fact that they did not run their own candidate for the governorship was a measure of their own weakness, but they remained sufficiently numerous to make a difference. On January 10, Elisha W. Keyes urged Senator Spooner to "keep all Stalwart candidates for Governor out of the field . . . and bunch our votes for Davidson. . . . He is the kind of man the party needs in this state after the strenuous times we have been having under Bob."[204] Even though Spooner himself expressed doubts about Davidson, many other stalwarts decided to help the governor quietly.[205] Echoing his 1894 "Scandinavian" strategy, "Hod" Taylor proposed to support Davidson in order to "get the Norwegian away from La Follette, and clean out the Bobolette machine."[206] The editor of the conservative *Janesville Gazette* even suggested that he might help Davidson by *not* boosting him in his newspaper.[207] Davidson and his closest allies, as it turned out, were extremely cautious in accepting stalwart support.[208] Yet, as Senator Spooner's son Willet reported, Davidson was cooperating actively with the stalwarts and even accepted 500 dollars from Philip Spooner, the senator's brother. Moreover, notwithstanding Davidson's official professions of friendship towards La Follette, he was reported to have admitted that "he hated Bob and would till he died for his insulting treatment, etc., etc."[209]

With political issues rather than personal record playing a central part in the campaign of 1906, if not in quite the clear-cut manner that La Follette and his allies visualized, did the direct primary also contribute to pushing the concept of merit to the fore in place of locality and nationality? The campaign definitely had a powerful impact on the traditional place of "locality" in Wisconsin politics. Lenroot and Davidson were both obliged to make their appeal statewide, for unlike 1894, when many leaders, if not Haugen and La Follette, were content with securing local political backing and hoping for the best at the state convention, in 1906 Davidson's and Lenroot's names figured on the primary ballots all over Wisconsin. To be sure, some respect for locality lingered on. Lenroot, after all, decided not to speak in Davidson's home county, Crawford, and Davidson likewise thought it "not strictly within the lines of propriety to make any outward stir in the home of a rival candidate."[210] The wide appeal of both candidates was remarkable. In 1906, Lenroot and Davidson each had access to statewide, grassroots-based organizations, arranging speaking tours, mass-mailing campaigns, and press releases.[211] By summer, both organizations were spewing out documents by the thousands, with the Davidson organization in that respect in no way falling behind Lenroot's. In June, William D. Connor, Davidson's running mate and head of the state Republican central committee, reported to Davidson that he was mailing 50,000 letters "over the entire state," and that he could increase the mailing list to 125,000 if necessary.[212]

With the direct primary contributing in great measure to reducing the formal geographical dimension to politics, how did ethnic considerations fare under the new system? In his Milwaukee address, La Follette contended that the national attachments and locality of a candidate now meant less than merit. La Follette even implied that Davidson's background as a typical immigrant politician made him less qualified than himself and Lenroot, both attorneys: "I am aware of the fact that it is not unusual with a certain order of intelligence to decry lawyers and lawmaking. . . . If there was ever a time in the history of this state when a man of superior ability, a man trained in the law and familiar with the important and far-reaching issues now pending, . . . could best serve the state, that time is now at hand."[213]

"In order to create a platform for his own candidate, Senator La Follette is attempting to prove that the next governor of the state ought to be an attorney. That is the only platform that he can think of for the moment." Thus spoke a powerful force among Wisconsin's Norwegian-American element, *Skandinaven* of Chicago.[214] The columns of that paper truly demonstrated the difficulty of rooting out the ethnic consideration from politics, especially now that Norway had just won her independence as a nation-state. Yet La Follette actually had reason to believe that editor Grevstad would side with Swedish-American Lenroot and hence largely neutralize the ethnic factor. Significantly, just four days before Lenroot officially announced his candidacy, Grevstad wrote Nils P. Haugen, "What do we think about the governorship of Wisconsin? We have been thinking the matter over and come to the conclusion that Mr. Lenroot is the man best fitted to be selected by the republicans of Wisconsin as a successor to

Mr. La Follette."[215] With such an assurance, and probably with the further knowledge that Lenroot could expect support from several Norwegian-American politicians, most notably Haugen himself, but also Assembly-men Herman L. Ekern, Andrew H. Dahl, and Ole G. Kinney, as well as Danish-American Henry Johnson, La Follette was hardly being foolish in believing that the Swedish American might in fact win.[216]

As it turned out, *Skandinaven* shifted horses quickly. Despite Lenroot's high hopes, no editorial in his favor appeared in the Chicago paper.[217] Just one week after Grevstad's letter to Haugen, John M. Nelson, hitherto a trusted La Follette ally, wrote Governor Davidson that John Anderson, the owner of *Skandinaven*, was having second thoughts about supporting Lenroot. "Skandinaven is going to take my advice and go slow, or I am greatly mistaken in Editor Grevstad."[218] In the following months, both parties wooed Anderson and Grevstad. In early November Assemblymen Dahl and Ekern, both favorable to Lenroot, traveled to Chicago to make overtures to *Skandinaven*, yet Davidson's allies were equally active, and in mid-January a Norwegian-American ex-assemblyman notified Davidson that Grevstad's "attitude towards your candidacy is all right as far as I can judge. Why, the first shot he made was to the effect that he did not think the Norwegians (in particular) desired a Swede for Governor."[219] By that point, Davidson could already rest assured that *Skandinaven* was on his side, for when in early January Ekern published a pro-Lenroot letter in the Wisconsin press signed by forty assemblymen, including all Scandinavian-American members save one, an editorial in *Skandinaven* blasted, "It begins with stupidity, and ends in about the same manner."[220] That same day, a grateful Davidson invited John Anderson to Madison. Both the latter and Grevstad soon paid the Governor's mansion a visit.[221] Thus, Grevstad and Anderson determined finally to support Davidson, with Anderson reportedly dismissing the Swedish American with the words, "Apparently Mr. L——'s candidacy is a flat failure, and this paper should not be expected to serve as a sort of testing vehicle to ascertain whether or not it is possible or advisable to push Mr. L in dead earnest."[222]

The defection of *Skandinaven* in early January was a bad blow to Lenroot and La Follette, whereas *Amerika*'s support for Davidson under the editorship of Rasmus B. Anderson was predictable.[223] La Follette indeed felt betrayed by *Skandinaven*: "Do you think G[revstad] wrote this? If so, I cannot understand or explain it. It seems to me that those fellows have pretty nearly played the game double."[224] In this way, the attempt by Lenroot and La Follette to neutralize the most powerful voice among the Norwegian Americans foundered, and the primary campaign soon took a strongly ethnic turn. At first glance, it seemed almost like the 1894 campaign all over again, but with the roles reversed, La Follette posing as the opponent of the Norwegian-American element, and the Norwegian-American gubernatorial candidate endeavoring to prove that he was a good American. Yet there were significant differences.

Arguably the Davidson forces first introduced the ethnic issue to the contest. La Follette at least thought so. In late May, Atley Peterson, Davidson's friend and neighbor from Soldiers Grove, published a letter in both *Skandinaven* and the *Milwaukee Free Press* citing Davidson's loyalty to La Follette, as well as political custom, as the main reason why the Republican Party should offer Davidson a full term as governor. Without directly referring to ethnicity, Peterson still asserted, "It may not be amiss to state that Senator La Follette was very generously supported by the people who are asking for Gov. Davidson's nomination, and without such support Mr. La Follette never could have become governor of the state."[225] La Follette and his allies immediately caught the implicit meaning: "By 'the people asking for Gov. Davidson's nomination,'" wrote Lenroot's campaign manager to the *Milwaukee Free Press*, "Mr. Peterson, of course, means Mr. Davidson's Norwegian supporters."[226] Angered by the introduction of the ethnic factor to the campaign, La Follette fumed, "*They* make this issue by Atley's letter. *We are not responsible for it.* But let us make the *most* of it."[227] Accordingly, Ekern wrote an open letter to the *Free Press* condemning Atley Peterson's missive: "Every true American citizen through whose veins throbs independent Viking blood resents this imputation, which Mr. Peterson, himself a Norwegian, should have been the last to cast upon all of us."[228]

The standard of nationality had been raised. At the rhetorical level, it is true, Davidson kept quiet on the question and actually insisted that Atley Peterson's letter made no direct reference to national attachments.[229] Even Grevstad of *Skandinaven*, while supporting Davidson strongly, was cautious: "It is also necessary for me to be careful in respect to the nationality issue which the other fellows are trying to raise."[230] Lenroot and La Follette, on the other hand, discussed the issue intensively, but only in negative

terms. To be sure, Lenroot did show up at at least one function staged spe-
cifically for Swedish Americans, a midsummer night's celebration at Ashland.[231] On this occasion, he sang his praise to the old country, yet
according to one report was quick to assert pointedly, "A Swede who will
vote for a Swede solely because of his nationality is not only false to the
oath of allegiance he has taken to this country, but is untrue to his own nationality as well."[232] And within minutes Lenroot had switched to the language of progressivism, asking his audience, "Shall this be a government
by and for and of the corporations, or a government by and for and of the
people?" In fact, nothing indicates that Lenroot made any effort to get the
backing of any of the major Swedish-American newspaper editors in
America. His main ethnic strategy consisted simply in endeavoring to neutralize *Skandinaven.*

When La Follette went on the stump in August 1906, he condemned
the ethnic issue sharply. "The other night in one of the Norwegian centers
where La F was talking," reported Willet M. Spooner to his father, "he
brought up to a climax the Lenroot talk and there wasn't a murmur for the
damned Swede. Bob stalked to the extreme front of the platform and
roared out, 'What is the matter with you Norwegians. Can't you throw off
your social prejudice and be good Americans?' He was drowned in a storm
of groans and cat calls and left the meeting abruptly. He is a nervy devil."[233]
Similar reports about La Follette's appeals to the Norwegian Americans
came from other meetings. In late August, Davidson's campaign manager
reported from Viroqua, Vernon County: "Not less than six times during
his address did he turn to that nationality, and lecture and scold them for
paying any attention to nationality in this campaign." As Davidson's ally
further noted, La Follette was in fact shooting himself in the foot, for "I
think many of them resent the imputation that nationality has any effect
on them at this time."[234]

Despite the centrality of ethnic issues to the 1906 campaign, this was
not simply the 1894 scenario in reverse. For one thing, Davidson made
more unabashed use of his Scandinavian-American connections than had
Haugen in 1894. Back then, La Follette and Haugen had devised a strategy
of only involving *Skandinaven* a good while *after* Haugen had made his
candidacy announcement in various English-language papers. Davidson,
on the other hand, worked to ensure that when his announcement was re-

leased, "the Skandinaven may use it among the very first."[235] In his campaign letters to Norwegian-American party activists, if not in his speeches, Davidson did not shrink from making clear ethnic appeals either. No public servant having served the people reasonably had in the past been turned out without an endorsement, he asserted, adding, "Do you think it fair to make an exception when one of our countrymen is in a position of honor and responsibility?"[236] In another letter mailed only to Norwegian Americans, Davidson acknowledged "especially the support accorded me by my countrymen."[237] He even told one supporter that he had succeeded in deflecting Norwegian-American Assemblyman Ole G. Kinney from Lenroot's cause by telling him to his face that he "was not only doing me a great injustice, but was bringing discredit upon our nationality."[238]

Overall, La Follette and Lenroot made only limited attempts to play dirty ethnic tricks on Davidson in the manner that conservative Republicans had on Haugen back in 1894. Herman L. Ekern, it is true, did suggest that rumors about Davidson actually being of Swedish heritage ought to be investigated, yet nothing more came of that.[239] Moreover, when at an early point Andrew H. Dahl announced himself a candidate for the state treasurership, Davidson correctly interpreted this as the La Follette-Lenroot faction's attempt to promote a Norwegian American at the expense of his own candidacy, at that point not yet announced.[240] As it turned out, however, with the direct primary in place, both Davidson and Dahl were eventually nominated, each, indeed, with the backing of *Skandinaven*.[241] La Follette and Lenroot made no further reversions to the traditional politics of party, nationality, personality, and locality.

Precisely because they refused to view ethnic issues as anything but an evil, La Follette and his allies saw no inconsistency in on the one hand backing Haugen in 1894 and on the other refusing to support Davidson in 1906. After all, was not Haugen, like Lenroot, an educated man, an attorney, a professional, a representative of the dynamic element within the Republican Party, whereas Davidson, like Hans B. Warner twelve years earlier, represented the uneducated, non-visionary, *typical immigrant politician*? "Mr. La Follette championed Mr. Haugen for governor," asserted Lenroot's campaign manager in his above-quoted letter to the *Milwaukee Free Press*, "because as his colleague in congress he had learned to know his commanding abilities. . . . Mr. La Follette in making appointments to important positions of trust and responsibility, has given recognition to men of Norwegian name and blood, but always in recognition of ability and fitness, – never because of their nationality."[242] Even though Alfred T. Rogers's letter was clearly a campaign document, there was nevertheless substance to his argument.

In early May, the same Rogers, referring to the duplicity of *Skandinaven*, wrote La Follette, "I'd like to tell Mr. Anderson to his face – and the whole Norwegian bunch for that matter – that if they and their damned dollar-and-cut paper [think] that they can tell Wisconsin she is too German they are a lot of chumps. This Norwegian business is being worked entirely too hard, and they will wake up election day to learn that there are some Irish, Dutch, Germans, *Swedes*, and plain 'United States' in good, old Wisconsin."[243] As it turned out, however, on 4 September 1906, in the first test of the statewide direct primary, Davidson defeated Lenroot resoundingly. In mock irony of the endeavor by La Follette and Lenroot to root out nationality and locality from politics, Lenroot won only in his home county of Douglas and in two heavily Swedish-American counties, Burnett and Price.[244] Davidson's appeals for moderation, for harmony within the Republican Party, for his traditional "rights" as an incumbent governor, for his personal record, for an end to La Follette "bossism," together with a low-key but highly efficient campaign to get the Norwegian-American vote, secured him of victory.

The irony of 1906 was amplified when compared with 1894, for back then the La Follette and Haugen forces had confronted opponents who proposed to fight out the battle along explicitly ethnic lines, even though the determining power struggle, as it turned out, centered on factional strife rooted in the emergence of corporate power in American politics, a struggle appearing the more urgent with America locked in the stranglehold of a depression. In 1906, on the other hand, with the economy actually booming, the battle was carried on in a language that was aggressively issue-oriented and anticorporate in tone, and where rhetorical reference to ethnic questions was extremely negative. Yet that year the nationality issue proved to be very powerful. La Follette and his allies had succeeded in changing the rules and the language of the political game, but not sufficiently to assure an outcome in defiance of underlying structures of tradition and power. La Follette was greatly disappointed, for he had expected that altering the rules and the language of the political process would assure what he considered the rightful outcome of the battle, despite his awareness of "the risk I run personally because the Scandinavians have always been my supporters and friends."[245]

In terms of political results, La Follette could easily be criticized for blunders. The defection from his ranks of a large segment of the Norwegian Americans was devastating, and he also had to face the wrath of Milwaukee's leading reformers who had been persuaded to stake everything on Lenroot's candidacy. As a result of the Lenroot debacle, Francis E. McGovern, their leader, later governor of Wisconsin, lost his fight for the prestigious Milwaukee district attorneyship.[246] Yet La Follette was determined to throw most pragmatic considerations overboard simply because he believed that he was instituting nothing less than a new political order in Wisconsin, an order in which blind partisan loyalty meant less than universal, nonpartisan principles, in which the nationality and locality of the candidate for political office counted for less than pure merit, in which the personality of the candidate in terms of his past record was not as important as the reform issues that he stood for. In La Follette's mind, *he* had been correct all along, and it was just too bad that *the voters* had blundered. "Aside from the sorrow that I feel for you and your dear family," he wrote to the defeated Lenroot, "my greatest disappointment is in the way the people abused the opportunity which the primary election law offered to every citizen to exercise his right of franchise independently and conscientiously. I believed that long years of educational work in our campaigns had established higher standards of citizenship. I believed that the principles of democracy were more highly valued than is apparent at this time. It would seem that there is much work still to be done."[247]

Davidson's victory did not, however, simply represent the triumph of tradition and conservatism over visionary political experiments. His candidacy had proven that La Follette and Lenroot could not bend the new rules and language of politics at will. Davidson, too, had to abide by those rules and that language. For one thing, the governor had to accept the fact that he could not reward very many of his warmest supporters with patronage positions now that the new Civil Service Act had taken effect. Moreover, despite the political success of the Norwegian-American element, the old ethnically and geographically balanced state ticket of the Republican Party was falling into disarray. Davidson himself indeed had to accept that another Norwegian American, Andrew H. Dahl of Vernon County, a Lenroot supporter, had also appeared on the Republican state ticket. As one observer further noted, besides two Norwegian Americans winning Republican nominations, German Americans and Milwaukeeans were conspicuously absent from the state ticket. "Had this been the action of a convention it would have been very hard to overlook, but coming as it does as a result of the primary election, the influence is not so impressive."[248] In 1908, the event was repeated: with La Follette not interfering, Davidson won renomination, as did Dahl, and no German American appeared on the state ticket. In 1910, moreover, whereas Dahl secured an unprecedented third term as state treasurer, Norwegian-American Herman L. Ekern, the former assembly Speaker, won the state insurance commissionership. Again, no German American appeared on the Republican state ticket. In 1912, finally, no Norwegian American was nominated for state office, whereas Danish-American Henry Johnson won the state treasurership. As usual, no German American received a nomination. From that point, some people began to worry both about the absence of German Americans on the state ticket and about what one commentator called "the practice of crowding the republican ticket into the west half of the state."[249]

Thus, notwithstanding Lenroot's crushing defeat, the new rules of the game did make a difference. To be sure, the substitution of nonpartisan principles for blind partisan loyalty, of merit for nationality and locality, of reform issues for personal record did not have quite the results envisioned by La Follette and his allies. Although the 1906 contest proved that party label was becoming increasingly irrelevant, since everybody knew that the main battle would be fought out in the Republican primaries, not in the general election between Davidson and John A. Aylward, his Irish Catholic Democratic adversary; although the gubernatorial race had highlighted that real political issues were now central to the debate and that the geographical factor had been all but eliminated from politics, consideration of nationality lingered on.

Particularly the Scandinavian Americans experienced changes in the terms of the ethnic debate. In neighboring Minnesota, this had become apparent in the late spring of 1905 when on the eve of the split between Norway and Sweden U.S. Senator Knute Nelson uttered the vain hope that

Denmark might *join* the Union, rather than that Norway leave it. He was met by a barrage of criticism from the Norwegian-American press for catering to his Swedish-American voters.[250] By 1906, with the recent break between Norway and Sweden in the background, the otherwise so frequent appeals in *Skandinaven* to Wisconsin's "Scandinavian" voters had ceased, at least temporarily. As Ole A. Buslett noted, "Events in the Nordic countries impinge on political life here in the West; that is a fact, whether we are willing to admit it or not. We are Norwegians and Swedes now, not Scandinavians; Norwegian and Swedish citizens in Wisconsin."[251]

According to the manuscript of his speech at the midsummer night's celebration in Ashland, Irvine Lenroot had intended to address his listeners as "Scandinavians," but a short report of the actual speech indicates that he pleaded with the "Swedes" not to vote ethnically.[252] By August, when he spoke at New Richmond in St. Croix County, Lenroot had dropped any illusion of addressing the "Scandinavians" collectively. As one observer noted, "What struck me was the Nationality [issue], he said the Republican [Party] is divided on Nationality[;] the Germans wants [*sic*] a German for Governor, the Norwegians wants their own, the Swedes wants their own[;] he said we are Americans and all that ought to be left out, so he begins to see that he is going to be left the moment the people looks upon nationality and I hope such will be the case."[253] Even though pleas to the "Scandinavians" would reappear in later election campaigns, for instance in that of 1910, when Buslett himself employed the label, and even though Yankees generally continued to lump Norwegian Americans, Swedish Americans, and Danish Americans into one common Scandinavian-American cluster, pan-Scandinavianism in the United States had faltered.[254]

La Follette and his political allies always stopped far short of questioning the moral validity of the ethnic institutions, first of all the press, but also the church and the secular societies, that all helped sustain networks of Scandinavian-American politicians and voters. All that the progressive politicians wanted was to deny the ethnic factor a formal expression in American politics, because they regarded such an expression as demeaning and irrelevant, even humiliating, to the ethnic groups involved. They believed that American politics should be reoriented, if not toward the kind of class-based politics that during those years was beginning to flourish in the European democracies, then at least toward a politics that put a premium on social and economic issues. They wanted to ensure that the economic, geographical, and ethnic integration of American society into a new whole would not be left to the ever growing corporations and their agents in the American political system, but be given "back to the people" and their representatives in the expanding state machinery. With the ethnic institutions left intact by the progressives, the nationality consideration was not rooted out of politics completely, even though it was weakened. In 1914, with the clouds of Europe darkening, the all-out assault on ethnicity was finally launched. It left La Follette and at least some of his progressive allies utterly disgusted.

PART THREE

Values:
A Set of Scandinavian-American
Political Principles?

CHAPTER EIGHT

Scandinavian-American Identity and Political Values

ARGUING AN IDENTITY

In late October 1894, with a depressed America on the verge of entering another winter of despair, and with the congressional elections looming, women from Eleva, neighbor to Strum, staged a bazaar to collect funds for a new Norwegian-American church building.[1] On hand at the event, which lasted from ten o'clock in the morning till midnight and included a menu of *lutefisk* and other Norwegian specialties, were several speakers, among them a couple of prohibition lecturers. Pastor Carl Johan Helsem of Strum was also present and was elected "president" of the occasion, and Miss Helsem's famed choir impressed the audience with songs both from the old fatherland and the adopted country. The main event of the day, however, was the arrival at Clausen Hall of Civil War General and Republican candidate for Congress Michael Griffin and a band of veterans, who entered to the sound of "Marching through Georgia" performed by the local brass band. The Republican overtones of the affair were further emphasized by the cannon adorning the table at which the special guests were seated. The inscription on it read, "Protection, boys!" to remind everyone of the GOP's high-tariff ideals. Thus, even a women's bazaar might be used as a staging ground for celebrating the Republican Party and warning against the Democratic policy of free trade, which, so it now seemed to many a worried soul, threatened America with material ruin.

Among Scandinavian Americans the depression strengthened already powerful Civil War-era bonds with the Republican Party, ties that, much to the dismay of *Skandinaven* editor Nicolai Grevstad, had otherwise weakened markedly in the Midwest in the early 1890s due both to the populist challenge and to resurgent Democrats who benefited from widespread opposition to the Republican McKinley tariff, and, in Illinois and Wisconsin, from sentiment against nativist-tinged English-language school laws.[2] From 1894 on, however, with the partial exception of the Danish Americans whose networks of ethnic institutions were looser than those of their Norwegian- and Swedish-American counterparts, and whose largest newspaper usually supported the Democrats, a culture of Republicanism permeated Scandinavian-American life. This political culture interlocked with several strands of Lutheranism, as well as with the mutual-aid associations, the temperance movement, and the press.

Did Scandinavian-American, or at least Norwegian-American and Swedish-American, if only partially Danish-American, identities actually incorporate certain political values associated with the Republican Party? Did representatives of class-ridden, quarrelsome European nations unite behind specific sets of political ideals in America? Some historians and cultural geographers have argued forcefully that at the *local* level, ethnic groups did tend to coalesce around certain systems of cultural values imported from the old home and adapted to and reexpressed in the new environment, although over time those values hardly remained fixed. Yet was something similar also true of *national* or perhaps even *Scandinavian* traditions?[3] Or did the ethnic label in this case refer less to well-defined cultural and political outlooks than to sets of social markers that helped maintain boundaries vis-à-vis other ethnic groups?[4] La Follette had emphasized the irrational quality of the ethnic factor and of blind partisanship and had insisted on devising a new political language focused on substantial social and economic issues, rather than on what he saw as empty ethnic symbolism, which could be seen as a subterfuge for corporate interests intent on disguising the true nature of power relationships in industrial America.

Nevertheless some debaters at least were attempting to argue the existence of a Scandinavian-American political identity. Attention here will focus on leaders rather than election data from the ethnic enclaves. Our analysis shall concentrate, first, on ways in which politics and ethnicity were actually discussed in the letters published in the Scandinavian-language press, letters that were frequently altered by the newspaper editors. Second, we shall study the manner in which the vocabulary from arguments in the ethnic press concerning the struggle for democratic reform in the Scandinavian countries carried over into a debate about progressivism in the United States. Due to the peculiar ethnic composition of Wisconsin, our analysis will focus particularly on the Norwegian-American case, with side glances at the Swedish Americans and Danish Americans. Finally, going one step further, a brief analysis of the voting patterns among the Scandinavian-American members of the Wisconsin Assembly may indicate whether or not possible political cohesion among Scandinavian Americans also created real legislative muscle.

LETTERS FROM THE PEOPLE

"The other day Mathias Lee had three teeth knocked out when he attempted to load a box into his horse carriage. Mrs. Børresen was going on a little visit with one of her neighbors and sprained one of her wrists badly. William T. Anderson was digging a well, and then a spade lying on the edge of the well slid and hit William on his nose, so that he got some bruises. Mud Creek is now overflowing here at Hanson, so that the carpenters working on the smithy had to build a boat to reach the other bank."[5] While many Scandinavian immigrants continued to look inward toward their local community, a larger world was also opening up to them. The very act of crossing the Atlantic Ocean had suggested this possibility, but so did Ole Skari's above-quoted letter, for no matter how local his point of view, he was communicating it to all the readers of the weekly edition of *Skandinaven* in that paper's special page, "Letters from the People." By 1890, that page was already an established weekly feature with *Skandinaven*, remaining so until the end of 1910, when it was discontinued abruptly.[6]

   Skandinaven was not the only Scandinavian-American newspaper to print letters on a regular basis, even though it claimed to be the first Danish-Norwegian paper to do so.[7] *Decorah-Posten, Den Danske Pioneer,* and *Svenska Amerikanska Posten,* to name but a few, also did so, and others, like *Reform* and *Superior Tidende,* printed such communications occasionally. The letters were very popular, and *Skandinaven* on at least two occasions expanded its number of pages to publish as many letters as possible.[8] Because *Skandinaven* was by far the most influential Scandinavian-language newspaper in Wisconsin politically, our discussion will focus on that paper's reader letters, with an occasional glance at the Swedish-language *Hemlandet*.[9] Since the depression years 1893–1897 formed a watershed both in terms of the electoral realignment taking place in the Midwest and in terms of preparing the ground for progressivism, our analysis will concentrate especially on that era. In all, we will examine 1,109 depression-era reader letters to *Skandinaven*, or about twenty-eight percent of all letters printed in that paper during those years.[10] Supplementing this investigation, smaller samples of pre- and post-depression letters will be analyzed, as will be 249 letters to *Hemlandet*.[11]

The majority of this total of 2,223 letters originated in the Midwest, with Minnesota and Wisconsin dominating among the *Skandinaven* letters, and Illinois and Minnesota among the letters in *Hemlandet*.[12] By far the majority of the letters bore a rural or small-town postmark, whereas cities like Chicago, Minneapolis-St. Paul, and Milwaukee were underrepresented. Twice as many letters to *Skandinaven* came out of rural Trempealeau County in Wisconsin as from Chicago, despite the fact that the paper was published in the latter city.[13]

Because a large share of correspondents did not disclose their names, the identity of the letter writers is hard to pin down. Particularly in *Hemlandet*, a culture of anonymity prevailed.[14] A few basic facts about the letter writers may, however, be established. First, among those correspondents revealing their gender, males predominated, particularly in *Skandinaven*. Relatively more women may, of course, actually have preferred to remain anonymous.[15] Second, a number of correspondents wrote more than one letter to *Skandinaven* or *Hemlandet*. Of the 1,234 non-anonymous letters studied, 341 (27.6 percent) represented 111 "repeaters."

The social status of the letter writers is especially hard to determine. It appears that the majority belonged to the well-established layers of society, from the farmer and middle-class town dweller and up. These seem to have been the people who wrote about themes including the social and economic characteristics of the local area, prospects for the harvest, land investment possibilities, educational matters, church celebrations, the temperance question, European affairs, as well as a welter of religious and political issues. These were the topics most often debated in both papers. Sometimes, top ethnic leaders also chipped in. Among the contributors to

Skandinaven were thus Norwegian Americans like Congressman Nils P. Haugen, Madison machine manufacturer John A. Johnson, and Assemblymen Ole A. Buslett and Bjørn Holland. In similar fashion, Tufve Nilsson Hasselquist, president of the Augustana Synod, wrote letters to *Hemlandet*, the paper that he in fact founded.[16]

Only on exceptional occasions was the distinct voice of a city or rural laborer heard. Peder Langbach of Milwaukee characterized himself as a worker and meditated on Milwaukee socialism, if only in negative terms. His well-known leadership within the Norwegian-American *bygdelag* movement, however, and his discussion of plans by various Milwaukee leaders to go on a vacation to Norway hardly qualify him as the proto-typical exemplar of the downtrodden masses.[17] Other debaters dwelled on the plight of the Scandinavian-American Chicago laborer from a philan-thropic perspective. One correspondent suggested that despite the exis-tence of a Swedish-American network of cultural institutions, and notwithstanding the abundance of ethnic celebrations, "the thousands of Swedish youths who are compelled to make their living in the large facto-ries and commercial houses hardly benefit. . . . When they come home to their miserable room in the boarding house, exhausted from the thunder of the machines, they have neither the energy nor the desire for self-education. If they want company, then the saloon is virtually their only meeting place."[18] If the opinions of city laborers were infrequently ex-pressed, the voices of rural laborers were heard almost as rarely. "I have seen that when the farmer is in need of laborers, he will welcome a man with a knapsack over his shoulder," noted one correspondent bitterly. "But when he does not need anyone, he says in his Norwegian-English, 'There comes a tramp.'"[19] Other letters written from the perspective of ru-ral laborers defended existing wage levels against farmer complaints.[20] Such communications represented the exception rather than the rule.

Even though the correspondents covered a broad range of topics, usually from a local perspective, just over half of all the sampled letters, in all 1,121, dealt with politics.[21] Some did so only perfunctorily, for instance touching briefly upon the strength of the political parties in an overall presentation of some particular locality, or referring in passing to the de-pression as "these Democratic times." Others dealt with political matters at much greater length.[22]

How trustworthy as a historical source are the letters to *Skandinaven* and *Hemlandet*? Both papers insisted that their letter sections represented the genuine voices of "the people."[23] At the same time, both papers made clear that some types of information would not be printed. On occasion, *Skandinaven* refused to publish letters threatening to create unnecessary discord in a locality, particularly on matters of religion. *Hemlandet* rejected letters that offended public morality or common decency.[24] *Skandinaven*, moreover, accepted letters only in Danish and Norwegian, as well as brief ones in Swedish. *Hemlandet* apparently followed a Swedish-only policy.[25] Finally, both papers urged correspondents to write brief letters, and it is clear that at least *Skandinaven* often abbreviated the letters. Indeed, when one correspondent complained that his missive had been abridged beyond recognition, the editor answered that letters almost invariably were condensed, yet offered to print the omitted portions.[26]

Did the editorship of *Skandinaven* and *Hemlandet* also fabricate their own reader letters? The large proportion of anonymous letters might suggest this. A communication from one correspondent applauding *Skandinaven* for always having the good of the people in mind was hardly reassuring: "I know full well that there are soreheads and cranks who accuse the editors of writing the 'Letters from the People' themselves. But nobody needs to pay attention to that."[27] That letter reads, after all, very much like an advertisement for *Skandinaven*, and one suspects strongly that it was written by the editorial staff. Other short letters, often printed in small type and sometimes appearing in several issues, sang their praise of the *Skandinaven* mail-order shop. These advertisements may well have been written by newspaper employees.[28]

Equally disturbing is one letter signed by S. O. Rundal that discussed a temperance club in Liberty Pole, Vernon County, Wisconsin. This letter reported that many young people had recently been hit by Cupid's arrow, and is identical, almost word for word, to a previous letter by L. S. Cranemo detailing events in Minneota, Goodhue County, Minnesota.[29] If Rundal was an editorial ghostwriter, however, *Skandinaven* concealed this fact remarkably well, for over the next eighteen years, despite shifting editorships, Rundal time and again wrote letters to *Skandinaven*.[30] Probably Rundal was a genuine correspondent who simply imitated L. S. Cranemo's language because he liked it. In Denmark, at least, nineteenth-century letter-writing peasants tended to borrow phrases, if not from each other, then from the Bible, because to them, "reading was an effort and writing a problem."[31] Other correspondents were definitely "real." On one occasion, assembly Speaker Herman L. Ekern thanked N. J. Hagen, an especially prolific scribe from Ekern's native village of Pigeon Falls, Trempealeau County, for a letter to *Skandinaven* on his behalf.[32]

Undoubtedly, letters about politics were often manipulated.[33] Both *Skandinaven* and *Hemlandet*, after all, were Republican newspapers that shared an economic interest in cooperating with the GOP's national committee. Indeed, the majority of letters about politics are partisan and Republican in sympathy.[34] Now and again, however, a letter identifying with the Democrats or Populists did appear, but then it would typically be cut down to size by a scathing editorial comment.[35] In one case, the *Skandinaven* editorship met the allegation that pro-Democratic letters were being treated unfairly with the accusation that the plaintiff was posing as a schoolmaster and making "infamous or idiotic accusations against 'Skandinaven.'"[36] When during the gubernatorial campaign of 1894 *Skandinaven* opened its columns to at least one attack on Nils P. Haugen, that correspondent was likewise criticized promptly, as were the forty assemblymen underwriting Irvine L. Lenroot's candidacy for the governorship twelve years later. The assemblymen's announcement, moreover, appeared in *Skandinaven* only months after other papers had printed it.[37] Indeed, Herman L. Ekern complained that *Skandinaven* tended deliberately to postpone printing letters at odds with editorial policy.[38]

While political reader letters were frequently tampered with by the editor, politicians, on the other hand, also organized letter-writing drives. Again, Nils P. Haugen's 1894 campaign and the 1906 Davidson-Lenroot battle provide some interesting clues. In June 1894, Haugen, worrying about Hans B. Warner's strength in Pierce County, urged an ally to have "Soren Rasmussen to write Skandinaven a good vigorous letter in my favor. He need not have his name appear in the communication unless he desires it."[39] Indeed, in Haugen's letter-books containing his own outgoing correspondence, figures a letter signed by "XXXX" and addressed "To the editor," decrying William H. Upham, the victor of 1894, as the willing tool of Sawyer and Spooner.[40]

Likewise, shortly after Irvine L. Lenroot announced his candidacy for the Republican gubernatorial nomination of 1906, some of his allies began planning a letter campaign to *Skandinaven*. "Something must be done at once," suggested Andrew H. Dahl. "Letters to 'Skandinaven' will be effective, and letters to the [Milwaukee] Free Press must be sent also. Davidson claims Judge Gilbertson – can you not see him? If he is off, fix him; if he is right, a letter to 'Skandinaven' would do us a great deal of good and would be quite a 'stunner' for Jim [Davidson]."[41] As it turned out, John Anderson of *Skandinaven* refused to print the anonymous letter that Dahl himself submitted.[42] Ed. Emerson of Chippewa Falls, who championed Davidson's cause, was more successful: a letter by him was indeed published in *Skandinaven*.[43] In July and August 1906, prior to the holding of the direct primaries in early September, another twelve pro-Davidson letters appeared in *Skandinaven*. No letters in Lenroot's support were printed, however.

POLITICAL ARGUMENTS IN THE READER LETTERS

Letters about politics were manipulated both by the editors of the newspapers and by leading politicians. The letters represented an effort on the part of the editorship, with the aid of many actual letter writers, to shape opinion among Scandinavian-American readers. This was done by mimicking the level and form of debate as it took place among everyday Scandinavian Americans in the countryside, the towns, and the cities.

These 1,121 political letters reflected the political party's two main functions: they focused on organizational matters, on *connections*, or they described the issues and *values* that the party supposedly represented. Several letters were written in a purely practical and "organizational" style. They centered on the relative strength of the political parties, on getting the voters to the polls, on electing individual politicians to office, or on factional battles. Some of these letters were neutral in tone. Some, for example, reported in a detached manner about the strength of the political parties in a given locality. In many other cases, however, the organizational letters were strongly biased. Even then value considerations were not made explicit, but silently taken for granted. No need to explain why "it would be a good thing if Norwegian-American citizens now finally could unite and vote for their reputable and clever Norwegian-American fellow citizens."[44] The mention of nationality, along with the labels of party, locality, and personality, sufficed as arguments in themselves. One suspects strongly that many of these biased missives were written by local politicians intent on mobilizing voter support for specific candidates for office. Of all 984 political letters to *Skandinaven*, one in five was written in the organizational mode, whereas the corresponding figure for the 137 political letters to *Hemlandet* was nearly one in four.[45]

Another group of letters, slightly more than one in four of all political letters to both papers, likewise dealt with practical matters and connections, but in these letters values would also be discussed, often in quite vague terms.[46] Why not, for instance, *both* praise Knute Nelson on Norwegian-American grounds *and* blame the Democrats for the depression?[47] Again, to the degree that the aim was to elect someone to office, undoubtedly these letters were often written by people with a material interest in politics. The largest proportion of the political letters, however, focused exclusively on values and issues, with no discussion whatsoever of organizational matters. About half of all political letters to both papers were written in that vein.[48] These letters need not necessarily have been written by politicians, for they were not composed with the intent of getting people to the polls. Sighing about the depression in a general presentation of a locality or moralizing about the saloon traffic was not the exclusive prerogative of politicians.

What exactly were the political issues and values discussed in these latter two categories of letters? Given a systematic reading, every letter may be broken down into its main argumentative components, subject by subject, making it possible to provide an overview of the *topics* most frequently discussed, and of various broader *categories* of topics debated (fig. 8.1, Appendix I).[49]

Even a quick glance at the topics debated in the reader letters dispels any notion that correspondents dealt only with ethnocultural matters.[50] In fact, many of the issues associated with the general "American" political debate were taken up by the Scandinavian-American letter writers. Concentrating first of all on the most intensely sampled depression-era letters to *Skandinaven*, it turns out that during those dark years the most commonly discussed category of topics was *economic affairs*.[51] By far the most popular subject was the depression itself, and most correspondents agreed that the Democratic Party and president Cleveland should be held responsible for America's present misery.[52] Other correspondents discussed the perennial tariff issue or the currency question, the latter overshadowing everything else in the memorable Bryan-McKinley contest of 1896.[53] As one letter writer, poking fun at the ever recurrent comments about the weather, noted shortly before the election, "We have no weather here, nor does anyone have time to talk about it this fall. Silver and gold are the themes discussed everywhere, no matter where we go."[54] Finally, some correspondents debated the growth of trusts and corporations and a few pondered other economic matters having to do with banking, taxation, and business generally.

The second-most popular category of subjects debated in these 476 depression-era letters to *Skandinaven* comprehended *ethnocultural matters*. By far the most commonly discussed topic was the inescapable one of temperance. Some letters were devoted wholly to this theme, whereas several others simply broached it in passing. The writer might, for example, deplore the amount of money locals wasted in the saloon.[55] Often, broad religious considerations and temperance arguments went hand in hand. One teetotaler thus insisted that drunkards did not go to heaven, and another asserted that whereas Lincoln had abolished slavery and Luther had cleansed the church, prohibition would reform Christianity. A third writer queried whether temperance was really primarily a political or a religious matter.[56] These letters were phrased in such broad terms that they did not in any obvious manner invite religious controversy among different Scandinavian-American churches.

The ethnic slur represented another important topic of ethnocultural discourse. Catholics were targeted most frequently. One supporter of the anti-Catholic American Protective Association for instance sang praise of all efforts "to counter the Catholic church and the spread of the pope's power in America," and another presented President Cleveland as "an honest and diligent man. When he is not negotiating with the pope or the Black Queen, he goes fishing or duck hunting."[57] From a Scandinavian-American perspective, this type of ethnocultural argument was not divisive, since most Scandinavian Americans, after all, were not Catholics. Other population groups likewise came under fire occasionally, especially the Jewish Americans, who were sometimes identified with English capitalism.[58] Now and again, people of German or Yankee background were also criticized.[59] From time to time, finally, two other ethnocultural subjects were discussed. The one referred to the language used in the public schools, the other to the immigration question. Who, asked one correspondent, found America first? The Americans or the immigrants?[60]

During the depression, *class-related matters* were discussed almost as frequently as ethnocultural ones. One very popular topic revolved around agricultural matters, including populism, another around labor questions, including socialism, and a third around the vices of the "plutocracy," the "moneyed men," and the "capitalists." One North Dakota Populist combined all these three themes in his discussion of the tariff: "Do you not see now that our representatives work for the factory owners, the moneyed men, and the gold kings in the east? . . . contemplate the position of the laborer and the farmer."[61]

Another sizeable subject category referred to *pure politics*, to matters concerning the basic rules of the American democracy. This debate centered on the supposed corruption of the "political machine," on the one hand, and on the honesty and wisdom required of good politicians and voters, on the other. Frequently, those two topics were combined. Nils P. Haugen lost the gubernatorial nomination in 1894, reasoned one correspondent, because "he was honest and poor," and "the money power" was too strong.[62] Other letter writers discussed such measures to enhance democracy as the initiative and the referendum, whereas a few used terms such as "reactionary" and "progressive" to label politicians or movements.[63] Finally, a very few letter writers discussed women's suffrage, one of them employing the classic argument that giving women the vote would help eradicate the saloon.[64] A much smaller subject category centered on *Scandinavian matters*, a topic expanded upon below, and yet another included *other matters*: foreign affairs or strictly local issues. Whereas some letter writers pondered Turko-Greek tensions or Cuba's fight for independence, others debated the location of the neighborhood post office or the construction of a courthouse.[65]

A comparison of the depression-era letters to *Skandinaven* with the more limited samples for the pre-depression and post-depression years suggests how over time the relative sizes of the *categories* of topics changed. Prior to the 1893 downturn, economic considerations played a smaller, and ethnocultural issues, especially temperance and to some extent the language question, a dramatically larger role in the debate. After the depression ended, on the other hand, many political exchanges revolved around pure politics. Whereas an increasing number of letter writers still pondered questions of honesty and wisdom, as well as of corruption, an almost equally large proportion of commentators now discussed the rise of the progressive movement. Thus, judging by the letter samples, even though ethnocultural subjects definitely played a prominent role in the political debate, only in the early years, prior to the depression, did that category tower above all others. Among the individual *topics* discussed, the temperance question was immensely important during the whole period 1890–1910, although in the years of economic crisis it was superseded very clearly by the depression issue. Down through the two decades, as it turned out, farmer matters constituted the next most popular topic, followed by the more diffuse "honesty-and-wisdom" theme in the third place.[66]

One category of letters blended issues and organizational matters and thus fused values and connections. In these letters, practical politics and more abstract matters were treated side by side. In the pre-depression years and during the economic downturn itself, such letters comprised just over half of all those touching upon organizational matters.[67] Significantly, in three out of five such cases, reflections on values were vague.[68] Thus, in one letter Knute Nelson of Minnesota received praise simply for being independent of "the capitalists' bribes," and in another Nils P. Haugen was presented as a poor and honest friend of the people who fought against "the money power."[69] In a third letter, Andrew T. Lund of Minnesota was portrayed as "a genuine farmer, a friend of the people, and a defender of the poor."[70] Only in two out of five cases was a direct link between political organization and somewhat more *substantial* political issues established. For instance, one correspondent criticized Knute Nelson for his tariff views and for that was promptly scolded by the editorship of *Skandinaven*; another suggested that Nils P. Haugen's defeat in 1894 was caused by corrupt people involved in the 1894 treasurer scandal and added that La Follette was a supporter of the McKinley tariff, whereas a third letter writer insisted that the local member of the assembly was a coward who had stayed away from the legislature on several important occasions, for instance when a bill to prohibit the sale of liquor in the vicinity of the soldiers' home in Milwaukee had come up for a vote.[71]

Significantly, in the post-depression years the share of letters to *Skan-*

dinaven dealing both with practical politics and value considerations increased to nearly two-thirds of all letters touching on organizational matters.[72] Moreover, in more than half the cases the issues dealt with were now substantial rather than diffuse.[73] For instance, one correspondent urged the Republican gubernatorial nomination of Captain William M. Lewis in Wisconsin, not only because he boasted a strong progressive record, but because he favored county option.[74] Another letter writer asked Scandinavian Americans to support H. B. Dahle for Congress, for besides being a good, honest Norwegian and a successful businessman, he favored high tariffs, the gold standard, and Cuban independence of Spain.[75] A third correspondent promoted La Follette as the people's gubernatorial favorite, because he fought for the direct primary, improved railroad rates, and good roads.[76]

This development towards a greater degree of integration between practical politics and a discussion of values implied by a chronological analysis of the letters supports the thesis that with the ascendancy of the Republican Party in the wake of the 1893–1897 depression, and with the subsequent advent of progressivism, politicians became increasingly identified with clearly defined, substantial political questions. Conversely, the promotion of politicians for office on the basis of empty labels and diffuse value judgments fell out of fashion. The letter samples also indicate, however, that in an ethnic paper like *Skandinaven*, structures of argument changed only slowly and incompletely. By 1910, it was still perfectly possible to promote a candidate for office on the basis of party, nationality, locality, and personality.[77]

How was ethnicity treated in the 984 political letters to *Skandinaven*? Generally speaking, ethnic labels were employed frequently. They occurred in more than half of the letters, and as a direct part of a political argument in more than one-third.[78] Especially the pre-depression and post-depression letters were marked by ethnopolitical arguments. Many depression-era letters, on the other hand, focused on hard economic times, with no reference at all to national attachments.[79] Some of these ethnopolitical letters contained slurs against Catholics, Jews, and other groups. The use of Scandinavian labels was much more frequent, occurring in nine out of ten such epistles.[80]

In these 326 "Scandinavian" letters, Norwegian Americans were discussed by far the most frequently, whereas Danish Americans and Swedish Americans received considerably less attention. *Skandinaven* remained first of all a Norwegian-American newspaper. Predictably, sixty-one "Scandinavian" letters to *Hemlandet* revealed a similar Swedish-American slant.[81] These circumstances gave the "Scandinavian" concept a somewhat hollow ring. Still, that exact term was invoked in more than one-third of the 326 letters to *Skandinaven*, if only in barely one-tenth of the sixty-one letters to *Hemlandet*.[82] Conceivably, Norwegian Americans, sharing their written language with the Danish Americans, found the employment of the Scandinavian name especially convenient. One Swedish-American correspondent in fact accused the Norwegian Americans of monopolizing the label.[83]

On some occasions, the Scandinavian term was employed in connection with the promotion of just one of the three Scandinavian-American groups. Why not ask all "Scandinavian Americans" rather than simply the "Norwegian Americans" to support a Norwegian-American political candidate for office? In most cases where the Scandinavian label was employed, however, explicit reference was made either to more than one of the three groups or to no specified group at all.[84] In one instance, a *Skandinaven* correspondent, writing in the *Norwegian* language, recommended John Lind of Minnesota for a seat in Congress. The letter did not refer to his *Swedish*-American background, but claimed that "we Scandinavians" ought to be proud of "our fellow national," and that "Blood is thicker than water."[85] Despite such pleas, whenever a conflict between the "national" and the "Scandinavian" commitment arose, the former invariably won out, as was the case in the 1906 Davidson-Lenroot struggle.

Regional labels below the level of European nationality were employed only rarely.[86] On one occasion Syver E. Brimi of Wisconsin was portrayed not only as "a complete Norwegian," but also as a "genuine Gudbrandsdøl"; in another, two North Dakota politicians were introduced as good Gudbrandsdøler who had been completely Americanized.[87] It would have been naïve, however, to expect to win political office above the local level on the basis of regional commitments.

Generally speaking, ethnic labels were invoked far more frequently when discussing connections than when debating values. To support a politician because he was of Norwegian, Swedish, or Danish background was a much simpler matter than to discuss the political *meaning* of being Scandinavian-American. In the 192 purely "organizational" letters to *Skandinaven*, reference to some kind of Scandinavian-American identity was made in nearly three out of five cases. If we further include the letters that boosted a candidate with a Scandinavian-sounding name for office, but without mentioning his national attachments explicitly, we are dealing with almost three in four of all the "organizational" letters.[88]

Likewise, Scandinavian-American identity was often invoked in the 273 letters to *Skandinaven* blending connections and values, more than half of the total.[89] Why not add, for instance, that since he served the people, not the corporations, "as Scandinavians we ought especially to give our good N. P. Haugen our support"?[90] Why not urge "our own fellow nationals" to vote for Halvor Stenerson and Knute Nelson of Minnesota, partly because they served the people rather than capitalists, banks, and corporations, partly because they carried good, Norwegian names?[91] Why not ask people to support La Follette not only because he favored the direct primary, increased corporate taxation, and fairer railroad rates, but also simply because most Norwegian Americans in Richland county were "all right" with La Follette?[92]

Conversely, in the 519 purely issue- and value-oriented letters to *Skandinaven*, only in slightly more than one in seven letters was Scandinavian-American identity invoked.[93] Thus, when letter writers turned from practical politics to a discussion of values and issues, ethnic arguments were employed much less frequently. While this result hardly refutes the thesis that ethnic labels usually were employed simply as a politically convenient rhetorical device, it is clear that some attempts were obviously being made to actually reason about issues and values by applying a distinctly ethnic point of view, if only in a minority of cases.

An analysis of the only 170 letters to *Skandinaven* establishing a link between Scandinavian-American identity and political issues or values suggests that some topics were easier to argue on ethnic grounds than others (fig. 8.2, Appendix I).[94] Concentrating again primarily on the depression years, the largest category among just sixty-six letters consisted of those discussing *pure politics*. The main, and very vague, idea promoted in these letters was that Scandinavian Americans were unusually honest, sometimes verging on the naïve, yet open to rational argument, indeed, in many respects particularly wise and, of course, strongly opposed to corruption. "We Norwegians must show these 'Rings' that we will not dance to their music," urged one correspondent, who further insisted that the Norwegian Americans were independent people, not voting cattle, and that they therefore ought to vote Republican.[95] Criticizing the corrupt "money power" and the "trusts," another correspondent uttered the hope that in the upcoming elections people would vote patriotically, and that not all "*Jomsvikings*" had perished.[96] Yet another writer complained that at present the "mighty men" [*Storgubberne*] were simply legislating in favor of each other and ignoring the poor people. Expressing his fear that "the majority of the Scandinavian voters will again cast their ballot for the same rotten government," he exclaimed, "Fellow nationals! Is it not about time that we start thinking independently and stop letting others do our thinking?"[97] In the opinion of another writer, Scandinavian Americans tended to be more thoughtful than the Yankees and, besides, "honest by nature."[98]

The second-largest category of letters consisted of those discussing *Scandinavian affairs*. Sometimes an argument was made along purely Scandinavian lines. A number of pre-1905 writers, for instance, discussed the political crisis between Norway and Sweden.[99] In other cases, Scandinavian topics were viewed from a U.S. perspective. What, for instance, were readers to make of the fact that whereas the Republican Party in America generally identified with protection, at least until 1897 Norway practiced a low-tariff policy?[100] One correspondent recommended that Norway introduce a protective tariff, and another even proposed, rather condescendingly, to let Norwegian Americans shower Norway with tariff pamphlets. This, of course, implied that the Norwegian Americans were more sophisticated politically than Norwegians.[101] The editorship of *Skandinaven*, on its part, acknowledged that due to Norway's limited productive capacity, "she cannot do without a pretty liberal dose of free trade," yet was quick to side with Norwegian protectionists when a debate on the tariff developed in Norway in the mid-1890s, and to praise Sweden for introducing protective principles.[102] Usually, the underlying message of this "Scandinavian" tariff discussion was simply to confirm Republican protectionist policies in the United States.

Other "American" issues could also be considered from a "Scandinavian" angle. Thus, the question of the currency might be viewed from a

Norwegian-American perspective. The result of abolishing the gold standard in Norway in 1875, warned one writer in 1896, was that "the money disappeared."[103] Even Nils P. Haugen's 1894 defeat could be presented in European terms: If Norway had never been willing to sell her independence to Sweden, reasoned one reader, why should Norwegian Americans feel obliged to sell their souls to the Republican Party? Predictably, *Skandinaven* urged its readers to be good sports and support the GOP nevertheless.[104]

Despite the fact that *economic affairs* played such a powerful overall role in the political debate of the depression years, attempts to align economic considerations with Scandinavian views sometimes proved painful. As noted above, the tariff and currency questions would now and again be discussed from a Scandinavian angle. Less convincing, however, were letters arguing that Norwegian Americans who supported the free coinage of silver ought simply to be ashamed, or those merely urging "fellow nationals" to reflect on the weakness of the pro-silver argument or to aid in the fight against the corporations.[105] Strikingly, even though in the mid-nineties the depression itself was the single most debated topic, it proved almost impossible to give that debate a Scandinavian dress, at least beyond an occasional urging of "Fellow nationals!" to ponder the Democratic Party's part in the economic downturn. Yet even this was the rare exception and occurred in just four out of 199 depression-era letters dealing with the crisis.[106] Thus, not all arguments to reinforce Scandinavian-American Republican allegiances were ethnic: the depression itself could be invoked as a powerful reason.

Hardly surprisingly, *ethnocultural matters* could easily be given a Scandinavian twist. Not only did God oppose the saloon, insisted one letter writer, but the Yankees expected the support of the Scandinavian element in the crusade for prohibition.[107] A Swedish-American writer in *Hemlandet*, on the other hand, noted that Jesus drank wine, and that therefore no person of Swedish background ought to vote for total prohibition.[108] P. N. Peterson posed as a Norwegian when he sought political advancement, lamented yet another correspondent. "It surprises and hurts me that the Norwegians in the vicinity are going to vote for a man like Peterson who has stated in public that he can get a Norwegian vote for a glass of beer and a Polish for 25 cents."[109] Shortly afterward, Peterson was in fact elected to the Wisconsin Assembly. This caused another writer to complain that the legislator was supporting the saloon element in spite of his Scandinavian background.[110] Being Scandinavian-American, of course, also implied being non-Catholic, and ethnic slurs against especially the Catholics were fairly common: "Dear Scandinavians!" warned one writer discussing the perceived Catholic menace, "a foreign power is penetrating [America] and threatens to destroy our schools, our religion and, I might add, our business life."[111]

Occasionally, *class-related matters* were also given a "Scandinavian" coloring. When this happened, one device was to contrast American egalitarian ideals with Scandinavian class divisions. Thus, noted one correspondent bitterly, the idea was being floated of sending the Norwegian king a present. Why not instead make a donation to Norway's cotters?[112] Undoubtedly inspired by rather parallel motives, quite a few other letter writers expected Scandinavian Americans to side with the "people" or the "farmers" against the "plutocracy." Whereas Scandinavians in Europe were split along class lines, in America, supposedly, they were all part of the common "people" and thus, by implication, precisely Scandinavian *Americans.* In the post-depression years, yet another type of Scandinavian-American class identification crept into a few reader letters which made reference to the fledgling Socialist movement back in the Scandinavian countries. One of these letter writers observed that socialism and patriotism were in fact antagonistic forces, yet when post-depression letter writers discussed politics in Scandinavia, they tended to pause and comment on the labor movement.[113] Only few depression-era letter writers established a connection between Scandinavian identity and *other matters* (local and foreign affairs). The sole exception includes letters already discussed about tensions between Norway and Sweden.

Over time and judging by the very limited number of letters, the manner in which Scandinavian-American identity was argued politically changed considerably. One persistent trend was the frequent invocation of *pure politics.* That topic, in fact, figured as the most commonly debated one in the depression and post-depression years. The popularity of that theme, and especially of the single topic of "honesty and wisdom," may have had to do with its convenient vagueness: reasoning about honesty and wisdom might be employed by *any* ethnic group seeking self-assurance.[114] In four out of five cases, this theme was invoked in the letters blending value considerations with practical politics. Thus, appeals to the integrity and acumen of Scandinavian-American voters and politicians represented simply one means of promoting candidates for office.[115] The emphasis on honesty and wisdom was undoubtedly bolstered by the attachment of a large share of the ethnic group to the supposed virtues of rural life and by their estrangement from the cities.

No other overall letter category displayed a similar constancy as did that of *pure politics*. The *ethnocultural* category showed volatility, figuring as the most popular category prior to the depression but dropping to fourth place during the depression and only climbing to third place after. Thus, particularly following the Republican victories in the Midwest in 1894–1896, ethnocultural arguments were becoming awkward to invoke in the discussion of Scandinavian-American political identity, as the nexus of the political battle moved from the Democratic-Republican struggle to internal Republican factionalism. Finally, despite the general popularity of *class-related matters* and *economic affairs* as categories of debate (touched upon in nearly two-thirds of all 476 value-oriented depression-era letters to *Skandinaven*), only in a relatively small proportion of cases did reasoning about those subjects lead to reflections on Scandinavian-American identity.

In all three periods under consideration, some individual topics, more than overall letter categories, retained considerable strength. As popular as the honesty-and-wisdom theme, for example, was the one revolving around politics in Scandinavia. A relationship between Scandinavian and Scandinavian-American identity was retained when discussing the political situation in the old country. Almost as frequently, the temperance question was brought up as part of a discussion of Scandinavian-American identity, even if the correspondents hardly agreed on remedies to the alcohol question. This type of reasoning reflected values of both Scandinavian-American Lutheranism and Anglo-American Protestantism as a whole.

Many different political topics were discussed in the reader letters to *Skandinaven*. These letters reflected the general "American" debate as well as ethnocultural characteristics. When ethnocultural matters were actually discussed, as happened most frequently prior to the depression of 1893–1897, they tended to be presented in a manner so as not to cause division internally within the ethnic group. The invocation of Norwegian-American, or Scandinavian-American, identity was particularly popular in unreflecting "organizational" letters, as well as in letters blending practical politics with value considerations. In those letters, thoughts about identity often took the form of vague reasonings about honesty and wisdom.

A minority of letters did nevertheless grapple with Scandinavian-American political identity in more substantial fashion. Attempts were occasionally made to argue that this was more than a matter of empty labels. Such letters set off the Norwegian Americans, or the Scandinavian Americans, both from other ethnic groups and, sometimes, from people back in Scandinavia. To prove their point, such letter writers would turn to a wide array of issues, including, for instance, an indictment of the "plutocracy," or even a discussion of the free coinage of silver. Over time, the categories employed to make this tendentious Scandinavian-American case tended to change. Nevertheless, in many instances the letter writers touched on two specific subject matters: politics in Scandinavia and, almost as frequently, the perennial temperance issue. Both themes, but especially that involving Scandinavian politics, had implications for the development of a peculiarly Norwegian-American, and conceivably Scandinavian-American, argument about reform and about progressivism.

SCANDINAVIAN-AMERICAN IDENTITY AND
THE PROGRESSIVE MOVEMENT

As a number of reader letters to *Skandinaven* in the post-depression era indicate, considerations of Scandinavian-American identity often went hand in hand with a discussion of progressivism. When political arguments revolved around Scandinavian-American identity, the progressive movement was the topic second-most frequently invoked. The case was made in a variety of ways. Support Lawrence Grimsrud for the Wisconsin Assembly both on account of his Norwegian background and because "he cherishes La Follette's policies and thus is a progressive in the full meaning of the word."[116] Vote for Captain William M. Lewis for the Wisconsin governorship, not only due to his progressive stance but also because of his interest in county option: "It is exactly such men that we Nordics like."[117] In North Dakota, noted one observer, Norwegian Americans made up 80 percent of the Republican "insurgents."[118] In Wisconsin, "The Norwegians have always stood for progress in state government, and some of the progressive laws of this state have been founded upon statutes in existence in Norway."[119] In Congress, "As is well known, all our fellow countrymen belong to the progressive group within the Republican Party, and the majority of them have felt the anger of Speaker Cannon."[120]

Several other political observers tended to agree with *Skandinaven's* letter writers. In Wisconsin, noted a conservative commentator in 1903, "The legislature is made up largely of native born Americans and Scandinavians, and it seems that where these control they must do a certain amount of populistic experimentation, such as they have done in the Dakotas and Nebraska."[121] "I suppose you are pretty well aware of what particular sections in this part of the state are heavily Scandinavian," wrote another observer to a would-be Norwegian-American governor of Wisconsin in 1914. "I refer to that fact, not so much because of your nationality, but because of the fact that about ninety percent of them are Republicans, and of that ninety percent, about ninety percent are progressive, and finally, because they *go to the polls*, when other people stay at home."[122] During the Davidson campaign of 1906, one conservative politician proposed translating a folder boosting the *stalwart* Dr. Hidershide into the Norwegian language: "You notice," he added, "it is flavored a good deal with La Folletteism but that is necessary to get the votes from the half breeds."[123] According to a 1910 editorial in *Svenska Amerikanska Tribunen* of Superior, Swedish Americans all as one supported the progressive cause.[124]

Similar comments were also heard outside Wisconsin. In July 1907, the conservative Republican U.S. Senator H. C. Hansbrough of North Dakota noted, "The insurgent contingent are doing all they can to induce one or more Scandinavians to run against me. . . . I have been surprised that our Scandinavian friends do not get on to the game of these politicians." Indeed, soon he was complaining that he had been portrayed as a "corporation tool" in *Normanden* of North Dakota, later adding that it was impossible to find a Scandinavian-American candidate for governor friendly to himself: "Unfortunately, the educated and capable Scandinavians of this state took themselves temporarily out of the Republican party last fall and are insurgents."[125]

A closer look at three key aspects of Wisconsin progressivism helps account for this apparent Scandinavian-American affinity for the movement. First, one of progressivism's defining features was its strongly insurgent quality; second, it was associated widely with activist progress; third, it made a powerful invocation of reform. If anything characterized Wisconsin progressivism, and to quite an extent the midwestern brand of the movement generally, it was its insurgent quality. "Fighting Bob" La Follette, more so than most politicians, believed in confrontation and pitched political battle not only to defeat his opponents but also to secure reform. In the La Follette mythology, not only did he win power in Wisconsin by smiting his enemies, but he was also willing to battle unto death for specific issues to ensure the ultimate victory of "the people" over "the interests." Never, he averred, would he accept half a loaf.[126] From a Scandinavian-American point of view, one of the most stirring features of Wisconsin progressivism was the fight over the direct primary, La Follette's defining issue from 1897 through 1903. Arguably, that fight resembled the battles being waged in each of the Scandinavian countries for enhanced democratic rights. When La Follette shouted, "Control by the machine is without exception the rule of the minority. Every machine victory is the triumph of despotism over democracy," conceivably this would ring a special bell for Scandinavian-American listeners.[127]

Scandinavian-American observers were dismayed on occasion at the slower pace of democratic development in the Scandinavian countries and at the class-ridden nature of society back home. "We left our country, our father, and our mother, because we were treated like children and incapable citizens, to find a place that gave all of us equal civil rights," wrote one correspondent to *Skandinaven*. "But even if we left our native countries, we remember them; we follow them, we are interested in what is going on back home. We watch, have indeed for years been watching, the fight that our liberty-loving people have fought and are fighting."[128] Reasoning of this type also served to instill pride in Scandinavian *Americans*, for by implication, after all, they had matured faster politically than their compatriots back home. In a similar vein, another letter writer suggested that had members of Denmark's liberal Left party [*Venstre*] identified with the Republican Party, they would have been imprisoned.[129] Reflections on class distinctions back home also served to emphasize the supposedly superior, egalitarian quality of life in the Middle West. One man wrote to *Skandinaven* that he had petitioned the Norwegian parliament to abolish the status of cotter.[130]

Misgivings about the class-ridden and semi-democratic state of the Scandinavian countries and sympathy for the ongoing fight to democratize them were also sometimes aired in the private correspondence of prominent Wisconsin Scandinavian Americans. When in 1885 Rasmus B. Anderson was appointed minister to Denmark, then a semi-dictatorship under the leadership of J. B. S. Estrup, one Norwegian American wrote Anderson, "I should think you would get heartily sick of staying in poor, distracted, crazy Denmark. . . . the Danish king is trying to rule not with but against the wishes of the people. . . . If America had been ruled by the Czar of Russia – or the king of Denmark – our civilization, progress, energy, development, would have been about on a par with that of Russia."[131] When later that same year a Danish typographer fired two gunshots at Estrup, Nils P. Haugen noted laconically, "Cranks should not be permitted to carry firearms. They are too poor marksmen."[132]

The continuing battle for democratic reform in the Scandinavian countries was sometimes discussed in editorials in the Scandinavian-American press. In 1900, the year that full male suffrage was first introduced to Norway, *Skandinaven* suggested that this development ought likewise to encourage suffrage reformers in Sweden, a theme naturally debated also in the Swedish-American press.[133] As far as *Den danske Pioneer*, the best-selling Danish-American paper, was concerned, its editorials were so critical of Estrup's government and of the Danish monarchy that the paper was banned from Denmark.[134]

We may go one step further. Sometimes *Skandinaven*, whose editor Nicolai Grevstad had been an active and prominent supporter of Norway's liberal Left party [*Venstre*], directly linked that party and the insurgent element within the GOP. He thus employed decidedly Norwegian political terminology to discuss the American situation. Defending his anticorporate attacks on the conservative U.S. Senator John C. Spooner in 1894, the editor asserted, "Our objections against Mr. Spooner have been dictated by the same fundamental view that would move us to join the ranks of the Left party in Norway or the Republicans in France."[135]

Four years later, *Skandinaven*, congratulating the La Follette faction on its reform-packed Republican state platform, again employed Norwegian political language: "The Left men [*Venstremændene*] within the party have thus not fought in vain; they have forced upon the party a platform that it cannot retreat from."[136] In the same issue of the paper, James O. Davidson was identified as "one of the leading men within the Left flank of the party in Wisconsin." In 1910, in similar fashion, *Skandinaven* equated Wisconsin's stalwarts with Norway's Rightists (*"Høiremændene"*).[137]

With arguments of this nature being trumpeted in the press, it should come as no surprise that many Scandinavian Americans supported La Follette's fight for the direct primary. Election returns from the 1904 referendum on the direct primary indicate that support for the proposal was strong in Scandinavian-American enclaves.[138] *Skandinaven*, as well as *Superior Tidende*, presented that reform as a democratic measure approved by "the people" and feared by party bosses.[139] Remarkably, when in the spring of 1901 the legislative battle over the direct primary warmed up in the Wisconsin legislature, *Skandinaven* printed a letter, and *Superior Tidende* an editorial, criticizing those few Scandinavian-American assemblymen, two Danish Americans and one Norwegian American, who opposed the reform.[140] One Norwegian-American organ, Rasmus B. Anderson's conservative *Amerika*, rose to their defense, lauding especially Norwegian-American Halvor Cleophas for his stand against the direct primary, yet Anderson himself was the first to admit that his own antiprogressivism cost him the support of many a Norwegian American.[141] One correspondent reported to *Skandinaven*, "We cannot understand those Norwegians who have come to the free America and still carry with them and preserve such reactionary thoughts as you find among some Norwegian Americans."[142]

To the degree that Scandinavian-American support for Wisconsin progressivism may be discussed in terms of values, rather than simply as a function of the factional logic of ethnic networks, the insurgent quality of the progressive movement proved vital. Again and again, La Follette and his allies hammered home the message that an awful struggle was at hand, a struggle pitting the people against corporate power. "In the long battle between popular government and corporate domination," insisted *Skandinaven* in 1904, "the Scandinavians have constituted the flower of the people's army."[143]

Wisconsin progressivism, moreover, like similar movements in other states, aspired to progressive activism. Even before the term "progressive" was invoked to cover insurgent, issue-oriented politics and activist statesmanship, it expressed a certain worldview, "a progressive tendency of human culture, i.e., a general development from worse to better."[144] In politics, the concept was first employed in 1844, and soon it was used by reformers as an alternative to laissez-faire politics, the philosophy being that humanly instigated change formed a natural part of evolution.

Undoubtedly it was in this more limited sense of non-laissez-faire evolution that Nils P. Haugen employed the phrase, when as early as 1894 he introduced the editor of *Skandinaven* to La Follette with the words, "You will find Mr. Grevstad a very wide-awake and progressive fellow, who is naturally in sympathy with your idea of politics."[145] That same year, long before the emergence of actual progressivism, a correspondent to *Skandinaven* promoted Haugen himself as "the man of progress" [*Fremskridtsmanden*] and as a "progressive Republican" [*progressiv Republikaner*].[146]

In this broad understanding of progress, a clear parallel between Norway and America actually existed: the liberal Left party in Norway represented "progress" [*Fremskridt*], and the Right, reaction [*Bagstræverideer*]. Again in 1894, a Norwegian American visiting Stavanger in Norway reported, "There is much unrest in political life, and the Right and the Left are fighting a bitter battle for supremacy. As I understand it, the Left wants to go ahead, the Right backwards. . . . the progressive party [*Fremskridtspartiet*] must be liberated, no matter what the cost."[147] That same year, a closer identification of the Norwegian Left party with both progress and reform was suggested by another observer: "Whenever the Left has worked for reform (such as the jury law, the school law, etc.), the Right has raised an outcry. . . . I hope that the progressive party [*Fremskridtspartiet*] will gain such an advantage at the next election that in the future the Right will realize that they cannot continue to break the law and sustain a government against the will of the people."[148]

Sometimes, the term "progressive" could also be invoked to identify the Left party with the struggle for Norwegian independence from, or for equal rights with, Sweden. When Viggo Ullman, president of the Norwegian Parliament, visited America in 1898, one communication to the little paper *Folkevennen* of La Crosse, Wisconsin, suggested that Ullman be invited to La Crosse, for "it would constitute no small aid to the Left party back home to know that behind their efforts to insist on Norway's equal rights, thousands upon thousands of compatriots on this side of the ocean watch with hope, admiration, and pleasure the progressive work of the Left party [*Venstres Fremskridtsarbeide*]."[149]

With this link between "progress" and the Left party in Norway in place, a similar connection between "progress" and the concept of reform in American politics could be made. "What our country needs today is a new political party," suggested a correspondent to *Reform*, the Prohibition organ of Eau Claire, in 1890. "A party that can unite all friends of reform irrespective of rank, a party of principles, a progressive party. The Prohibition party is the magnet."[150] In 1894, moreover, *Skandinaven* employed the concepts of "progress" and "reform" to characterize Nils P. Haugen's gubernatorial candidacy, notwithstanding that he was *not* running on an issue-oriented political platform, and that Wisconsin's progressive movement had not yet received its name: "In reality, he is the leading representative of the younger element, of the progressive faction [*Fremskridtsfløien*] within the Republican Party. . . . The reform element will coalesce around Haugen, and there is every reason to believe that he will be nominated."[151] Criticizing the "old corporate ring," the editorial further asserted, "It is not necessary to ask on whose side the Nordics will stand in the upcoming struggle. They are men of progress [*Fremskridtsmænd*], and all as one they will join the progressive band [*Fremskridtsflokken*]." Two years later, the same paper praised La Follette as the representative of "the band of progressive men" within the GOP and further asserted that he was the favorite candidate of "the Nordics."[152] In 1901, when La Follette sent a stinging veto message to the state legislature in condemnation of its emasculation of the original, administration-sponsored direct-primary bill, *Superior Tidende*, referring to Nordic mythology, insisted, "Anyone who believes in reform must join the ranks of the progressive band [*Fremskridtsflokken*] and prepare for next year's major battle on the political Braavalla battlefield."[153]

By the time that a distinctly "progressive movement" emerged after the turn of the century, the term "progressive" had a positive connotation in the Norwegian-American political vocabulary. This usage evoked not only the banal rationalistic sense that "progress" in itself connoted something good, but also brought to mind the attitudes of the Left party back home. In the Norwegian-American political argot, "progress" and "insurgency" constituted two sides of the same liberal coin. This was felt compatible with the "American" understanding of those concepts.

In the Norwegian-American press, direct parallels between the American opponents of reform and Norwegian "reactionaries" [*Bagstrævere*] were also sometimes made explicit.[154] In 1893, Peer O. Strømme, the editor of *Posten* in Superior, realized that his support of an injunction against American railroad laborers on strike might earn him the reputation of being a "plutocrat" and a "reactionary" [*Bagstræver*].[155] Eight years later, Ole A. Buslett asserted that even though the majority of Scandinavian Americans in the state favored La Follette, some of the Scandinavian-American legislators "nevertheless support the Phister-Payne reactionary machine [*Phister-Payne Bagstrævermaskinen*]."[156]

Related both to the "insurgent" and "progressive" sides of progressivism was a third fundamental tenet, the identification of that movement with moral integrity and with the concept of political reform. Tapping the nonpartisan tradition traceable to the days of the Founding Fathers, the progressives insisted that theirs was a battle for "Righteousness" and "the Truth." An early ambition of the progressives was to "purify" politics, to "clean up" nominations and elections, and to "purge" the political system of corporate money. In Wisconsin, right from the 1890s and until the outbreak of World War I, that ambition remained central to the movement. Gradually, nonpartisanship came to be expressed even more strongly in terms of "scientific" rather than simply "pure" politics.[157] By 1914, this "scientific" approach came under attack for being elitist, yet prior to this few people saw a strong contradiction between "pure" and "scientific" politics, between grassroots democracy and Bismarckean-style rule by the expert, because both were held together under the aegis not only of Robert M. La Follette but also of *reform*.[158]

If both "pure politics" and "scientific politics" represented a search for truth and righteousness in politics, the concept of reform added a further powerful moral dimension to that quest. This sometimes acquired broad religious overtones. According to one scholar, "Coincidence in the fortunes of Protestantism and reform was not an accident. Progressivism was the sensitive conscience of American Protestantism during its most expansive and optimistic era, a time when American idealism was practically synonymous with Protestant idealism."[159] Not only did La Follette himself refer to primary-election reform as "this great field of political reformation," but E. Ray Stevens, author of the ill-fated 1901 direct-primary bill, suggested to La Follette five years later, "I feel that when the historian shall [look] into the record of these years in which we live, he must place this period of struggle beside that of the Civil War as one of the epoch making periods of our history; and he must call you the Luther of this new Reformation."[160]

Did the moral tenor of progressivism have a special appeal in Scandinavian-American political debate? An affirmative answer to that question does not so much presuppose the assertion of a fundamental, class-based unity among Scandinavian immigrants, as the discussion of the insurgent and "progressive" qualities of the movement highlighted. Rather, it assumes a morally and religiously based concord. Sometimes the concept of reform was in fact treated by Scandinavian-American observers in a manner to suggest a peculiarly Scandinavian-American moral and religious commitment to the term. Between 1890 and 1914, Wisconsin boasted exactly three newspapers carrying the word "reform" in their titles.[161] The first was *The Reformer*, an English-language Populist paper; the second was the German-language *Reformer und Volksblatt*, likewise Populist; the third was *Reform*, the Norwegian-American Prohibition organ of Eau Claire. To the degree that "reform" among progressives generally described the journey of a concept from the fringes of the political universe to center stage, with a certain emphasis on basic Protestant values, something similar was true of the "Scandinavian-American" understanding of the concept. In this case, a particular emphasis was placed on temperance, especially among Norwegian-American and Swedish-American commentators.

John Lind of Minnesota described the evolution of the concept. In 1886, Lind, running for election to Congress, asserted, "The prohibitionists are agitators and reformers and as such are extremists. Every reform has been inaugurated by that class of men. A true reformer is a sort of a crank on the subject he devotes his attention to. It is necessary that he should be such – if he were not, he would not have the zeal to brave the opposition he meets. Even Luther was an extremist."[162] Lind further claimed that the prohibitionists, despite their impractical fanaticism, served a vital role as forerunners of his own party, the Republican. Eight years later, Lind wrote Nils P. Haugen, "When I retired from politics I reformed – absolutely."[163] The immediate meaning of Lind's statement was simply that he had not been active politically since he left Congress in 1893, yet just two months after writing Haugen, Lind was nominated for the Minnesota governorship on a Democrat-Populist fusion ticket. Significantly, Lind now accepted the nomination with the words that he was running "not as a Democrat, not as a Populist, nor a Republican, but as a citizen of our great state in hearty sympathy with the aims and endeavors of the united reform forces."[164] In that speech, however, Lind identified "reform" not with temperance, but with the ambition to resuscitate Minnesota's antitrust law. In Lind's world, Lutheranism, temperance agitation, and antitrust legislation all belonged together under the umbrella of reform.

In the view of the Norwegian-American journal *Nordmanden*, the status of the term by 1895, as a halfway house between temperance and other types of political radicalism, was unsettling: "'Reform' is becoming fashionable. We don't mean the paper *Reform*, for that is all right. But we mean this stereotyped label that some journals and politicians use. For people are gradually beginning to see that reform is just a bluff, and that most of the political adventurers and reform heroes are to be found in the so-called reform parties."[165] Despite such apprehensions, by 1912 the concept of reform pointed especially to "those so-called reform parties," more than simply to the temperance movement. Nevertheless, broad, noncontroversial religious conviction could still be invoked. That year, *Svenska Amerikanaren*, promoting Theodore Roosevelt for the presidency, insisted, "The progressive party is to the Republican party what Protestant teaching is to Catholic doctrine. The progressives are nothing else than the Protestants of American national politics."[166]

A SCANDINAVIAN-AMERICAN LEGISLATIVE MUSCLE?

Progressivism could be sold to Scandinavian-American voters by stressing its insurgent nature, its basic aspiration to progress, and its association with reform. The first two qualities carried echoes of the class-based struggle for enhanced political rights back home, a fight followed sympathetically not only by the Norwegian-American press but also by its Danish-American and Swedish-American counterparts. Especially the Danish Americans may have identified easily with Norwegian-American political arguments, because Denmark towards the end of the nineteenth

century, like Norway, was experiencing a dramatic political struggle between a liberal Left and a conservative Right, with the Danish parties even
carrying the same names as their Norwegian counterparts. Whereas reference to the political stage in Scandinavia occurred fairly frequently and
was personified in the editorship of Nicolai Grevstad of *Skandinaven*, only
on rare occasions did the secular press invoke the powerful Scandinavian-
American identification with Lutheranism, despite often discussing reform.
Overall, the argument was made in secular terms that Scandinavian-
American identity had special progressive connotations.

Might it even be that Scandinavian-American sympathies for progressivism spilled over into legislative action, as some of the *Skandinaven*
letter writers had suggested? Certainly only on very rare occasions did actual Scandinavian legislation inspire Scandinavian-American political
initiatives in America. The United States, after all, boasted stronger democratic traditions than Denmark, Norway, and Sweden. Politically, few
Scandinavian Americans viewed their old home as a "city upon a hill." In
a very few areas of legislation, it is nevertheless true, the Scandinavian
countries did serve as models for Scandinavian-American reform efforts.
In this respect, the temperance field was by far the most important, with
several attempts being made to introduce the Gothenburg system to
America.[167]

Other "Scandinavian" political ideas were floated only occasionally.
Whereas the cooperative movement, especially powerful in Denmark,
undoubtedly served as a general inspiration for some Scandinavian-
American farmers, specific legislative proposals rarely followed. Certainly,
two correspondents did comment favorably upon Danish experiments
with cooperative banking and discussed the possibility of transplanting
such institutions to America, but nothing appears to have come of that.[168]
Another Scandinavian idea did actually gain access to the statute books:
at the suggestion of Norwegian-born James D. Reymert, the Wisconsin
Constitution of 1848 provided for courts of conciliation in line with
those in existence in Denmark and Norway, and in 1893 the system was
introduced in North Dakota, causing *Skandinaven* to exult, "every Nordic has a right to be proud that this reform is a Nordic flower."[169] That
year, *The Atlantic Monthly* even featured an enthusiastic plea by Nicolai
Grevstad for the reform.[170]

One might perhaps have expected Scandinavian-American political initiatives in the field of railroad regulation, the issue that played so powerful a role not only among the progressives but also among their Granger and Populist forebears. In America, the debate over the ideal relationship between the government and the railroads centered mainly on the establishment of strong railroad commissions, but the concept of government ownership, which by the late nineteenth century was being practiced in each of the Scandinavian countries, also often entered the discussion. Indeed, in 1916 La Follette, who for years had fought for stronger railroad commissions at the state and federal levels, came out in favor of government ownership, cooperating with Professor John R. Commons in preparing bills along those lines.[171] Only on rare occasions, however, did Scandinavian Americans refer to the Scandinavian situation when discussing railroad regulation.

John Lind, the Swedish-American member of Congress, constituted the major exception proving the rule. In March 1887, he wrote Rasmus B. Anderson in Copenhagen, asking for a compilation of the laws and regulations for the management of railroads in Denmark, yet Lind's intention remains unclear.[172] On a very few occasions, correspondents to *Skandinaven* also took up the topic. One person thus suggested that if the United States, like Norway, owned the railroad companies, the latter would not require such large tracts of land, which could then instead be given to needy farmers.[173] Another correspondent, this one railing against the "plutocracy," argued that since Norway, Sweden, India, and Australia practiced government ownership, the United States ought also to do so.[174] The small Norwegian-American temperance paper *Rodhuggeren* suggested, finally, that "When poor Norway can afford to own her own railroads, ought not this be more than ample reason for America to do so?"[175]

To be sure, pro-regulation attitudes were occasionally voiced by Scandinavian-American politicians, as Haugen's little feud with railroad manager Roswell Miller over the scope of the Interstate Commerce Act had demonstrated.[176] Yet Haugen's immediate inspiration for quarreling with Miller was not the Norwegian system but *The Railway Problem*, an 1891 book by Alpheus Beede Stickney, the broad-minded president of the Chicago and Alton Railway Company. In October 1891, Haugen in fact wrote Stickney, commending him for his book and asking him to help draft a railroad regulation bill.[177] In June of the following year, Representative Haugen actually introduced a bill to establish a new federal department of railroads with powers to seize companies breaking the law. "We have to give up the idea that the railroads are articles of commerce that the owner can do with as he likes," Haugen insisted. "The aim is not to destroy the railroads but to remove from them those powers of government that they have arrogated and hand them back to the people with whom they belong."[178] Thus, Haugen's immediate inspiration was Stickney, and without doubt also A. R. Hall, his zealous, railroad-reforming friend in Dunn County.[179] Later, La Follette and Irvine L. Lenroot, too, would be influenced by Stickney's ideas.[180]

In one last area of political reform, the Scandinavian inspiration was unmistakable but the political results in America meager. Especially after the turn of the century, many Scandinavian immigrants, inspired by the growth of the labor movement back home, brought Socialist ideas with them to America. Generally speaking, however, the Scandinavian-American Socialist movement that budded in Chicago and New York City existed in isolation from rural and small-town Scandinavian America and hardly explains progressive sympathies among Scandinavian Americans generally, not to speak of the political success of the German-dominated Social Democratic party in Milwaukee.[181] Many Scandinavian Americans seem to have had fewer scruples about supporting laborers back home than about participating in labor activities in the United States. Some of the greatest positive achievements of Scandinavian-American labor sympathizers in fact consisted in channeling money *back* to Scandinavia. During the Great Lockout in Denmark in 1899, Danish Americans reportedly collected more than 9,000 dollars in funds for locked-out laborers. During the Great Strike in Sweden in 1909, Swedish Americans avowedly gathered more than 30,000 dollars for their comrades back in Sweden.[182] To the degree that representatives of rural Scandinavian America also participated in this philanthropy, however, it is highly possible that such action merely confirmed them in the belief that the Scandinavian countries remained more class-ridden than America.

Some studies have indicated that in congressional politics, at least, Scandinavian Americans tended to join ranks with insurgent Republicans.[183] A limited investigation of 199 roll calls regarding sixty-seven of the most famous legislative proposals in the history of Wisconsin progressivism, 1895–1913, suggests that Scandinavian-American legislators and constituencies did in fact play an important role in the progressive movement, at least prior to 1911. Several consistent patterns emerge from this analysis (fig. 8.3, Appendix I).[184] First, judging by the session-by-session "progressive" scores on a scale from zero to 100, Democratic assemblymen proved less enthusiastic about progressive reform than their Republican counterparts in all sessions but the two-party tie of 1909. Nevertheless, the Democratic Party also had its own progressive insurgents. In the legislative session of 1901, the Canadian-born Democratic farmer-politician Alfred Cook of Marathon County in central Wisconsin voted "progressively" on all the twenty-five roll calls studied. This put him alongside pioneer A. R. Hall and two other Republicans as the session's most zealous reformers. Indeed, this placed Cook slightly ahead of five Scandinavian-American Republicans, including Swedish-American Irvine L. Lenroot, Norwegian-American Andrew H. Dahl, and Danish-American Henry Johnson.[185] Eight of Cook's nineteen Democratic associates, on the other hand, differed with their progressive colleague on all but one roll call.

Second, except for ties in 1907 and 1913 and a turnabout in 1911, Republicans from the state's twenty-three westernmost counties voted more progressively than their Republican colleagues from other parts of the state. Subdividing Wisconsin into nine sections along north-central-south and west-central-east axes, it turns out that among those geographical units the northwestern took first "progressive" place in four of the ten legislative sessions, the central western in three, and the southwestern in one.[186] Thus, on a session-by-session average, those three western areas were the state's highest-ranking in terms of progressive sympathies, the northwestern region topping the list, the southwestern coming in second place, and the central western in third, whereas at the other extreme the central eastern and southeastern areas shared last place.[187]

Milwaukee's Republican assemblymen displayed especially conservative sympathies. Introducing Milwaukee as a tenth independent geographical variable places the metropolitan Republican assemblymen in the bottom tenth "progressive" place in four sessions and in the ninth in three, even if they climbed to sixth place in 1899 and to fourth in 1909 and 1911. Thus, even in the heyday of the Municipal League in the mid-1890s, Milwaukee's Republican assemblymen remained hostile to reform. When the League's famed corrupt-practices bill 35 S came up for a vote on 18 April 1895, four Milwaukee Republicans voted against the bill, another four abstained, and only three pronounced an aye.[188]

Despite the overall progressive sympathies among assemblymen from the western section, their ranks also included some staunch conservatives. Thus, in the dramatic legislative session of 1901, two prominent stalwarts, Charles A. Silkworth of Eau Claire and Philo O. Orton of Lafayette, were westerners.[189] In that session, even though the northwestern section took first place and the southwestern second, the central western section ended up only in the sixth place among the nine geographical regions. In the memorable session of 1911, arguably the most "progressive" state legislative session in U.S. history, the western assemblymen scored poorly, the southwesterners ending in fifth, the northwesterners in seventh, and the centralwesterners in the bottom ninth place. Obviously, some westerners had difficulty stomaching the urban-labor turn of progressivism in that session, when Wisconsin Republicans under the energetic leadership of Governor Francis E. McGovern of Milwaukee, and under pressure from the Social Democrats, passed the first graduated income-tax measure in U.S. history and established a Workmen's Compensation Board and an Industrial Commission.[190]

A third trend among Wisconsin's assemblymen during 1895–1913 was that in a majority of sessions the Scandinavian-American Republicans displayed greater progressive sympathies than did their colleagues of other ethnic origins, even though the two groups tied in 1897, 1907, 1911, and 1913.[191] This hardly precludes the existence of groups of progressives among the Republicans of non-Scandinavian background, but cumulatively at least the Scandinavian Americans emerge as an easily identifiable force on the side of progressive reform. Some scope for variation existed. Notwithstanding that the 1901 session included five Scandinavian Americans yielding almost perfect "progressive" scores, at the other extreme Danish-American Andrew Jensen, a lumberman-farmer from Waupaca County, figured among the session's most stalwart members. His conservatism was so marked that even the generally impartial *Blue Book of Wisconsin* made a point of it.[192] Halvor Cleophas, the Norwegian-American member scolded by both *Superior Tidende* and *Skandinaven* for his hostility to the direct primary, likewise belonged to the conservative faction within the Republican Party.[193] Generally speaking, the majority of Scandinavian-American Republican assemblymen came out on the side of progressive reform and, unlike the minority of their more conservative fellow ethnics, several of them subsequently staked out impressive political careers for themselves, men such as the Norwegian-American Herman L. Ekern, later state insurance commissioner and state attorney general; James O. Davidson, the future governor of Wisconsin; and Andrew H. Dahl, soon-to-be state treasurer and would-be Republican gubernatorial candidate, as well as the Swedish-American Irvine L. Lenroot, destined to be U.S. senator; and Danish-born Henry Johnson, who was to become state treasurer.[194] As far as internal differences based on Old World national attachments are concerned, finally, no clear patterns emerge among the Scandinavian-American assemblymen, among other things because we are dealing with very small numbers.[195]

The regional and the Scandinavian-American factors overlapped: many westerners were progressives, and many Scandinavian-American legislators were westerners. One might ask, therefore, how western Scandinavian-American Republicans compared with other western Republicans? The picture is clear: in five sessions the two groups tied; in the remaining five, the Scandinavian Americans came out on top. Of forty-six assembly seats occupied by western Scandinavian-American Republicans, only three belonged to decidedly nonprogressive politicians, among them Albert T. Twesme of Trempealeau County, the stalwarts' favorite who in the election of 1908 defeated the strongly progressive Herman L. Ekern.[196] With the Scandinavian Americans adding their shade to the western region politically, the region seems also to have colored them: in each legislative session except the tying ones in 1909 and 1911, the western Scandinavian-American Republicans proved more progressively inclined than their fellow ethnics from other parts of Wisconsin.[197] Nevertheless, overall, those non-western Scandinavian-American Republicans, in turn, proved to be more friendly to progressivism than their non-western Republican colleagues of other ethnic origins, even though the difference was not as marked.[198]

Did areas with large Scandinavian-American *constituencies* also tend to support progressivism? Statewide, the picture was clear: in all legislative sessions save a tie in 1907 and a reversal in 1911, Republican assembly-men representing constituencies at least twenty percent Scandinavian-American proved more progressively inclined than their Republi-can colleagues representing constituencies less than twenty percent Scandinavian-American.[199] That tendency did not appear in the western section of the state, however (fig. 8.3, Appendix I). In six of the ten legisla-tive sessions, the two groups tied, with the Republicans representing con-stituencies at least twenty percent Scandinavian-American coming out ahead of their colleagues representing constituencies less than twenty per-cent Scandinavian-American in three cases, the reverse happening once.[200] Thus, in the progressive west, at least, Scandinavian-American assembly-men were somewhat stronger guarantors of progressive reform than were large Scandinavian-American constituencies.[201]

A limited roll call analysis of temperance attitudes among the Wis-consin assemblymen during 1895–1913, based on sixty-five roll calls on twenty-two temperance bills, paints a similar picture but in somewhat stronger colors (fig. 8.4, Appendix I). Predictably, in each legislative ses-sion Republicans averaged higher pro-temperance scores than their Democratic opponents. Equally predictably, in each session western Re-publicans proved more inclined towards temperance legislation than their fellow Republicans hailing from other areas of the state. Hardly sur-prisingly, assemblymen from Milwaukee averaged particularly low pro-temperance scores: of seventy-nine assembly seats occupied by Republi-cans from America's beer capital, only six represented scores above ninety, whereas forty-six represented scores below ten.[202]

In every legislative session the Scandinavian-American Republican assemblymen averaged more adamant pro-temperance positions than their non-Scandinavian-American colleagues. This does not preclude the existence also of other equally determined pro-temperance minority groups within the Republican Party. As far as discrepancies among the Scandinavian-American assemblymen based on their different national at-tachments are concerned, the picture blurs, simply because so few legisla-tors of each national background were involved.[203]

Among the western members, in five sessions the Scandinavian-American Republicans averaged a higher pro-temperance score than their non-Scandinavian-American colleagues, a lower score in two, and ties in three. In five sessions, moreover, western Scandinavian-American Republicans proved more susceptible to temperance reform than their non-western fellow ethnics, with the reverse being the case in two sessions and draws resulting in three.[204] Even though western Republican Scandinavian-American assemblymen thus proved somewhat drier in their views than their non-western Scandinavian-American brethren, outside the west the latter nevertheless turned out to be more temperance-minded than their non-Scandinavian-American colleagues.[205] Thus, both regional and ethnic factors colored general Republican attitudes to temperance. In only two out of the ten legislative sessions, finally, did western Republicans representing large Scandinavian-American constituencies display stronger pro-temperance attitudes than their colleagues from not-so-Scandinavian-American western districts, with the reverse being the case in five sessions and with ties in three. In the generally dry west, Scandinavian-American Republican assemblymen were somewhat stronger guarantors of temperance reform than heavily Scandinavian-American constituencies.

This limited dual analysis of roll calls on progressive issues and the temperance question confirms the picture of Wisconsin as a state divided into regionally rooted, ethnically oriented political cultures. The western part of Wisconsin was more predictably Republican, more rural, less economically dynamic, more Protestant, more Scandinavian-American than especially the industrial, densely populated, German-dominated southeast. The western part of the state also tended to boast more progressively inclined legislators than especially the southeast, at least until 1911, when southeastern Republicans under the dual pressure from the Milwaukee Socialists and the energetic Republican Governor McGovern contributed to giving Wisconsin progressivism a distinctly urban-industrial cast. Similarly, the western legislators tended to be more favorably inclined to temperance legislation than especially their southeastern colleagues. Both in the case of progressivism and of temperance, the behavior of the Scandinavian-American Republicans supports the thesis that this group, on an average, added its own support to reform legislation, both inside and outside the west.

This coincidence between legislative behavior and the highly visible ethnic factor was taken by some commentators, both then and later, to suggest that the Scandinavian Americans in fact represented their own sets of values on progressivism and on temperance legislation. Two important qualifications need to be made, however. First, in the west, Scandinavian-American Republican legislators tended to display stronger progressive inclinations and more marked pro-temperance attitudes than did their fellow ethnics in other regions, suggesting that regional considerations, in the widest sense, also helped to inform legislative attitudes. In the more Protestant, more rural, and economically less dynamic Wisconsin west, regional and ethnic identities interlocked.

Second, neither was the coincidence between progressive inclinations and pro-temperance attitudes complete, nor was the connection simple and direct.[206] The coincidence was not complete, because some Scandinavian-American legislators clearly favored one type of reform over the other. In their resistance to La Follette progressivism, legislators like the Danish-American Andrew Jensen and the Norwegian-American Halvor Cleophas emerged as stalwarts in 1901, but nevertheless supported temperance legislation.[207] Conversely, at least a few assemblymen, like the second-generation Scandinavian Americans E. F. Nelson in 1907 and Lawrence Grimsrud in 1913, turned out to be rather enthusiastic progressives but more cautious on temperance reform.[208] Nor was the connection between temperance and progressivism simple and direct, at least not in an ethnic sense. To be sure, both temperance and progressivism were related to the idea of reform, and both were colored by Protestantism in the broadest sense. Yet temperance remained much more "ethnic" than progressivism. Many Scandinavian immigrants, especially among those of Norwegian and Swedish origins, formed clear ideas about the temperance question even before voyaging to the United States, and the midwestern environment only offered reinforcement of such views along powerful ethnic and religious lines. Arguably, to some extent the temperance movement was submerged by progressivism, and only when the progressive movement fell apart did the temperance issue truly resurface.

In its political aims, progressivism was much less ethnocultural in character than the temperance movement and much more secular. The struggles for more democracy in the Scandinavian countries, as well as the association of progressivism with progress and reform, might reverberate among Scandinavian Americans and inspire them to support American progressivism, but in this case the connection was indirect and not, as in the case of temperance, supported by networks of ethnic clubs and churches. For Scandinavian-American political leaders, the distinction between the temperance issue and progressivism was especially dramatic. Particularly Wisconsin's western Scandinavian-American politicians had little choice but to support temperance legislation, since not doing so might spell their political death among the generally dry, Protestant grass roots of that region, be they Scandinavian-American or not. At the same time, however, Scandinavian-American legislators tended to be wary of the temperance question, for that issue might prove fatal to any ambition of reaching beyond the assembly level and into state and national politics among an enlarged, ethnically more diverse constituency.

One of the charms of the progressive movement was that it entailed no similar ethnocultural risk. To the degree that progressivism was indeed associated positively with Scandinavian America, this hardly caused particular resentment among other ethnic groups. Scandinavian-American politicians could easily boast of their own group's progressive inclinations without risking a backlash from the multicultural environment. At most, venomous tongues might point out that numerous Scandinavian-American politicians had joined forces with La Follette even *before* his movement acquired a distinctly ideological character beyond mere insurgency against the old Republican machine, and that several of them later, in the Davidson-Lenroot campaign of 1906, proved willing to sacrifice progressive principles for the ethnic consideration. At the level of leadership, the assertion that ethnic networks counted for more than genuine Scandinavian-American political values was usually correct.

In the final analysis, as much as progressivism evoked Scandinavian-American memories of political struggles back home, from an ethnic perspective the movement represented nothing less than a benign attempt to de-ethnicize politics, to rechannel political argument along a more meaningful course by confronting tangible social problems and real economic issues, rather than to deal in empty labels. For that reason, Scandinavian-American support for progressivism always had an ambiguous quality to it: the more enthusiastically Scandinavian Americans championed it, the more they embraced politics on "American" terms.

Conclusion

With the elevation of Emanuel L. Philipp, a Republican stalwart, to the governor's chair after the 1914 elections, Wisconsin's progressive movement fell apart. A devastating split had opened up already in 1912, when Governor Francis E. McGovern decided to support Theodore Roosevelt rather than Robert M. La Follette for the presidency.[1] Even though Philipp's 1914 victory resulted first of all from the split among progressives, enthusiasm for reform was definitely waning, with complaints about high taxes, about university domination, about rule by commission being heard ever more frequently.[2] "The complaint about high taxes seems to be quite universal and undoubtedly will have a strong effect on the political situation next fall," noted one observer.[3] "I may say," commented another, "that the farmers and others hereabouts are exceedingly incensed at the high taxes and the party which caused them (or which they think caused them); the commissions, which they think entail added expense; and the State University, for which they appear to have no use whatever."[4] "Personally I am radical, very radical," insisted a third commentator; "- some people call me a socialist, and strange to say I don't feel insulted at the epithet. At the same time I believe in evolution rather than revolution, and am inclined to think we in Wisconsin have been hitting too fast a pace for the average citizen to follow."[5]

Another indication of progressivism's declining fortunes was the souring of Wisconsin's, and America's, ethnic temper.[6] In the senatorial primaries of 1914, Lieutenant Governor Tom Morris, a Canadian-born lawyer from La Crosse backed strongly by La Follette, thus ran for the U.S. Senate against ex-Governor McGovern. Morris, however, was a Catholic.

"The agitation against the Catholics that is sweeping the state is certainly going to cut [a] considerable figure in the primary and election," warned one observer.[7] Indeed, anti-Catholicism retained a powerful appeal among Scandinavian Americans in Wisconsin—the anti-Catholic *The Menace* circulating in Trempealeau County and *Skandinaven*, since 1911 under the editorship of John Benson, participating actively in the anti-Morris campaign.[8] "Aside from the economical and business administration of our government there is yet another issue which at the present time needs more than passing consideration," wrote one Scandinavian-American voter to would-be Governor Andrew H. Dahl. "That is the Catholic issue. . . . I would like to have a fair and square statement as to whether your candidacy or your position as governor would be in any way hampered or influenced by Catholic interests in any manner whatsoever."[9] True, Herman L. Ekern uttered his disgust at this turn of politics, yet the tide proved impossible to turn, and Morris was trounced in the Republican primaries and shortly afterward announced his decision to leave politics completely.[10]

With the beginning of World War I, the conscious progressive attempt to leniently root out the ethnic issue from politics was succeeded by a much harsher kind of patriotism. Only at this point was the head-on assault on American ethnic institutions that the progressives had always stopped far short of undertaking finally launched. Now the idea that old and new identities complemented each other, the idea that Norway be the mother and America the bride, for example, was challenged by the assertion that "hyphenated" allegiances smacked too much of disloyalty to the adopted fatherland.[11] Indeed, no longer might one propose, as had a professed newspaper subscriber back in 1897, that the ethnic institutions in fact contributed to Americanization: "*Skandinaven* another couple of years, and I will be a complete American."[12] Instead, American entry into the conflict in 1917 signaled the arrival of "one-hundred percent Americanism."[13]

The Wisconsin progressives had aimed at something quite different. They had identified a political system that, rather than facing squarely the problems of industrializing America, dealt in symbols and labels of limited consequence to the true power struggle that in their view ought to be waged against corporate power. This hardly represented emergent European-style class politics writ large, for the progressives, employing a nonpartisan mode of thinking that harked back to the era of the Founding

Fathers, always made their case before the whole "people." Yet they did hope to purify the political system of whatever distortions they found and hence make it more responsive to the social and economic needs of the day. Thus they launched their attack on "traditional politics."

We may add that this progressive assault on traditionalism also unfolded in other states in the Middle West, and that in each case the Scandinavian-American politicians, as well as the leaders of the ubiquitous Scandinavian-American ethnic institutions, faced some tough choices in groping towards a modern political agenda. Nowhere else, however, did the progressive struggle reach such intensity and dramatic heights as in La Follette's Wisconsin. In that state, the struggle between traditionalism and progressivism was thus painted in stronger colors than anywhere else in the Middle West.

Originally, the old style of politics that so often focused on such labels as party, nationality, locality, and personality suited some Scandinavian-American leaders quite well. First, by the early 1890s this type of politics afforded the ethnic group a certain niche within the political system. In local, county, and assembly-level politics, the raw numerical strength of the group sometimes elevated one of their leaders to a position of prominence, occasionally in cooperation with other local interests. In state and federal politics, moreover, "Scandinavians," in Wisconsin almost invariably Norwegian Americans, were granted at least symbolic representation on the Republican state ticket and usually took seats in the state delegation in the House of Representatives (although not in the less important state senate).

Second, in their electoral battle, Scandinavian-American politicians, and in Wisconsin particularly those of Norwegian background, had ethnic institutions and their networks of leaders and grass roots to validate their "national" credentials. Those institutions and networks resulted from processes of ascription and adversity that taught Scandinavian Americans to stick together in the rarely hostile but nevertheless strange, Yankee-dominated New World, and even to build their own sense of ethnic pride. As the numbers of Scandinavian immigrants in the Midwest rose during the second half of the nineteenth century, moreover, the churches, the secular societies, and the press tended to branch out from pan-Scandinavian-American beginnings to "national" independence, a development more successfully pursued by Norwegian and Swedish immigrants than by the Danish, who remained too few and too scattered to organize as strongly—yet with particularly the Norwegian Americans sometimes sustaining a rough sense of Old World national attachments by bickering internally with each other over matters of religion and culture.[14]

Many a Scandinavian-American politician viewed the ethnic institutions as sources of strength, and several leaders of the latter indeed felt attracted to the political arena. Lutheran pastors often entered the political fray with a certain embarrassment. How ought one aspire to secular leadership and deal with less-than-pious politicians in a country that prided itself on the separation of church and state? Nor were leaders of the mutual-aid societies free from inhibitions, for their institutions typically boasted strict political neutrality, yet they might still stage rallies headed by Scandinavian-American politicians or attempt to build political careers for themselves. Temperance activists entered the political struggle freely, but to the degree that they did so as representatives of the Prohibition Party, their success was very limited. Only the newspaper editors could engage in politics completely openly *and* upon election victory expect their share of the plums. A few of them, most notably Nicolai A. Grevstad of *Skandinaven*, experienced remarkable political success.

The third reason that the old style of politics suited some Scandinavian-American politicians well was that the ethnic appeal usually remained wonderfully vague: reference to the European nationality label often functioned as an argument in itself. What Edward W. Said wrote of modern-day appeals to nationalism in the Middle East would have made perfect sense to many a late-nineteenth-century Scandinavian-American politician in the Middle West: "My impression is that more effort is being spent in sustaining *the connection*, bolstering the idea that to be Syrian, Iraqi, Egyptian, or Saudi is a sufficient end, rather than in thinking critically, even audaciously, about the national programme itself."[15] In many a Scandinavian-American politician's view, therein precisely lay the charm of the appeal to Scandinavian national attachments: in day-to-day practical politics, the *values* purportedly associated with being Norwegian-, Swedish-, Danish-, or simply Scandinavian-American mattered less than the *connections* opened up by communication with the leaders of the ethnic institutions and their networks of grassroots supporters.

More than this, from the politician's point of view, the invocation of this form of ethnicity functioned as a means of *defusing* certain highly explosive issues, for instance the language or temperance questions, which amateur politicians like ex-Governor William Dempster Hoard or opportunistic leaders like Democratic boss Edward C. Wall sometimes touched off, and which mattered deeply to influential groups of the Lutheran clergy. Quite simply, the political elite met the grassroots-based ethnocultural threat that a politics of religious and cultural division posed with a much tamer and more secular—indeed oftentimes avowedly nonreligious—appeal to national background, not wholly devoid of meaning, yet still imprecise. Thus, the near-primordial type of ethnic identity, revolving around religiously colored local or regional European attachments that affected the lives of so many ordinary Scandinavian Americans was met by the elite with a much more constructed type of appeal to Norwegian-American, Swedish-American, Danish-American, or even pan-Scandinavian-American identity. Even though the Scandinavian-American grass roots hardly got what at least some of them wanted in terms of, for example, temperance legislation, an issue that under all circumstances caused much internal division, the political leadership could nevertheless boast that several Scandinavian Americans had been elevated to prominent positions within the political system. To some extent, this establishment of "national" niches in American politics functioned as compensation for the unwillingness by the elite to act aggressively on the ethnocultural issues that so absorbed and divided large parts of the grass roots, even though many a Republican Scandinavian-American assemblyman obligingly voted pro-temperance.

Of course, the endeavor to root out, or at least neutralize, the volatile ethnocultural issues politically was only partially successful, as the Bennett English-language school law campaign of 1890 illustrated clearly, and the pressure not only from grassroots organizations but also from large parts of the Lutheran pastorate for temperance reform often proved irresistible. Under all circumstances, by the mid-1890s a culture of Republicanism, constructed in the Civil War era and strengthened after the outbreak of the 1893 depression, permeated political and institutional life among Norwegian Americans and Swedish Americans, if only in part among Danish Americans. Again, the ethnic leadership hardly *created* these Republican attachments, for originally they had much to do with the general American debate over the Civil War issues of slavery (among Norwegian Americans originally a divisive matter) and the general Northern cause. The Republican Party's overall pro-temperance ethnocultural profile only strengthened those bonds, as did the GOP's economic policies, with the Democrats receiving the blame for the economic crisis. By and large, the ethnic institutions and networks sustained these Republican attachments powerfully, the press, parts of it funded by the GOP, playing an especially aggressive role.

The 1893 depression had the effect of changing the Wisconsin political debate from a Democratic-Republican struggle into an internal Republican affair, since Wisconsin became in 1894–1896 and for a generation to come remained nearly a one-party state. Under these circumstances, the progressive struggle against politics-as-usual was launched. Rebelling against the Republican leadership as early as 1891, Robert M. La Follette soon built his own organization within the GOP. In doing so, he relied on his own oratorical genius, as well as on new techniques of mass communication and mobilization to reach into every nook and cranny of Wisconsin's traditionally unwieldy political landscape of island communities. In late 1896, at the same point in time that the Municipal League of Milwaukee was experiencing its short-lived statewide influence, La Follette, following in the footsteps of his ally Albert R. Hall, finally converted to reform. Thus began his powerful challenge to what he and his associates perceived as the corporate menace to American politics, the supposed stranglehold of "the machine" upon the Republican organization of the state.

As early as 1894, La Follette and Haugen demonstrated their ambition to change the terms of the political debate, to reorient politics away from old symbols and labels towards something that had not yet clearly been identified as reform. During the 1894 campaign, they launched their first attack on the matrix of party, nationality, locality, and personality. The assault failed, however, and La Follette and Haugen's attempt to underplay the role played by nationality misfired badly. By 1906, however, the progressives had succeeded in reforming the language of the political debate. They offered a reorientation of politics away from symbols and labels towards matters of substance, attacking the old rhetoric focusing on loyalty to the party, the national and local attachments of the candidate, and his personal qualities. Instead, they proposed to introduce an essentially nonpartisan, merit-based, and issue-oriented approach that promised to make politics "pure" or, in a later phrase, "scientific." The novel approach to politics found institutionalized expression in a number of reforms, the most important of which was the enactment in 1903–1904 of the direct primary law that turned the nomination process into an intraparty general election and the party itself into a public utility rather than a semiprivate organization.

A remarkable circumstance attending the progressive upheaval in Wisconsin was that so many Scandinavian Americans participated in it. From an elite perspective, this constituted something of a paradox. On the one hand, joining La Follette made perfect sense, for he had demonstrated a willingness to recognize Scandinavian-American leaders as his equals. He accepted Congressman Nils P. Haugen on his merits as a fellow young professional and even promoted him for the governorship. La Follette did not condescend in his interaction with Scandinavian-American politicians. The maneuvering space afforded the Scandinavian Americans under the traditional system of politics, after all, was predicated on a system of basic inequality that granted them only a special niche within the Republican Party, better than no slot at all, of course, but still only a narrowly defined place. La Follette proposed to break that pattern by accepting the Scandinavian Americans on equal terms.

On the other hand, in theory at least, La Follette thus proposed to destroy the consideration of ethnic identity in politics. In practice, it is true, he understood that winning over the Scandinavian Americans would strengthen his cause immensely, and few Scandinavian-American political leaders, on their part, were willing to break their bonds with the Scandinavian-American institutions, not least the press, that had helped elevate them to prominence in the first place. Nevertheless, the fact remained that La Follette was intent on downplaying the ethnic factor dramatically and on institutionalizing a new political order in Wisconsin based upon a system of direct primaries that ideally would eradicate it. It is, perhaps, no coincidence that although so many Scandinavian-American politicians and grass roots joined forces with La Follette, some of those leaders who never converted to La Folletteism, or who did so less than wholeheartedly, were those who proved most stubbornly nationally minded, individuals not only like Rasmus B. Anderson, Ole A. Buslett, and Peer O. Strømme but also such persons as Atley Peterson and James O. Davidson, the latter two indeed representing the kind of typical immigrant politician of common-school background whom Haugen and La Follette particularly loathed.

Our investigation suggests that despite the formidable role played by *connections* in fostering Scandinavian-American allegiances with the La Follette movement in Wisconsin, *values*—as vaguely as the concept of Scandinavian-American identity was usually presented by vote-desiring politicians—also played a part. To be sure, nothing much about Scandinavian-American ethnicity can be concluded from the fact that Nils P. Haugen personally was a close friend of Albert R. Hall, Wisconsin's progressive pioneer, and indeed began flirting with reform as early as 1892.[16] Perhaps more telling is the circumstance that in 1895 the same Hall, notwithstanding his non-Scandinavian background, undertook to write weekly reports to *Skandinaven* about the proceedings in the Wisconsin legislature together with Hans Borchsenius, a Danish-born assemblyman.[17] Truly significant was the fact that prior to the coining of the phrase "progressivism," the politically influential Norwegian-American *Skandinaven* under the editorship of Nicolai A. Grevstad was using a "progressive-reactionary" vocabulary borrowed directly from the secular struggle by the liberal party in Norway for political reform and was applying it to the Wisconsin battle.

Both inside and outside Wisconsin some argued that Scandinavian-American identity had "progressive" connotations. They contended that the insurgent nature of the struggle in America, as well as the basic aspiration to progress, echoed the class-based fight between liberals and conservatives in Norway over political reform. This line of reasoning could easily be extended to the political situation in Denmark, and conceivably also to that in Sweden. To be sure, the Danish Americans would not react with the same kind of unified, institutionalized Republicanism as would their Norwegian-American counterparts, nor would the Swedish Americans respond with the same levels of nationalistically inspired enthusiasm, not to speak of political activism.

Usually this progressive argument was presented in purely secular terms, but occasionally reference to Lutheranism or Protestantism was also made. However, to the same extent that under the traditional system of politics the consideration of nationality had helped defuse ethnoculturally explosive issues, the modernizing politics of progressivism contributed to rechanneling ethnocultural energies into nonreligious and constructive areas of political action. After the turn of the century, grassroots arguments stating that ethnic identity ought politically to be understood in terms of pro-temperance attitudes were met by the political elite with the secular claim that Scandinavian-American identity entailed having positive views on progressivism. When bills on temperance legislation came up in the assembly they were often supported by Scandinavian Americans, not least by those living in the western, rural, overall Protestant section of the state. Still, the relationship between the attitudes of Scandinavian-American assemblymen on temperance and on progressivism was not always straightforward, even though especially western Republican Scandinavian-American assemblymen proved friendly to progressive reform.

The overall strength of "national" Scandinavian-American values in explaining Scandinavian-American attachments to progressivism should not be exaggerated—the political elite, including the editorship of particularly *Skandinaven*, first articulated the nature of the relationship between Scandinavian-American identity and progressivism, even though it reverberated quite strongly among the grass roots. In fact, in the campaign of 1906, when Norwegian-born James O. Davidson was pitted against Swedish-American Irvine L. Lenroot in the first test of the statewide direct primary, appeals to ethnic identity played an important part in Davidson's quiet campaign among his fellow Norwegian-American ethnics, yet not as a system of carefully argued political or cultural values meshing well with progressivism but simply as a label that invoked a sense of ethnic pride, especially now that Norway had just broken her union with Sweden. Had the Norwegian Americans truly opted for progressivism in 1906, they would have chosen Lenroot over Davidson, as indeed editor Grevstad and Nils P. Haugen had originally signaled that they would do, and as politicians like Herman L. Ekern and Andrew H. Dahl in fact did. The campaign of 1906 demonstrated first of all the strength of ethnic *connections* and laid bare the elusiveness of the *values* associated with it, even though for a while those values became identified with progressivism and to some extent offered a "national" secular alternative, or complement, to the religiously colored

attachments that so many Scandinavian Americans felt to Old World locality or region.

From the progressive leadership's point of view, from the vantage
point of La Follette, Scandinavian-American sympathies for progressivism
came in handy, but only because they fit a cause that in its very nature was
nonethnic. To La Follette, the main aim was to purify the political language of all distortions based on unreflecting appeals to party, nationality,
locality, and personality, and hence be in position to wage an all-out struggle against the corrupting forces of corporate power that in his view were
threatening democratic America with moral ruin. In the short term, the
extent of La Follette's success may be measured by the fact that whereas in
1894, even with America gripped in a depression, the true nature of the
struggle between the insurgents and the entrenched Republican leadership
was veiled behind a rhetoric focusing on the national background of the
candidates for state office, by 1906, with prosperity having returned long
ago, and with La Follette reigning triumphant, the political language was
couched in strongly anticorporate terms. Indeed, overt acknowledgment
of the nationality consideration in politics now appeared hopelessly old-
fashioned. In the longer term, the degree of progressivism's success may be
gauged by the fact that in their attempt to cleanse politics of what they
viewed as a meaningless recognition of empty labels and symbols, despite
their failure to root out the nationality consideration, they stopped far
short of launching an all-out campaign against the ethnic institutions and
networks that were sustaining the nationality factor in politics.

Only with America's entry into World War I would shrill demands
for one-hundred-percent Americanism eliminate the nationality consideration from politics, but then it happened in so brutal and traumatizing a
fashion that several progressives, including La Follette, who opposed
American entry into the war, were thoroughly disgusted. Seen in this light,
midwestern progressivism represents a bright period in the history of the
United States, an era when a number of reformers, with the backing of an
awakened citizenry, insisted on imparting new social and economic democratic meaning to the practice of politics, both by challenging tradition as
expressed through the matrix of party, nationality, locality, and personality, and by attacking expanding corporate power. They may have failed in
their latter endeavor, and they were only partially successful in their

former. Yet they insisted all along, not least in their attack on the ethnic factor in politics, on moving ahead gently, on playing by the rules of the democratic game, indeed, on transforming and strengthening those rules through careful and tolerant argument and persuasion. From an ethnic point of view, therein lay their claim to greatness.

Appendices

I. Maps, Charts, and Tables

II. Wisconsin's Elected State and Federal Officials, 1890–1914

III. Roll-Call Analysis

Figure 1.1. Gross migration from Europe and Scandinavia to the USA, 1840–1915.

a. Danish, Norwegian, Swedish, and Scandinavian gross migration to the USA, 1840–1915.

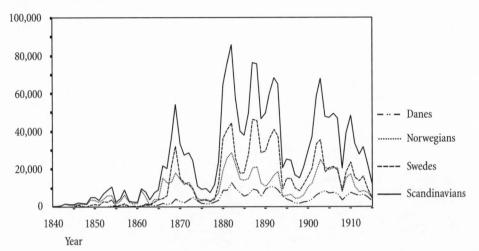

b. Scandinavian and European gross migration to the USA, 1840–1915

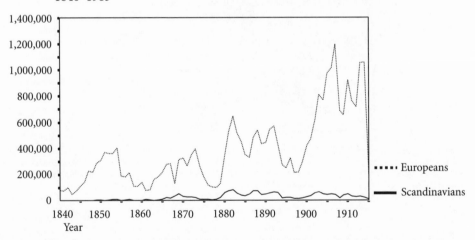

Note: The charts were computed from official migration statistics in Danmarks Statistik, *Statistisk Tabelværk*, 5. række, litra A:5 (Copenhagen, 1905), 42–43; Danmarks Statistik, *Statistiske Undersøgelser* 19 (Copenhagen, 1966), 117; Adolph Jensen, "Migration Statistics of Denmark, Norway, and Sweden," in *International Migrations*, ed. Imre Ferenczi and Walter Willcox, 2 vols. (New York, 1929), 1:747 and 752; Nils William Olsson and Erik Wikén, *U.S. Passenger Arrival Statistics for Swedes* (Stockholm, 1995), 27–140; Sten Carlsson, "Chronology and Composition of Swedish Emigration," in *From Sweden to America: A History of the Migration*, ed. Harald Runblom and Hans Norman (Uppsala, 1976), 117–119; U.S. Bureau of the Census, *Historical Statistics of the United States: From Colonial Times to the Present* (New York, 1976), 105–106. The Scandinavian data are based on Scandinavian sources; the cumulative European on American.

Figure 1.2. The counties in Wisconsin with most family heads of Scandinavian origins, based on parents' nativity; ten counties per ethnic group, State Census of 1905.

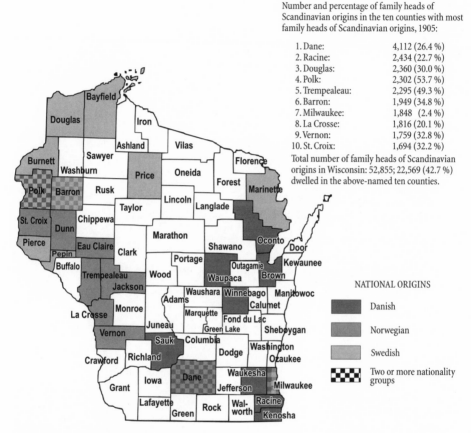

Number and percentage of family heads of Scandinavian origins in the ten counties with most family heads of Scandinavian origins, 1905:

1. Dane:	4,112 (26.4 %)
2. Racine:	2,434 (22.7 %)
3. Douglas:	2,360 (30.0 %)
4. Polk:	2,302 (53.7 %)
5. Trempealeau:	2,295 (49.3 %)
6. Barron:	1,949 (34.8 %)
7. Milwaukee:	1,848 (2.4 %)
8. La Crosse:	1,816 (20.1 %)
9. Vernon:	1,759 (32.8 %)
10. St. Croix:	1,694 (32.2 %)

Total number of family heads of Scandinavian origins in Wisconsin: 52,855; 22,569 (42.7 %) dwelled in the above-named ten counties.

NATIONAL ORIGINS

Danish

Norwegian

Swedish

Two or more nationality groups

Number and percentage of family heads of Danish origins in the ten counties with most family heads of Danish origins, 1905:

1. Racine:	1,775	(16.5 %)
2. Polk:	597	(13.9 %)
3. Waupaca:	583	(8.4 %)
4. Brown:	390	(4.0 %)
5. Winnebago:	384	(3.0 %)
6. Kenosha:	353	(6.5 %)
7. Milwaukee:	312	(0.4 %)
8. Dane:	257	(1.7 %)
9. Oconto:	216	(4.8 %)
10. Waukesha:	198	(3.0 %)

Total number of family heads of Danish origins in Wisconsin: 8,010; 5,075 (63.4 %) dwelled in the above-named ten counties.

Number and percentage of family heads of Norwegian origins in the ten counties with most family heads of Norwegian origins, 1905:

1. Dane:	3,766	(24.2 %)
2. Trempealeau:	2,189	(47.1 %)
3. Vernon:	1,724	(32.2 %)
4. La Crosse:	1,688	(18.7 %)
5. Barron:	1,397	(25.0 %)
6. Dunn:	1,367	(26.4 %)
7. Eau Claire:	1,245	(19.2 %)
8. Milwaukee:	1,191	(1.6 %)
9. St. Croix:	1,187	(22.5 %)
10. Jackson:	1,161	(32.9 %)

Total number of family heads of Norwegian origins in Wisconsin: 33,995; 16,915 (49.8 %) dwelled in the above-named ten counties.

Number and percentage of family heads of Swedish origins in the ten counties with most family heads of Swedish origins, 1905:

1. Douglas:	1,251	(15.9 %)
2. Polk:	1,088	(25.4 %)
3. Burnett:	839	(42.1 %)
4. Marinette:	693	(11.2 %)
5. Pierce:	668	(13.9 %)
6. Price:	533	(21.1 %)
7. Bayfield:	502	(16.9 %)
8. Barron:	438	(7.8 %)
9. Milwaukee:	345	(0.5 %)
10. Pepin:	342	(22.0 %)

Total number of family heads of Swedish origins in Wisconsin: 10,850; 6,699 (61.7 %) dwelled in the above-named ten counties.

Note: The map was created on the basis of data from "A Retabulation from the Wisconsin State Census of 1905."

Figure 2.1. A rough estimate of the communicant membership of the Scandinavian-American churches, ca. 1900/1906.

Denomination	Year of establishment /reorganization	No. of congregations	Communicant members
United Norw. Luth. Church	1890	900	185027
Swedish Lutheran Augustana Synod	1848/1851/1860/70	c. 1000	121446
Synod of the Norw. Ev. Luth. Church	1843/1851/1853/1867	813	107712
Hauge's Norw. Ev. Luth. Synod	1839/1843/1846/1875	194	33268
Norwegian Lutheran Free Church	1893/1897	296	26928
United Danish Ev. Luth. Church	1894/1896	151	16340
Swedish Free Mission	1868	400	15000
Swedish Ev. Mission Covenant	1868/1873/1874–75/1885	140	12000
Danish Ev. Luth. Church	1872/74	80	4000
Eielsen's Synod	1839/1843/1846	10	500
TOTAL LUTHERAN		3984	522221
Swedish Baptists	1852	310	21500
Swedish Methodists	1845	170	16000
Norw.-Danish Methodists	1851	115	8000
Scandinavian Congregationalists	1884	109	7000
Norw.-Danish Baptists	1856	80	5000
Scandinavian Adventists	1849	30	3000
Swedish Episcopalians	1849	25	3000
Scandinavian Salvationists	1887	55	1500
Scandinavian Moravians	1849	15	800
Scandinavian Unitarians	1882	5	400
Scandinavian Disciples of Christ	1888	6	200
TOTAL NON-LUTHERAN		920	66400
GRAND TOTAL		**4904**	**588621**

Sources: Hugo Söderström, *Confession and Cooperation* (Lund, 1973), 94; U.S. Bureau of the Census, *Special Reports: Religious Bodies, 1906, Part One: Summary and General Tables* (Washington, D.C., 1910), 288–290, 371–373, 529–531; O. N. Nelson, "Statistics Regarding the Scandinavians in the United States," in *History of the Scandinavians and Successful Scandinavians in the United States*, ed. O. N. Nelson, 2 vols., rev. ed. (1904; reprint, New York, 1969), 1:263; Peder Kjølhede, "Den danske, evangelisk-lutherske Kirke i Amerika," in *Danske i Amerika*, ed. Peter Sørensen Vig, 2 pts. in 1 vol. (Minneapolis, 1908), 2:112. The figures are only rough estimates, for even the census count was based on the reports of the congregations rather than of the individuals; in their own reports, moreover, the church bodies only counted those congregations that affiliated *formally* with them. It must be noted that the churches were also open to many churchgoers (including minors) who were not communicant members. See Robert C. Ostergren, "The Immigrant Church as a Symbol of Community and Place in the Upper Midwest," *Great Plains Quarterly* 1 (Fall 1981), 237, note 1; G. O. Brohough, "Historical Review of Hauge's Evangelical Lutheran Synod in America," in Nelson, *History of the Scandinavians*, 1:180–181.

Figure 4.1. The lifespan of the Scandinavian-American newspapers printed in Wisconsin, 1891–1913[1]

Newspaper	National background	Place of publication	County	Orientation	Frequency
Ashland Bladet	Swedish	Ashland	Ashland	Republican	Weekly
Ashland Posten	Swedish	Ashland	Ashland	Republican	Weekly
American Scandinavian	Norwegian	Stoughton	Dane	Independent	Weekly
Amerika	Norwegian	Madison	Dane	Republican[2]	Weekly
Danskeren	Danish	Neenah	Winnebago	Republican	Weekly
Folkets Avis	Danish	Racine	Racine	Independent	Weekly
Folkevennen	Norwegian	La Crosse	La Crosse	Republican	Weekly
For Gammel og Ung	Norwegian	Wittenberg	Shawano	Religious	Weekly
Fram	Norwegian	Milwaukee	Milwaukee	Independent	Weekly
Freja	Danish	Marinette	Marinette	Literary	Weekly
Fremad	Norwegian	Marinette	Marinette	Independent	Weekly
Förposten	Swedish	Marinette	Marinette	Republican	Weekly
La Crosse Tidende	Norwegian	La Crosse	La Crosse	Republican	Biweekly
Marinette Tribunen	Swedish	Marinette	Marinette	Republican	Weekly
Norden	Norw-Dan.	Racine	Racine	Literary	Monthly
Nordvestern Härold	Swedish	Superior	Douglas	Independent	Weekly
Normannen	Norwegian	Stoughton	Dane	Independent	Weekly
Posten	Norwegian	Superior	Douglas	Republican[3]	Weekly
Reform	Norwegian	Eau Claire	Eau Claire	Prohibition	Weekly
Scandinavian Tribune	Norwegian	Stoughton	Dane	Independent	Weekly
Superior Tidende	Norwegian	Superior	Douglas	Republican[4]	Weekly
Svenska Am. Tribunen	Swedish	Superior	Douglas	Republican[5]	Weekly
Søndagsskoleblad	Norwegian	Wittenberg	Shawano	Religious	Weekly
Telskuden	Danish	Neenah	Winnebago	Republican	Weekly
Varden	Norwegian	La Crosse	La Crosse	Republican	Weekly
Wisconsin Journalen	Swedish	Amery	Polk	Republican	Weekly
Wisconsin Val. Posten	Swedish	Merrill	Lincoln	Independent	Weekly
Wittenberg Herald	Norwegian	Wittenberg	Shawano	Republican	Weekly
28 newspapers	Da. 4.5	13 localities	12 counties	Republ. 15	Wkly :
	Nor. 15.5	= 11 cities +		Democr. 0	Biwkly
	Sw. 8.0	2 villages		Prohib. 1	Mnthly
				Indepen. 8	
				Other 4	

[1]Source: *Blue Book of Wisconsin*, 1891:331–340, 1893:351–361, 1895:395–406, 1897:334–346, 1899: 401–413, 1901:408–423, 1903:648–663, 1905:598–612, 1907:673–687, 1909:595–610, 1911:383–397, 1913:318–332.

[2]Democratic in 1897.

Year mentioned in the *Blue Book of Wisconsin*												Total number of hits in the *Blue Book*
91	93	95	97	99	01	03	05	07	09	11	13	
								x				1
			x	x	x							3
					x	x	x					3
			x	x	x	x	x	x	x	x	x	9
x	x	x	x									4
x	x	x	x	x	x	x	x	x	x	x	x	12
	x											1
					x	x	x	x	x	x		6
		x	x									2
			x	x								2
		x	x	x	x							4
x	x	x	x	x	x	x	x	x	x			10
		x										1
		x	x	x	x	x	x	x	x	x	x	10
								x	x	x	x	4
					x	x	x					3
x	x	x										4
x												2
x	x	x	x	x	x	x	x	x	x	x	x	12
												1
		x	x	x	x	x	x	x	x	x	x	10
x	x	x	x	x	x	x	x	x	x	x	x	12
					x	x	x	x	x			5
					x							1
x												2
			x									1
	x											1
				x								1
8	10	13	12	14	12	12	12	11	9	7		127

[3]Democratic in 1893.

[4]Independent in 1895, Independent Republican in 1913.

[5]Independent Republican in 1913.

Figure 4.2. Circulation figures for the Scandinavian-American press inside and outside Wisconsin, 1900

a. All Scandinavian-American publications with an estimated circulation above 10,000 (twenty-six newspapers)

Newspaper (weeklies unless otherwise stated)	National background	Place of publication	State	Orientation	Est. circulation
Skandinaven (semiweekly)	Norwegian	Chicago	Illinois	Republican	44468
Svenska Amerikanaren	Swedish	Chicago	Illinois	Independent	38500
Decorah-Posten	Norwegian	Decorah	Iowa	Family	36238
Svenska Amerikanska Posten	Swedish	Minneapolis	Minnesota	Independent	35864
Svenska Kuriren	Swedish	Chicago	Illinois	Independent Republican	35000
Svenska Tribunen	Swedish	Chicago	Illinois	Republican	30000
Minneapolis Tidende	Norwegian	Minneapolis	Minnesota	Independent	28038
Hemlandet	Swedish	Chicago	Illinois	Republican	26784
Den danske Pioneer	Danish	Omaha	Nebraska	Independent Democrat	25135
Humoristen	Swedish	Chicago	Illinois	Humor	22500
Svenska Folkets Tidning	Swedish	Minneapolis	Minnesota	Liberal	20000
Kvinden og Hjemmet (monthly)	Norwegian	Cedar Rapids	Iowa	Family	18500
Skandinaven (daily)	Norwegian	Chicago	Illinois	Republican	17526
Missions-Wännen	Swedish	Chicago	Illinois	Religious (Evangelical)	17316
Fosterlandet	Swedish	Chicago	Illinois	No mention	15900
Nordvesten	Norwegian	Minneapolis	Minnesota	Independent Republican	14000
Christelige Talsmand	Norwegian	Chicago	Illinois	Religious (Methodist)	13500
Augustana	Swedish	Rock Island	Illinois	Religious (Lutheran)	13009
Bladet	Swedish	Chicago	Illinois	Religious	12700
Svenska Roman Bladet	Swedish	Minneapolis	Minnesota	Family	12500
Minnesota Stats Tidning	Swedish	Minneapolis	Minnesota	Republican	12000
Lutheraneren	Norwegian	Minneapolis	Minnesota	Religious (Lutheran)	11646
Nya Wecko Posten	Swedish	Chicago	Illinois	Religious (Baptist)	10600
Weckoblad	Swedish	Minneapolis	Minnesota	Republican	10430
Skördemannen (semimonthly)	Swedish	Minneapolis	Minnesota	Agricultural	10000
Sändebudet	Swedish	Chicago	Illinois	Religious (Methodist)	10000

b. Scandinavian-language newspapers published in Wisconsin

Newspaper	National background	Place of publication	County	Orientation	Est. circulation
Amerika	Norwegian	Madison	Dane	Independent	7000
Wisconsin Svenska Tribun	Swedish	Superior	Douglas	Independent	6000
Reform	Norwegian	Eau Claire	Eau Claire	Prohibition	4768
Förposten	Swedish	Marinette	Marinette	Republican	3800
Folkets Avis	Norwegian	Racine	Racine	Independent	3000
Superior Tidende	Norwegian	Superior	Douglas	Independent Republican	2700
Marinette Tribunen	Swedish	Marinette	Marinette	Republican	1400
Fremad	Norwegian	Marinette	Marinette	Independent	850

Source: N. W. Ayer & Son's American Newspaper Annual (Philadelphia), 1900:1411–1413. Generally, *N.W. Ayer & Son* relied on light evidence for circulation figures, in several cases simply the publisher's claim; nor were all newspapers enumerated. In 1900, Wisconsin boasted thirteen Scandinavian-American papers, yet *N. W. Ayer & Son* only listed eight.

Figure 4.3. The party affiliation of the Scandinavian-language press in America in 1900 according to *N. W. Ayer & Son's American Newspaper Annual* (103 newspapers)

NUMBER OF PAPERS	Danish	Norwegian	Swedish	Sum: Scandinavian
Republican papers	0	15	23	38
Democratic papers	1	1	0	2
Socialistic papers	0	1	0	1
Prohibition papers	0	1	0	1
Independent papers	5	9	6	20
Other types of publications	2	18	21	41
Total number of papers	8	45	50	**103**

ESTIMATED CIRCULATION	Danish	Norwegian	Swedish	Scandinavian
Republican circulation	0	115829	184614	300443
Democratic circulation	25135	2000	0	27135
Socialistic circulation	0	2800	0	2800
Prohibition circulation	0	4768	0	4768
Independent circulation	14552	63707	96664	174923
Other circulation	3250	122184	180588	306022
Total estimated circulation	42937	311288	461866	**816091**

Source: N.W. Ayer & Son's American Newspaper Annual, 1900:1411–1413. All figures calculated by me. "Other types of publications" were those that were not strictly newspapers, i.e., religious, literary, agricultural, humoristic, or family-oriented journals. "Independent Republican" and "Independent Democratic" papers were counted under the respective party labels, Republican and Democratic. Thus, the only large Danish-American newspaper in the USA, *Den danske Pioneer*, was listed as "Independent Democratic" and therefore placed under the Democratic party label. An additional twenty Scandinavian-American papers were listed by *N.W. Ayer & Son*, but without circulation figures, including two from Wisconsin, the Norwegian-American *Freja* of Marinette, and the Danish-American *Nye Dansker* of Neenah.

Figure 5.1. Scandinavian Americans and other ethnic groups in the Wisconsin Assembly, 1891–1914

a. Nativity of the immigrant members (308 seats)

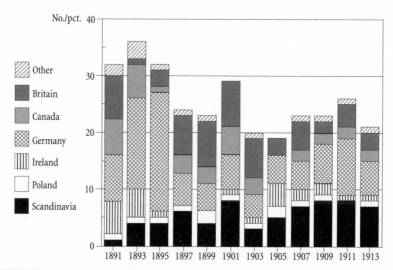

Country/region of birth	Representation in the Assembly, 1891–1914 (1204 seats)	Share of the state population in 1900 (total size of the population: 2,069,042)
USA	74.4 %	75.1 %
Germany	8.2 %	11.7 %
Scandinavia	5.4 %	5.1 %
Britain	4.9 %	1.3 %
Canada	2.9 %	1.7 %
Ireland	2.0 %	1.1 %
Poland	1.1 %	1.5 %
Other	1.1 %	2.5 %

b. Number and percentage of first- and second-generation Scandinavian Americans (125 seats)

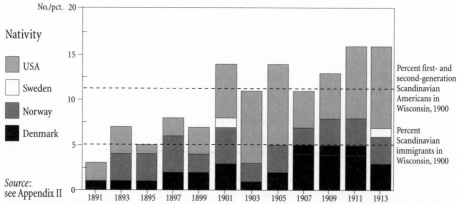

Source: see Appendix II

Figure 5.2. Wisconsin's assemblymen by national background, age, type of residence, and profession, 1891–1914

a. Wisconsin's assemblymen by profession and nativity (1,204 seats)

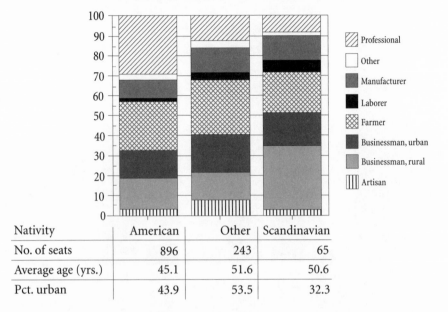

Nativity	American	Other	Scandinavian
No. of seats	896	243	65
Average age (yrs.)	45.1	51.6	50.6
Pct. urban	43.9	53.5	32.3

b. American-born assemblymen by profession and ascertainable parents' nativity (392 seats)

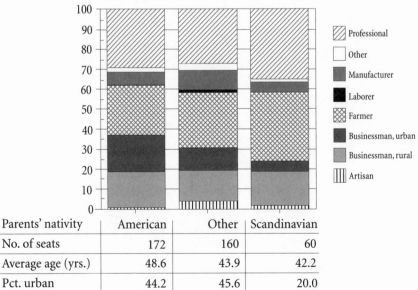

Parents' nativity	American	Other	Scandinavian
No. of seats	172	160	60
Average age (yrs.)	48.6	43.9	42.2
Pct. urban	44.2	45.6	20.0

Source: see Appendix II

Figure 5.3. The political affiliation of the Scandinavian-American members of the Wisconsin Assembly, 1891–1914 (125 seats)

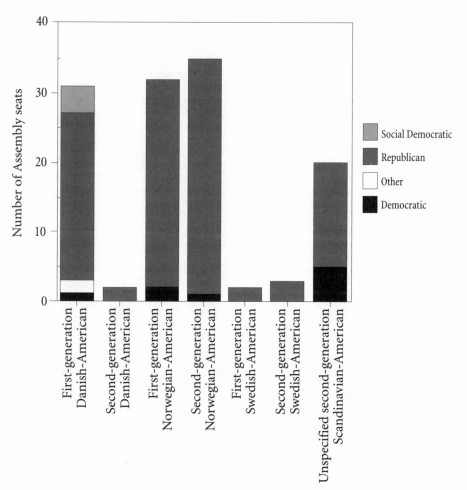

Source: see Appendix II

Figure 5.4. Wisconsin's elected state and federal officials by occupation and type of residence, 1891–1914

a. Profession (1,626 seats)

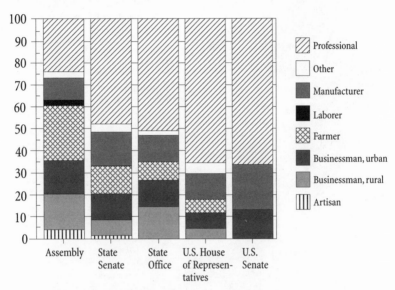

b. Type of residence (1,626 seats)

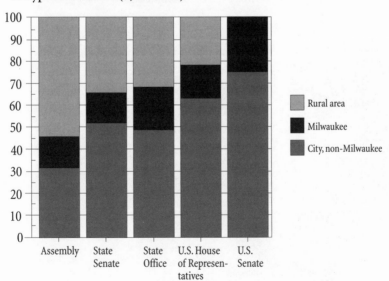

Note: In the years 1890 through 1912, 1204 seats were up for election in the assembly; 198 in the state senate; 91 for state office; 125 for the Wisconsin delegation in the U.S. House of Representatives; and 8 for the Wisconsin delegation in the U.S. Senate.

Source: see Appendix II

Figure 7.1. Nils P. Haugen's areas of support at the Republican state convention in Wisconsin, 1894

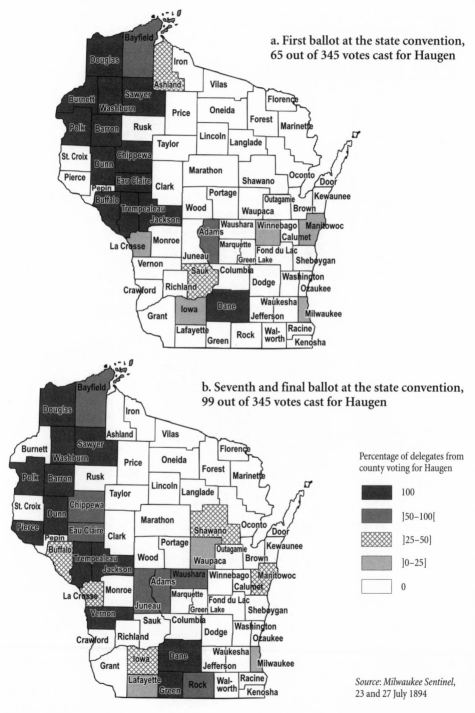

a. First ballot at the state convention, 65 out of 345 votes cast for Haugen

b. Seventh and final ballot at the state convention, 99 out of 345 votes cast for Haugen

Percentage of delegates from county voting for Haugen

- 100
-]50–100[
-]25–50]
-]0–25]
- 0

Source: *Milwaukee Sentinel*, 23 and 27 July 1894

Figure 8.1. Political topics discussed in 792 value-oriented letters to *Skandinaven*, 1890–1910

a. Individual topics

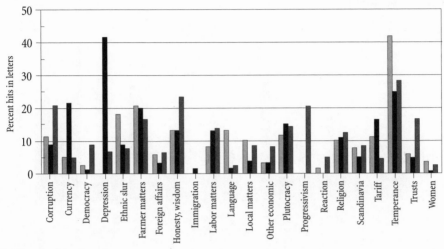

b. Categories of topics

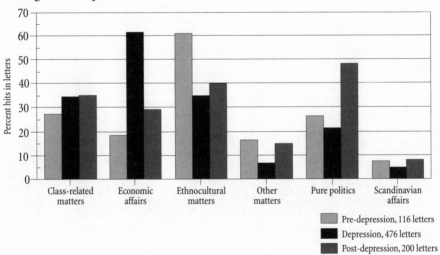

Note: In figure 8.1.b the *topics* of figure 8.1.a have been conflated into broader *categories*.

Class-related matters refer to "Farmer matters," "Labor matters," and "Plutocracy." *Economic affairs* refer to "Currency," "Depression," "Other economic," "Tariff," and "Trusts." *Ethnocultural matters* refer to "Ethnic slur," "Immigration," "Language," "Religion," and "Temperance." *Other matters* refer to "Foreign affairs" and "Local matters." *Pure politics* refers to "Corruption," "Democracy," "Honesty, wisdom," "Progressivism," "Reaction," and "Women." *Scandinavian affairs* refer to "Scandinavia." If one letter contained two or more *topics* within the same *category*, the topics would be counted individually in figure 8.1.a but once, collectively, in figure 8.1.b. In all, the 792 letters touched upon 1,759 topics.

Figure 8.2. Political topics associated with being Scandinavian American in 170 value-oriented reader letters to *Skandinaven*, 1890–1910

a. Individual topics

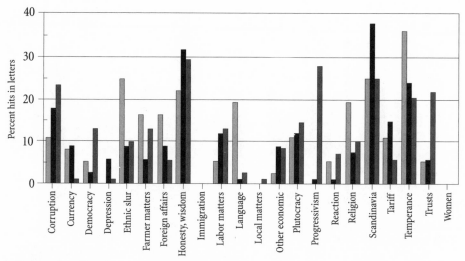

b. Categories of topics

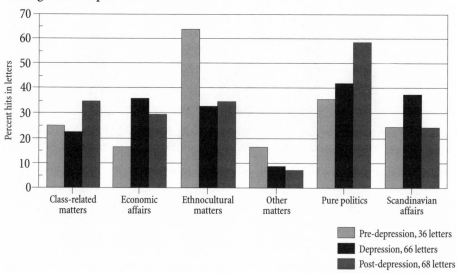

Note: In figure 8.2.b the *topics* of figure 8.2.a have been conflated into broader *categories*, as in figure 8.1.

Figure 8.3. Ranking of groups in the Wisconsin Assembly by degree of progressivism, 1895–1913 (five pairs of groups)

Year	1895	1897	1899	1901	1903	1905	1907	1909	1911	1913
Number of bills investigated	8	4	7	5	6	7	8	7	7	8
Number of roll calls investigated	10	9	26	25	25	16	20	12	23	33
Democrats	0	0	0	0	0	0	0	½	0	0
	33.5	*49.0*	*49.7*	*25.0*	*54.7*	*30.3*	*49.2*	*39.8*	*26.6*	*36.5*
	13	7	14	19	23	10	11	17	25	32
Republicans	1	1	1	1	1	1	1	½	1	1
	40.8	*57.5*	*73.0*	*48.9*	*64.0*	*71.5*	*68.4*	*43.6*	*84.7*	*72.7*
	61	88	69	79	71	83	66	73	54	53
Non-western Republicans	0	0	0	0	0	0	½	0	1	½
	34.4	*53.5*	*68.7*	*42.9*	*54.4*	*63.5*	*68.1*	*42.0*	*86.7*	*71.2*
	42	63	47	54	47	59	46	51	36	33
Western Republicans	1	1	1	1	1	1	½	1	0	½
	55.1	*67.7*	*82.0*	*62.0*	*82.8*	*90.9*	*69.1*	*47.1*	*80.9*	*75.3*
	19	25	22	25	24	24	20	22	18	20
Non-Scandinavian-American Republicans	0	½	0	0	0	0	½	0	½	½
	39.9	*57.3*	*71.7*	*45.9*	*62.2*	*69.4*	*68.4*	*42.2*	*84.9*	*73.1*
	56	81	63	66	61	70	59	62	42	39
Scandinavian-American Republicans	1	½	1	1	1	1	½	1	½	½
	51.6	*59.7*	*86.5*	*64.3*	*75.2*	*82.5*	*68.7*	*51.5*	*84.2*	*71.6*
	5	7	6	13	10	13	7	11	12	14
Western non-Scandinavian-American Republicans	0	0	0	0	½	½	0	½	½	½
	53.3	*67.0*	*79.9*	*59.5*	*81.8*	*90.1*	*67.6*	*46.7*	*80.2*	*75.4*
	18	23	18	18	18	17	18	19	12	12
Western Scandinavian-American Republicans	1	1	1	1	½	½	1	½	½	½
	88.0	*75.0*	*91.5*	*68.4*	*85.5*	*93.0*	*83.0*	*50.0*	*82.3*	*75.1*
	1	2	4	7	6	7	2	3	6	8
Western Republicans representing a constituency less than twenty percent Scandinavian-American	1	0	½	½	½	0	½	½	½	0
	57.1	*60.6*	*84.1*	*60.5*	*81.2*	*87.1*	*69.0*	*48.5*	*83.2*	*68.8*
	12	13	11	13	12	12	11	12	9	9
Western Republicans representing a constituency at least twenty percent Scandinavian-American	0	1	½	½	½	1	½	½	½	1
	51.7	*75.3*	*79.9*	*63.7*	*84.3*	*94.8*	*69.2*	*45.5*	*78.6*	*80.6*
	7	12	11	12	12	12	9	10	9	11

Note: The *top figure* in each triple cell gives the relative progressive ranking of the group in question in the legislative session in question on the basis of the calculation of progressive scores. "1" represents the higher progressive ranking, "0" the lower, and "½" indicates a tie, i.e., that less than five points separate the exact progressive scores of the two groups.

The *middle figure* in each triple cell gives the exact progressive score of the group in question on a scale from zero to 100; see Appendix III.

The *bottom figure* in each triple cell gives the number of actively voting assemblymen within the group in question.

Figure 8.4. Ranking of groups in the Wisconsin Assembly by temperance attitudes, 1895–1913 (five pairs of groups)

Year	1895	1897	1899	1901	1903	1905	1907	1909	1911	1913
Number of bills investigated	2	1	2	1	1	1	3	2	5	4
Number of roll calls investigated	10	1	4	3	1	11	4	7	14	10
Democrats	0	0	0	0	0	0	0	0	0	0
	25.6	0.0	8.3	42.1	10.5	10.0	29.5	2.9	28.4	18.9
	19	6	12	19	19	11	11	17	25	34
Republicans	1	1	1	1	1	1	1	1	1	1
	75.6	82.5	49.6	74.7	43.3	57.9	74.2	44.2	62.2	59.8
	74	80	68	79	60	85	60	61	53	58
Non-western Republicans	0	0	0	0	0	0	0	0	0	0
	70.1	75.4	37.2	64.8	31.6	47.1	66.4	33.9	58.4	47.4
	51	57	47	55	38	61	43	42	36	37
Western Republicans	1	1	1	1	1	1	1	1	1	1
	87.8	100.0	77.4	97.2	63.6	85.5	94.2	66.8	70.2	81.7
	23	23	21	24	22	24	17	19	17	21
Non-Scandinavian-American Republicans	0	0	0	0	0	0	0	0	0	0
	74.3	81.3	47.2	69.7	42.0	51.7	72.8	42.8	58.7	54.2
	69	75	62	66	50	72	52	53	41	44
Scandinavian-American Republicans	1	1	1	1	1	1	1	1	1	1
	94.0	100.0	75.0	100.0	50.0	92.0	83.4	53.1	74.1	77.4
	5	5	6	13	10	13	8	8	12	14
Western non-Scandinavian-American Republicans	0	½	0	½	1	0	0	1	0	½
	87.3	100.0	72.1	96.1	75.0	83.9	93.4	67.8	66.3	80.2
	22	21	17	17	16	17	15	18	11	13
Western Scandinavian-American Republicans	1	½	1	½	0	1	1	0	1	½
	100.0	100.0	100.0	100.0	33.3	89.1	100.0	50.0	77.5	84.1
	1	2	4	7	6	7	2	1	6	8
Western Republicans representing a constituency less than twenty percent Scandinavian-American	1	½	0	0	1	½	½	1	1	1
	91.4	100.0	75.0	94.4	83.3	86.2	93.4	75.5	74.6	93.3
	12	12	12	12	12	12	10	11	9	9
Western Republicans representing a constituency at least twenty percent Scandinavian-American	0	½	1	1	0	½	½	0	0	0
	83.9	100.0	80.6	100.0	40.0	84.8	95.3	55.0	65.4	72.9
	11	11	9	12	10	12	7	8	8	12

Note: The *top figure* in each triple cell gives the relative temperance ranking of the group in question in the legislative session in question on the basis of the calculation of temperance scores. "1" represents the drier view, "0" the wetter, and "½" indicates a tie, i.e., that less than five points separate the exact temperance scores of the two groups.

The *middle figure* in each triple cell gives the exact temperance score of the group in question on a scale from zero to 100; see Appendix III.

The *bottom figure* in each triple cell gives the number of actively voting assemblymen within the group in question.

APPENDIX II.
WISCONSIN'S ELECTED STATE AND FEDERAL OFFICIALS, 1890–1914

The present book includes an overview of all Wisconsin's state and federal officials winning seats in the elections of 1890 through 1912. That overview is based
principally on the information found in the biennial *Blue Book of Wisconsin*,
1891-1913.[1] On the basis of the biographical material in the *Blue Book*, a database
was constructed providing data on each politician's name, address, type of residence (rural, urban, metropolitan), age, occupation (618 types of job descrip-
tions being boiled down to eight general categories: artisan, businessman (rural),
businessman (urban), farmer, laborer, manufacturer, other, professional), country of birth, year of arrival in Wisconsin and age at arrival, partisan affiliation, political body elected to, and the number of terms. Furthermore, the *Blue Book*
allowed an investigation of the career patterns of politicians *across* legislative bodies even prior to 1890, because the 1911 volume included a complete list of all
elected state and federal legislators 1848–1911.[2]

Since the *Blue Book* generally does not provide information on the religious
background of the politicians, nor on their second-generation ethnicity,
seventy-six county histories in the possession of the Wisconsin Historical Society
were gleaned in a time-consuming and often vain search for further information
on at least the assemblymen occupying the 1204 seats in the Assembly 1891–
1914; additional biographical material on Scandinavian Americans was found in
the Scandinavian-language press and in the correspondence of politicians.[3] In
this manner, the religious affiliation of assemblymen occupying 379 seats (31.5
percent of all seats) was established, as was the second-generation ethnicity of
members taking 700 seats (58.1 percent of all seats), 392 of which were filled by
American-born individuals. In my estimate, all second-generation Scandinavian-
American assemblymen were thus detected (sixty members). The parental nativity of the "non-Scandinavian," American-born politicians who together took
836 seats 1891–1914, however, was found in only 332 cases (39.7 percent of the
cases).

Besides the personal data, each assemblyman's constituency was investigated for its proportion of Scandinavian-American voters by matching the data
on the geographical makeup of the often changing assembly districts found in the
biographical section of the *Blue Book of Wisconsin* with the information on ethnic
groups at the minor civil divisions level provided by the typewritten "A Retabula-

tion of Population Schedules from the Wisconsin State Census of 1905," table 26, again a truly time-consuming task. A geographical variable was also introduced by dividing the state into nine regions, from the northwest to the southeast.[4]

[1]*Blue Book of Wisconsin*, 1891:571–605, 1893:619–661, 1895:657–695, 1897:652–700, 1899:743–795, 1901:721–769, 1903:1069–1112, 1905:1065–1123, 1907:1115–1177, 1909:1083–1146, 1911:727–786, 1913:629–689.

[2]*Blue Book of Wisconsin*, 1911:542–622.

[3]I counted 1204 rather than 1200 assemblymen, because four died in office. For a list of the seventy-six county histories, see Jørn Brøndal, "National Identity and Midwestern Politics: Scandinavian-American Involvement in the Progressive Movement of Wisconsin, c. 1890-1914," 3 vols. (PhD diss., University of Copenhagen, 1998), 2:79–83; see also *Skandinaven*, 20 January 1891, 25 January, 15 February 1893, 20 February 1895, 10 May 1899, 18, 22 January, 6, 8 March, 22 May 1901, 9 July 1902, 12 October 1904, 12 April 1911; *Normannen*, 13 January 1893; *Reform*, 8 December 1896; *Superior Tidende*, 29 October 1896; George Olson to O. A. Buslett, 9 March 1909; O. A. Buslett to Anlaug Buslett, 9 May 1909, in Ole A. Buslett Papers, Archives of the Norwegian-American Historical Association, St. Olaf College, Northfield, MN; clipping dated "January, 1899," in Bjørn Holland Papers, Archives of the Norwegian-American Historical Association; J. O. Davidson to B. Anundsen, 11 February 1903, in James O. Davidson Papers, Library-Archives, Wisconsin Historical Society, Madison, WI.

[4]The "Northwest" consisted of Barron, Burnett, Chippewa, Douglas, Dunn, Polk, St. Croix, and Washburn counties; the "Central West" of Buffalo, Clark, Eau Claire, Jackson, Pepin, Pierce, and Trempealeau counties; the "Southwest" of Crawford, Grant, Iowa, La Crosse, Lafayette, Monroe, Richland, and Vernon counties; the "North Central" of Ashland, Bayfield, Iron, Lincoln, Price, Rusk, Sawyer, and Taylor counties; the "Central Central" of Adams, Green Lake, Juneau, Marathon, Marquette, Portage, Waushara, and Wood counties; the "South Central" of Columbia, Dane, Dodge, Green, Rock, Jefferson, Sauk, and Walworth counties; the "Northeast" of Door, Florence, Forest, Langlade, Marinette, Oconto, Oneida, and Vilas counties; the "Central East" of Brown, Calumet, Kewaunee, Manitowoc, Outagamie, Shawano, Waupaca, and Winnebago counties; the "Southeast" of Fond du Lac, Kenosha, Milwaukee, Ozaukee, Racine, Sheboygan, Washington, and Waukesha counties.

Appendix III.
Roll-Call Analysis

The roll-call analysis was limited to investigating the behavior of a few clearly defined categories of legislators, first of all those of Scandinavian-American background. For this reason, a full-fledged analysis employing Guttman scaling,
aiming at identifying groups of legislators, was not undertaken (and might easily
have required an additional volume). Instead, a simple "progressive" ranking system was devised. Sixty-five legislative bills (199 roll calls), all deemed central to
Wisconsin progressivism, were selected for analysis.[1] The bills were picked on the
basis, first, of a reading of *Skandinaven's* weekly summaries of the proceedings in
the Wisconsin legislature 1895–1913, together with the *Milwaukee Sentinel's*
evaluation of the legislature's performance at the end of each session, and, second, of the present writer's general knowledge of Wisconsin progressivism.[2] Bills
were easier to select for the later sessions than for the earlier, simply because roll
calls became increasingly popular as a political weapon after 1900. Moreover,
only roll calls in which the minority vote constituted at least ten percent of the
majority vote were picked for analysis, and only legislators voting on at least seventy percent of the issues were counted.

On each roll call, each voting legislator scored either a progressive "1" or a
conservative "0." If one legislative bill involved more than one roll call, each legislator's "bill score" would be found by adding up the individual roll-call scores
and dividing by the number of active votes. Thus, in the session of 1901, Assemblyman Charles Barker of Milwaukee, known for his strong opposition to the direct primary, scored "0" on all fourteen votes on bill 98 A, thus averaging a score
of 0.[3] A. R. Hall of Dunn County, on the other hand, scored "1" on all fourteen
votes and thus averaged a 1; P. G. Duerrwaechter of Washington County, finally,
scored "0" on nine votes and "1" on five, thus averaging a score of 0.4.

After each assemblyman's score on each legislative bill was calculated, the
average scores on all selected bills of the session were added up and divided by the
number of bills, the resulting figure expressing the assemblyman's "progressive"
performance during the legislative session. By multiplying by a factor of 100, that
figure was reexpressed on a scale ranging from 0 (conservative) to 100 (progressive). When comparing the average scores of two groups of legislators, whenever
the difference in the score amounted to less than five points, it was considered insignificant, indicating a tie between the two. A parallel analysis of sixty-five roll

calls on twenty-two temperance bills was also performed, the degree of enthusiasm for temperance legislation being measured on a scale from zero (wet) to 100 (dry).

Despite the simplicity of the roll-call analysis, the relative consistency of the results in figures 8.3 and 8.4 suggests that for our limited purposes (i.e., of adding a statistical dimension to a generally nonstatistical argument by identifying the behavior of some clearly defined groups of legislators) this method suffices.

[1]The bills were found in State of Wisconsin, *Assembly Bills*, 1895–1913 (Madison, 1895–1913), and State of Wisconsin, *Senate Bills*, 1895–1913 (Madison, 1895–1913), and the roll calls in the *Journal of the Assembly*, 1895–1913 (Madison, 1895–1913).

[2]*Milwaukee Sentinel*, 20, 21, 22 April 1895, 24, 25 April 1897, 2 May 1899, 16, 17 May 1901, 23 May 1903, 15, 16, 19, 21, 22, 23 June 1905, 16 December 1905 (the extra legislative session of 1905), 17, 18 July 1907, 19 June 1909, 15, 16 July 1911, 7, 9 August 1913; *Normannen*, 19 May 1893. See also the explanatory notes with the legislative bills listed in the present appendix.

[3]On Charles Barker's stalwart stance, see the *Milwaukee Daily News*, 22 March 1901; *Milwaukee Sentinel*, 23 March 1903; *Milwaukee Journal*, 23 May 1903.

Legislative bills of relevance to Wisconsin progressivism picked for roll-call analysis

Year	Bill no.	Bill text, with explanatory comment in brackets	Number of roll calls analyzed
1895	Jt. Res. 3 A	*Joint resolution… relating to free passes* (introduced by A. R. Hall; on Hall's pioneering fight against free passes and for a railroad commission, see chapter 7).	2
	Jt. Res. 71 A	*Joint resolution relating to the constitutionality of the way in which the railroads of the state are taxed and providing for an investigation…* (introduced by A. R. Hall; see the comment to Jt. Res. 3 A).	1
	146 A	*A bill to establish a board of railroad commissioners,… and for the appointment of a secretary for such board…* (introduced by A. R. Hall; see the comment to Jt. Res. 3 A).	1

	148 A	*A bill to regulate railway corporations and other common carriers in this state and to define the powers and duties of the board of railroad commissioners in relation to the same and to prevent and punish extortion and unjust discrimination in the rates...* (introduced by A. R. Hall; see the comment to Jt. Res. 3 A).	1
	722 A	*A bill relating to an investigation of railroad companies* (introduced by A. R. Hall; see the comment to Jt. Res. 3 A; see also Kenneth C. Acrea, "Wisconsin Progressivism: Legislative Response to Social Change, 1891–1909" [PhD diss., University of Wisconsin, 1968], 177).	1
	35 S	*A bill to prevent the improper and corrupt use of money in elections* (see chapter 8; also David P. Thelen, *The New Citizenship: Origins of Progressivism in Wisconsin, 1885–1900* [Columbia, MO, 1971], 170).	1
	212 S	*A bill for the relief of Henry Baetz and Ferdinand Kuehn, ex-state treasurers, and their sureties* (relating to the treasurer cases; see chapters 6 and 7).	2
	425 S	*A bill authorizing the attorney general to satisfy and discharge certain judgments in favor of the state and against Edward C. McFetridge, et al.* (relating to the treasurer cases; see the comment to 212 S).	1
1897	Jt. Res. 8 A	*Proposing an amendment to the constitution prohibiting the granting of free passes...* (introduced by A. R. Hall; see the comment to Jt. Res. 3 A, 1895).	5
	Res. 33 A	*Proposing that the members of the assembly be requested to deliver to the chief clerk of the assembly all the railway passes they have in their possession...* (an anti-railroad pass measure in A. R. Hall's spirit).	1
	110 A	*A bill to establish a board of railroad commissioners, prescribe their qualifications,... and for the appointment of a secretary for such board...* (introduced by A. R. Hall; see the comment to Jt. Res. 3 A, 1895).	1
	129 A	*A bill to define express companies and to prescribe the mode of taxing the same, and to fix the rate of taxation thereon* (introduced by J. O. Davidson; see chapter 7 and Albert O. Barton, *La Follette's Winning of Wisconsin (1894–1904)* [Madison, WI, 1922], 99–103).	2
1899	Jt. Res. 12 A	*Proposing an amendment to article 13 of the constitution of the State of Wisconsin to prohibit the pass system* (an anti-pass measure strongly supported by A. R. Hall; see the comment to Jt. Res. 3 A, 1895).	9
	19 A	*A bill for a tax on gifts, inheritances, bequests and legacies in certain cases* (introduced by A. R. Hall; on the role of inheritance taxation for progressivism, see Frederic C. Howe, *Wisconsin: An Experiment in Democracy* [New York, 1912], 136; Robert S. Maxwell, *La Follette and the Rise of the Progressives in Wisconsin* [Madison, WI, 1956], 93).	1

	111 A	*A bill… relating to the amount of license fees to be paid by railroad companies* (see Acrea, "Wisconsin Progressivism: Legislative Response to Social Change," 315; Emanuel L. Philipp, *Political Reform in Wisconsin*, ed. and abr. Stanley P. Caine and Roger E. Wyman [1910; Madison, WI, 1973], 117).	8
	290 A	*A bill to tax certain railroads, and to provide free passes thereon to certain public officials therein mentioned* (a bill to circumvent anti-free pass legislation).	1
	388 A	*A bill to establish a board of railroad commissioners, prescribing their qualifications… and for the appointment of a secretary for such board…* (introduced by A. R. Hall; see the comment to Jt. Res. 3 A, 1895).	1
	16 S	*A bill to prohibit the pass system and to provide punishment for the violation thereof* (with this bill that was enacted into law the distribution by the railroad companies of free railroad passes to public officials was finally forbidden; see the comment to Jt. Res. 3 A, 1895).	5
	356 S	*A bill creating the office of commissioner and assistant commissioners of taxation…* (see Maxwell, *La Follette and the Rise of the Progressives in Wisconsin*, 11).	1
1901	78 A	*A bill to regulate railway corporations and other common carriers in this state, to create a board of railway commissioners and define its powers and duties, to prevent and punish excess rates and unjust discriminations in the rates charged for the transportation of passengers and freights…* (introduced by A. R. Hall; see the comment to Jt. Res. 3 A, 1895).	2
	98 A	*A bill to abolish political caucuses and conventions and provide for political nominations by direct vote* (La Follette's pet measure in 1901, introduced by E. Ray Stevens, aiming at introducing the direct primary; see Robert M. La Follette, *La Follette's Autobiography : A Personal Narrative of Political Experiences*, rev. ed. [Madison, WI, 1913], 247; Jørn Brøndal, "The Quest for a New Political Order: Robert M. La Follette and the Genesis of the Direct Primary in Wisconsin, 1891–1904" [master's thesis, University of Copenhagen, 1993], 79–99).	14
	164 A	*A bill providing for the* ad valorem *taxation of railroads…* (see La Follette, *La Follette's Autobiography*, 245–247; John D. Buenker, *The Progressive Era, 1893–1914*, vol. 4 of *The History of Wisconsin*, ed. William Fletcher Thompson [Madison, WI, 1998], 464–465).	1
	165 A	*A bill relating to license fees for the operation of railroads in this state…* (see La Follette, *La Follette's Autobiography*, 245–247; Maxwell, *La Follette and the Rise of the Progressives in Wisconsin*, 37).	3
	73 S	*A bill relating to nominations of county officers by direct vote* (the stalwart "Hagemeister bill"; see La Follette, *La Follette's Autobiography*, 267–268).	5

1903	Jt. Res. 18 S	*Asking congress to call a constitutional convention for the purpose of submitting to the states for ratification, an amendment to the federal constitution providing for the election of United States senators by direct vote of the people* (electing U.S. senators by popular elections was a pet direct-democracy measure of the progressives).	2
	97 A	*A bill to provide for party nominations by direct vote* (the direct primary bill that finally was enacted into law; see also the comment to 98 A, 1901).	11
	531 A	*A bill to prohibit political lobbyists from attempting to personally influence the votes of members of the legislature, the votes of individual electors for nominees or for candidates for the nomination for any elective office; the appointment or discharge of any appointive officer, and from receiving or soliciting money from corporations and other sources for personal uses in return for influence for or against any nominee or any candidate for the nomination for any elective office* (a bill introduced by the stalwart Charles Barker to highlight La Follette's use of state employees for political work; see the *Milwaukee Sentinel*, 14 and 25 February 1903).	3
	600 A	*A bill to provide for the taxation of railroad companies...* (enacted into law, this bill established the principle of taxing railroad companies on an *ad valorem* basis; see La Follette, *La Follette's Autobiography*, 124; Buenker, *The Progressive Era*, 470–473).	3
	623 A	*A bill to regulate railroad corporations and other common carriers in this state, to create a board of railroad commissioners,... define its duties and powers, prevent the imposition of excessive rates, prevent unjust discrimination in rates charged for the transportation of passengers and freights...* (on this railroad commission bill, see La Follette, *La Follette's Autobiography*, 278–287).	4
	695 A	*A bill to prohibit any increase in the rates of railroad companies in force June 15th, 1902, for the transportation of property in Wisconsin, and providing for the filing of tariff schedules* (a bill introduced immediately after La Follette's dramatic special message to freeze railroad rates; see the *Milwaukee Sentinel*, 9 May 1903).	2
1905	132 A	*A bill relating to the civil service of Wisconsin* (enacted into law, this bill reformed Wisconsin's civil service; see chapter 5).	4
	413 A	*A bill prohibiting legislative counsel and agents from attempting to influence members of the legislature, other than by appearance before the committees thereof* (this bill resulted in an anti-lobby law hailed in Howe, *Wisconsin: An Experiment in Democracy*, 27–28).	2

	444 A	*A bill to regulate railroad corporations and other common carriers in this state, to create a board of railroad commissioners,… define their duties and powers, prevent the imposition of unreasonable rates, prevent unjust discriminations,… and prescribing penalties for the violation of the provisions of this act* (on this railroad commission bill, see Stanley P. Caine, *The Myth of a Progressive Reform: Railroad Regulation in Wisconsin 1903–1910* [Madison, WI, 1970], 76).	4
	724 A	*A bill to provide for the taxation of the property of telephone and telegraph companies or any combination thereof…* (enacted into law, this bill extended the *ad valorem* principle of taxation to telephone and telegraph companies).	2
	99 S	*A bill creating a forestry board…* (on the centrality of reforestation to progressivism, see La Follette, *La Follette's Autobiography*, 364).	1
	268 S	*A bill to regulate railroads and other common carriers in this state, create a board of railroad commissioners,… define their duties, prevent the imposition of unreasonable rates, prevent unjust discriminations,… prescribe penalties for violations…* (the bill that led to the establishment of Wisconsin's railroad commission, the main topic in Caine, *The Myth of a Progressive Reform*).	1
	11 A (extra session)	*A bill… relating to primary elections* (the aim of the bill was to add the "second-choice" principle to the direct primary in cases of no candidate receiving a majority of votes; the defeat of the bill dramatized La Follette's struggle with William D. Connor; see chapter 7).	2
1907	Jt. Res. 16 A	*A joint resolution asking for the passage by congress of (S. 5133) "An act to promote the safety of employes upon railroads by limiting the hours of service thereon"* (efforts to reduce working hours and thereby improve safety for employees formed an important part of progressive labor reform; see also the comment to bill no. 12 S, 1911).	1
	Jt. Res. 33 A	*Joint resolution… relating to legislative power* (the resolution aimed at introducing the initiative to Wisconsin, a direct-democracy measure favored by many progressives; see also Roger E. Wyman, "Voting Patterns in the Progressive Era: Wisconsin as a Test Case" [PhD diss., University of Wisconsin, 1970], 455).	1
	Jt. Res. 68 A	*Joint resolution making application to the congress of the United States to call a convention for proposing amendments to the constitution of the United States* (a call for the direct election of U.S. senators; see the comment to Jt. Res. 18 S, 1903).	1
	15 A	*A bill… relating to passenger rates* (one of Governor Davidson's pet measures, this bill to establish a two-cent flat railroad rate was opposed by some progressives; see chapter 7).	7
	367 A	*A bill… relating to the form of official ballots* (this bill proposed to abolish the "straight" ballot, i.e., the possibility of voting by making just one mark on the ballot; see Brøndal, "The Quest for a New Political Order," 41–42).	3

	575 A	A bill... *relating to child labor* (on efforts to reduce the hours of woman and child labor, see Buenker, *The Progressive Era*, 266–269; also the 1911 Republican platform, the *Blue Book of Wisconsin*, 1911:675).	1
	626 A	A bill... *relating to license fees to be paid by life insurance companies* (on the importance of the regulation of insurance companies to progressives, see Albert Erlebacher, "Herman L. Ekern: The Quiet Progressive" [PhD diss., University of Wisconsin, 1965], 112–153; Buenker, *The Progressive Era*, 502–503).	2
	933 A	A bill... *giving the Wisconsin railroad commission jurisdiction over public utilities, providing for the regulation of such public utilities,... and repealing certain acts in conflict with the provisions hereof* (the 1906 Republican state platform recommended expanding the functions of the railroad commission; see the *Blue Book of Wisconsin*, 1907:1071).	4
1909	Jt. Res. 21 A	*Joint resolution requesting Isaac Stephenson to file an account of expenditures made by him or for him as a candidate for the nomination of United States senator in the primary campaign of 1908* (a device by La Follette allies to question Isaac Stephenson's right to re-election to the U.S. senatorship; see Herbert F. Margulies, *The Decline of the Progressive Movement in Wisconsin, 1890–1920* [Madison, WI, 1968], 115).	2
	20 A	A bill... *relating to hours of labor for women in manufacturing establishments* (see the comment to bill no. 575 A, 1907).	1
	317 A	A bill... *relating to primary elections* (introduced by the stalwart Norwegian-American Assemblyman Twesme to "close" the Wisconsin direct primaries to nonparty members; on the open primary, see chapter 6).	1
	836 A	A bill... *relating to primary elections* (another second-choice proposal; see the comment to bill no. 11 A, 1905, extra legislative session).	1
	122 S	A bill to *confer self government on cities of the first class* (the bill aimed at introducing home rule to Milwaukee, a favorite idea among municipal reformers; see Thelen, *The New Citizenship*, 244–246; Howe, *Wisconsin: An Experiment in Democracy*, 62–63).	3
	123 S	A bill to *provide for non-partisan elections in cities of the first class* (this bill not only promised to make elections less partisan, a popular progressive principle [see chapter 6] but also aimed at weakening Milwaukee's Social Democratic movement).	3
	124 S	A bill to *prohibit corrupt practices in elections in cities of the first class* (a typical progressive pure-politics bill aiming at reducing graft in Milwaukee).	1

1911	29 A	*To provide for the nomination of judicial officers in counties having a population of over 100,000 inhabitants by a non-partisan primary election* (the effort to make judicial elections nonpartisan was in line with progressive ideals of nonpartisanship and pure politics).	4
	230 A	*A bill... relating to primaries and providing for majority nominations by enabling the voter to designate his first and second choice of candidates* (this bill finally established the principle of the "second choice" in the direct primaries; see also Robert S. Maxwell, *Emanuel L. Philipp: Wisconsin Stalwart* [Madison, WI, 1959], 105; and the comment to bill no. 11 A, 1905, extra legislative session).	3
	476 A	*A bill... relating to corrupt practices in primaries and elections and to the publication of information relative to such primaries and elections...* (on this corrupt-practices measure that was enacted into law, see Charles C. McCarthy, *The Wisconsin Idea* [New York, 1912], 101–116; Buenker, *The Progressive Era*, 161).	3
	963 A	*A bill... creating an industrial commission, transferring to such commission the powers and duties of the commissioner of labor and the bureau of labor and industrial statistics, granting such commission certain other powers, and providing for safe and hygienic conditions...* (on the establishment of the Industrial Commission, see McCarthy, *The Wisconsin Idea*, 163; Howe, *Wisconsin: An Experiment in Democracy*, 104–117; Buenker, *The Progressive Era*, 549–550).	2
	12 S	*A bill... relating to the liability of employers for injuries or death sustained by their employes, providing for compensation for the accidental injury or death of employes, establishing an industrial accident board, defining its powers, providing for a review of its awards...* (on the Workmen's Compensation Act, see McCarthy, *The Wisconsin Idea*, 156–166; Robert Asher, "The 1911 Workmen's Compensation Law: A Study in Conservative Labor Reform," *Wisconsin Magazine of History* 57 [Winter 1973–1974], 123–140; Buenker, *The Progressive Era*, 544–546).	2
	45 S	*A bill... relating to the election of senators in congress, and providing for a statement by candidates for the legislature at primary and general election as to whether or not they will promise to support the people's choice for senator in congress* (see the comment to Jt. Res. 18 S, 1903).	4
	573 S	*A bill... relating to the taxation of incomes* (the passage of this income tax bill was considered one of the main progressive achievements of the 1911 legislature; see Howe, *Wisconsin: An Experiment in Democracy*, 137–139; Buenker, *The Progressive Era*, 551–554).	5

1913	Jt. Res. 4 A	*To… give to the people the power to propose laws and to enact or reject the same at the polls, and to approve or reject at the polls any act of the legislature; and… providing for the submission of amendments to the constitution upon the petition of the people* (the aim was to establish the initiative in Wisconsin; see also Wyman, "Voting Patterns in the Progressive Era," 455).	1
	Jt. Res. 38 A	*A joint resolution… relating to state insurance* (on this resolution, aiming at introducing a system of state fire and life insurance, see Erlebacher, "Herman L. Ekern," 162–169).	1
	107 A	*A bill… relating to majority nominations at primaries* (the aim of this bill was to abolish the second-choice amendment to the direct primary; see the comment to bill no. 230 A, 1911).	8
	477 A	*A bill… relating to aid for needy and neglected children, and… providing a penalty* (an early attempt at social welfare legislation).	9
	1086 A	*A bill… creating a market commission, prohibiting monopoly and unfair trade, promoting coöperative enterprises,… and providing penalties* (on Governor McGovern's pet measure of creating a marketing commission, see Margulies, *The Decline of the Progressive Movement in Wisconsin*, 119–121; Buenker, *The Progressive Era*, 644).	1
	347 S	*A bill… relating to time of purchase of street railways by municipalities* (this bill, enacted into law, provided for public ownership of street railways, a pet measure of some urban reformers).	5
	454 S	*A bill… relating to the improvement of the navigation of navigable waters; to the construction, maintenance, and operation of dams and other works necessary therefor; to the inspection of all dams and works and a fee therefor; to a survey of the navigable waters of the state; to the creation of special corporations for the improvement of navigation, and the development of hydraulic power and hydroelectric energy for sale…* (this bill provided for state development of water power in Wisconsin; see also the Republican platform of 1912, the *Blue Book of Wisconsin*, 1913:575; Buenker, *The Progressive Era*, 555–557).	6
	572 S	*A bill… relating to the promotion of economical and efficient production, storage, distribution, and to the reduction of cost and waste therein, providing for direct marketing and for investigation by the industrial commission of methods of production, storage and distribution…* (this bill constituted a vain attempt to save parts of Governor McGovern's pet marketing commission proposal; see also Margulies, *The Decline of the Progressive Movement in Wisconsin*, 119–121; Buenker, *The Progressive Era*, 644).	2

Legislative bills picked for roll-call analysis of attitudes
on temperance legislation

Year	Bill no.	Bill text	Number of roll calls analyzed
1895	208 A	*A bill to restrict the liquor traffic within one-half mile of the bounda-ries of the National Soldiers' Home in Wisconsin.*	9
	183 S	*A bill... relating to penalty for evading law, selling to minors or at prohibited places.*	1
1897	499 A	*A bill to restrict the liquor traffic to within one-half mile of the boundaries of the national soldiers' home in Wisconsin.*	1
1899	103 A	*A bill to prevent the sale of intoxicating liquors within one mile of the grounds of the Soldiers' Home in Milwaukee county.*	1
	155 A	*A bill to prohibit the licensing of saloons within a radius of two hun-dred and fifty feet of any church or school house, from and after the passage of this act...*	3
1901	79 A	*A bill to define the words "intoxicating liquors"... relating to the ex-cise and sale of intoxicating liquors.*	3
1903	77 A	*A bill concerning excise, and the sale of intoxicating liquors, and amendatory of certain sections of the Wisconsin statutes of 1898, re-lating to that subject.*	1
1905	171 A	*A bill to enable qualified electors of any residence district in any town, village or city of the state, to prevent by remonstrance the granting of license for the sale of spirituous, malt, ardent or intoxicat-ing liquors or drinks as a beverage in such district.*	11
1907	589 A	*A bill... authorizing municipal corporations to dispose of all licenses for the sale of intoxicating liquors to a private corporation upon a vote of a majority of the electors thereof.*	1
	916 A	*A bill... prohibiting the granting of saloon licenses near the univer-sity.*	1
	358 S	*A bill... relating to the sale of intoxicating liquors.*	2
1909	633 A	*A bill... relating to minimum liquor license.*	2

	905 A	A bill... relating to excise and providing for a state board of license revocations.	5
1911	Jt. Res. 96 A	*Relating to the use of intoxicating liquors by the students of the university of Wisconsin.*	1
	84 A	A bill... providing for county option elections as to the sale of intoxicating liquors.	4
	188 A	A bill... relating to the sale of intoxicating liquors near a state university, state normal school or county agricultural school.	5
	263 A	A bill... relating to the sale of liquor at public auctions.	2
	1003 A	A bill... authorizing municipal corporations to dispose of all licenses for the sale of intoxicating liquors to a private corporation upon a vote of a majority of the electors thereof.	2
1913	33 A	A bill... relating to excise.	5
	81 A	A bill... relating to the sale of liquors, and providing a penalty.	3
	85 A	A bill... prohibiting treating to intoxicating liquors, and providing a penalty therefor.	1
	411 A	A bill... relating to the issuance of licenses for the sale of intoxicating liquor within one mile of the main building of the state university.	1

Notes

NOTES TO THE INTRODUCTION

[1] A. C. Hurst to Nils P. Haugen, 19 May 1890; Nils P. Haugen to A. C. Hurst, 23 May 1890, in Nils P. Haugen Papers, Library-Archives, Wisconsin Historical Society, Madison, WI.

[2] Jon Gjerde, "The Effect of Community on Migration: Three Minnesota Townships 1885–1905," *Journal of Historical Geography* 5/4 (1979), 406.

[3] The "uprooted" metaphor is first of all associated with Oscar Handlin, *The Uprooted: The Epic Story of the Great Migrations That Made the American People* (Boston, 1951). For the newer perspective, see Frank Thistlethwaite, "Migration from Europe Overseas in the Nineteenth and Twentieth Centuries," in *Population Movements in Modern European History*, ed. Herbert Moller (New York, 1964), 73–92; Charles Tilly and C. Harold Brown, "On Uprooting, Kinship, and the Auspices of Migration," *International Journal of Comparative Sociology* 8 (1967), 139–164; John Bodnar, *The Transplanted: A History of Immigrants in Urban America* (Bloomington, IN, 1985); Jon Gjerde, *From Peasants to Farmers: The Migration from Balestrand, Norway, to the Upper Middle West* (Cambridge, 1985); Jon Gjerde, *The Minds of the West: Ethnocultural Evolution in the Rural Middle West, 1830–1917* (Chapel Hill, NC, 1997); Ann M. Legreid, "The Exodus, Transplanting, and Religious Reorganization of a Group of Norwegian Lutheran Immigrants in Western Wisconsin, c. 1836–1900" (PhD diss., University of Wisconsin, 1985); Robert C. Ostergren, *A Community Transplanted: The Trans-Atlantic Experience of a Swedish Immigrant Settlement in the Upper Middle West, 1835–1915* (Madison, WI, 1988); Jette Mackintosh, *Danskere i Midtvesten: Elk Horn-Kimballton bosættelsen 1870–1925* (Copenhagen, 1993); and Torben Grøngaard Jeppesen, *Dannebrog på den amerikanske prærie: Et dansk koloniprojekt i 1870'erne—landkøb, bygrundlæggelse og integration* (Odense, 2000).

[4] Kathleen Neils Conzen et al., "The Invention of Ethnicity: A Perspective from the USA," *Journal of American Ethnic History* 12 (1992), 4–5. On ethnic identity as a shared sense of peoplehood, see Milton M. Gordon, *Assimilation in American Life: The Role of Race, Religion, and National Origins* (New York, 1964), 23–24. I agree with Yinger's sharpened definition of the ethnic group, requiring

291

that the members share in various activities based on their common origins and culture; see J. Milton Yinger, "Ethnicity," *Annual Review of Sociology* 11 (1985), 159.

[5]Eric Hobsbawm, "Introduction: Inventing Traditions," in *The Invention of Tradition*, ed. Eric Hobsbawm and Terence Ranger (Cambridge, 1983), 1–14; Benedict Anderson, *Imagined Communities: Reflections on the Origin and Spread of Nationalism*, rev. ed. (London, 1991), 205; Werner Sollors, "Introduction: The Invention of Ethnicity," in *The Invention of Ethnicity*, ed. Werner Sollors (New York, 1989), viii–xx; April R. Schultz, *Ethnicity on Parade: Inventing the Norwegian American through Celebration* (Amherst, MA, 1994); H. Arnold Barton, *A Folk Divided: Homeland Swedes and Swedish Americans, 1840–1940* (Carbondale, IL, 1994); Per Nordahl, *Weaving the Ethnic Fabric: Social Networks Among Swedish-American Radicals in Chicago, 1890–1940* (Umeå, 1994); Dag A. Blanck, *Becoming Swedish-American: The Construction of an Ethnic Identity in the Augustana Synod, 1860–1917* (Uppsala, 1997); Daniel Lindmark, ed., *Swedishness Reconsidered: Three Centuries of Swedish-American Identities* (Umeå, 1999).

[6]Philip Gleason, "American Identity and Americanization," in *Harvard Encyclopedia of American Ethnic Groups*, ed. Stephan Thernstrom (Cambridge, MA, 1980), 31.

[7]Nils P. Haugen to J. H. McCourt, 14 April 1892, in Haugen Papers.

[8]We may add that usually the "Scandinavian" and "Scandinavian-American" (or, say, "Norwegian" and "Norwegian-American") labels were used interchangeably, but occasionally a difference could be detected, with the "American" hyphen adding a distinctly New World flavor to the ethnic term. On the one hand, the ethnic churches, the strongest representatives of Old World traditions, never used the "American" mark in their names. On the other hand, an 1892 reader letter in the Norwegian-language paper *Skandinaven* expressed resentment at the fact that a political candidate of German origins was being promoted by a German-language newspaper as a "German American," whereas one of his rivals was being presented only as a "Norwegian" rather than a "Norwegian American"; see "Milwaukier" to *Skandinaven*, 19 October 1892. For a discussion of pan-Scandinavian-American identity, see John R. Jenswold, "The Rise and Fall of Pan-Scandinavianism in Urban America," in *Scandinavians and Other Immigrants in Urban America: The Proceedings of a Research Conference, October 26–27, 1984*, ed. Odd S. Lovoll (Northfield, MN, 1985), 162; Odd S. Lovoll, "A Scandinavian Melting Pot in Chicago," in *Swedish-American Life in Chicago*, ed. Philip J. Anderson and Dag Blanck (Uppsala, 1991), 60–67; Harald Runblom, "A Nordic Melting Pot or 'Unmelting Pot' in North America," in *On Distant Shores: Proceedings of the Marcus Lee Hansen Immigration Conference, Aalborg, Denmark, June 29–July 1, 1992*, ed. Birgit Flemming Larsen, Henning Bender, and Karen Veien (Aalborg, 1993), 231–242; Briant Lindsay Lowell, "The Scandinavians," in *Encyclopedia of American Social History*, ed. Mary Kupiec Cayton, Elliott T. Gorn, and Peter W. Williams (New York, 1993), 2:701–709; and Jørn Brøndal and Dag Blanck, "The

Concept of Being Scandinavian-American," *American Studies in Scandinavia* 34/2 (2002), 14–23.

[9]Some of the pioneering works of this "New Political History" or "ethnocultural interpretation" of American political history are Lee Benson, *The Concept of Jacksonian Democracy: New York as a Test Case*, rev. ed. (New York, 1967); Samuel P. Hays, *American Political History as Social Analysis: Essays by Samuel P. Hays* (Knoxville, TN, 1980); Paul Kleppner, *The Cross of Culture: A Social Analysis of Midwestern Politics 1850–1900* (New York, 1970); Richard J. Jensen, *The Winning of the Midwest: Social and Political Conflict, 1888–1896* (Chicago, 1971); see also Gjerde, *Minds of the West*, 309. For an historiographical overview and spirited defense of the "New Political History," see Ronald P. Formisano, "The New Political History," *International Journal of Social Education* 1 (1986), 5–21. For critiques of the ethnocultural interpretation on methodological grounds, see James E. Wright, "The Ethnocultural Model of Voting: A Behavioral and Historical Critique," *American Behavioral Scientist* 16 (1973), 653–674; J. Morgan Kousser, "The 'New Political History': A Methodological Critique," *Reviews in American History* 4 (1976), 1–14.

[10]On the significance of ethnic labeling to the process of "ethnicization," see Jonathan D. Sarna, "From Immigrants to Ethnics: Toward a New Theory of 'Ethnicization,'" *Ethnicity* 5 (1978), 371–374.

[11]E. C. Wall to William F. Vilas, 18 May 1892, in William F. Vilas Papers, Library-Archives, Wisconsin Historical Society, Madison, WI.

[12]Historiographically, the present study thus provides a possible answer to one central question that a critic of the "ethnocultural" interpretation posed: "Given the deep importance of cultural concerns to voters, it is surprising how minimal were the fruits of their prejudices and values. Only a small proportion of public policies in the nineteenth century were culturally oriented, and the question arises as to why the American electorate was so strikingly unsuccessful at getting results on the ethnoreligious and ethnocultural factors that mattered most." Richard L. McCormick, *The Party Period and Public Policy: American Politics from the Age of Jackson to the Progressive Era* (New York, 1986), 55.

[13]Richard Hofstadter, *The Age of Reform: From Bryan to F.D.R.* (New York, 1955), 35–36; Robert C. Nesbit, *Wisconsin: A History* (Madison, WI, 1973), 6–7.

[14]Quoted from David P. Thelen, *The New Citizenship: Origins of Progressivism in Wisconsin, 1885–1900* (Columbia, MO, 1971), 54.

[15]Frederic C. Howe, *Wisconsin: An Experiment in Democracy* (New York, 1912), vii.

[16]Stanley P. Caine, *The Myth of a Progressive Reform: Railroad Regulation in Wisconsin 1903–1910* (Madison, WI, 1970), 85–95, 202–203.

[17]Roger E. Wyman, "Voting Patterns in the Progressive Era: Wisconsin as a Test Case" (PhD diss., University of Wisconsin, 1970), 296–297; Turner quoted from John D. Buenker, *The Progressive Era, 1893–1914*, vol. 4 of *The History of*

Wisconsin, ed. William Fletcher Thompson (Madison, WI, 1998), 566; Theodore Roosevelt, "Introduction," in Charles C. McCarthy, *The Wisconsin Idea* (New York, 1912), viii; Howe, *Wisconsin: An Experiment in Democracy*.

[18]Peter G. Filene, "An Obituary for 'The Progressive Movement,'" *American Quarterly* 22/1 (1970), 20–34; for the historiography of progressivism, see William G. Anderson, "Progressivism: An Historiographical Essay," *History Teacher* 6/3 (May 1973), 427–452; David M. Kennedy, "Overview: The Progressive Era," *Historian* 37/3 (May 1975), 453–468; Arthur S. Link and Richard L. McCormick, *Progressivism* (Arlington Heights, IL, 1983), 1–25; Steven J. Diner, "Linking Politics and People: The Historiography of the Progressive Era," *OAH Magazine of History* 13/3 (Spring 1999), 5–9.

[19]Gabriel Kolko, *The Triumph of Conservatism: A Reinterpretation of American History, 1900–1916* (Chicago, 1963), 285; Robert H. Wiebe, *The Search for Order, 1877–1920* (New York, 1967), 180.

[20]Among Wisconsin scholars, the proposition that reform was basic to progressivism is hardly controversial, not even among those who during the 1960s and 1970s grew increasingly cynical about La Follette's personal contributions to the movement; see Caine, *The Myth of a Progressive Reform*, xii; Thelen, *The New Citizenship*, 4; Herbert F. Margulies, *The Decline of the Progressive Movement in Wisconsin, 1890–1920* (Madison, WI, 1968), v; Robert S. Maxwell, *La Follette and the Rise of the Progressives in Wisconsin* (Madison, WI, 1956), vii; Robert C. Twombly, "The Reformer as Politician: Robert M. La Follette in the Election of 1900" (master's thesis, University of Wisconsin, 1964), ii. See also Louis Filler, *Progressivism and Muckraking* (New York, 1976), 62. More recent works have been somewhat more favorable to La Follette, e.g., Wyman, "Voting Patterns in the Progressive Era," 243–245, 299; Fred Greenbaum, *Robert Marion La Follette* (Boston, 1975), 43, 62, 226; Carl R. Burgchardt, *Robert M. La Follette, Sr.: The Voice of Conscience* (New York, 1992), 6; Jørn Brøndal, "The Quest for a New Political Order: Robert M. La Follette and the Genesis of the Direct Primary in Wisconsin, 1891–1904" (master's thesis, University of Copenhagen, 1993), 5–6, 58–61; Bernard A. Weisberger, *The La Follettes of Wisconsin: Love and Politics in Progressive America* (Madison, WI, 1994), 324–326. Finally, the older "panegyrical" literature on La Follette and progressive reform in Wisconsin includes Robert M. La Follette's colorful yet distorted *La Follette's Autobiography: A Personal Narrative of Political Experiences*, rev. ed. (Madison, WI, 1913); Albert O. Barton, *La Follette's Winning of Wisconsin (1894–1904)* (Madison, WI, 1922); Belle C. La Follette and Fola La Follette, *Robert M. La Follette, June 14, 1855–June 18, 1925*, 2 vols. (New York, 1953).

[21]For an earlier discussion of the progressive break with tradition, see David P. Thelen, "Robert La Follette's Leadership, 1891–1896: The Old and New Politics and the Dilemma of the Progressive Politician," *Pacific Northwest Quarterly* 62 (July 1971), 97.

[22]On the composite nature of progressivism, see George E. Mowry, "The

Progressive Era, 1900–1920: The Reform Persuasion," *American Historical Association Pamphlets* 212 (1958), 34; Link and McCormick, *Progressivism*, 9; David P. Thelen, "Social Tensions and the Origins of Progressivism," *Journal of American History* 56 (1969), 223–241; Buenker, *The Progressive Era*, 611–612. On Scandinavian-American support for progressivism, see Jørgen Weibull, "The Wisconsin Progressives, 1900–1914," *Mid-America* 47 (July 1965), 209–211; David L. Brye, "Wisconsin Scandinavians and Progressivism, 1900–1950," *Norwegian-American Studies* 27 (Northfield, MN, 1977), 163–193; David L. Brye, *Wisconsin Voting Patterns in the Twentieth Century, 1900-1950* (New York, 1979), 225–295; Lowell J. Soike, *Norwegian Americans and the Politics of Dissent, 1880–1924* (Northfield, MN, 1991), 119–126; Wyman, "Voting Patterns in the Progressive Era," 624–644, 653–660, 662–671; and Jon Wefald, *A Voice of Protest: Norwegians in American Politics, 1890–1917* (Northfield, MN, 1971).

[23]John Higham, "From Process to Structure: Formulations of American Immigration History," in *American Immigrants and Their Generations*, ed. Dag Blanck and Peter Kivisto (Urbana, IL, 1989), 14.

[24]Peter A. Munch, "Segregation and Assimilation of Norwegian Settlements in Wisconsin," *Studies and Records* 18 (Northfield, MN, 1954), 105–106; Gordon, *Assimilation in American Life*, 74–83; Fredrik Barth, "Introduction," in *Ethnic Groups and Boundaries: The Social Organization of Culture Difference*, ed. Fredrik Barth (Bergen, 1969), 14–15.

NOTES TO CHAPTER ONE

[1]"The Diary and Account Book of Kristoffer O. Skauge, 1888–1896," Library-Archives, Wisconsin Historical Society, Madison, WI. The following account of Skauge's voyage and arrival in America is based on this Norwegian-language source.

[2]Ingrid Semmingsen, *Veien mot vest: Utvandringen fra Norge til Amerika, 1825–1865* (Oslo, 1941), 158.

[3]On the history of the *Adriatic*, see the Norway Heritage Project, "One Hundred Years of Emigrant Ships from Norway," n.p., http://www.norwayheritage .com/p_ship.asp?sh=adri1 (accessed 9 January 2004).

[4]Actually, king Magnus Barefoot of Norway was killed by the Irish during a looting expedition in 1103.

[5]If we take the year 1875 as the first in which steam totally dominated the trans-Atlantic passenger traffic from Europe (see Maldwyn A. Jones, *American Immigration* [Chicago, 1960], 184), then, using official American immigration data, 73.2 percent of all European trans-Atlantic migrants from 1820 to 1920 traveled by steam. Calculated from data in U.S. Bureau of the Census, *Historical Statistics of the United States: From Colonial Times to the Present* (New York, 1976), 105–106.

[6]J. D. Gould, "European Inter-Continental Emigration 1815–1914: Patterns

and Causes," *Journal of European Economic History* 8 (1979), 596–696. According to my calculations from the official Scandinavian statistics, 97.2 percent of the Norwegian migrants, 99.2 percent of the Swedish, and 94.7 percent of the Danish headed for the USA. See Danmarks Statistik, *Statistisk Tabelværk*, 5. række, litra A:5 (Copenhagen, 1905), 42–43; Danmarks Statistik, *Statistiske Undersøgelser* 19 (Copenhagen, 1966), 117; Adolph Jensen, "Migration Statistics of Denmark, Norway, and Sweden," in *International Migrations*, ed. Imre Ferenczi and Walter Willcox, 2 vols. (New York, 1929), 1:747, 752; Nils William Olsson and Erik Wikén, *U.S. Passenger Arrival Statistics for Swedes Landing in the U.S., 1840–1850* (Stockholm, 1995), 27–140; and Sten Carlsson, "Chronology and Composition of Swedish Emigration to America," in *From Sweden to America: A History of the Migration*, ed. Harald Runblom and Hans Norman (Uppsala, 1976), 117–119.

[7]Theodore Blegen, *Norwegian Migration to America, 1825–1860* (Northfield, MN, 1931), 46–48; Semmingsen, *Veien mot vest, 1825–1865*, 16.

[8]George M. Stephenson, *The Religious Aspects of Swedish Immigration: A Study of Immigrant Churches* (Minneapolis, 1932), 49–73; Kjell Söderberg, *Den första massutvandringen: En studie av befolkningsrörlighet och emigration utgående från Alfta socken i Hälsingland 1846–1895* (Umeå, 1981), 225–226.

[9]Between 1850 and 1904, some 16,800 Danish Mormons emigrated to America; see Kristian Hvidt, *Flugten til Amerika eller Drivkræfter i masseudvandringen fra Danmark 1868–1914* (Århus, 1971), 280–300, and *Danske veje vestpå—en bog om udvandringen til Amerika* (Copenhagen, 1976), 48–51.

[10]On the evasion of military duties as a cause of migration, see Hvidt, *Flugten til Amerika*, 263–266; Ann-Sofie Kälvemark, "Fear of Military Service—A Cause of Emigration?" in Runblom and Norman, *From Sweden to America*, 174; Lars Ljungmark, *Swedish Exodus* (Evanston, IL, 1979), 41; Blegen, *Norwegian Migration to America, 1825–1860*, 171–172; and Ingrid Semmingsen, *Veien mot vest: Utvandringen fra Norge til Amerika, 1865–1915* (Oslo, 1950), 496–497.

[11]Hvidt, *Flugten til Amerika*, 273–280; Blegen, *Norwegian Migration to America, 1825–1860*, 287–307; Semmingsen, *Veien mot vest, 1865–1915*, 392–415; Terje I. Leiren, *Marcus Thrane: A Norwegian Radical in America* (Northfield, MN, 1987), 15. On people agitating for emigration for political reasons, see Peter Sørensen Vig, "Efterretninger om nogle af de første danske Nybyggere i Wisconsin," in *Danske i Amerika*, ed. Peter Sørensen Vig, 2 pts. in 1 vol. (Minneapolis, 1908), 1:252; Hvidt, *Flugten til Amerika*, 270–273; William J. Orr, "Rasmus Sørensen and the Beginnings of Danish Settlement in Wisconsin," *Wisconsin Magazine of History* 65/3 (Spring 1982), 209; Semmingsen, *Veien mot vest, 1865–1915*, 68–70; H. Arnold Barton, *A Folk Divided: Homeland Swedes and Swedish Americans, 1840–1940* (Carbondale, IL, 1994), 74; Ljungmark, *Swedish Exodus*, 37–39; Lars-Göran Tedebrand, "Strikes and Political Radicalism in Sweden and Emigration to the United States," in *American Labor and Immigration History, 1877–1920s: Recent European Research*, ed. Dirk Hoerder (Urbana, IL, 1983), 221–234; Björn Rondahl, "Ljusne 1906—en politiskt motiverad utvandring," in

Utvandring: Den svenska emigrationen till Amerika i historiskt perspektiv, ed. Ann-Sofie Kälvemark (Stockholm, 1973), 119–129.

[12]Blegen, *Norwegian Migration to America, 1825–1860,* 84–85; Semmingsen, *Veien mot vest, 1865–1915,* 74; Barton, *Folk Divided,* 13, 15, 23–25.

[13]Hvidt, *Flugten til Amerika,* 237–245.

[14]Carlsson, "Chronology and Composition of Swedish Emigration," 141–147; Hvidt, *Flugten til Amerika,* 118. Semmingsen argued that migration in stages often caused rurals to dwell in cities for a while before leaving for America; Nilsson insisted that many such individuals stayed in urban areas for so long that they were urbanized. See Semmingsen, *Veien mot vest, 1865–1915,* 195, 236, 498–499; Ingrid Semmingsen, "Emigration from Scandinavia," *Scandinavian Economic History Review* 20 (1972), 52–54; Fred Nilsson, *Emigrationen från Stockholm til Nordamerika 1880-1893: En studie i urban utvandring* (Stockholm, 1970), 11, 61–87.

[15]Semmingsen, *Veien mot vest, 1825–1865,* 50, 192–195, 215; David C. Mauk, *The Colony That Rose from the Sea: Norwegian Maritime Migration and Community in Brooklyn, 1850–1910* (Northfield, MN, 1997), 4.

[16]Hans Try, *To kulturer, en stat, 1851–1884,* vol. 11 of *Norges historie,* ed. Knut Mykland (Oslo, 1979), 153–201; Kristian Hvidt, *Det folkelige gennembrud og dets mænd, 1850–1900,* vol. 11 of *Gyldendal og Politikens Danmarkshistorie,* ed. Olaf Olsen (Copenhagen, 1990), 19; W. R. Mead, *An Historical Geography of Scandinavia* (London, 1981), 269.

[17]Hvidt, *Flugten til Amerika,* 353–375, 460–478; Semmingsen, *Veien mot vest, 1825–1865,* 139. Berit Brattne and Sune Åkerman, "The Importance of the Transport Sector for Mass Emigration," in Runblom and Norman, *From Sweden to America,* 199, asserted that Hvidt exaggerated the aggressive activities of the steamship company agents but ignored Hvidt's suggestion that the behavior of the agents was more moderate after 1880; cf. Hvidt, *Flugten til Amerika,* 478.

[18]Lars Ljungmark, *For Sale, Minnesota: Organized Promotion of Scandinavian Immigration 1866–1873* (Göteborg, 1971).

[19]Theodore Blegen, *Norwegian Migration to America: The American Transition* (Northfield, MN, 1940), 383–385.

[20]Gould, "European Inter-Continental Emigration," 653; Jette D. Søllinge and Niels Thomsen, *De danske aviser 1634–1989,* 3 vols. (Odense, 1989), 2:29–42; Try, *To kulturer, en stat,* 394–398; Thomas von Vegesack, "Den snabba nyheten," in *Industri och folkrörelser 1866–1920,* vol. 9 of *Den svenska historien,* ed. Gunvor Grenholm (Stockholm, 1968), 284–285.

[21]Blegen, *Norwegian Migration to America, 1825–1860,* 196–213, 239–266; Erik Helmer Pedersen, *Drømmen om Amerika* (Copenhagen, 1985), 22.

[22]Among the Swedes perhaps 50 percent of all emigrants traveled on prepaid tickets; among the Norwegians and Danes somewhat lower percentages; see Hvidt, *Flugten til Amerika,* 348–349.

[23]Lars Ljungmark, "The Organized Stock Effect," in *From Scandinavia to America: Proceedings from a Conference at Gl. Holtegaard*, ed. Steffen Elmer Jørgensen, Lars Scheving, and Niels Peter Stilling (Odense, 1987), 104–116.

[24]K. P. Boyd to *Skandinaven*, 2 September 1896.

[25]Quoted from Blegen, *Norwegian Migration to America: The American Transition*, 472; see also Semmingsen, *Veien mot vest, 1865–1915*, 496.

[26]Sune Åkerman, "Theories and Methods of Migration Research," in Runblom and Norman, *From Sweden to America*, 27–32.

[27]Sven Lundkvist, *Folkrörelserna i det svenska samhället, 1850–1920* (Uppsala, 1977), 2, 45, 153–160.

[28]Quoted from Richard Hofstadter, *The American Political Tradition and the Men Who Made It* (New York, 1948), 31.

[29]Timothy J. Hatton and Jeffrey T. Williamson, "What Drove the Mass Migrations from Europe in the Late Nineteenth Century?" *Population and Development Review* 20/3 (September 1994), 539–540, 556.

[30]Sten Carlsson, "Från familjeutvandring till ensamutvandring: En utvecklingslinje i den svenska emigrationens historia," in *Emigrationer: En bok till Vilhelm Moberg 20.8.1968*, ed. Magnus von Platen (Stockholm, 1968), 115–117; Ingrid Semmingsen, "Family Emigration from Bergen, 1874–1892," *Americana Norvegica* 3 (1971), 40; Hvidt, *Flugten til Amerika*, 195–197; Semmingsen, *Veien mot vest, 1865–1915*, 492–493.

[31]Semmingsen, *Veien mot vest, 1865–1915*, 62; Dorothy Swaine Thomas, *Social and Economic Aspects of Swedish Population Movements, 1750–1933* (New York, 1941), 95.

[32]Hvidt, *Det folkelige gennembrud*, 19; Andreas A. Svalestuen, "Nordisk emigrasjon: En komparativ oversikt," in *Emigrationen fra Norden indtil 1. Verdenskrig: Rapporter til det nordiske historikermøde i København, 9–12 August 1971* (Copenhagen, 1971), 9–11, 19, 22–23; Rondo Cameron, *A Concise Economic History of the World: From Paleolithic Times to the Present* (New York, 1989), 191.

[33]Hvidt, *Flugten til Amerika*, 244–245; Hvidt, *Det folkelige gennembrud*, 26–28, 169; Sten Carlsson, "Why Did They Leave?" in *Perspectives on Swedish Immigration: Proceedings of the International Conference on the Swedish Heritage in the Upper Midwest, April 1–3, 1976, University of Minnesota, Duluth*, ed. Nils Hasselmo (Chicago, 1978), 26.

[34]Svalestuen, "Nordisk emigrasjon," 13–14. In Europe in 1850–1900, Norwegian emigration intensity was second only to Irish.

[35]Carlsson, "Why Did They Leave?" 27; Hvidt, *Det folkelige gennembrud*, 171.

[36]Carlsson, "Från familjeutvandring till ensamutvandring," 115–117; Hvidt, *Flugten til Amerika*, 195–197; Semmingsen, *Veien mot vest, 1865–1915*, 492–493.

[37]Cameron, *A Concise Economic History*, 252; Hvidt, *Det folkelige gennem-*

brud, 304–305; Try, *To kulturer, en stat,* 259–260; Sten Carlsson, "Rationalisering inom jordbruket 1870–1920," in Grenholm, *Industri och folkrörelser,* 138.

[38]William Ashworth, *A Short History of the International Economy since 1850,* 3rd ed. (London, 1975), 21–22.

[39]John Michael Quigley, "An Economic Model of Swedish Emigration," *The Quarterly Journal of Economics* 86 (February 1972), 126; Semmingsen, *Veien mot vest, 1865–1915,* 507–508.

[40]John Bodnar, *The Transplanted: A History of Immigrants in Urban America* (Bloomington, IN, 1985), 6.

[41]Semmingsen, *Veien mot vest, 1865–1915,* 506–507; Lars-Göran Tedebrand, "Remigration from America to Sweden," in Runblom and Norman, *From Sweden to America,* 209.

[42]Martin A. Egge to *Skandinaven,* 14 July 1897.

[43]My calculation from a database lent me courtesy of Danes Worldwide Archives, Aalborg, Denmark, based upon the information entered into police protocols on Danes departing for the New World; see also Christian D. Nokkentved, "Danes, Denmark and Racine, 1837–1924: A Study of Danish and Overseas Migration" (PhD diss., University of Illinois, 1984). Reports of Danish patterns of chain migration and of provincial loyalties and suspicions do exist, to be sure, for instance that of Jutlanders in the town of Viborg, Minnesota, regarding people from Funen and Zealand with disdain; see Henrik Cavling, *Fra Amerika,* 2 vols. (Copenhagen, 1897), 2:143–144; see also Steffen Elmer Jørgensen, "'Emigration Fever': The Formation of an Early Rural Emigration Tradition on Lolland-Falster and Møn, Three Danish Islands, c. 1830–1871" (PhD diss., European University Institute, Florence, 1991).

[44]Robert C. Ostergren, *A Community Transplanted: The Trans-Atlantic Experience of a Swedish Immigrant Settlement in the Upper Middle West, 1835–1915* (Madison, WI, 1988); Jon Gjerde, *From Peasants to Farmers: The Migration from Balestrand, Norway, to the Upper Middle West* (Cambridge, 1985).

[45]Peer O. Strømme, *Erindringer* (Minneapolis, 1923), 45.

[46]J. O. Taylor to *Skandinaven,* 17 February 1897.

[47]Norway was a little Illinois settlement southwest of Chicago; see Olaf M. Norlie, *History of the Norwegian People in America* (Decorah, IA, 1925), 211.

[48]In the present work, whenever a European-American ethnic group is referred to, in a statistical sense we are dealing with *two generations of ethnics*: the immigrants themselves and those born in America having either both parents born in the same European country or one born in that European country, the other in America. As far as *Scandinavian* Americans are concerned, included are also individuals of mixed Scandinavian parentage.

[49]My calculations from the U.S. Bureau of the Census, *Eleventh Census of the*

United States, 1890: Population, Part One (Washington, D.C., 1895), clxvi–clxvii and 698–699.

[50]*Eleventh Census of the United States, 1890,* clxvi–clxvii, 45, 667–668; Robert C. Nesbit, *Wisconsin: A History* (Madison, WI, 1973), 548.

[51]Carlton C. Qualey, *Norwegian Settlement in the United States* (Northfield, MN, 1938), 47–51; Blegen, *Norwegian Migration to America, 1825–1860,* 118–132.

[52]Blegen, *Norwegian Migration to America, 1825–1860,* 194–195.

[53]Robert C. Ostergren, "The Euro-American Settlement of Wisconsin, 1830–1920," in *Wisconsin Land and Life,* ed. Robert C. Ostergren and Thomas R. Vale (Madison, WI, 1997), 154–155; Robert C. Nesbit, *Urbanization and Industrialization, 1873–1893,* vol. 3 of *The History of Wisconsin,* ed. William Fletcher Thompson (Madison, WI, 1985), 46; John D. Buenker, *The Progressive Era, 1893–1914,* vol. 4 of *The History of Wisconsin,* ed. William Fletcher Thompson (Madison, WI, 1998), 82.

[54]Norlie, *History of the Norwegian People in America,* 349; Thomas J. Archdeacon, *Becoming American: An Ethnic History* (New York, 1983), 110.

[55]In 1905, 68.6 percent of Stoughton's family heads were of Norwegian parentage; city wards 4, 7, 8, 9, and 10 of Eau Claire were all more than 30 percent Norwegian-American, as were city wards 7, 9, and 10 of La Crosse. These data were calculated from the 11-volume typewritten "A Retabulation of Population Schedules from the Wisconsin State Census of 1905," table 26, "Number and Distribution of Family Heads by Nativity and Minor Civil Divisions," Library-Archives, Wisconsin Historical Society, Madison, WI. That table gives the national composition of all the family heads in Wisconsin's 1,654 minor civil divisions on the basis of parents' nativity. In the present work, all the data and calculations from "A Retabulation from the Wisconsin State Census of 1905" derive from a database I created on the basis of this table.

[56]Arnold Strickson and Robert A. Ibarra, "The Changing Dynamics of Ethnicity: Norwegians and Tobacco in Wisconsin," *Ethnic and Racial Studies* 6/2 (April 1983), 180–182.

[57]The exact share of family heads of Norwegian parentage was 84.4 percent in Pleasant Springs; 82.7 percent in Christiana; 88.3 percent in Pigeon; 85.4 percent in Unity; 85.4 percent in Scandinavia; 90.2 percent in Westby; and 94.9 percent in Coon; see "A Retabulation from the Wisconsin State Census of 1905."

[58]My calculations on the basis of "A Retabulation from the Wisconsin State Census of 1905"; see also Jørn Brøndal, "Etniske enklaver i det amerikanske Midtvesten," *1066: Tidsskrift for historie* 29/2 (1999), 3–12.

[59]The *Eleventh Census of the United States, 1890,* 668, counted 17,660 Polish immigrants in Wisconsin but did not enumerate people of Polish parentage; probably the share of second-generation Polish Americans was small, however, since Polish migration to America only truly took off after 1890.

[60]Albert O. Barton, "The Scandinavian Element in Wisconsin," in *Wiscon-*

sin: Its History and Its People, 1634–1924, ed. Milo M. Quaife, 4 vols. (Chicago, 1924), 2:118.

[61]Norlie, *History of the Norwegian People in America*, 349.

[62]My calculation on the basis of "A Retabulation from the Wisconsin State Census of 1905." City ward 2 of Ashland was more than 30 percent Swedish-American, whereas wards 5 and 9 in Superior and 1 and 2 in Marinette were more than 25 percent Swedish-American.

[63]Ostergren, *A Community Transplanted*, 161.

[64]My calculation on the basis of "A Retabulation from the Wisconsin State Census of 1905." Stockholm was 88.9 percent Swedish-American, Trade Lake 91.7 percent. On real estate values in Wisconsin in 1900, see Thomas J. Pressly and William H. Scofield, eds., *Farm Real Estate Values in the United States by Counties, 1850–1959* (Seattle, 1965), 32.

[65]Torben Grøngaard Jeppesen, *Dannebrog på den amerikanske prærie: Et dansk koloniprojekt i 1870'erne—landkøb, bygrundlæggelse og integration* (Odense, 2000), 43–47; see also Thomas P. Christensen, "Danish Settlement in Wisconsin," *Wisconsin Magazine of History* 12/1 (September 1928), 26.

[66]Nesbit, *Urbanization and Industrialization*, 15.

[67]My calculation on the basis of "A Retabulation from the Wisconsin State Census of 1905"; Norlie, *History of the Norwegian People in America*, 349.

[68]A. Bobjerg, *En dansk Nybygd i Wisconsin: 40 Aar i Storskoven (1869–1909)* (Copenhagen, 1909), 17. According to "A Retabulation from the Wisconsin State Census of 1905," Luck was 88.5 percent Danish American, Withee/Hixon 58.1 percent, and New Denmark 50.2 percent.

[69]Calculation on the basis of "A Retabulation from the Wisconsin State Census of 1905."

[70]It is true that, according to "A Retabulation from the Wisconsin State Census of 1905," 8.3 percent of the family heads in Milwaukee's eighth ward were of Norwegian parentage.

[71]According to calculations on the basis of "A Retabulation from the Wisconsin State Census of 1905," only 2.3 percent of Wisconsin's family heads of English parentage clustered together in minor civil divisions that were dominated by more than 50 percent of their own ethnic group; among Irish Americans the corresponding figure was just 0.4 percent; among Polish Americans, on the other hand, 35.6 percent; and among German Americans fully 59.6 percent. See Brøndal, "Etniske enklaver," 8.

[72]The sense of continuity is conveyed by the fact that of the top ten favorite Danish-American counties in 1900, eight were also favorites in 1890 and 1920, whereas something similar was true of seven of ten counties among the Norwegian Americans and Swedish Americans; see *Eleventh Census of the United States, 1890*, 667; U.S. Bureau of the Census, *Twelfth Census of the United States, 1900*,

vol. 1, *Population, Part One* (Washington, D.C., 1901), 357–367; U.S. Bureau of the Census, *Fourteenth Census of the United States, 1920,* vol. 1, *Population,* 1135–1136; see also Guy-Harold Smith, "Notes on the Distribution of the Foreign-Born Scandinavian in Wisconsin in 1905," *Wisconsin Magazine of History* 14/4 (June 1931), 425.

[73]Blegen, *Norwegian Migration to America: The American Transition,* 97. According to "A Retabulation from the Wisconsin State Census of 1905," Garfield boasted an 82.6 percent Scandinavian-American presence (7.9 percent Danish-American, 36.5 percent Norwegian-American, and 38.2 percent Swedish-American); Baronette was 72.1 percent Scandinavian-American (29.4 percent Danish-American, 10.3 percent Norwegian-American, and 32.4 percent Swedish-American).

[74]*Hemlandet,* 20 October 1892; Einar Haugen, "Language and Immigration," *Studies and Records* 10 (Northfield, MN, 1938), 19–20.

[75]Nils P. Haugen, *Pioneer and Political Reminiscences* (Madison, 1929), 18.

[76]Einar Haugen, *The Norwegian Language in America: A Study in Bilingual Behavior,* 2 vols. (Bloomington, IN, 1969), 1:94; Nils Hasselmo, *Amerikasvenska: En bok om språkutvecklingen i Svensk-Amerika* (Lund, 1974), 110; Bobjerg, *En dansk Nybygd i Wisconsin,* 70–71.

[77]*Arbeideren,* 23 February 1886. According to a local history, Strum took shape as early as 1877; its post office, however, dated from 1885. See Roy Matson, "A History of Strum and the Town of Unity," 29, http://www.norhemian.com/0529strumhistory.html (accessed 8 January 2004).

[78]Sivert Rekstad to *Skandinaven,* 27 February 1897.

[79]See the figures for Unity Township in "A Retabulation from the Wisconsin State Census of 1905"; Martin Ulvestad, *Norge i Amerika, med Kart* (Minneapolis, 1901), 494.

[80]Olaf M. Norlie, ed., *Norsk Lutherske Menigheter i Amerika, 1843–1916,* 2 vols. (Minneapolis, 1918), 1:230.

[81]*Reform,* 14 April 1896.

[82]"The Diary and Account Book of Kristoffer O. Skauge," 14.

[83]Mead, *An Historical Geography of Scandinavia,* 225, 250; Try, *To kulturer, en stat,* 292–300; Hvidt, *Flugten til Amerika,* 139.

[84]Try, *To kulturer, en stat,* 365–373.

[85]Søllinge and Thomsen, *De danske aviser,* 44; Gro Hageman, *Det moderne gjennombrud, 1870–1905,* vol. 9 of *Aschehougs Norgeshistorie* (Oslo, 1997), 202–203; von Vegesack, "Den snabba nyheten," 284–287.

[86]Per Fuglum, *Norge i støpeskjeen,* vol. 12 of *Norges Historie,* ed. Knut Mykland (Oslo, 1978), 83–130.

[87]Dag A. Blanck, *Becoming Swedish-American: The Construction of an Ethnic Identity in the Augustana Synod, 1860–1917* (Uppsala, 1997), 21–22. According to

George M. Stephenson, "The Mind of the Scandinavian Immigrant," *Studies and Records* 4 (Northfield, MN, 1929), 71, "Norway in the nineteenth century experienced a renaissance of nationalism dating from the 'Seventeenth of May,' but the Swedish immigrant left his country when national feeling was at a very low ebb."

[88]Lundkvist, *Folkrörelserna i det svenska samhället*, 20, 59, 159, 189; Hans Try, *Assosiasjonsånd og foreningsvekst i Norge: Forskningsoversyn og perspektiv* (Bergen, 1985), 22–30; Peter Gundelach, *Sociale bevægelser og samfundsændringer: Nye sociale grupperinger og deres organisationsformer ved overgangen til ændrede samfundstyper* (Århus, 1988), 124–128.

[89]Uffe Østergård, "Peasants and Danes: The Danish National Identity and Political Culture," *Comparative Studies in Society and History* 34/1 (January 1992), 5; Try, *To kulturer, en stat*, 365–373; Richard Hofstadter, *The Age of Reform: From Bryan to F.D.R.* (New York, 1955), 23–59.

[90]The figures were calculated by taking all males above the age of 20 in each country as a starting point and then reducing by age and income/status requirements in order to find the actual share of eligible voters. My calculations are based on the information on national age and income/status requirements in Stein Kuhnle, *Patterns of Social and Political Mobilization: A Historical Analysis of the Nordic Countries* (London, 1975), 10–28, and Kjeld Winding, Pirko Rommi, Rolf Danielsen, and Per Hultquist, "Framveksten av de politiske partier i de nordiske land på 1800-tallet," in *Rapporter til det nordiske historikermøte i Bergen 1964* (Bergen, 1964), 78–186; as well as on the data on age cohorts in the 1860s and 1870s in Det Statistiske Bureau, *Statistisk Tabelværk*, 3. række:1 (Copenhagen, 1863), 46–47; Kungl. statistiska Centralbyrån, *Statistisk årsbok för Sverige* 1 (Stockholm, 1914), 8; and Det Statistiske Centralbureau, *Resultaterne af Folketællingen i Norge i Januar 1876*, 1 (Oslo, 1878), 97. In Sweden, women were actually granted suffrage in communal elections in 1862.

[91]Henrik Becker-Christensen, *Skandinaviske drømme og politiske realiteter: Den politiske skandinavisme i Danmark 1830–1850* (Århus, 1981), 267; Hvidt, *Det folkelige gennembrud*, 119–120; Try, *To kulturer, en stat*, 51–52; Sten Carlsson, "Neutralitetspolitik och unionstvister 1864–1885," in Grenholm, *Industri och folkrörelser*, 73.

[92]J. D. Beck to Andrew H. Dahl, 23 July 1914, in Andrew H. Dahl Papers, Library-Archives, Wisconsin Historical Society, Madison, WI.

[93]V. C. S. Topsøe, *Fra Amerika* (Copenhagen, 1872), 213.

[94]Henrik Cavling, *Fra Amerika*, 1:156.

[95]See Jonathan D. Sarna, "From Immigrants to Ethnics: Toward a New Theory of 'Ethnicization,'" *Ethnicity* 5 (1978), 371–374.

[96]Bayrd Still, "Norwegian-Americans and Wisconsin Politics in the Forties," *Studies and Records* 8 (Northfield, MN, 1934), 58–59; Blegen, *Norwegian Migration to America, 1825–1860*, 259.

[97]B. E. Bergesen to *Amerika*, 29 August 1902. See also Jørn Brøndal and Dag

Blanck, "The Concept of Being Scandinavian-American," *American Studies in Scandinavia* 34/2 (2002), 14–15.

[98]Barton, *Folk Divided*, 27; Merle Curti, *The Making of an American Community: A Case Study of Democracy in a Frontier Community* (Stanford, 1959), 97–98.

[99]Topsøe, *Fra Amerika*, 213.

[100]On the ethnic temper during World War I, see Carl H. Chrislock, *Ethnicity Challenged: The Upper Midwest Norwegian-American Experience in World War I* (Northfield, MN, 1981); Sture Lindmark, *Swedish America, 1914–1932: Studies in Ethnicity with Emphasis on Illinois and Minnesota* (Uppsala, 1971), 134–136; John Higham, *Strangers in the Land: Patterns of American Nativism, 1860–1925*, rev. ed. (New Brunswick, NJ, 1988), 21–22, 68, 234–235.

[101]Quoted from Frederick Hale, *The Swedes in Wisconsin* (Madison, WI, 1983), 13.

[102]Nils Holm to Nils P. Haugen, 12 June 1894, in Nils P. Haugen Papers, Library-Archives, Wisconsin Historical Society, Madison, WI.

[103]B. Dahley to *Skandinaven*, 28 February 1894.

[104]M. A. Sommer to *Skandinaven*, 24 January 1894; "A.O." to *Hemlandet*, 18 October 1894.

[105]*Skandinaven*, 24 January 1891.

[106]For a similar dating of ethnic assertiveness among Norwegian Americans and Swedish Americans, see Barton, *Folk Divided*, 43; Blanck, *Becoming Swedish-American*, 211–212; Odd S. Lovoll, *The Promise of America: A History of the Norwegian-American People* (Minneapolis, 1984), 177.

[107]Indeed, the Swedish-American press alone was America's second-largest foreign-language press; see Anna Williams, *Skribent i Svensk-Amerika: Jakob Bonggren, journalist och poet* (Uppsala, 1991), 31.

[108]Examples of filiopietistic works are Norlie, *History of the Norwegian People in America*; C. F. Peterson, *Sverige i Amerika: Kulturhistoriska och Biografiska Teckningar* (Chicago, 1898); Vig, *Danske i Amerika*; and O. N. Nelson, ed., *History of the Scandinavians and Successful Scandinavians in the United States*, 2 vols., rev. ed. (1904; reprint, New York, 1969).

[109]Quoted from Odd S. Lovoll, ed., *Cultural Pluralism versus Assimilation: The Views of Waldemar Ager* (Northfield, MN, 1977), 46–49. In a similar vein, a prominent Norwegian American of Minneapolis suggested, "Had you not better leave off bolstering our reputation and furnishing us a certificate of character from the old country, and see to it that we establish one here ourselves by our own merits?" A. Ueland to Rasmus B. Anderson, 4 December 1887, in Rasmus B. Anderson Papers, Library-Archives, Wisconsin Historical Society, Madison, WI.

[110]Quoted from from H. Arnold Barton, "Clio and Swedish America," in

Hasselmo, *Perspectives on Swedish Immigration*, 6; see also Blanck, *Becoming Swedish-American*, 217–218.

[111]On *Syttende Mai* celebrations, see David Mauk, "Syttende Mai Vignettes from Minneapolis-St. Paul: The Changing Meaning of Norway's Constitution Day in the Capital of Norwegian America, 1869–1914," *American Studies in Scandinavia* 34/2 (Fall 2002), 32–53; also, for instance, "O.F." to *Skandinaven*, 28 May 1890.

[112]Lloyd Hustvedt, *Rasmus Bjørn Anderson: Pioneer Scholar* (Northfield, MN, 1966), 311.

[113]*Skandinaven*, 30 May 1894; *Folkets Avis*, 14 June 1900.

[114]Blanck, *Becoming Swedish-American*, 196–199; "Ung svensk" to *Hemlandet*, 18 September 1890; "En närvärande" to *Hemlandet*, 25 September 1890; "Kansas-Olle" to *Hemlandet*, 20 October 1892; "Svensk-amerikan" to *Hemlandet*, 26 October 1898.

[115]Chr. Ravn to Nils P. Haugen, 23 March 1893, in Haugen Papers; Dag Blanck, "Swedish Americans and the 1893 Columbian Exposition," in *Swedish-American Life in Chicago*, ed. Philip J. Anderson and Dag Blanck (Uppsala, 1991), 284.

[116]See pages 3–4 in the Introduction.

[117]*Superior Tidende*, 25 August 1898.

[118]*Superior Tidende*, 28 July 1911; see also Brøndal and Blanck, "Concept of Being Scandinavian-American," 21.

[119]*Amerika*, 26 August 1910; see also Milton M. Gordon, *Assimilation in American Life: The Role of Race, Religion, and National Origins* (New York, 1964), 135; Jon Gjerde, *The Minds of the West: Ethnocultural Evolution in the Rural Middle West, 1830–1917* (Chapel Hill, NC, 1997), 59–60, 324–325; Peter A. Munch, "The Church as Complementary Identity," in *The Scandinavian Presence in North America*, ed. Erik J. Friis (New York, 1973), 63–66.

[120]Gjerde, *Minds of the West*, 154–156; Nesbit, *Wisconsin: A History*, 321–328; Robert H. Wiebe, *The Search for Order, 1877–1920* (New York, 1967), xiii–xiv.

[121]Martin Hov to *Skandinaven*, 26 October 1910.

[122]Hans A. Anderson, "Autobiography," 17, in Hans A. Anderson Papers, Library-Archives, Wisconsin Historical Society, Madison, WI. The manuscript bears no date but ends in 1894.

[123]Blanck, *Becoming Swedish-American*, 46–47.

NOTES TO CHAPTER TWO

[1]Robert C. Ostergren, "The Immigrant Church as a Symbol of Community and Place in the Upper Midwest," *Great Plains Quarterly* 1 (Fall 1981), 227.

[2]"Republikaner" to *Skandinaven*, 24 January 1894.

[3]"En Abonent" to *Skandinaven*, 24 July 1894.

[4]See the anonymous letter to *Skandinaven*, 10 August 1892; A. J. Nilsson to

Skandinaven, 13 May 1896; S. J. Steffenson to Skandinaven, 3 June 1896; and an anonymous letter from Luck, Polk County, Wisconsin, to Danskeren, 28 August 1895.

[5]J. I. Seder to Herman L. Ekern, 15 July 1908, in Herman L. Ekern Papers, Library-Archives, Wisconsin Historical Society, Madison, WI.

[6]Anders Pontoppidan Thyssen, "Indledning," in Väckelse och kyrka i nordiskt perspektiv: Nordiska studier över brytningarna mellan kyrklig ordning och religiös folkrörelse under 1800-talet, ed. Anders Pontoppidan Thyssen (Copenhagen, 1969), 22; E. Clifford Nelson and Eugene L. Fevold, The Lutheran Church among Norwegian-Americans: A History of the Evangelical Lutheran Church, 2 vols. (Minneapolis, 1960), 1:17, 32–34; J. L. Balling and P. G. Lindhardt, Den nordiske kirkes historie, 2nd ed. (Copenhagen, 1967), 310; George M. Stephenson, The Religious Aspects of Swedish Immigration: A Study of Immigrant Churches (Minneapolis, 1932), 235–236.

[7]Jon Gjerde, "Conflict and Community: A Case Study of the Immigrant Church in America," Journal of Social History 19 (1986), 692–693.

[8]"Farmer" to Skandinaven, 27 May 1896. For a Swedish-American Baptist example of an Old World congregation nearly splitting in the New, see Robert C. Ostergren, A Community Transplanted: The Trans-Atlantic Experience of a Swedish Immigrant Settlement in the Upper Middle West, 1835–1915 (Madison, WI, 1988), 216.

[9]Theodore Blegen, Norwegian Migration to America: The American Transition (Northfield, MN, 1940), 173; Erik Helmer Pedersen, Drømmen om Amerika (Copenhagen, 1985), 223.

[10]Stephenson, Religious Aspects of Swedish Immigration, 313–314; Hugo Söderström, Confession and Cooperation: The Policy of the Augustana Synod in Confessional Matters and the Synod's Relations with Other Churches up to the Beginning of the Twentieth Century (Lund, 1973), 75–76, 100–101; Nelson and Fevold, The Lutheran Church among Norwegian-Americans, 1:161–162; Blegen, Norwegian Migration to America: The American Transition, 248–270; Johs. Ylvisaker, "Tilslutning til den ev.-luth. Synodalkonferens," in Festskrift til Den norske Synodes Jubilæum, 1853–1903, ed. H. Halvorsen (Decorah, IA, 1903), 229.

[11]"X" to Skandinaven, 7 April 1897.

[12]B. E. Lerud to Skandinaven, 31 March 1897.

[13]E. Arntsen to Skandinaven, 14 September 1904.

[14]Blegen, Norwegian Migration to America: The American Transition, 172; Ann M. Legreid, "The Exodus, Transplanting, and Religious Reorganization of a Group of Norwegian Lutheran Immigrants in Western Wisconsin, c. 1836–1900" (PhD diss., University of Wisconsin, 1985), 362–363.

[15]Jette Mackintosh, Danskere i Midtvesten: Elk Horn-Kimballton bosættelsen 1870–1925 (Copenhagen, 1993), 124–125.

[16]Henrik Bredmose Simonsen, *Kampen om danskheden: Tro og nationalitet i de danske kirkesamfund i Amerika* (Århus, 1990), 22.

[17]Peder Kjølhede, "Den danske, evangelisk-lutherske Kirke i Amerika," in *Danske i Amerika*, ed. Peter Sørensen Vig, 2 pts. in 1 vol. (Minneapolis, 1908), 2:74–75. After the division of the Danish church in 1894, some pastors from Denmark also opted for the Inner-Mission United Danish Church; see Paul C. Nyholm, *The Americanization of the Danish Lutheran Churches in America* (Copenhagen, 1963), 164.

[18]Gisle Bothne, "Bestræbelser paa at faa Prester fra Norge," in Halvorsen, *Festskrift til Den norske Synodes Jubilæum*, 121–123; Olaf M. Norlie, *History of the Norwegian People in America* (Decorah, IA, 1925), 197; Blegen, *Norwegian Migration to America: The American Transition*, 141.

[19]Stephenson, *Religious Aspects of Swedish Immigration*, 147, 237.

[20]Stephenson, *Religious Aspects of Swedish Immigration*, 226.

[21]Dag A. Blanck, *Becoming Swedish-American: The Construction of an Ethnic Identity in the Augustana Synod, 1860–1917* (Uppsala, 1997), 52.

[22]Einar Haugen, "Language and Immigration," *Studies and Records* 10 (Northfield, MN, 1938), 27.

[23]Nyholm, *The Americanization of the Danish Lutheran Churches*, 79, 242, 260; Bredmose Simonsen, *Kampen om danskheden*, 86; Stephenson, *Religious Aspects of Swedish Immigration*, 255; Jørn Brøndal, "Dansk-amerikansk politisk kultur i Midtvesten ca. 1890–1914," in *Nye Perspektiver i Dansk Udvandringshistorie*, ed. Birgit Flemming Larsen (Aalborg, 2002), 17–18.

[24]J. Johansen, "De danske Brødre og deres Deltagelse i Arbeidet," in Halvorsen, *Festskrift til Den norske Synodes Jubilæum*, 447–453.

[25]*Kvartalskrift*, April 1909, 6–21.

[26]*Reform*, 20 April 1897, 6 October 1891; O. N. Nelson et al., "Biographies of Scandinavians in Minnesota," in *History of the Scandinavians and Successful Scandinavians in the United States*, ed. O. N. Nelson, 2 vols., rev. ed. (1904; reprint, New York, 1969), 1:404–405; see also Blanck, *Becoming Swedish-American*, 196–199.

[27]Peter A. Munch, "Authority and Freedom: Controversy in Norwegian-American Congregations," *Norwegian-American Studies* 28 (Northfield, MN, 1980), 30; see also Lowell J. Soike, *Norwegian Americans and the Politics of Dissent, 1880–1924* (Northfield, MN, 1991), 39–40.

[28]Stephenson, *Religious Aspects of Swedish Immigration*, 158–159, 174; quoted from Munch, "Authority and Freedom," 24–25.

[29]*Reform*, 22 December 1896; *Skandinaven*, 20 March 1895.

[30]*Arbeideren*, 16 February 1886.

[31]See, for instance, "X" to *Skandinaven*, 7 April 1894; "Farmer" to *Skandinaven*, 24 April 1897.

[32]Some sects found surprise parties too frivolous; see S. J. Steffenson to *Skandinaven*, 3 June 1896.

[33]"En Deltager" to *Skandinaven*, 11 November 1896.

[34]"J.F." to *Skandinaven*, 5 November 1890.

[35]"O.S." to *Skandinaven*, 10 August 1892; anonymous letter to *Förposten*, 18 August 1892.

[36]S. R. Hovland to *Skandinaven*, 27 May 1896, 3 November 1897; "W" to *Skandinaven*, 6 October 1897.

[37]Ingrid Semmingsen, *Veien mot vest: Utvandringen fra Norge til Amerika, 1865–1915* (Oslo, 1950), 74; Stephenson, *Religious Aspects of Swedish Immigration*, 389.

[38]Peer O. Strømme, *Erindringer* (Minneapolis, 1923), 193 (italics added).

[39]The question of the political influence of the Scandinavian-American pastor is important to answer, not only because the church played so vital a role in the daily lives of many Scandinavian Americans but also because the part played by religion has been stressed so emphatically by proponents of the "new political history," yet thus far the actual involvement of the ethnic clergy in politics has not been illuminated by historical research.

[40]C. K. Preus to Nils P. Haugen, 28 March 1890, in Nils P. Haugen Papers, Library-Archives, Wisconsin Historical Society, Madison, WI.

[41]Nelson et al., "Biographies of Scandinavians in Minnesota," 1:387–391.

[42]"Svensk-Amerikan" to *Hemlandet*, 1 November 1894.

[43]Other examples are Pastor P. A. Cederstam, Chisago County, Minnesota (see Sten Carlsson, *Skandinaviska politiker i Minnesota 1882–1900: En studie rörande den etniske faktorns roll vid politiska val i en immigrantstat* [Uppsala, 1970], 17–18); Rev. J. I. Welo, South Dakota (see Nils P. Haugen to J. I. Welo, 24 January 1892, in Haugen Papers); and Rev. M. Falk Gjertsen (see *Reform*, 4 November, 1890).

[44]T. N. Hasselquist and C. O. Olander to *Hemlandet*, 23 October 1890; Stephenson, *Religious Aspects of Swedish Immigration*, 393. For a view of Hasselquist as an out-and-out Republican, see Roger Kvist, "Religious Perfectionism, Early Swedish Immigrant Political Identification, and T. N. Hasselquist," in *Swedishness Reconsidered: Three Centuries of Swedish-American Identities*, ed. Daniel Lindmark (Umeå, 1999), 56.

[45]Joshua Hasselquist to *Hemlandet*, 30 October 1890; "Svensk amerikan" to *Hemlandet*, 30 October 1890.

[46]O. Risvold to J. O. Davidson, 19 May 1908, in James O. Davidson Papers, Library-Archives, Wisconsin Historical Society, Madison, WI.

[47]Carl G. O. Hansen, "Pressen til Borgerkrigens Slutning," in *Norsk-Amerikanernes Festskrift 1914*, ed. Johs. B. Wist (Decorah, IA, 1914), 14–16.

[48]Hansen, "Pressen til Borgerkrigens Slutning," 14; Johs. B. Wist, "Pressen efter Borgerkrigen," in Wist, *Norsk-Amerikanernes Festskrift*, 110–111; Stephenson, *Religious Aspects of Swedish Immigration*, 183, 197–199, 333–334; Ulf A. Beijbom, "The Swedish Press," in *The Ethnic Press in the United States*, ed. Sally M. Miller (New York, 1987), 380; Kjølhede, "Den danske, evangelisk-lutherske Kirke i Amerika," 2:33; Marion Tuttle Marzolf, "The Danish Press," in Miller, *The Ethnic Press in the United States*, 64; John M. Jensen, *The United Evangelical Lutheran Church: An Interpretation* (Minneapolis, 1964), 66–68, 152. In 1872, the Augustana Synod sold *Hemlandet*, but the paper remained loyal to the Synod under the new editorship; see Blanck, *Becoming Swedish-American*, 140, 151.

[49]Wist, "Pressen efter Borgerkrigen," 195–199. From 1866, Hauge's Synod published *Budbæreren*, whereas the Norwegian Free Church was responsible for *Luthersk Tidsskrift*, established in 1906.

[50]Chr. Christiansen to Andrew H. Dahl, 18 July 1914, in Andrew H. Dahl Papers, Library-Archives, Wisconsin Historical Society, Madison, WI.

[51]J. Linnevold to Andrew H. Dahl, 20 July 1914; Dahl to Linnevold, 21 July 1914, in Dahl Papers.

[52]F. Kammholz to Andrew H. Dahl, 25 July 1914, in Dahl Papers.

[53]Sigurd Gryttenholm to J. O. Davidson, 22 May 1906, in Davidson Papers.

[54]Nils P. Haugen to Gjermund Hoyme, 7 June 1894; also Haugen to Robert M. La Follette and to Nils Holm, 7 June 1894, in Haugen Papers; Nils Holm to Samuel A. Harper, 4 June 1894, in Robert M. La Follette Papers, Library-Archives, Wisconsin Historical Society, Madison, WI.

[55]Nils Holm to Nils P. Haugen, 12 June 1894, in Haugen Papers.

[56]Ole Larson to Nils P. Haugen, 22 June 1894, in Haugen Papers.

[57]Sigurd Gryttenholm to J. O. Davidson, 7 May 1906, in Davidson Papers.

[58]J. O. Davidson to Sigurd Gryttenholm, 8 May 1906, in Davidson Papers.

[59]Blegen, *Norwegian Migration to America: The American Transition*, 241–276; Robert James Ulrich, "The Bennett Law of 1889: Education and Politics in Wisconsin" (PhD diss., University of Wisconsin, 1965), 156, 166, 173–174, 182; Stephenson, *Religious Aspects of Swedish Immigration*, 330–331; Nyholm, *The Americanization of the Danish Lutheran Churches*, 252–256; Roger E. Wyman, "Wisconsin Ethnic Groups and the Election of 1890," *Wisconsin Magazine of History* 51 (Summer 1968), 282–290.

[60]E. C. Wall to William F. Vilas, 12 May 1893, in William F. Vilas Papers, Library-Archives, Wisconsin Historical Society, Madison, WI; Wall is also quoted in Paul Kleppner, *The Cross of Culture: A Social Analysis of Midwestern Politics 1850–1900* (New York, 1970), 252. See also Richard J. Jensen, *The Winning of the Midwest: Social and Political Conflict, 1888–1896* (Chicago, 1971), 222.

[61]E. C. Wall to William F. Vilas, 15 March, 11 December 1890, in Vilas Papers.

[62]*Skandinaven*, 13, 15, 18 June 1890; *Reform*, 8 July 1890.

[63] *Skandinaven*, 20 August 1890; *Reform*, 25 March, 6 May, 19 August 1890.

[64] *Højskolebladet* 22 (1897), 20–21; quoted from Frederick Hale, *Danes in Wisconsin* (Madison, 1981), 30; see also Bredmose Simonsen, *Kampen om danskheden*, 77.

[65] *Svenska Amerikanska Posten*, 15 July 1890; *Fædrelandet og Emigranten*, 6 August 1890; Stephenson, *Religious Aspects of Swedish Immigration*, 411.

[66] As suggested by Jensen, *Winning of the Midwest*, 64–66, and Kleppner, *The Cross of Culture*, 69–76, such religiously colored splits sometimes informed voting behavior at grassroots level. I am arguing that the creation of personal coalitions between pastors and politicians at the *elite* level were not always the outcome solely of theological considerations.

[67] O. M. Kalheim (editor of *Amerika*) to Nils P. Haugen, 25 July, 8 April, 18 September 1890, in Haugen Papers.

[68] W. A. Emery to J. O. Davidson, 17 March 1907, in Davidson Papers.

[69] C. J. Lamb to E. W. Keyes, 25 July 1906, in Elisha W. Keyes Papers, Library-Archives, Wisconsin Historical Society, Madison, WI.

[70] Millard L. Gieske and Steven J. Keillor, *Norwegian Yankee: Knute Nelson and the Failure of American Politics, 1860–1923* (Northfield, MN, 1995), 31, 35, 56–57.

[71] George M. Stephenson, *John Lind of Minnesota* (Minneapolis, 1935), 127–128; see also *Hemlandet*, 9 September 1896.

[72] C. K. Preus to Nils P. Haugen, 28 March 1890; Nils P. Haugen to Preus, 6 April 1890; Belle Haugen to Nils P. Haugen, 13 October 1893; also N. L. Blomholm to Nils P. Haugen, 4 September, 13 November 1906, in Haugen Papers.

[73] Belle Haugen to Nils P. Haugen, 1 October 1893, in Haugen Papers.

[74] Nils P. Haugen to Miller Winterbotham, 8 May 1892; also Arthur Gough to Haugen, 29 April 1892, in Haugen Papers.

[75] J. O. Davidson to August Klagstad, 12 January 1906, in Davidson Papers.

[76] J. O. Davidson to F. L. Frelstad, 29 May 1906, in Davidson Papers.

[77] Elisabeth Ekern to Herman L. Ekern, 9 June 1901, in Ekern Papers.

[78] Hans A. Anderson, "Autobiography," 28, 44, in Hans A. Anderson Papers, Library-Archives, Wisconsin Historical Society, Madison, WI.

[79] O. A. Buslett to Anlaug Buslett, 15 March 1909, in Ole A. Buslett Papers, Archives of the Norwegian-American Historical Association, St. Olaf College, Northfield, MN.

[80] C. J. Helsem to Nils P. Haugen, 29 August 1900, in Haugen Papers.

[81] Nils P. Haugen to Robert M. La Follette, 27 May 1900, in Haugen Papers.

[82] W. A. Emery to J. O. Davidson, 17 March 1907, in Davidson Papers.

[83] C. G. Lundell to J. O. Davidson, 21 September 1900; H. E. Erffmeyer to J.

O. Davidson, 12 September 1902; J. E. Linner to J. O. Davidson, 8 October 1906, in Davidson Papers.

[84]H. A. Preus to William F. Vilas, 24 January 1893; Vilas to Rasmus B. Anderson, 24 September 1888; Vilas to Calvin S. Brice, 15 October 1888, in Vilas Papers.

[85]Nils P. Haugen to J. P. Peterson, 6 February 1897, in Haugen Papers.

[86]Soike, *Norwegian Americans and the Politics of Dissent*, 37. Soike disagrees with Kleppner, *The Cross of Culture*, 51–53, 334, and Jensen, *Winning of the Midwest*, 81, each of whom had argued that religious differences among Norwegian Americans had a certain electoral impact.

[87]Kleppner, *The Cross of Culture*, 51–53; for three independent discussions of Danish-American voting patterns, all focusing on the Elkhorn-Kimballton settlement in Iowa, see Bjarne Gade Johansen, "Danske emigranters vælgeradfærd i Iowa: En case-study af fem danske townships i 90'erne" (master's thesis, University of Copenhagen, 1982), 50; Stephen H. Rye, "Danish American Political Behavior: The Case of Iowa, 1887–1936," *The Bridge: Journal of the Danish American Heritage Society* 2 (1979), 36–37; and Jette Mackintosh, "Politik, kultur og religion i et indvandrersamfund," *1066: Tidsskrift for historisk forskning* 23/4 (March, 1994), 6–7.

[88]E. C. Wall to William F. Vilas, 24 November 1896, in Vilas Papers.

NOTES TO CHAPTER THREE

[1]A. B. Johnson to *Skandinaven*, 1 June 1892.

[2]Anonymous letter to *Reform*, 2 April 1895. In fact, Hayward's Methodists were Danish-Norwegian; see John Mortensen to *Reform*, 16 April 1890.

[3]*Superior Tidende*, 8 February 1899.

[4]The existence of ethnic institutions other than the church is a circumstance usually ignored by researchers dealing with the combination of ethnicity and politics.

[5]Carl G. O. Hansen, "Det norske Foreningsliv i Amerika," in *Norsk-Amerikanernes Festskrift 1914*, ed. Johs. B. Wist (Decorah, IA, 1914), 273; Wesley Westerberg, "Swedish-American Religious and Secular Organizations," in *Perspectives on Swedish Immigration: Proceedings of the International Conference on the Swedish Heritage in the Upper Midwest, April 1–3, 1976, University of Minnesota, Duluth*, ed. Nils Hasselmo (Chicago, 1978), 200; Odd Lovoll, *A Folk Epic: The Bygdelag in America* (Boston, 1975), 74–75.

[6]Dag A. Blanck, *Becoming Swedish-American: The Construction of an Ethnic Identity in the Augustana Synod, 1860–1917* (Uppsala, 1997), 36; Ulf Beijbom, *Swedes in Chicago: A Demographic and Social Study of the 1846–1880 Immigration* (Växjö, 1971), 266–287; Odd S. Lovoll, *The Promise of America: A History of the*

Norwegian-American People (Minneapolis, 1984), 179; Hansen, "Det norske Foreningsliv i Amerika," 290.

[7]*Reform,* 17 June, 26 August, 14 October, 25 November 1890; Aksel H. Holter to J. O. Davidson, 17 August, 11 September 1906; G. N. Risjord to Davidson, 18 January 1907; Carl Tellefson to Davidson, 19 January 1907, in James O. Davidson Papers, Library-Archives, Wisconsin Historical Society, Madison, WI; see also Hansen, "Det norske Foreningsliv i Amerika," 288.

[8]Anders Pontoppidan Thyssen, *Vækkelse, kirkefornyelse og nationalitetskamp i Sønderjylland 1815–1850,* vol. 7 of *Vækkelsernes frembrud i Danmark i første halvdel af det 19. århundrede,* ed. Anders Pontoppidan Thyssen (Åbenrå, Denmark, 1977), 389; see also Anders Pontoppidan Thyssen, "Indledning," in *Väckelse och kyrka i nordiskt perspektiv: Nordiska studier över brytningarna mellan kyrklig ordning och religiös folkrörelse under 1800-talet,* ed. Anders Pontoppidan Thyssen (Copenhagen, 1969), 14.

[9]Hans Try, *To kulturer, en stat, 1851–1884,* vol. 11 of *Norges historie,* ed. Knut Mykland (Oslo, 1979), 432–445; Sven Lundkvist, *Folkrörelserna i det svenska samhället, 1850–1920* (Uppsala, 1977), 47–58, 61–62; Peter Gundelach, *Sociale bevægelser og samfundsændringer: Nye sociale grupperinger og deres organisationsformer ved overgangen til ændrede samfundstyper* (Århus, 1988), 124–128.

[10]Thorkild Kjærgård, *Den danske revolution 1500–1800: En økohistorisk tolkning* (Copenhagen, 1991), 220–224; Kristian Hvidt, *Det folkelige gennembrud og dets mænd, 1850–1900,* vol. 11 of *Gyldendal og Politikens Danmarkshistorie,* ed. Olaf Olsen (Copenhagen, 1990), 103, 309; Per Fuglum, *Norge i støpeskjeen,* vol. 12 of *Norges Historie,* ed. Knut Mykland (Oslo, 1978), 225; Lundkvist, *Folkrörelserna i det svenska samhället,* 153–160.

[11]Albert Erlebacher, "Herman L. Ekern: The Quiet Progressive" (PhD diss., University of Wisconsin, 1965), 174–175.

[12]*Skandinaven,* 7 February 1906.

[13]Hansen, "Det norske Foreningsliv i Amerika," 287–288.

[14]Hansen, "Det norske Foreningsliv i Amerika," 281–284.

[15]J. P. Paulsen, "Det Danske Brodersamfund i Amerika," in *Danske i Amerika,* ed. Peter Sørensen Vig, 2 pts. in 1 vol. (Minneapolis, 1908), 2:222.

[16]Sture Lindmark, *Swedish America, 1914–1932: Studies in Ethnicity with Emphasis on Illinois and Minnesota* (Uppsala, 1971), 305; Timothy J. Johnson, "The Independent Order of Svithiod: A Swedish-American Lodge in Chicago," in *Swedish-American Life in Chicago,* ed. Philip J. Anderson and Dag Blanck (Uppsala, 1991), 345–346.

[17]See, for instance, *Folkets Avis,* 14 June 1900.

[18]*Superior Tidende,* 30 August, 30 November 1898, 1 August 1901.

[19]See fig. 4.2, Appendix I.

[20]Hansen, "Det norske Foreningsliv i Amerika," 284.

[21] *Superior Tidende*, 21, 25 February 1901. "Rural" lodges were those found in townships and villages according to "A Retabulation of Population Schedules from the Wisconsin State Census of 1905," table 26, Library-Archives, Wisconsin Historical Society, Madison, WI.

[22] Hansen, "Det norske Foreningsliv i Amerika," 284; *Svenska-Amerikanska Tribunen*, 15 June, 3 August 1906; *Superior Tidende*, 18 January 1900, 31 July 1902, 21 August 1908, 28 July 1911; P. J. Smith to J. A. Frear, 5 January 1924; A. M. Smith to Jens Heilskov, 8 January 1924, in Peter J. Smith Papers, Library-Archives, Wisconsin Historical Society, Madison, WI.

[23] Beijbom, *Swedes in Chicago*, 266; Westerberg, "Swedish-American Religious and Secular Organizations," 201–202; Paulsen, "Det Danske Brodersamfund i Amerika," 2:216; Lovoll, *The Promise of America*, 188.

[24] *Arbeideren*, 16 February 1888; *Skandinaven*, 17 June 1890; *Reform*, 12 November 1895.

[25] F. A. Scawie to *Skandinaven*, 26 October 1900.

[26] Westerberg, "Swedish-American Religious and Secular Organizations," 203; *Reform*, 21 January 1890; "En Afholdsmand" to *Reform*, 21 February 1899; "Lars fra Landet" to *Reform*, 14 March 1899.

[27] *Superior Tidende*, 1 August 1901.

[28] The meetings of local churches and fraternal orders were announced regularly in the Scandinavian-language press; see, for instance, *Reform*, 6 November 1894; *Superior Tidende*, 24 September 1896.

[29] According to Paulsen, "Det Danske Brodersamfund i Amerika," 2:219, in 1902 the Danish Brotherhood boasted 145 lodges with 8,347 male members, whereas according to fig. 3.1, Appendix I, the United Danish Church two years earlier had 16,340 male *and* female members.

[30] Martin Olsen to *Skandinaven* and Ebert Olsen to *Skandinaven*, 24 March 1897.

[31] S. J. Rasmussen to *Skandinaven*, 23 June 1897; F. A. Scawie to *Skandinaven*, 26 October 1900.

[32] N. J. Hagen to *Skandinaven*, 12 May, 18 August 1897.

[33] J. P. Paulsen, "Det Danske Brodersamfund i Amerika," 2:216; George R. Nielsen, *The Danish Americans* (Boston, 1981), 174; Lovoll, *The Promise of America*, 188–189; Anna Williams, *Skribent i Svensk-Amerika: Jakob Bonggren, journalist och poet* (Uppsala, 1991), 167.

[34] Fred Peterson to *Skandinaven*, 12 May 1897.

[35] F. A. Scawie to *Skandinaven*, 26 October 1900.

[36] *Superior Tidende*, 25 January, 23 February 1899. Lodge 23, on the other hand, was named "Concord" (*Enighed*).

[37] *Reform*, 14 September 1897. See also *Reform*, 21 September 1897.

[38]*Arbeideren*, 25 May 1886.

[39]*Superior Tidende*, 1 August 1901; *Svenska Amerikanska Tribunen*, 3 August 1906; Peter J. Smith [ISWA Grand Lodge Secretary] to J. O. Davidson 12 December 1905 ("Brotherly greetings") and 11 January 1907 ("Dear Sir and Bro."), in Davidson Papers.

[40]*Superior Tidende*, 3 August 1899.

[41]*Superior Tidende*, 16 February 1899.

[42]H. P. Peterson to J. O. Davidson, 26 June 1905, in Davidson Papers.

[43]Peterson had in fact been president of the ISWA back in 1901; see *Superior Tidende*, 24 January 1901.

[44]H. P. Peterson to J. O. Davidson, 8 August 1905, in Davidson Papers.

[45]H. P. Peterson to Robert M. La Follette, 1 March 1906, in Robert M. La Follette Papers, Library-Archives, Wisconsin Historical Society, Madison, WI.

[46]Ed. Emerson to J. O. Davidson, 3 June 1906; Davidson to H. P. Peterson, 6 June 1906; Peterson to Davidson, 18 June 1906, in Davidson Papers.

[47]*Superior Tidende*, 3 October 1901, 12 June, 17 July 1902.

[48]T. M. Thorson to Nils P. Haugen, 26 May, 7 August 1890, 10 August 1896, in Nils P. Haugen Papers, Library-Archives, Wisconsin Historical Society, Madison, WI; *Superior Tidende*, 3 August 1899, 12 June 1902.

[49]*Superior Tidende*, 31 July 1902.

[50]*Superior Tidende*, 3 August 1899, 19 June 1902.

[51]H. P. Peterson to J. O. Davidson, 24 July 1905; P. J. Smith to Davidson, 6 June 1906; Julius Howland to J. O. Davidson, 20 December 1905, in Davidson Papers.

[52]Julius Howland to J. O. Davidson, 6 June 1906; Davidson to Howland, 11 June 1906, in Davidson Papers.

[53]Julius Howland to J. O. Davidson, 23 July 1906; Davidson to Howland, 24 July 1906, in Davidson Papers.

[54]Julius Howland and Peter J. Smith to J. O. Davidson, 25 July 1906. Davidson did participate in the meeting; see Julius Howland to Davidson, 30 July 1906, in Davidson Papers.

[55]John J. Jenkins to O. G. Munson, 27 July 1906, in Davidson Papers; *Svenska Amerikanska Tribunen*, 3 August 1906.

[56]A copy of Julius Howland's official message is found under the date of 20 June 1906, in Ekern Papers.

[57]*Skandinaven*, 10 August 1910.

[58]J. O. Davidson to P. J. Smith, 7 February 1907, in Davidson Papers. Postmasterships were federal, not state, positions.

[59]See the draft of a resolution to Governor John J. Blaine under the date of 13 February 1923, in Smith Papers.

[60]Peter J. Smith to Nils P. Haugen, 24 June 1905, in Haugen Papers.

[61]P. J. Smith to Robert M. La Follette, 19 March 1906; H. P. Peterson to Robert M. La Follette, 27 March 1906, in La Follette Papers.

[62]J. O. Davidson to Peter J. Smith, 31 January 1906, in Davidson Papers.

[63]Andrew H. Dahl to Peter J. Smith, 26 June 1914; also Smith to Dahl, 12 June 1914, in Andrew H. Dahl Papers, Library-Archives, Wisconsin Historical Society, Madison, WI. Apparently Smith opposed Dahl's candidacy; see Smith to Henry Johnson, 30 July 1914, and Johnson to Smith, 31 July 1914, in Henry Johnson Papers, Library-Archives, Wisconsin Historical Society, Madison, WI.

[64]"The Diary and Account Book of Kristoffer O. Skauge, 1888–1896," Library-Archives, Wisconsin Historical Society, Madison, WI, 5.

[65]*Reform*, 14 April 1896.

[66]Roy Matson, "A History of Strum and the Town of Unity," 29, http://www.norhemian.com/ 0529strumhistory.html (accessed 8 January 2004).

[67]"Fra Westby" to *Skandinaven*, 3 July 1890.

[68]Among 1,974 letters to *Skandinaven*, 13.6 percent referred to alcohol-related topics, whereas the corresponding figure for 249 letters to *Hemlandet* was 8.8 percent. For a discussion of the reader letters, see pages 209–226 in chapter 8. Neither *Skandinaven* nor *Hemlandet* was a prohibition paper.

[69]Hans E. Lie to *Skandinaven*, 18 April 1890.

[70]Erik O. Stalheim to *Skandinaven*, 24 April 1891. One temperance reformer suggested that the saloon victory resulted from fraud; see anonymous correspondent to *Skandinaven*, 23 April 1891.

[71]*Arbeideren*, 13 April 1886.

[72]*Reform*, 21 January 1890, included the complete text of the local-option law.

[73]C. J. Hanson to *Reform*, 19 June 1894; anonymous writer from Lake Park, Minnesota, to *Skandinaven*, 28 February 1890; "S.P." to *Skandinaven*, 19 March 1890.

[74]Richard J. Jensen, *The Winning of the Midwest: Social and Political Conflict, 1888–1896* (Chicago, 1971), 75, 84; Kathleen Neils Conzen, *Immigrant Milwaukee, 1836–1860* (Cambridge, MA, 1976), 210.

[75]*Reform*, 21 October 1890; P. H. H. McGovern to J. O. Davidson, 1 May 1908, in Davidson Papers; Leo Stern to Herman L. Ekern, 5 August 1908, in Herman L. Ekern Papers, Library-Archives, Wisconsin Historical Society, Madison, WI.

[76]Waldemar Ager, "The Norwegian-American Temperance Movement," 1, manuscript typed by E. B. Ager ca. 1936 on the basis of Waldemar Ager's handwritten manuscript, box 2 in Waldemar Ager Papers, Archives of the Norwegian-

American Historical Association, St. Olaf College, Northfield, MN. Hansen, "Det norske Foreningsliv i Amerika," 286, suggested that the earliest Norwegian-American temperance society dated from 1877.

[77]Jon Gjerde, *The Minds of the West: Ethnocultural Evolution in the Rural Middle West, 1830–1917* (Chapel Hill, NC, 1997), 292. For a Danish traveler's account of the role played by women in the temperance movement, see K. Rovsing, *Træk af Livet i Amerika—Af Breve til Hjemmet fra en dansk Reisende* (Copenhagen, 1874), 26–41.

[78]In 1890, and again in 1894 and 1896, the Wisconsin Prohibition Party urged suffrage reform, but not, for instance, in 1892 and 1898; see the *Blue Book of the State of Wisconsin* (Madison, WI), 1891:396, 1893:426, 1895:458, 1897:636, 1899:725; *Reform*, 12 February 1895, 11 October 1898.

[79]Lowell J. Soike, *Norwegian Americans and the Politics of Dissent, 1880–1924* (Northfield, MN, 1991), 62.

[80]Waldemar Ager, "The Norwegian-American Temperance Movement," 7; Martin Havdal to *Reform*, 6 January 1891; *Reform*, 2 September 1890. One Danish-American temperance club in Waupaca, Wisconsin, was mentioned in a letter by "A.C." to *Skandinaven*, 20 September 1890.

[81]*Svenska Amerikanska Posten*, 15 July 1890; George M. Stephenson, *The Religious Aspects of Swedish Immigration: A Study of Immigrant Churches* (Minneapolis, 1932), 19–20.

[82]*Reform*, 11 February, 1 April 1890, 24 October 1893, 24 November 1896; Soike, *Norwegian Americans and the Politics of Dissent*, 62–68.

[83]*Reform*, 24 June, 26 August, 30 December 1890, 8 January, 19 November 1895, 26 January 1897.

[84]Einar Haugen, *Immigrant Idealist: A Literary Biography of Waldemar Ager, Norwegian American* (Northfield, MN, 1989), 21; undated clipping, "Af historisk Interesse" from *Reform*, by N. L. Hansen, in Ager Papers; *Reform*, 10 June 1890, 27 November 1894.

[85]Chr. Omann to *Reform*, 26 August 1890; P. M. Zachariassen to *Skandinaven*, 24 January 1894; Haugen, *Immigrant Idealist*, 9.

[86]See Peder Kjølhede, "Den danske, evangelisk-lutherske Kirke i Amerika," in *Danske i Amerika*, ed. Peter Sørensen Vig, 2 pts. in 1 vol. (Minneapolis, 1908), 2:31–113; P. S. Vig and I. M. Hansen, "Den forenede danske evangelisk-lutherske Kirke i Amerika," in Vig, *Danske i Amerika*, 2:117–164; Paul C. Nyholm, *The Americanization of the Danish Lutheran Churches in America* (Copenhagen, 1963).

[87]P. G. Lindhardt, *Vækkelse og kirkelige retninger* (Copenhagen, 1959), 66–67; Jette Mackintosh, *Danskere i Midtvesten: Elk Horn-Kimballton bosættelsen 1870–1925* (Copenhagen, 1993), 111–112; Sidsel Eriksen, "Vækkelse og afholdsbevægelse: Et bidrag til studiet af den svenske og den danske folkekultur," *Scandia* 54/2 (1988), 269, 274–275, 283–284.

[88]Ulf Jonas Björk, "*Svenska Amerikanska Posten*: An Immigrant Newspaper with American Accents," in *Swedes in the Twin Cities: Immigrant Life and Minnesota's Urban Frontier*, ed. Philip J. Anderson and Dag Blanck (St. Paul, MN, 2001), 211; Johs. B. Wist, "Pressen efter Borgerkrigen," in Wist, *Norsk-Amerikanernes Festskrift*, 136, 142–143. Marzolf, *The Danish-Language Press in America* (New York, 1979), makes no mention of Danish-American temperance papers.

[89]Ager, "The Norwegian-American Temperance Movement," 6–7; Hansen, "Det norske Foreningsliv i Amerika," 286.

[90]J. I. Seder to Herman L. Ekern, 15 July 1908, in Ekern Papers.

[91]Eriksen, "Vækkelse og afholdsbevægelse," 277–279; Ulf Beijbom, *Utvandrarna och Svensk-Amerika* (Stockholm, 1986), 148.

[92]Beijbom, *Utvandrarna och Svensk-Amerika*, 149–150; Waldemar Ager, "The Norwegian-American Temperance Movement," 2.

[93]Waldemar Ager, "The Norwegian-American Temperance Movement," 2–3.

[94]*Reform*, 30 July 1889.

[95]See Ager's obituary in *Reform*, 7 August 1941.

[96]Peter J. Smith to James A. Frear, 5 January 1924, in Smith Papers.

[97]Peter J. Smith to Henry Johnson, 12 September 1914, in Henry Johnson Papers.

[98]Quoted from Lloyd Hustvedt, *Rasmus Bjørn Anderson: Pioneer Scholar* (Northfield, MN, 1966), 174.

[99]Soike, *Norwegian Americans and the Politics of Dissent*, 65.

[100]*Skandinaven*, 3 December 1890, 31 January, 13 June 1894, 8 February 1906, 6 July 1910.

[101]*Reform*, 23 September 1890, 6 January 1891, 6 November 1894, 22 September 1896.

[102]See fig. 4.2, Appendix I.

[103]*Svenska Amerikanaren*, 7 August 1890.

[104]*Den danske Pioneer*, 11 October 1894; *Reform*, 29 September 1896.

[105]Peer O. Strømme, *Erindringer* (Minneapolis, 1923), 203.

[106]*Superior Tidende*, 8 September 1898.

[107]*Folkets Avis*, 14 June 1900.

[108]*Folkets Avis*, 2 August 1900.

[109]"Odin" to *Reform*, 16 April 1895.

[110]A. P. Eikjarud to *Reform*, 12 November 1895.

[111]*Reform*, 25 November 1890.

[112]*Reform*, 7 October 1890.

[113]*Reform*, 19 June 1894. The American Protective Association, it is true,

never came out wholly on the side of the drys; see Jensen, *Winning of the Midwest*, 237.

[114]*Reform*, 13 August 1889, 25 August 1896.

[115]*Reform*, 9 April 1895, 31 August 1897.

[116]C. A. Larsen, Oslo (Kristiania), to *Reform*, 26 November 1895; anonymous letter from Røros to *Reform*, 12 November 1895.

[117]*Reform*, 13 August 1889.

[118]Waldemar Ager, "The Norwegian-American Temperance Movement," 4–5.

[119]*Reform*, 12 November 1895.

[120]Clipping from *Menneskevennen*, 26 May 1900; *Afholdsvennernes Aarbog for 1903*, boxes 10 and 11 in Ager Papers.

[121]A list of Ager's literary productions is found in Haugen, *Immigrant Idealist*, 170–173; see also Orm Øverland, *The Western Home: A Literary History of Norwegian America* (Northfield, MN, 1996), 324–345.

[122]On Ager's nationalism and prominence, see also Haugen, *Immigrant Idealist*, 3, 49–50.

[123]*Reform*, 7 August 1941; see also Haugen, *Immigrant Idealist*, 110, 115, 186. Ager also wrote a book about Heg: *Colonel Heg and His Boys*, trans. Della Kittleson Catuna and Clarence A. Clausen (Northfield, MN, 2000).

[124]See note 76, above.

[125]Olaf M. Norlie, *History of the Norwegian People in America* (Decorah, IA, 1925), 491.

[126]My calculation on the basis of the *Blue Book of Wisconsin*, 1891:575, 1893:623, 1895:661, 1897:656, 1899:748, 1901:725, 1903:1069, 1905:1069, 1907:1120, 1909:1088, 1911:732, 1913:633.

[127]In 1890, Andrew Peterson ran for insurance commissioner, as did Thomas Edward, likewise Scandinavian-American, in 1894; in 1896, Ole A. Christensen ran for railroad commissioner; in 1898, William Larson ran for state treasurer and Edward Berg for insurance commissioner; in 1900, Thorvild K. Thorvildson ran for lieutenant governor; in 1902, H. H. Moe ran for insurance commissioner; in 1904, John A. Berg ran for state treasurer; in 1910, Chris. Nordby ran for insurance commissioner; see the *Blue Book of Wisconsin*, 1891:575–577, 1893:623–625, 1895:661–663, 1897:656–658, 1899:748–751, 1901:725–727, 1903:1069–1072, 1905:1069–1072, 1907:1116–1119, 1909:1088–1090, 1911:731–733, 1913:633–635; and Thomas Edward to Nils P. Haugen, 24 June 1894, in Haugen Papers.

[128]See page 130 in chapter 5.

[129]*Blue Book of Wisconsin*, 1895:661, 1909:1088–1089.

[130]J. S. Holland to *Reform*, 5 August 1890.

[131]Pastor Holseth to *Reform*, 24 September 1895.

[132]*Reform*, 21 July 1896.

[133]Nils P. Haugen to Torger Olson, ca. 10 November 1891 (date illegible, but the letter was placed in a letterbook among letters dated 9 November and 10 November 1891), in Haugen Papers.

[134]*Reform*, 20 August 1889.

[135]John A. Johnson to Rasmus B. Anderson, 23 December 1886; by 1888, Johnson was back in the Republican fold; see Johnson to Anderson, 11 December 1888; both letters in Rasmus B. Anderson Papers, Library-Archives, Wisconsin Historical Society, Madison, WI.

[136]E. W. Keyes to Philip L. Spooner, 14 July 1894, in Elisha W. Keyes Papers, Library-Archives, Wisconsin Historical Society, Madison, WI; Johnson's activism within the Prohibition Party escaped his biographer; cf. Agnes M. Larson, *John A. Johnson: An Uncommon American* (Northfield, MN, 1969), 246.

[137]E. C. Wall to William F. Vilas, 1 May 1891, in William F. Vilas Papers, Library-Archives, Wisconsin Historical Society, Madison, WI.

[138]E. C. Wall to William F. Vilas, 29 March 1892, in Vilas Papers.

[139]Jensen, *Winning of the Midwest*, 270.

[140]*Reform*, 21 July 1896, 13 September 1898; see also S. C. Morgan to *Reform*, 25 October 1898.

[141]*Blue Book of Wisconsin*, 1897:620–641. Paul Kleppner has suggested that the Swedish- and Norwegian-American minorities supporting the Democratic Party were larger in 1896 than at any other point since 1876, and that they thus participated in a more general "cross of culture" involving several pietistically inclined ethnic groups crossing over to the Democrats. Lowell Soike's extensive analysis of voting patterns among Norwegian Americans in 189 Midwestern ethnic enclaves, however, does not indicate a particular low in the Norwegian-American Republican gubernatorial vote of 1896; see Paul Kleppner, *The Cross of Culture: A Social Analysis of Midwestern Politics 1850–1900* (New York, 1970), 317, 334; and the chart in Soike, *Norwegian Americans and the Politics of Dissent*, 52.

[142]John A. Johnson to Rasmus B. Anderson, 1 November 1888, in R. B. Anderson Papers; J. E. McConnell and James Thompson to J. O. Davidson, 27 October 1906, in Davidson Papers; J. Line to *Hemlandet*, 3 November 1892.

[143]*Reform*, 2 September 1890.

[144]These Danish-American assemblymen were Christian Wellengard (1907–1910) and Ferdinand Wittig (1909–1910). Another eleven "saloon" seats were occupied by Democrats and one by a Social Democrat. All these assemblymen lived in the eastern half of Wisconsin. On the biographical database on Wisconsin politicians, see Appendix II.

[145]Nils P. Haugen to A. F. F. Jensen, 14 April 1892, in Haugen Papers.

[146]P. H. McGovern to J. O. Davidson, 1 May 1908, in Davidson Papers.

[147]Nils P. Haugen to Nils Holm, 20 June 1892; Samuel A. Harper to Nils P. Haugen, 14 January 1896, in Haugen Papers.

[148]J. O. Davidson to Edgar E. Clough, 20 February 1905, in Davidson Papers.

[149]Peter J. Smith to J. O. Davidson, 7 May 1906, in Davidson Papers; see also *Reform*, 11 September 1906.

[150]A translation of the *Germania* article is found in Davidson Papers under the date of 8 December 1905. See also Herbert F. Margulies, *Senator Lenroot of Wisconsin: A Political Biography, 1900–1929* (Columbia, MO, 1977), 27, 67.

[151]Charles Smith to Nils P. Haugen, 20 October 1905, in Haugen Papers.

[152]O. G. Munson to E. L. Tracy, 21 August 1906, in Davidson Papers.

[153]On the 1908 Ekern-Twesme battle, see also Erlebacher, "Herman L. Ekern," 141–145; Soike, *Norwegian Americans and the Politics of Dissent*, 141–146.

[154]Erlebacher, "Herman L. Ekern," i.

[155]Herman L. Ekern to J. F. Rhodes, 10 January 1905; to E. G. Updike, 4 February 1905; to P. B. Knox, 6 February 1905; to N. K. Larson, 17 February 1905; to "Dear Sir," 18 February 1905; to J. G. Thorpe, 21 February 1905; to N. L. Sweet, 4 March 1905; to S. G. Messmer, 6, 7, 15 March 1905; to Martin Tollach, 26 May 1905; to L. C. Foss, 8 July 1905; E. A. Warner to Ekern, 16 December 1904; N. L. Sweet to Ekern, 3 March 1905, in Ekern Papers.

[156]Herman L. Ekern to H. A. Anderson, 6 February 1905; Ekern to John Koren, 26 April 1907, in Ekern Papers.

[157]Andrew H. Dahl to Herman L. Ekern, 27 June, 24 August 1908; W. S. Irvine to Ekern, 20 July 1908; O. J. Hawkeson to Ekern, 15, 22 August 1908; W. P. Massuere to Ekern, 24 August 1908; A. J. Bautch to Ekern, 27 August 1908; James N. Hunter to Ekern, 28 August, 2 September 1908; J. T. Qualle to Ekern and F. M. Jackson to Ekern, 3 September 1908; Ekern to John E. Holden, 18 August 1908, in Ekern Papers.

[158]W. P. Massuere to Herman L. Ekern, 25 August 1908, in Ekern Papers.

[159]J. I. Seder to Herman L. Ekern, 4 July 1908, in Ekern Papers. Apparently, Seder did not know that Ekern, as noted above, opposed a county option bill in 1907.

[160]J. I. Seder to Herman L. Ekern, 15 July 1908, in Ekern Papers.

[161]S. S. Urberg to Herman L. Ekern, 26 August 1908, in Ekern Papers.

[162]Herman L. Ekern to J. I. Seder, 26 August 1908, in Ekern Papers.

[163]Herman L. Ekern to Robert M. La Follette, 2 September 1908; Ekern to Irvine L. Lenroot, 3 September 1908, in Ekern Papers.

[164]Irvine L. Lenroot to A. T. Rogers, 14 April 1910, in Irvine L. Lenroot Papers, Manuscript Division, Library of Congress, Washington, D.C.

[165]A. T. Torge to John M. Nelson, 5 May 1910, in John M. Nelson Papers, Library-Archives, Wisconsin Historical Society, Madison, WI.

[166]E. F. Kileen to Herman L. Ekern, 2 September 1910, in Ekern Papers.

[167]*Skandinaven*, 10 October 1910.

[168]*Skandinaven*, 6 July, 19, 31 August 1910; *Reform*, 30 August 1910.

[169]O. A. Buslett to *Skandinaven*, 20 July 1910.

[170]*Normannen*, 15 March 1895.

[171]J. O. Davidson to O. A. Buslett, 20 September 1910, in Ole A. Buslett Papers, Archives of the Norwegian-American Historical Association, St. Olaf College, Northfield, MN.

[172]Robert M. La Follette to Nils P. Haugen, 25 February 1892, in Haugen Papers.

[173]Nils P. Haugen to O. I. Ronning, 23 June 1892, in Haugen Papers.

NOTES TO CHAPTER FOUR

[1]Sivert Rekstad to *Skandinaven*, 24 February 1897; see also page 29 in chapter 1.

[2]C. J. Helsem to Herman L. Ekern, 22 October 1908, in Herman L. Ekern Papers, Library-Archives, Wisconsin Historical Society, Madison, WI; see also Helsem to J. O. Davidson, 23 October 1908, in James O. Davidson Papers, Library-Archives, Wisconsin Historical Society, Madison, WI. Helsem's mission in Chicago was to secure the support of *Skandinaven* if Ekern chose to run as an independent for the assembly, now that he had been beaten by Albert T. Twesme in the Republican primaries.

[3]P. O. Strømme to Rasmus B. Anderson, 24 February 1893, in Rasmus B. Anderson Papers, Library-Archives, Wisconsin Historical Society, Madison, WI; Peer O. Strømme, *Erindringer* (Minneapolis, 1923), 311–319.

[4]P. O. Strømme to Waldemar Ager, 15 January 1918, in Waldemar Ager Papers, Archives of the Norwegian-American Historical Association, St. Olaf College, Northfield, MN.

[5]John L. Erickson to Nils P. Haugen, 8 March 1905, in Nils P. Haugen Papers, Library-Archives, Wisconsin Historical Society, Madison, WI.

[6]O. M. Kalheim to Nils P. Haugen, 8 April 1890; Belle Haugen to Nils P. Haugen, 11 April 1890, in Haugen Papers; Strømme, *Erindringer*, 292.

[7]N. W. Ayer & Son's American Newspaper Annual and Directory (Philadelphia), 1889:1001–1002, 1900:1411–1413, 1910:1161–1164; unless otherwise indicated, the newspaper circulation figures in the present chapter derive from this source. A fourth paper, *Amerika*, was in existence in the whole period 1891–1913; it had moved to Wisconsin in 1896.

[8]Anna Williams, *Skribent i Svensk-Amerika: Jakob Bonggren, journalist och poet* (Uppsala, 1991), 31.

[9]On yellow journalism, see Daniel J. Boorstin, *The Americans: The National Experience* (New York, 1965), 133.

[10]*Skandinaven*, 5 November 1898.

[11]Examples of Wisconsin four-page papers were the Danish-American *Folkets Avis* of Racine, the Swedish-American *Förposten* of Marinette, and the Norwegian-American *Posten* of La Crosse; the Norwegian-language Socialist *Gaa Paa* of Minneapolis also used this format.

[12]*Norden*, 3 June 1890, 28 April 1891, 9 August 1892, 22 April 1893, 5 May 1894.

[13]Jette D. Søllinge and Niels Thomsen, *De danske aviser 1634–1989*, 3 vols. (Odense, 1989), 29–42; Thomas von Vegesack, "Den snabba nyheten," in *Industri och folkrörelser 1866–1920*, vol. 9 of *Den svenska historien*, ed. Gunvor Grenholm (Stockholm, 1968), 284–287; Gro Hageman, *Det moderne gjennombrud, 1870–1905*, vol. 9 of *Aschehougs Norgeshistorie* (Oslo, 1997), 202–203.

[14]On the Scandinavian-American Socialist and Populist press, see Jørn Brøndal, "Socialister, fagforeninger og broderskaber i skandinavisk Amerika, 1870–1914," *Arbejderhistorie* 1999/1 (1999), 33–50.

[15]See, for instance, *Den Danske Pioneer*, 3 November 1898; *Danskeren*, 11 October 1894.

[16]Theodore Blegen, *Norwegian Migration to America, 1825–1860* (Northfield, MN, 1931), 132; Marion Tuttle Marzolf, *The Danish-Language Press in America* (New York, 1979), 29–30.

[17]H. Arnold Barton, *A Folk Divided: Homeland Swedes and Swedish Americans, 1840–1940* (Carbondale, IL, 1994), 34. Barton mistakenly calls *Skandinaven* the first Scandinavian-American newspaper.

[18]Carl G. O. Hansen, "Pressen til Borgerkrigens Slutning," in *Norsk-Amerikanernes Festskrift 1914*, ed. Johs. B. Wist (Decorah, IA, 1914), 10; Finis Herbert Capps, *From Isolationism to Involvement: The Swedish Immigrant Press in America, 1914–1945* (Chicago, 1966), 16.

[19]Nils P. Haugen to John J. Jenkins, 7 September 1894, in Haugen Papers.

[20]Marzolf, *The Danish-Language Press*, 31; Hansen, "Pressen til Borgerkrigens Slutning," 16–17, 27–28; Johs. B. Wist, "Pressen efter Borgerkrigen," in Wist, *Norsk-Amerikanernes Festskrift*, 42.

[21]Nels Jensen to J. O. Davidson, 24 August 1906, in Davidson Papers.

[22]On Hans Mattson, see Lars Ljungmark, *For Sale: Minnesota: Organized Promotion of Scandinavian Immigration 1866–1873* (Gothenburg, 1971), 267–268. On Jaeger, see O. N. Nelson et al., "Biographies of Scandinavians in Minnesota," in *History of the Scandinavians and Successful Scandinavians in the United States*, ed. O. N. Nelson, 2 vols., rev. ed. (1904; reprint, New York, 1969), 1:416–418.

[23]Luth Jaeger to Rasmus B. Anderson, 23 February 1889; Anderson appeared uninterested in the newspaper project; see Jaeger to Anderson, 17 April, 31 December 1889, 8 January 1890, all in R. B. Anderson Papers.

[24]Luth Jaeger to Rasmus B. Anderson, 18 December 1888, in R. B. Anderson Papers.

[25]Nils P. Haugen to Nicolai A. Grevstad, 26 March 1896, in Haugen Papers.

[26]See the reverse side of the letter from Luth Jaeger to Rasmus B. Anderson, 14 October 1891, in R. B. Anderson Papers.

[27]Luth Jaeger to Rasmus B. Anderson, 25 January, 17 December 1890, in R. B. Anderson Papers.

[28]Wist, "Pressen efter Borgerkrigen," 164.

[29]Luth Jaeger to Rasmus B. Anderson, 17 February 1894, in R. B. Anderson Papers.

[30]N. L. Bendz to Nils P. Haugen, 7 October 1890, in Haugen Papers.

[31]Nils P. Haugen to "General Passenger Agent" (name illegible), 16 March 1893; Haugen to N. L. Bendz, 31 May 1895, in Haugen Papers.

[32]*Svenska Amerikanska Tribunen*, 1, 8, 29 June, 6, 13, 20 July, 3, 10, 24, 31 August 1906.

[33]*Svenska Amerikanska Tribunen*, 31 August 1906.

[34]*Svenska Amerikanska Tribunen*, 7, 13 September 1906.

[35]*Förposten*, 4 August, 28 September, 19 October 1892.

[36]*Förposten* made no mention of the 1900 Republican state convention that nominated Robert M. La Follette for the governorship, nor of the dramatic 1904 Republican convention, when conservative "stalwarts" bolted the GOP. The paper did not even cover Swedish-American Irvine L. Lenroot's 1906 primary-election campaign; see *Förposten*, 10, 17, 24 August 1900, 29 April, 6, 13, 20, 27 May, 3, 10 June 1904, 17, 24, 31 August 1906.

[37]*Marinette Tribunen* and *Förposten*, 31 August 1906. The only difference between the front pages of the two papers was the name of the paper.

[38]G. L. Forsen to Herman L. Ekern, 16 August 1910, in Ekern Papers.

[39]Lloyd Hustvedt, *Rasmus Bjørn Anderson: Pioneer Scholar* (Northfield, MN, 1966), 3.

[40]Wist, "Pressen efter Borgerkrigen," 169; Hustvedt, *Rasmus Bjørn Anderson*, 235–236.

[41]Hustvedt, *Rasmus Bjørn Anderson*, 163–172, 181, 195–199, 212–213, 348; Merle Curti and Vernon Carstensen, *The University of Wisconsin, 1848–1925: A History*, 2 vols. (Madison, WI, 1949), 1:340–343.

[42]Hustvedt, *Rasmus Bjørn Anderson*, 236–237.

[43]V. Koren to Rasmus B. Anderson, 26 March 1910, in R. B. Anderson Papers; see also Hustvedt, *Rasmus Bjørn Anderson*, 235, 239, 249, 296–298.

[44]Hustvedt, *Rasmus Bjørn Anderson*, 106–107; see also *The Scandinavian American* (quoting the *Mt. Horeb Times*), 13 May 1904.

[45]*Amerika*, 10, 31 October 1900. See also Hustvedt, *Rasmus Bjørn Anderson*, 237.

[46]J. C. Gaveney to E. W. Keyes, 20 June 1901, in Elisha W. Keyes Papers, Library-Archives, Wisconsin Historical Society, Madison, WI.

[47]Rasmus B. Anderson and Albert O. Barton, *Life Story of Rasmus B. Anderson, Written by Himself with the Assistance of Albert O. Barton*, rev. ed. (Madison WI, 1917), 649.

[48]Those four papers were *Den Danske Pioneer* and *Nordiske Blade* (Democratic), *Arbejderen* (Socialist), and *Reform* (Prohibitionist).

[49]The five Democratic papers were *Tidende*, Minneapolis (1889), *Budstikken* (1889), *Michigan Skandinav* (1889), *Vikingen* (1889), and *Norske Amerikaner* (1910), all Norwegian-American. The Norwegian-American *Norden* of Chicago was listed by *N. W. Ayer & Son's American Newspaper Annual* as Republican in 1889, yet in 1888 it actually turned Democratic; see Rasmus B. Anderson to William F. Vilas, 3 August 1888, in William F. Vilas Papers, Library-Archives, Wisconsin Historical Society, Madison, WI; also *Norden*, 11 October 1890. The five Socialist papers were *Gaa Paa* (1910) and *Ny Tid* (1910), both Norwegian-American; *Forskaren* (1910) and *Svenska Socialisten* (1910), both Swedish-American, and *Revyen* (1910), which was Danish-American. The temperance papers were *Feltraabet* (1889), *Afholdsbasunen* (1889), and *Statstidende* (1910), all Norwegian-American, and *Svenska Familje Vännen* (1889), Swedish-American. The Populist journal, finally, was *Fremad* (1910), Norwegian-American.

[50]S. E. Olson, Charles Kittelson, M. A. Paulson, A. J. Blothen, Charles Reese, Odin Moe, J. A. Peterson, and Nicolai A. Grevstad to Nils P. Haugen, 15 February 1892, in Haugen Papers.

[51]*Skandinaven*, 29 October 1890. By 1892, *Skandinaven* was clearly back on the Republican track; see *Skandinaven*, 13 July 1892.

[52]Ulf Beijbom, *Utvandrarna och Svensk-Amerika* (Stockholm, 1986), 185.

[53]Hustvedt, *Rasmus Bjørn Anderson*, 285.

[54]*Svenska Amerikanaren*, July-August 1906; *Svenska Amerikanska Posten*, July-August 1906.

[55]In the masses of correspondence among Wisconsin politicians consulted by the present writer, no reference was made to *Svenska Tribunen*, whereas *Svenska Kuriren* found only scant mention (Alex J. Johnson to Nicolai A. Grevstad, 12 December 1912, 21 August 1913, 19 October 1913, in Nicolai A. Grevstad Papers, Archives of the Norwegian-American Historical Association, St. Olaf College, Northfield, MN); thus, those two papers did not undergo further analysis.

[56]*Hemlandet*, June-July 1894, 28 August 1890, 15 August 1900.

[57]*Hemlandet*, May-August 1906; 11 September 1906.

[58]Arlow W. Andersen, *Rough Road to Glory: The Norwegian-American Press Speaks Out on Public Affairs, 1875–1925* (Philadelphia, 1975), 45–56; *Den danske Pioneer*, 17 November 1887.

[59]Marzolf, *The Danish-Language Press*, 41, 58, 73, 77.

[60]Marzolf, *The Danish-Language Press*, 41.

[61]Indeed, in 1894, the *Pioneer* expressed sympathy for the People's Party, and two years later it vouched for William Jennings Bryan and the cause of free silver; see *Den danske Pioneer*, 18 October 1894, 29 October 1896; *Norden*, 5 May 1893.

[62]*Den danske Pioneer*, 2 August 1894.

[63]*Den danske Pioneer*, August 1896, May-June 1901.

[64]On these papers generally, see also Odd S. Lovoll, "*Decorah-Posten:* The Story of an Immigrant Newspaper," in *Norwegian-American Studies* 27 (Northfield, MN, 1977), 77–100; Wist, "Pressen efter Borgerkrigen," 102–110.

[65]*Decorah-Posten*, 11 September 1906; see also *Decorah-Posten*, 7 September 1906; *Minneapolis Tidende* 3, 10, 17, 24, 31 August 1906.

[66]Knute Nelson to Nicolai A. Grevstad, 12 March 1912, in Grevstad Papers.

[67]Wist, "Pressen efter Borgerkrigen," 45–46.

[68]See also Agnes M. Larson, "The Editorial Policy of Skandinaven, 1900–1903," *Studies and Records* 8 (Northfield, MN, 1934), 117; Jean Skogerboe Hansen, "*Skandinaven* and the John Anderson Publishing Company," *Norwegian-American Studies* 28 (Northfield, MN, 1979), 35.

[69]Theodore Blegen, *Norwegian Migration to America: The American Transition* (Northfield, MN, 1940), 241–275.

[70]See, for instance, *Skandinaven* 13 September 1890, 7 March 1891, 28 February 1894.

[71]Strømme, *Erindringer*, 254; see also Wist, "Pressen efter Borgerkrigen," 50.

[72]Peter Hendrickson to Rasmus B. Anderson, 1 August 1893, in R. B. Anderson Papers.

[73]Wist, "Pressen efter Borgerkrigen," 54–55; S. C. Hammer, "Grevstad, Nicolai Andreas," in *Norsk biografisk Leksikon*, ed. Edvard Bull and Einar Jansen, 19 vols. (Oslo, 1929), 4:596–597; biographical clipping from an unknown newspaper, 1 May 1917, box 1, in Grevstad Papers.

[74]*Skandinaven*, 8 June 1890.

[75]Nicolai A. Grevstad to Nils P. Haugen, 28 March 1890; Haugen to Grevstad, 4 April 1890, in Haugen Papers.

[76]Nicolai A. Grevstad to Nils P. Haugen, 28 March, 30 April 1890, in Haugen Papers.

[77]Nils P. Haugen to Nicolai A. Grevstad, 1 May 1895, in Haugen Papers.

[78]Nicolai A. Grevstad to Nils P. Haugen, 8 November 1890, in Haugen Papers; *Nordvesten*, 6 November 1890.

[79]Nicolai A. Grevstad to Nils P. Haugen, 6 June 1892, in Haugen Papers.

[80]Nils P. Haugen to Nicolai A. Grevstad, 29 February, 26 March, 21 May 1896; Grevstad to Haugen, 17 May 1896; undated letter from Grevstad to Haugen placed under June 1896; Haugen to Samuel A. Harper, 18 April 1896; Haugen to B. J. Castle, 7 January 1897, in Haugen Papers.

[81]Nils P. Haugen to Nicolai A. Grevstad, 29 February 1896; Haugen to A. R. Hall, 18 April, 21 May 1896; Hall to Haugen, 25 May 1896; Haugen to Samuel A. Harper, 4 March, 18 April 1896; Harper to Haugen, 13 April, 5 December 1896; Grevstad to Harper, 17 April 1896, in Haugen Papers.

[82]William Howard Taft to Philander C. Knox, 17 April 1911, in Grevstad Papers.

[83]J. C. Gaveney to E. W. Keyes, 20 June 1901, in Keyes Papers; A. N. Freng to Herman L. Ekern, 27 August 1906, in Ekern Papers.

[84]J. O. Davidson to John Anderson, 7 September 1906, in Davidson Papers.

[85]*Normannen*, 30 November 1894.

[86]H. P. Peterson to Robert M. La Follette, 26 February 1903; La Follette to Peterson, 3 March 1903, in Robert M. La Follette Papers, Library-Archives, Wisconsin Historical Society, Madison, WI. For counterassertions that *Superior Tidende* was under the influence of La Follette's enemies, see Nicolai A. Grevstad to Haugen, 17 April 1896, in Haugen Papers.

[87]Nils P. Haugen to "Mr. Parker," 13 April 1890; Haugen to Elias Jenson, 15 July 1892, in Haugen Papers.

[88]Rasmus B. Anderson to Pastor Fosmark, 17 August 1900, in R. B. Anderson Papers.

[89]James West Davidson et al., *Nation of Nations: A Narrative History of the American Republic* (New York, 1991), 708.

[90]Maldwyn A. Jones, *American Immigration* (Chicago, 1960), 238.

[91]Luth Jaeger to Rasmus B. Anderson, 17 December 1890, in R. B. Anderson Papers.

[92]A. J. Palmquist, *Ashland Bladet*, to J. O. Davidson, 18 August 1906, in Davidson Papers. See also A. B. Lange, *Scandia*, to Nils P. Haugen, 20 September 1892; J. L. Hjort, *La Crosse Tidende*, to Haugen, 5 May 1896; H. P. Peterson, *Superior Tidende*, to Haugen, 17 September 1900, in Haugen Papers; G. L. Forsen, *Marinette Tribunen*, to Herman L. Ekern, 16 August 1910; Ekern to C. J. Johnson, 19 August 1910, in Ekern Papers.

[93]Nils P. Haugen to Nicolai A. Grevstad, 26 January 1895, in Haugen Papers; Hansen, "Pressen til Borgerkrigens Slutning," 28; O. A. Buslett to Anlaug Buslett, 15 January 1909, in Ole A. Buslett Papers, Archives of the Norwegian-American Historical Association, St. Olaf College, Northfield, MN.

[94]Nicolai A. Grevstad to Herman L. Ekern, 31 July 1905; Ekern to Grevstad, 2 August 1905, in Ekern Papers.

[95]John M. Nelson to Herman L. Ekern, 4 May 1906; Herman L. Ekern to John Anderson, 9 May 1906, in Ekern Papers.

[96]Herman L. Ekern to Nils P. Haugen, 17 July 1906, in Haugen Papers; Ekern to Robert M. La Follette, 17 July 1906; Ekern to Andrew H. Dahl, 17 December 1905, in Ekern Papers.

[97]Herman L. Ekern to A. N. Freng, 28 August 1906, in Ekern Papers.

[98]Nils P. Haugen to A. B. Lange, 26 March 1895, in Haugen Papers.

[99]Rasmus B. Anderson to William F. Vilas, 3 August 1888, in Vilas Papers; Nicolai A. Grevstad to Nils P. Haugen, 13 April 1891, in Haugen Papers.

[100]S. E. Olson, Charles Kittelson, M. A. Paulson, A. J. Blothen, Charles Reese, Odin Moe, J. A. Peterson, and Nicolai A. Grevstad to Nils P. Haugen, 15 February 1892, in Haugen Papers. Actually, *Normannen* of Stoughton figured as "Independent" in the *Blue Book of Wisconsin*, 1893:353, and an editorial in *Normannen*, 11 May 1892, mildly criticized both major parties.

[101]L. S. Reque to Rasmus B. Anderson, 23 February 1893, in R. B. Anderson Papers.

[102]Nils P. Haugen to Elias Jenson, 15 July 1892, in Haugen Papers.

[103]Nils P. Haugen to John Anderson, 16 July 1892; Haugen to Nicolai A. Grevstad, 15 July 1892, in Haugen Papers. See also the thirty-seven letters dated 10 July 1892, and the eleven letters dated 15 July 1892, from Haugen to post office employees in Wisconsin, likewise in the Haugen Papers.

[104]The John Anderson Publishing Company to Nils P. Haugen, 25 August 1892; H. H. Rand to Haugen, 7 September 1892, in Haugen Papers.

[105]A. E. Johnson to Nils P. Haugen, 31 August 1892; Haugen to Johnson, 4 September 1892, in Haugen Papers.

[106]Nils P. Haugen to H. C. Thom, 19 September 1892, in Haugen Papers.

[107]Nicolai A. Grevstad to Nils P. Haugen, 21 October [1896; since Mark Hanna figured as national Republican chairman in the letter, it dates from 1896]; see also Haugen to Grevstad, 25 August 1896, both in Haugen Papers; "Per" to *Skandinaven*, 3 March 1897.

[108]*Hemlandet*, 21 October 1896.

[109]*Förposten*, 1, 8, 15, 22, 29 October, 1896. These announcements ceased in the 5 November 1896 issue, just after the general election.

[110]*Den danske Pioneer*, 15, 22 October 1896.

[111]William H. Taft to Nicolai A. Grevstad, 7 June 1911, in Grevstad Papers.

[112]Peter Hendrickson to Rasmus B. Anderson, 13 March 1889, in R. B. Anderson Papers; for assertions that Enander had served a prison sentence in Sweden, see Anderson and Barton, *Life Story of Rasmus B. Anderson*, 547–551. For mention of other Swedish-American editors receiving patronage plums, see Beijbom, *Utvandrarna och Svensk-Amerika*, 184–185.

[113]For an early discussion of the ethnic argument in the Scandinavian-

American press, see Kendrick C. Babcock, *The Scandinavian Element in the United States* (1914; reprint, New York, 1969), 173–178.

[114]*Förposten*, 24 August 1892; for similar Norwegian-American complaints, see *Superior Tidende*, 17 September 1896, 8 August 1902.

[115]*Superior Tidende*, 28 August 1914.

[116]*Svenska Amerikanska Tribunen*, 29 June 1906.

[117]*Folkets Avis*, 29 October 1896, 21 April 1902.

[118]*Svenska Amerikanaren*, 11 September 1890.

[119]*Hemlandet*, 2 November 1898.

[120]*Hemlandet*, 31 October 1912; see also *Hemlandet*, 26 October 1904; *Svenska Amerikanaren*, 1 November 1898, 31 October 1912; Sten Carlsson, *Skandinaviska politiker i Minnesota 1882–1900: En studie rörande den etniske faktorns roll vid politiska val i en immigrantstat* (Uppsala, 1970), 8.

[121]*Den danske Pioneer*, 11 October 1894; see also the reader letter from J. Mølgaard, Nebraska, to *Den danske Pioneer*, 30 October 1902, captioned, "Stem paa Danske" ("Vote for the Danish").

[122]*Norden*, 30 July 1894; *Amerika*, 4 July 1894. See also O. M. Kalheim to Nils P. Haugen, 30 May 1894, in Haugen Papers.

[123]*Skandinaven*, 27 July, 2 November 1890.

[124]*Skandinaven*, 28 October 1914.

[125]This argument was employed to support Knute Nelson in Minnesota (see *Nordvesten*, 23 July 1892), and Edmund Heg, son of Civil War veteran Hans C. Heg, in Wisconsin (see *Skandinaven*, 17 August 1892). The case of Edmund Heg is interesting, since he was in fact born in the United States and did not master the Norwegian language, yet stated that he was planning to learn it! The risk of having two "Norwegians" on the same state ticket was highlighted in Rasmus B. Anderson's *Amerika* fourteen years later: "If a Norwegian is also nominated for state treasurer, there is the risk that the other nationalities may view the ticket with anger"; see *Amerika*, 31 August 1906.

[126]*Posten*, 3 November 1892.

[127]*Skandinaven*, 7 September 1898.

[128]*Svenska Amerikanaren*, 1 November 1892. On Hertz's bossism, see also Strømme, *Erindringer*, 238.

[129]*Skandinaven*, 4 July 1894.

[130]According to *Skandinaven*, 19 February 1890, "The Roman church is rotten in its root; the trunk is hollow, even though the outer branches still are succulent and leafy." See also *Skandinaven*, 27 October 1914.

[131]*Skandinaven*, 13 September 1890, 7 March 1891.

[132]*Skandinaven*, 25 August 1897; the letter was by A. Søiseth.

NOTES TO CHAPTER FIVE

[1]One upstate New York paper did, however, mistakenly take the change of name back to Strum as an insult against the Democratic statesman; see Nils P. Haugen, *Pioneer and Political Reminiscences* (Madison, 1929), 92.

[2]O. Thomasgaard to Nils P. Haugen, 19 February, 7 April 1890; Haugen to H. A. Hayes, 13 March 1890, in Nils P. Haugen Papers, Library-Archives, Wisconsin Historical Society, Madison, WI; Haugen, *Pioneer and Political Reminiscences*, 92.

[3]Theodore Blegen, *Norwegian Migration to America: The American Transition* (Northfield, MN, 1940), 312.

[4]Roger Daniels, *Coming to America: A History of Immigration and Ethnicity in American Life* (New York, 1990), 114–115; *Blue Book of the State of Wisconsin* (Madison, WI), 1905:21–46.

[5]U.S. Bureau of the Census, *Eleventh Census of the United States, 1890: Population, Part One* (Washington, D.C., 1895), lxxiii. Among Polish and Hungarian immigrants, for instance, the corresponding figures were 20.9 percent and 37.4 percent, respectively; see also Harald Runblom, "Nordic Immigrants in the New World," in Hans Norman and Harald Runblom, *Transatlantic Connections: Nordic Migration to the New World after 1800* (Oslo, 1987), 218–219.

[6]Merle Curti, *The Making of an American Community: A Case Study of Democracy in a Frontier Community* (Stanford, CA, 1959), 227, 229.

[7]Curti, *The Making of an American Community*, 12–13, 96, 318–326, 334; for parallel Minnesota and Nebraska examples (the latter Danish-American), see Peer O. Strømme, *Erindringer* (Minneapolis, 1923), 178–180; Torben Grøngaard Jeppesen, *Dannebrog på den amerikanske prærie: Et dansk koloniprojekt i 1870'erne—landkøb, bygrundlæggelse og integration* (Odense, 2000), 241–244.

[8]"En Ven af Ret og Sandhed" to *Skandinaven*, 24 August 1900; N. J. Hagen to *Skandinaven*, 11 July, 19 September 1906; 17 August 1910; John Berg to *Skandinaven*, 22 August 1906.

[9]"F." to *Skandinaven*, 29 June 1900.

[10]"Flere Vælgere" to *Skandinaven*, 23 March 1901; see also A. Bobjerg, *En dansk Nybygd i Wisconsin: 40 Aar i Storskoven (1869–1909)* (Copenhagen, 1909), 16–17.

[11]"Svensk-amerikan" to *Hemlandet*, 29 September 1892.

[12]S. C. Nelson to *Skandinaven*, 20 May 1896; for pan-Scandinavian-American political reasoning, see also Olaf H. Green to Nils P. Haugen, 17 May 1892, in Haugen Papers.

[13]"A." to *Skandinaven*, 31 October 1894.

[14]"Idus Martii" to *Skandinaven*, 29 August 1894.

[15]On temperance as a local or state issue equivalent to the tariff, see Ballard

C. Campbell, *Representative Democracy: Public Policy and Midwestern Legislatures in the Late Nineteenth Century* (Cambridge, MA, 1980), 198.

[16]On the importance of party, nationality, locality, and personality to local politics, see also Curti, *The Making of an American Community*, 325–326.

[17]"Point Creek Voter" to *Skandinaven*, 3 November 1897.

[18]See pages 215–216, 225–226, and 235–236 in chapter 8.

[19]Richard J. Jensen, *The Winning of the Midwest: Social and Political Conflict, 1888–1896* (Chicago, 1971), 171–173. However, political clubs would sometimes greatly exaggerate their membership figures; see Edwin J. Gross, "A Political Grab Bag," typewritten manuscript in Edwin J. Gross Papers, Library-Archives, Wisconsin Historical Society, Madison, WI.

[20]O. E. Rasmus to L. B. Smith, 27 September 1892, in Rasmus B. Anderson Papers, Library-Archives, Wisconsin Historical Society, Madison, WI.

[21]*Reform*, 23 September 1890; *Skandinaven*, 9 March 1901; Carl G. O. Hansen, "Det norske Foreningsliv i Amerika," in *Norsk-Amerikanernes Festskrift 1914*, ed. Johs. B. Wist (Decorah, IA, 1914), 270. On club activities in rural areas, see *Amerika*, 1 August 1902; Peter T. Harstad and Bonnie Lindemann, *Gilbert N. Haugen: Norwegian-American Farm Politician* (Iowa City, 1992), 49.

[22]*Skandinaven*, 14 September 1892; "En Republikaner" to *Skandinaven*, 5 October 1892; *Hemlandet*, 20 October 1892; see also *Skandinaven*, 17 August 1892; E. R. Anderson to *Skandinaven*, 31 August 1892.

[23]W. D. Connor to Davidson, 14 June 1906, in James O. Davidson Papers, Library-Archives, Wisconsin Historical Society, Madison, WI. Connor ran for the lieutenant governorship.

[24]A. J. Peterson to J. O. Davidson, 22 June 1906, in Davidson Papers.

[25]Hansen, "Det norske Foreningsliv i Amerika," 270.

[26]E. C. Wall to William F. Vilas, 11 December 1890, in William F. Vilas Papers, Library-Archives, Wisconsin Historical Society, Madison, WI.

[27]See William F. Vilas to E. C. Wall, 23 April 1892 (date suggested by the Wisconsin Historical Society, Madison, WI); Wall to Vilas, 20 September 1894, in Vilas Papers.

[28]Leigh A. Smith to Rasmus B. Anderson, 8 October 1892, in R. B. Anderson Papers.

[29]Nicolai A. Grevstad to Nils P. Haugen, undated letter placed under March 1895, box 41 in Haugen Papers; Rasmus B. Anderson to O. A. Buslett, 10 August 1894, in Ole A. Buslett Papers, Archives of the Norwegian-American Historical Association, St. Olaf College, Northfield, MN.

[30]*Skandinaven*, 11 April 1894.

[31]Ulf Beijbom, *Swedes in Chicago: A Demographic and Social Study of the*

1846–1880 Immigration (Växjö, 1971), 330; Odd S. Lovoll, *A Century of Urban Life: The Norwegians in Chicago before 1930* (Northfield, MN, 1988), 167.

[32]Jørn Brøndal, "Socialister, fagforeninger og broderskaber i skandinavisk Amerika, 1870–1914," *Arbejderhistorie* 1999/1 (1999), 38–39.

[33]Lovoll, *A Century of Urban Life*, 270.

[34]Per Nordahl, *Weaving the Ethnic Fabric: Social Networks Among Swedish-American Radicals in Chicago, 1890–1940* (Umeå, 1994), 157–166.

[35]Hansen, "Det norske Foreningsliv i Amerika," 289.

[36]Odd S. Lovoll, *The Promise of America: A History of the Norwegian-American People* (Minneapolis, 1984), 164.

[37]Henry Bengston, *Skandinaver på vänstreflygeln i USA* (Stockholm, 1955), 36–37; *Blue Book of Wisconsin*, 1905:1109, 1913:671; Nordahl, *Weaving the Ethnic Fabric*, 42–46.

[38]In 1904, this federation was reorganized as Skandinaviska Socialistiska Arbetareförbundet (The Scandinavian Socialistic Labor Federation) with branch offices in both New York City, its stronghold, and Chicago. Bengston, *Skandinaver på vänstreflygeln*, 12, 42–43, 49; Nordahl, *Weaving the Ethnic Fabric*, 48–54.

[39]Bengston, *Skandinaver på vänstreflygeln*, 58–59; Nordahl, *Weaving the Ethnic Fabric*, 72; Odd-Stein Granhus, "Socialist Dissent among Norwegian Americans: Emil Lauritz Mengshoel, Newspaper Publisher and Author," *Norwegian-American Studies* 33 (Northfield, MN, 1992), 44–46.

[40]By 1914, according to Per Nordahl's figures, this organization consisted of 62 locals with 1,188 members in good standing. Nordahl, *Weaving the Ethnic Fabric*, 222–223 (my calculation on the basis of Nordahl's figures). According to Bengston, *Skandinaver på vänstreflygeln*, 65, the membership stood at 1,380 in 1914 and culminated in 1918 with 3,735 members.

[41]Bengston, *Skandinaver på vänstreflygeln*, 61, 68; Granhus, "Socialist Dissent among Norwegian Americans," 47.

[42]Those papers were the Norwegian-language *Gaa Paa/Folkets Røst*, Minneapolis 1903–1925; the Norwegian-Danish *Politiken/Ny Tid*, Minneapolis 1905–1910; the Danish-American *Revyen*, Chicago 1895–1953; and the Swedish-American *Forskaren*, Minneapolis 1894–1924, which in 1900 identified with populism but by 1910 had switched to socialism. See Brøndal, "Socialister, fagforeninger og broderskaber i skandinavisk Amerika," 40; also Michael Brook, "*Forskaren*: A Swedish Radical Voice in Minneapolis, 1894–1924," in *Swedes in the Twin Cities: Immigrant Life and Minnesota's Urban Frontier*, ed. Philip J. Anderson and Dag Blanck (St. Paul, MN, 2001), 198–209; Odd S. Lovoll, "*Gaa Paa*: A Scandinavian Voice of Dissent," *Minnesota History* 52/3 (Fall 1990), 86–99; Odd-Stein Granhus, "Scandinavian-American Socialist Newspapers with Emphasis on the Norwegian Contribution and E. L. Mengshoel's *Gaa Paa/Folkets Røst*," in *Essays on the Scandinavian-North American Radical Press, 1880s–1930s*, ed. Dirk Hoerder (Bremen, 1984), 79–99.

[43]Gary B. Nash et al., *The American People: Creating a Nation and a Society*, 2 vols. (New York, 1990), 2:637, 724–725.

[44]Nordahl, *Weaving the Ethnic Fabric*, 160–161, 171.

[45]Robert W. Ozanne, *The Labor Movement in Wisconsin: A History* (Madison, WI, 1984), 34–40; Robert Lewis Mikkelsen, "Immigrants in Politics: Poles, Germans, and the Social Democratic Party of Milwaukee," in *Labor Migration in the Atlantic Economies*, ed. Dirk Hoerder (Westport, CT, 1985), 284.

[46]Herbert F. Margulies, *The Decline of the Progressive Movement in Wisconsin, 1890–1920* (Madison, WI, 1968), 132–133; *Blue Book of Wisconsin*, 1911:729. Daniel De Leon's older Socialist Labor Party had a small presence in Wisconsin; see Ozanne, *The Labor Movement in Wisconsin*, 38.

[47]Mikkelsen, "Immigrants in Politics," 281, 283, 289; Donald Pienkos, "Politics, Religion, and Change in Polish Milwaukee, 1900–1930," *Wisconsin Magazine of History* 61 (Spring 1978), 181.

[48]Ozanne, *The Labor Movement in Wisconsin*, 39; *Blue Book of Wisconsin*, 1911:722.

[49]Bengston, *Skandinaver på vänstreflygeln*, 60–61, 64.

[50]Nordahl, *Weaving the Ethnic Fabric*, 222–223.

[51]On the size of the lumbering industry, see John D. Buenker, *The Progressive Era, 1893–1914*, vol. 4 of *The History of Wisconsin*, ed. William Fletcher Thompson (Madison, WI, 1998), 82.

[52]Ozanne, *The Labor Movement in Wisconsin*, 14–25.

[53]Terje I. Leiren, *Marcus Thrane: A Norwegian Radical in America* (Northfield, MN, 1987), 143–144.

[54]*Arbeideren*, 8 June 1886.

[55]*Folkevennen*, 18 August, 15 September, 6 October 1893.

[56]*Skandinaven*, 8 June 1890.

[57]*Superior Tidende*, 10 November 1898.

[58]*Superior Tidende*, 5 September 1901. On the paper's Socialist sympathies, see also H. P. Peterson (the former editor) to J. O. Davidson, 23 January 1906, in Davidson Papers.

[59]Nordahl, *Weaving the Ethnic Fabric*, 222–223.

[60]J. S. Stack to J. O. Davidson, 8 June 1906, in Davidson Papers.

[61]See fig. 4.2, Appendix I; and Lowell J. Soike, *Norwegian Americans and the Politics of Dissent, 1880–1924* (Northfield, MN, 1991), 103–104.

[62]Carl H. Chrislock, *The Progressive Era in Minnesota, 1899–1918* (St. Paul, MN, 1971), 106–113.

[63]Wisconsin State Board of Public Affairs, *Agricultural Co-operation* (Madison, WI, 1912), 51.

[64]Wisconsin State Board of Public Affairs, *Agricultural Co-operation*, 53–54. In 1905, Dodge County was 0.8 percent Scandinavian-American, Green County 2.5 percent; see "A Retabulation of Population Schedules from the Wisconsin State Census of 1905," table 26, Library-Archives, Wisconsin Historical Society, Madison, WI.

[65]In 1905, Polk County was 53.7 percent Scandinavian-American; see "A Retabulation from the Wisconsin State Census of 1905." Significantly, whereas Green and Dodge counties contained cooperatives organized on the principle of "one *share*, one vote" and others organized by "one *member*, one vote," the latter type of cooperative was much stronger in Polk County, as it was in the Scandinavian countries.

[66]Bobjerg, *En dansk Nybygd i Wisconsin*, 33–39; Johan Jørgensen to *Skandinaven*, 28 September 1898; Henrik Bredmose Simonsen, *Kampen om danskheden: Tro og nationalitet i de danske kirkesamfund i Amerika* (Århus, 1990), 91–92.

[67]*Skandinaven*, 26 February 1901.

[68]*Den danske Pioneer*, 16 August 1906, 13 August 1914; on William A. Henry, see also Merle Curti and Vernon Carstensen, *The University of Wisconsin, 1848–1925: A History*, 2 vols. (Madison, WI, 1949), 2:381–394.

[69]Wisconsin State Board of Public Affairs, *Agricultural Co-operation*, 91.

[70]Frederic C. Howe, *Denmark: The Coöperative Way* (New York, 1937), 258; Belle C. La Follette and Fola La Follette, *Robert M. La Follette, June 14, 1855–June 18, 1925*, 2 vols. (New York, 1953), 2:1085. In 1912, moreover, Charles McCarthy of the Legislative Reference Library dispatched John Sinclair, a member of his staff, to Denmark to study the cooperative movement; see Buenker, *The Progressive Era*, 644.

[71]Robert C. Nesbit, *Urbanization and Industrialization, 1873–1893*, vol. 3 of *The History of Wisconsin*, ed. William Fletcher Thompson (Madison, WI, 1985), 6.

[72]By 1901, Larsen indeed figured as a full-fledged Populist, and when he was reelected to the assembly in 1913, he entered as an "Independent." Larsen, who came to Wisconsin at the age of sixteen in company with his parents, not only married a Danish immigrant but was also a trustee of the Danish-American Dannebrog Society. Why he was elected twice to the assembly from an otherwise solidly Republican district remains unclear. Perhaps his status as a local hero who once saved seven people from drowning in a storm on Lake Superior contributed to his electoral success. See J. H. Beers et al., eds., *Commemorative Biographical Record of the West Shore of Green Bay* (Chicago, 1901), 634–635; *Blue Book of Wisconsin*, 1913:670; Mikkelsen, "Immigrants in Politics," 280–281.

[73]*Blue Book of Wisconsin*, 1893:622; *Skandinaven*, 26 October 1892.

[74]Soike, *Norwegian Americans and the Politics of Dissent*, 73.

[75]Robert C. Nesbit, *Wisconsin: A History* (Madison, WI, 1973), 452; Buenker, *The Progressive Era*, 76; Wisconsin State Board of Public Affairs, *Agricultural Co-operation*, 32.

[76]J. O. Davidson to John Zalurto, 1 May 1907, in Davidson Papers.

[77]*Amerika*, 24 July 1908.

[78]*Amerika*, 14 August 1908.

[79]*Amerika*, 18 June 1909; from 26 August 1910, *Amerika* ceased publishing material from the American Society of Equity, not stating why.

[80]Soike, *Norwegian Americans and the Politics of Dissent*, 144–146. Ekern himself became a member of the Society of Equity; see C. Meyer to Ekern, 2 October 1908; Ekern to Meyer, 7 November 1908, in Herman L. Ekern Papers, Library-Archives, Wisconsin Historical Society, Madison, WI.

[81]Chrislock, *The Progressive Era in Minnesota*, 108.

[82]Kenneth C. Acrea, "The Wisconsin Reform Coalition, 1892–1900: La Follette's Rise to Power," *Wisconsin Magazine of History* 52 (Winter 1968–1969), 138, 153, 157; Margulies, *The Decline of the Progressive Movement in Wisconsin*, 25–26, 96.

[83]W. D. Hoard to Alex. Corstvedt, 28 July 1894, in William Dempster Hoard Papers, Library-Archives, Wisconsin Historical Society, Madison, WI.

[84]Carl G. O. Hansen, "Pressen til Borgerkrigens Slutning," in *Norsk-Amerikanernes Festskrift 1914*, ed. Johs. B. Wist (Decorah, IA, 1914), 11–12; *Blue Book of Wisconsin*, 1911:551, 593.

[85]A two-page manuscript in the Albert O. Barton Papers, Library-Archives, Wisconsin Historical Society, Madison, WI, names Gabriel Bjornson of Christiana, Dane County, as the second Norwegian immigrant in America to be elected to a state legislature; he was member of the assembly in the 1851 session. See the *Blue Book of Wisconsin*, 1911:559.

[86]Peter Sørensen Vig, "Efterretninger om nogle af de første danske Nybyggere i Wisconsin," in *Danske i Amerika*, ed. Peter Sørensen Vig, 2 pts. in 1 vol. (Minneapolis, 1908), 1:250; Blegen, *Norwegian Migration to America: The American Transition*, 296, 322; *Blue Book of Wisconsin*, 1911:527–622; Millard L. Gieske and Steven J. Keillor, *Norwegian Yankee: Knute Nelson and the Failure of American Politics, 1860–1923* (Northfield, MN), 55. Henrik Cavling's assertion that Danish-born Soren Listoe was the first Danish American elected to an American legislature is incorrect: Listoe was only elected to the Minnesota legislature in 1875; cf. Henrik Cavling, *Fra Amerika*, 2 vols. (Copenhagen, 1897), 2:187–188.

[87]Blegen, *Norwegian Migration to America: The American Transition*, 322.

[88]Hansen, "Pressen til Borgerkrigens Slutning," 30.

[89]Haugen, *Pioneer and Political Reminiscences*, 53–56; Albert O. Barton, *La Follette's Winning of Wisconsin (1894–1904)* (Madison, WI, 1922), 165; Margulies, *The Decline of the Progressive Movement in Wisconsin*, 48.

[90]Leon D. Epstein, *Politics in Wisconsin* (Madison, WI, 1958), 35.

[91]For data on the membership of the state assembly and senate, see Appendix II.

[92]These figures are corrected for the circumstance that, in my estimate, the 60 seats taken by second-generation Scandinavian Americans represented *all* second-generation Scandinavian Americans in the assembly, 1891–1914; the 332 seats occupied by other members whose second-generation nativity could be traced, on the other hand, represented only 39.7 percent of the 836 seats taken by American-born assemblymen of non-Scandinavian background; see Appendix II.

[93]Due to the "Scandinavian" bias of the source material (see Appendix II), probably the Lutheran percentage is an overcount. For a penetrating analysis of the relationship between party and ethnocultural identity in the Wisconsin Assembly, 1886–1895, see Ballard C. Campbell, "Ethnicity and the 1893 Wisconsin Assembly," *Journal of American History* 62/1 (1975), 78–79, 83; Campbell, *Representative Democracy*, 36, 205–206. Likewise, several of Wisconsin's leading Scandinavian-American politicians had a lax attitude toward the Lutheran church. Of those fifty-six seats in Wisconsin's Assembly occupied by Scandinavian Americans with an identifiable religious affiliation between 1891 and 1914, eleven (19.6 percent) were taken by non-Lutherans, all Republicans.

[94]Of all the 294 professionals in the assembly in 1891–1914, 191 (65.0 percent) were attorneys. On the classification of job categories, see Appendix II.

[95]The exact figures were 29.0 percent for the native-born, 7.7 percent for the Scandinavian-born, and 11.9 percent for the other foreign-born assemblymen. Whereas according to Ballard C. Campbell between 1886 and 1895 10 percent of all assemblymen had a background as lawyers, I found that between 1897 and 1913 the figure had grown to 17 percent. See Campbell, *Representative Democracy*, 38.

[96]The exact share of rural businessmen and farmers among Scandinavian-American members was 52.3 percent; on the eminent community status of assemblymen, see also Campbell, *Representative Democracy*, 39.

[97]The 23 non-Republican young immigrant assemblymen included 14 individuals of Polish background, the Polish immigrants being a more recent immigrant group in Wisconsin than, say, the Scandinavian or the German.

[98]The exact figures were 32.3 percent for the Scandinavian-born, 53.5 percent for the other foreign-born, and 43.9 percent for the native-born members.

[99]On the role of the young attorneys in the assembly more generally, see also Epstein, *Politics in Wisconsin*, 113; Campbell, *Representative Democracy*, 38–39.

[100]According to U.S. Bureau of the Census, *Twelfth Census of the United States, 1900*, vol. 1, *Population, Part One* (Washington, D.C., 1901), 413, Rice Lake had a population of 3,002 individuals.

[101]*Reform*, 5 February 1895.

[102]O. A. Buslett to *Skandinaven*, 19 March 1909; "A. A-g" to *Hemlandet*, 5 October 1898.

[103]The average age among these Scandinavian-American professionals was 35.1 years; 23.8 percent of them were urban.

[104]Among the Danish-born legislators, three seats were taken by Danish immigrants born in German-occupied Slesvig.

[105]Of those twenty assembly seats occupied by second-generation Scandinavian-American assemblymen whose exact national background could not be specified, 75.0 percent were taken by Republicans.

[106]See Bayrd Still, "Norwegian-Americans and Wisconsin Politics in the Forties," *Studies and Records* 8 (Northfield, MN, 1934), 59; Blegen, *Norwegian Migration to America: The American Transition,* 554; Sten Carlsson, *Skandinaviska politiker i Minnesota 1882–1900: En studie rörande den etniske faktorns roll vid politiska val i en immigrantstat* (Uppsala, 1970), 7–8 (repeated in Sten Carlsson, "Swedes in Politics," in *From Sweden to America: A History of the Migration,* ed. Harald Runblom and Hans Norman [Uppsala, 1976], 291; Sten Carlsson, "Scandinavian Politicians in the United States," in *Scando-Americana: Papers on Scandinavian Emigration to the United States,* ed. Ingrid Semmingsen and Per Seyersted [Oslo, 1980], 153); Jon Wefald, *A Voice of Protest: Norwegians in American Politics, 1890–1917* (Northfield, MN, 1971), 27; Kendrick C. Babcock, *The Scandinavian Element in the United States* (1914; reprint, New York, 1969), 150; Beijbom, *Swedes in Chicago,* 315, 335; Sune Åkerman and Hans Norman, "Political Mobilization of the Workers: The Case of the Worcester Swedes," in *American Labor and Immigration History, 1877–1920s: Recent European Research,* ed. Dirk Hoerder (Urbana, IL, 1983), 242; Hans Norman, *Från Bergslagen til Nordamerika: Studier i migrationsmönster, social rörlighet och demografisk struktur med utgångspunkt från Örebro län 1851–1915* (Uppsala, 1974), 258–259, 270; Charles W. Estus, Kevin L. Hickey, and Kenneth J. Moynihan, "The Importance of Being Protestant: The Swedish Role in Worcester, Massachusetts, 1868–1930," in *Swedes in America: Intercultural and Interethnic Perspectives on Contemporary Research. A Report of the Symposium Swedes in America: New Perspectives,* ed. Ulf Beijbom (Växjö, 1993), 49–50.

[107]Stein Kuhnle, *Patterns of Social and Political Mobilization: A Historical Analysis of the Nordic Countries* (London, 1975), 10–28, 49; see also page 32 in chapter 1, above.

[108]See page 27 in chapter 1.

[109]Robert C. Ostergren, *A Community Transplanted: The Trans-Atlantic Experience of a Swedish Immigrant Settlement in the Upper Middle West, 1835–1915* (Madison, WI, 1988), 161.

[110]The same argument about the Minnesota influence cannot be made about Wisconsin's Norwegian Americans, since most Norwegian Americans in Minnesota settled in the *western* part of the state, on the borders of North and South Dakota; see Carlsson, *Skandinaviska politiker i Minnesota,* 14.

[111]Babcock, *The Scandinavian Element,* 150; Wefald, *A Voice of Protest,* 27; Blegen, *Norwegian Migration to America: The American Transition,* 554.

[112]Cavling, *Fra Amerika,* 2:66.

[113]Judging by "A Retabulation from the Wisconsin State Census of 1905," by far the majority of the assembly seats (991, or 82.3 percent) represented constituencies that were less than 20 percent Scandinavian-American. Among the thirty-seven seats representing constituencies more than 40 percent Scandinavian-American, fully 67.6 percent belonged to first-and second-generation Scandinavian-American legislators.

[114]See pages 25–28 in chapter 1.

[115]"En Vælger" to *Skandinaven*, 17 September 1890.

[116]A. H. Ratwick to *Skandinaven*, 22 October 1914.

[117]Sime was in fact nominated for the assembly by the Republican Party but lost in the general election; see the *Blue Book of Wisconsin*, 1915:506.

[118]"Ino" to *Skandinaven*, 25 April 1891. Scots-American Assemblyman Joseph Henderson was in fact not reelected to the assembly in 1892.

[119]"Norsk Republikaner" to *Skandinaven*, 16 September 1896. Beach was in fact elected to the assembly.

[120]"En Farmer" to *Skandinaven*, 26 October 1898. Løberg lost the election to his Republican Yankee rival, Fred J. Frost.

[121]Ed. Emerson to *Skandinaven*, 20 February 1895.

[122]"Korr." to *Skandinaven*, 20 January 1891.

[123]One exception was *Skandinaven*'s 1900 support for Bjørn Holland of Iowa County; see *Skandinaven*, 24 October 1900.

[124]*Superior Tidende*, 17, 24 September, 29 October, 5 November 1896; *Amerika*, 10 August 1906; *Förposten*, 28 October 1898.

[125]62.3 percent of all elective state offices taken by native-born politicians were occupied by professionals (76.7 percent of those professionals living in urban areas); the corresponding figure for immigrant politicians was 18.2 percent (with 100 percent living in urban areas); among members of both houses of Congress, the corresponding figures were 68.8 percent for the native-born (with 89.3 percent living in urban areas) and 52.0 percent for the foreign-born (with 84.6 percent living in urban areas), respectively.

[126]Haugen, *Pioneer and Political Reminiscences*, 5, 42; Gieske and Keillor, *Norwegian Yankee*, 10, 13, 54; George M. Stephenson, *John Lind of Minnesota* (Minneapolis, 1935), 6–7, 18; Richard B. Lucas, *Charles August Lindbergh, Sr.: A Case Study of Congressional Insurgency, 1906–1912* (Uppsala, 1974), 19–20. One Scandinavian-American farmer making it to Congress was Gilbert N. Haugen of Iowa; see Harstad and Lindemann, *Gilbert N. Haugen*, 201–202; another was Haldor E. Boen, the Populist from Minnesota.

[127]In the assembly the corresponding figure was significantly lower, 38.3 percent. None of the Canadian-born assemblymen and senators had French names; Assemblyman Gagnon (the sessions of 1899 and 1901) came closest, yet his first name was Jonas.

[128]Significantly, people born in Britain and Canada alone (excluding Ireland) made up 57.6 percent of the senate's immigrant body.

[129]"Norsk-født Amerikaner" to *Skandinaven*, 4 June 1906.

[130]Nils P. Haugen to G. L. Jones, 5 May 1892, in Haugen Papers.

[131]See for instance "Republikaner" to *Skandinaven*, 10 October 1894; H. T. Hanson to *Skandinaven*, 10 August 1910.

[132]The following Republican candidates, all Norwegian-American, were nominated between 1890 and 1904: Syver E. Brimi for railroad commissioner (1890); Atley Peterson for state treasurer and J. E. Heg for railroad commissioner (1892); Sewell A. Peterson for state treasurer (1894 and 1896); James O. Davidson for state treasurer (1898 and 1900); James O. Davidson for lieutenant governor (1902 and 1904). The following Democratic candidates were nominated: Thomas Thompson (Swedish-American) for railroad commissioner (1890 and 1892); P. O. Strømme (Norwegian-American) for state treasurer (1898); O. R. Skaar (Norwegian-American) for insurance commissioner (1894) and for attorney general (1902). See the *Blue Book of Wisconsin*, 1891:575–577, 1893:623–625, 1895:661–663, 1897:656–658, 1899:748–751, 1901:725–727, 1903:1069–1072, 1905:1069–1072.

[133]Haugen, *Pioneer and Political Reminiscences*, 56.

[134]Sewell A. Peterson to Nils P. Haugen, 31 May 1894, in Haugen Papers.

[135]J. O. Davidson to Andrew H. Dahl, 29 March 1898, in Davidson Papers.

[136]*Skandinaven*, 24 August 1898.

[137]Gieske and Keillor, *Norwegian Yankee*, 97–120; Stephenson, *John Lind of Minnesota*, 41–42. The first Danish American to be elected to Congress was Charles W. Woodman of Chicago, in one estimate a corrupt "machine" politician; see *Reform*, 20 November 1894.

[138]*Skandinaven*, 12 January, 14 February, 27 April, 18, 27, 31 July, 12, 16, 17 August, 1, 18, 25 October 1890; *Fædrelandet og Emigranten*, 23 July, 6, 20 August 1890; *Nordvesten*, 5 June, 13 November 1890; *Amerika*, 24 September, 28 October, 19 November 1890.

[139]Dahle was elected to Congress in 1898 and 1900; Nelson in 1906, remaining there with one interruption (1919–1921) until 1933; and Lenroot in 1908, remaining there until 1919, when he filled the vacancy in the United States Senate caused by the death of Paul Husting; he retained his seat there until 1927.

[140]"Flere Vælgere" to *Fædrelandet og Emigranten*, 23 July 1890.

[141]*Skandinaven*, 27 July, 12 August 1890. For a parallel Swedish-American argument, see *Hemlandet*, 23 September 1896.

[142]*Skandinaven*, 4 July 1894.

[143]Christian B. Nielsen, *Praktisk Raadgiver for Udvandrere til Amerika Udarbejdet med særligt Hensyn til Regeringens Friland og dets Erholdelse i de vestlige Stater*, rev. ed. (1871; reprint, Copenhagen, 1975), page 7 in chapter 3.

[144]Bruce Levine et al., *Who Built America? Working People and the Nation's Economy, Politics, Culture, and Society*, 2 vols. (New York, 1992), 2:99–100; Leon D. Epstein, *Political Parties in the American Mold* (Madison, WI, 1986), 135.

[145]Bryce here quoted from Nash et al., *The American People*, 2:648; Richard Hofstadter, *The American Political Tradition and the Men Who Made It* (New York, 1948), 169; see also Epstein, *Political Parties in the American Mold*, 137.

[146]Patrick F. Palermo, "The Rules of the Game: Local Republican Political Culture in the Gilded Age," *The Historian* 47/4 (August, 1985), 491.

[147]John A. Garraty, *The New Commonwealth, 1877–1890* (New York, 1968), 257–258; Nash et al., *The American People*, 2:650.

[148]Epstein, *Politics in Wisconsin*, 29.

[149]See the undated list, "Federal Employees and Appointees in and from Wisconsin," placed under 1903 in Robert M. La Follette Papers, Library-Archives, Wisconsin Historical Society, Madison, WI; see also the *Milwaukee Sentinel*, 29 January 1902, 1 June 1904; Lincoln Steffens, "The Story of Governor La Follette" (1904; reprint) in *La Follette*, ed. Robert S. Maxwell (Englewood Cliffs, NJ, 1969), 109; Robert S. Maxwell, *La Follette and the Rise of the Progressives in Wisconsin* (Madison, WI, 1956), 63–64.

[150]E. W. Keyes to Joseph V. Quarles, 6 January 1899, in Elisha W. Keyes Papers, Library-Archives, Wisconsin Historical Society, Madison, WI.

[151]W. D. Hoard to Robert M. La Follette, 5 December 1900, in La Follette Papers.

[152]Nils P. Haugen to J. J. Graslie, 1 February 1895, in Haugen Papers.

[153]Nils P. Haugen to Mert Herrik, 30 August 1890, in Haugen Papers.

[154]See the many patronage applications from 16 December through 25 December 1900, in box 51 in La Follette Papers, for instance E. O. Plummer to Robert M. La Follette, 16 December 1900.

[155]J. P. Peterson to J. O. Davidson, 22 March 1905, in Davidson Papers.

[156]R. J. Flint to Robert M. La Follette, 19 February 1906, in La Follette Papers; Nils P. Haugen to John A. Johnson, 7 December 1889, in Haugen Papers.

[157]A. A. Johnson to Nils P. Haugen, 24 November 1894, in Haugen Papers; P. C. Nelsen to J. O. Davidson, 19 November 1898, in Davidson Papers.

[158]Nils P. Haugen to R. J. Flint, 9 February 1889, in Haugen Papers.

[159]See page 98 in chapter 4.

[160]Nils P. Haugen to Benjamin Harrison, 23 December 1889, in Haugen Papers.

[161]Nils P. Haugen to Charles Foster, 1 September 1891, in Haugen Papers.

[162]Nils P. Haugen to Sewell A. Peterson, 8 September 1890; see also Haugen to John DeGroff, 30 November 1889, in Haugen Papers.

[163]Nils P. Haugen to Syver E. Brimi, 17 December 1889, in Haugen Papers.

[164]Nils P. Haugen to Griff O. Jones, 10 December 1889; see also Haugen to O. I. Ronning, 23 June 1892, in Haugen Papers.

[165]State of Wisconsin, *Journal of the Assembly* (Madison, WI, 1909), 1909:916–918.

[166]O. A. Buslett to Anlaug Buslett, 15, 19 January, 7 February, 31 March 1909, in Buslett Papers.

[167]Waldemar Ager to O. A. Buslett, 2 February 1909, in Buslett Papers.

[168]O. A. Buslett to Anlaug Buslett, 22 March 1909; L. Stavnheim to O. A. Buslett, 27 July 1909, in Buslett Papers.

[169]O. A. Buslett to Anlaug Buslett, 18, 26 April 1909, in Buslett Papers; see also O. A. Buslett to *Skandinaven*, 7 May 1909.

[170]Herman L. Ekern to Lily Ekern, 16 February 1903, in Ekern Papers; *Superior Tidende*, 25 April 1901; George A. Olson to O. A. Buslett, 9 March 1909; O. A. Buslett to Anlaug Buslett, 9 May 1909, in Buslett Papers.

[171]O. A. Buslett to *Skandinaven*, 28 March 1901.

[172]O. A. Buslett to *Skandinaven*, 19 March 1909.

[173]O. A. Buslett to *Skandinaven*, 3 August 1910. On Buslett's 1910 defeat, see also pages 79–80 in chapter 3.

[174]Lloyd Hustvedt, *Rasmus Bjørn Anderson: Pioneer Scholar* (Northfield, MN, 1966), 209.

[175]*Fædrelandet og Emigranten*, 18 June 1890.

[176]P. O. Strømme to Rasmus B. Anderson, 26 May 1891; see also Wilbur S. Tupper to Anderson, 22 May 1891, in R. B. Anderson Papers.

[177]Hustvedt, *Rasmus Bjørn Anderson*, 218, suggests that not even Anderson really believed in his own chances; on the other hand, if we are to trust Strømme's memoirs (not discussed by Hustvedt), Anderson was enthusiastic about his prospects.

[178]P. O. Strømme to Rasmus B. Anderson, 8 June 1891, in R. B. Anderson Papers.

[179]Strømme, *Erindringer*, 296.

[180]P. O. Strømme to Rasmus B. Anderson, 8 June 1891, in R. B. Anderson Papers.

[181]Strømme, *Erindringer*, 297; *Reform*, 15 September 1891.

[182]P. O. Strømme to Rasmus B. Anderson, 11 July 1891, in R. B. Anderson Papers.

[183]L. S. Reque to Rasmus B. Anderson, 27 June 1891, in R. B. Anderson Papers.

[184]Wilbur S. Tupper to Rasmus B. Anderson, 22 May, 27 August 1891, 18 January 1892; Andreas Ueland to Anderson, 17, 26 June 1891; Josiah Bayfield to Anderson, 8 August 1891, in R. B. Anderson Papers; Hustvedt, *Rasmus Bjørn Anderson*, 218.

[185]*Skandinaven,* 29 June 1892.

[186]Wilbur S. Tupper to Rasmus B. Anderson, 22 May 1891, in R. B. Anderson Papers.

[187]Quoted from Hustvedt, *Rasmus Bjørn Anderson,* 218.

[188]Mark Hanna to Nils P. Haugen, 10 October 1896, in Haugen Papers.

[189]Nils P. Haugen to Mark Hanna, 10 October 1896; on 13 January 1897, Haugen wrote a letter to his own mother in the English language; both letters in Haugen Papers.

[190]*Superior Tidende,* 8 October 1896.

[191]Nils P. Haugen to A. A. Johnson, 8 September 1894, in Haugen Papers; also quoted in Jensen, *Winning of the Midwest,* 137.

NOTES TO CHAPTER SIX

[1]Nils P. Haugen to Robert M. La Follette, 27 May 1900, in Nils P. Haugen Papers, Library-Archives, Wisconsin Historical Society, Madison, WI; Herman L. Ekern to Anton Rognlien, 26 October 1904; Ekern to A. Garthus, 5 May 1906; Ekern to La Follette, 25 July 1906; Ekern to A. B. Peterson, 6 June 1908; Ekern to Sivert Rekstad, 25 June, 2 November 1908; "Trempealeau County," a list placed under July 1908, all in Herman L. Ekern Papers, Library-Archives, Wisconsin Historical Society, Madison, WI.

[2]Robert M. La Follette to Nils P. Haugen, 15 April 1894, in Haugen Papers.

[3]On Oshkosh, see Randall Rohe, "Lumbering: Wisconsin's Northern Urban Frontier," in *Wisconsin Land and Life,* ed. Robert C. Ostergren and Thomas R. Vale (Madison, 1997), 225. On La Follette at the Plankinton, see Robert M. La Follette, *La Follette's Autobiography: A Personal Narrative of Political Experiences,* rev. ed. (Madison, WI, 1913), 139–148.

[4]Nils P. Haugen to Miller Winterbotham, 21 January 1891, in Haugen Papers; the appointment of Oakley happened at the expense of Rockwell J. Flint, an ally of Haugen; see also the very detailed discussion of the whole patronage affair in John C. Spooner to Philetus Sawyer, 29 January 1892, in John C. Spooner Papers, Manuscript Division, Library of Congress, Washington, D.C. According to R. La Follette, *La Follette's Autobiography,* 45, Oakley belonged to the so-called "Madison Ring," consisting also of Elisha W. Keyes, Philip Spooner (a brother of John C. Spooner), and Willet Main (a brother-in-law of John C. Spooner).

[5]Philetus Sawyer to John A. Johnson, 2 November 1891, in John A. Johnson Papers, Archives of the Norwegian-American Historical Association, St. Olaf College, Northfield, MN.

[6]Robert M. La Follette to Nils P. Haugen, 25 February 1892, the Haugen Papers. La Follette wrote that this meeting took place "sometime early last October." The public only learned about the clash after 24 October 1891, when Judge Siebecker caused a sensation by withdrawing from the treasurer cases; see Richard N.

Current, *Pine Logs and Politics: A Life of Philetus Sawyer, 1816–1900* (Madison, 1950), 261–264.

[7]Nils P. Haugen to Rockwell J. Flint, 2 February 1892, the Haugen Papers.

[8]On "island communities," see Robert H. Wiebe, *The Search for Order, 1877–1920* (New York, 1967), xiii and 44.

[9]Current, *Pine Logs and Politics*, 3–4.

[10]Current, *Pine Logs and Politics*, 140–142. See also N. P. H. [Nils P. Haugen] to [W. S.] Hidden, 4 June 1896, in La Follette Family Collection, Manuscript Division, Library of Congress, Washington, D.C.

[11]D. L. Agnew et al., eds., *Dictionary of Wisconsin Biography* (Madison, 1960), 335.

[12]David P. Thelen, *The New Citizenship: Origins of Progressivism in Wisconsin, 1885–1900* (Columbia, MO, 1971), 250–262.

[13]William T. La Follette to Robert M. La Follette, 2 November 1891, in La Follette Family Collection.

[14]Nils P. Haugen to H. T. Engoe, 27 March 1896, in Haugen Papers. La Follette quoted from Herbert F. Margulies, *The Decline of the Progressive Movement in Wisconsin, 1890–1920* (Madison, WI, 1968), 36.

[15]A. R. Hall to Samuel A. Harper, 12 October 1896, in Robert M. La Follette Papers, Library-Archives, Wisconsin Historical Society, Madison, WI; Kenneth C. Acrea, "The Wisconsin Reform Coalition, 1892–1900: La Follette's Rise to Power," *Wisconsin Magazine of History* 52 (Winter 1968–1969), 136–137.

[16]This point was stressed in the *New York Evening Post*, 14 October 1897, and in R. La Follette, *La Follette's Autobiography*, 222.

[17]Leon D. Epstein, *Political Parties in the American Mold* (Madison, WI, 1986), 158–163.

[18]Current, *Pine Logs and Politics*, 106.

[19]Epstein, *Political Parties in the American Mold*, 137.

[20]Current, *Pine Logs and Politics*, 199.

[21]*Milwaukee Sentinel*, 19 February 1901; Henry C. Payne to John C. Spooner, 7, 14 February 1901; Spooner to Payne, 11 February 1901; Charles F. Pfister to Spooner, 19 February 1901, in Spooner Papers.

[22]Acrea, "The Wisconsin Reform Coalition," 134–138; for an emphasis on the role played by Belle C. La Follette, see Lucy Freeman, Sherry La Follette, and George A. Zabriskie, *Belle: The Biography of Belle Case La Follette* (New York, 1986); Bernard A. Weisberger, *The La Follettes of Wisconsin: Love and Politics in Progressive America* (Madison, WI, 1994); Nancy C. Unger, *Fighting Bob La Follette: The Righteous Reformer* (Chapel Hill, NC, 2000).

[23]Robert M. La Follette to R. D. Rood, and to George F. Cooper, 7 September 1896, in La Follette Papers.

[24]Margulies, *The Decline of the Progressive Movement in Wisconsin*, 42, 83–163.

[25]Isaac Stephenson, *Recollections of a Long Life, 1829–1915* (Chicago, 1915), 199–201; Margulies, *The Decline of the Progressive Movement in Wisconsin*, 45–46.

[26]Robert S. Maxwell, *La Follette and the Rise of the Progressives in Wisconsin* (Madison, WI, 1956), 173–177.

[27]On the concept of the American political party as a public utility, see Epstein, *Political Parties in the American Mold*, 167–174.

[28]John C. Spooner to Henry C. Payne, 11 February 1901, in Spooner Papers.

[29]David P. Thelen, *The Early Life of Robert M. La Follette* (Chicago, 1966), 50.

[30]Belle C. La Follette and Fola La Follette, *Robert M. La Follette, June 14, 1855–June 18, 1925*, 2 vols. (New York, 1953), 1:134–135, 232, 2:1125; La Follette quoted from Carl R. Burgchardt, "The Will, the People, and the Law: A Rhetorical Biography of Robert M. La Follette, Sr." (PhD diss., University of Wisconsin, 1982), 187.

[31]R. La Follette, *La Follette's Autobiography*, 199–200; *Milwaukee Sentinel*, 23 February 1897. Apparently, the newspaper-supplement campaign passed at least the 100,000 mark; see John A. Butler to Robert M. La Follette, 3 March 1897, in La Follette Papers.

[32]Isaac Stephenson to Robert M. La Follette, 13 January 1905, in La Follette Family Collection.

[33]Stephenson, *Recollections of a Long Life*, 244–248; Maxwell, *La Follette and the Rise of the Progressives in Wisconsin*, 176–177.

[34]B. La Follette and F. La Follette, *Robert M. La Follette*, 1:263–265, 509–512.

[35]Samuel A. Harper to D. C. Owen, 5 October 1896; also A. R. Hall to Harper, 22 September 1894; Kirby Thomas to Harper, 25 September 1894; Nils P. Haugen to Harper, 21 September 1897; Robert M. La Follette to C. E. Buell, 8 July 1898, in La Follette Papers.

[36]Quoted from Albert O. Barton, *La Follette's Winning of Wisconsin (1894–1904)* (Madison, WI, 1922), 416; John M. Whitehead to Ralph H. Gabriel, 22 April 1914, in John M. Whitehead Papers, Library-Archives, Wisconsin Historical Society, Madison, WI.

[37]Robert M. La Follette to C. C. Gittings, 17 April 1900, in La Follette Papers.

[38]Leon D. Epstein, *Politics in Wisconsin* (Madison, WI, 1958), 35–36.

[39]See page 133 in chapter 5.

[40]Robert M. La Follette to R. D. Rood, and to George F. Cooper, 7 September 1896, in La Follette Papers.

[41]Waldo Schumacher, "The Direct Primary in Wisconsin" (PhD diss., University of Wisconsin, 1923), 78–80.

[42]*Milwaukee Journal*, 29 October 1904.

[43]Philip Gleason, *Speaking of Diversity: Language and Ethnicity in Twentieth-Century America* (Baltimore, 1992), 16–18.

[44]Belle C. La Follette to Nils P. Haugen, 30 June 1894; see also George C. Koeppen to Haugen, 23 June 1894; Haugen to Koeppen, 27 June 1894; Haugen to Robert M. La Follette, 28 June 1894, in Haugen Papers.

[45]Robert M. La Follette to Nils P. Haugen, 6 June 1894, in Haugen Papers.

[46]On this issue, see also Richard J. Jensen, *The Winning of the Midwest: Social and Political Conflict, 1888–1896* (Chicago, 1971), 130–131.

[47]John C. Spooner to Henry C. Payne, 25 February 1892, in Spooner Papers.

[48]Samuel A. Harper to J. Bassel, 10 October 1896, in La Follette Papers.

[49]A. R. Hall to Nils P. Haugen, 25 April 1894, in Haugen Papers.

[50]Nils P. Haugen to Robert M. La Follette, 23 February 1894, in Haugen Papers; see also Assemblyman William T. Lewis's statement in the *Milwaukee Sentinel*, 9 April 1897.

[51]Jørn Brøndal, "The Quest for a New Political Order: Robert M. La Follette and the Genesis of the Direct Primary in Wisconsin, 1891–1904" (master's thesis, University of Copenhagen, 1993), 86–90.

[52]*Milwaukee Sentinel*, 13, 14, 21 February 1901. The four speakers quoted here were, in sequence, H. C. Adams, Levi H. Bancroft, W. D. Corrigan, and James G. Monahan.

[53]Ira B. Bradford to Nils P. Haugen, 4 July 1896, in Haugen Papers.

[54]C. J. Smith to James A. Stone, 19 February 1898, in James A. Stone Papers, Library-Archives, Wisconsin Historical Society, Madison, WI.

[55]Quoted from Robert C. Twombly, "The Reformer as Politician: Robert M. La Follette in the Election of 1900" (master's thesis, University of Wisconsin, 1964), 45.

[56]Woodrow Wilson here quoted from Mary Beth Norton et al., *A People and a Nation: A History of the United States*, 2 vols. (Boston, 1982), 2:550; see also John A. Garraty, *The New Commonwealth, 1877–1890* (New York, 1968), 236.

[57]Current, *Pine Logs and Politics*, 199.

[58]Agnew, *Dictionary of Wisconsin Biography*, 335.

[59]Thelen, *The New Citizenship*, 255, 259.

[60]See John D. Hicks, *The Populist Revolt: A History of the Farmers' Alliance and the People's Party*, rev. ed. (Minneapolis, 1955), 378–379.

[61]*Blue Book of the State of Wisconsin* (Madison, WI), 1893:420.

[62]See the state platforms of the Democratic and Republican parties in the *Blue Book of Wisconsin*, 1895:456, 459.

[63]Robert M. La Follette to Nils P. Haugen, 15 December 1892, in Haugen Papers.

[64]Robert M. La Follette to H. C. Waite, 6 July 1896, in La Follette Papers.

[65]*Milwaukee Sentinel,* 16 February 1893.

[66]On this point, I thus disagree with Thelen, *The New Citizenship,* 257–260, 288–289, 309.

[67]Nils P. Haugen to A. R. Hall, 30 December 1892; Hall to Haugen, 5 January 1893, in Haugen Papers.

[68]John A. Butler to Robert M. La Follette, 3 January 1901; for the view that state and municipal politics traditionally were sharply separated, see Ralph M. Easley to Robert M. La Follette, 23 July 1897, both in La Follette Papers.

[69]John A. Butler to William F. Vilas, 22 May 1893, in William F. Vilas Papers, Library-Archives, Wisconsin Historical Society, Madison, WI.

[70]John A. Butler to William F. Vilas, 26 December 1892, in Vilas Papers.

[71]*Milwaukee Sentinel,* 13 February 1901. The speaker was H. C. Adams, who at this time sided with La Follette.

[72]See page 6 in the Introduction.

[73]Gardner P. Stickney to John C. Spooner, 8 March 1901, in Spooner Papers.

[74]Henry Fink to John C. Spooner, 20 May 1901, in Spooner Papers.

[75]C. A. Badlong to E. C. Minor, 20 April 1903, in Spooner Papers.

[76]E. W. Keyes to Marvin Hughitt, 26 April 1899; Keyes to John Hicks, 7 December 1907, in Elisha W. Keyes Papers, Library-Archives, Wisconsin Historical Society, Madison, WI.

[77]*Milwaukee Journal,* 3 February 1903; *Milwaukee Sentinel,* 2 September 1901.

[78]Robert M. La Follette to R. D. Rood, 4 July 1896, in La Follette Family Collection; H. E. Ticknor to Robert M. La Follette, 27 August 1897, in La Follette Papers.

[79]*Milwaukee Journal,* 1 October 1902.

[80]La Follette's speech here quoted from the *Milwaukee Journal,* 17 July 1902.

[81]*Milwaukee Free Press,* 3 September 1904.

[82]J. C. Gaveney to E. W. Keyes, 23 July 1902, in Keyes Papers.

[83]*Blue Book of Wisconsin,* 1905:459, 1911:670–676.

[84]John Milton Cooper, Jr., "Robert M. La Follette: Political Prophet," *Wisconsin Magazine of History* 69/2 (Winter 1985–1986), 91.

[85]The Beedle pamphlet is found under August 1910 in box 9 in Ekern Papers.

[86]Barton, *La Follette's Winning of Wisconsin,* 230.

[87]George E. Scott to Henry Johnson, 1 August 1911, in Henry Johnson Papers, Library-Archives, Wisconsin Historical Society, Madison, WI.

[88]La Follette's speech is found in box B 212 in La Follette Family Collection.

Notes to Chapter Seven

[1]"En Farmergut" to *Skandinaven*, 29 March 1893.

[2]Homer Fowler to Nils P. Haugen, 11 October 1893, in Nils P. Haugen Papers, Library-Archives, Wisconsin Historical Society, Madison, WI.

[3]Gary B. Nash et al., *The American People: Creating a Nation and a Society*, 2 vols. (New York, 1990), 2:663–665.

[4]*Den danske Pioneer*, 2 August 1894.

[5]John D. Buenker, *The Progressive Era, 1893–1914*, vol. 4 of *The History of Wisconsin*, ed. William Fletcher Thompson (Madison, WI, 1998), 10; David P. Thelen, *The New Citizenship: Origins of Progressivism in Wisconsin, 1885–1900* (Columbia, MO, 1971), 58–59; *Reform*, 30 April 1895.

[6]See, for instance, "Ein fraa Sjaak" to *Skandinaven*, 14 February 1894; "En af de 14" to *Skandinaven*, 5 September 1894; N. T. Larsen to *Skandinaven*, 16 January 1895.

[7]See, for instance, the anonymous letter from Ettrick, Trempealeau County, Wisconsin, to *Skandinaven*, 30 January 1894; "T.H.A." to *Skandinaven*, 16 January 1895; "K.H.S." to *Skandinaven*, 13 June 1894.

[8]Quoted from James West Davidson et al., *Nation of Nations: A Narrative History of the American Republic* (New York, 1991), 778–779.

[9]Bruce Levine et al., *Who Built America? Working People and the Nation's Economy, Politics, Culture, and Society*, 2 vols. (New York, 1992), 2:137–144; Richard J. Jensen, *The Winning of the Midwest: Social and Political Conflict, 1888–1896* (Chicago, 1971), 238–268.

[10]On the expanded activities of the Municipal League of Milwaukee in 1895 and 1896, see Thelen, *The New Citizenship*, 219–222, 262–268.

[11]Nils P. Haugen, *Pioneer and Political Reminiscences* (Madison, 1929), 4–66.

[12]Nils P. Haugen to Rasmus B. Anderson, 7 January 1886, also Haugen to Anderson, 22 March 1886, in Rasmus B. Anderson Papers, Library-Archives, Wisconsin Historical Society, Madison, WI.

[13]Nils P. Haugen to F. A. Husher, 25 November 1886, in Haugen Papers.

[14]John A. Johnson to Rasmus B. Anderson, 21 January 1887, in R. B. Anderson Papers.

[15]On Haugen's appointments, see pages 134–136 in chapter 5.

[16]Nils P. Haugen to Rasmus B. Anderson, 17 March 1887, in R. B. Anderson Papers; Nils P. Haugen to Nicolai A. Grevstad, 26 January 1895, in Haugen Papers.

[17]Haugen, *Pioneer and Political Reminiscences*, 75–76.

[18]Nils P. Haugen to Nicolai A. Grevstad, 25 August 1896, in Haugen Papers. Haugen mentioned Knute Nelson by name several times in the letter.

[19]Haugen, *Pioneer and Political Reminiscences*, 75–82.

[20]George M. Stephenson, *John Lind of Minnesota* (Minneapolis, 1935), 105–107, 117–118.

[21]Nils P. Haugen to O. J. Dahle, 2 November 1891, in Haugen Papers.

[22]Nils P. Haugen to John Lind, 16 September 1893, in Haugen Papers.

[23]John Lind to Nils P. Haugen, 23 August 1894, 7 June 1896, in Haugen Papers.

[24]Haugen, *Pioneer and Political Reminiscences*, 105–106.

[25]See pages 93–95 in chapter 4.

[26]Belle C. La Follette and Fola La Follette, *Robert M. La Follette, June 14, 1855–June 18, 1925*, 2 vols. (New York, 1953), 1:11. According to "A Retabulation of Population Schedules from the Wisconsin State Census of 1905," table 26, Library-Archives, Wisconsin Historical Society, Madison, WI, in 1905 Primrose was 58.6 percent Norwegian-American.

[27]Robert M. La Follette, *La Follette's Autobiography: A Personal Narrative of Political Experiences*, rev. ed. (Madison, WI, 1913), 75–80, 177–178, 207–208.

[28]Nils P. Haugen to Myron H. McCord, 13 July 1891, in Haugen Papers.

[29]W. W. Winterbotham to Nils P. Haugen, 3 July 1890; Haugen to A. R. Hall, 20 August 1890, in Haugen Papers; biographical clipping from the *Appleton Post*, 5 June 1905, in A. R. Hall Papers, Library-Archives, Wisconsin Historical Society, Madison, WI.

[30]Nils P. Haugen to Robert M. La Follette, 30 December 1892, in Haugen Papers; Albert O. Barton, *La Follette's Winning of Wisconsin (1894–1904)* (Madison, WI, 1922), 93–101; Stanley P. Caine, *The Myth of a Progressive Reform: Railroad Regulation in Wisconsin 1903–1910* (Madison, WI, 1970), 11–12; Buenker, *The Progressive Era*, 416.

[31]Roswell Miller to Nils P. Haugen, 15 December 1893; Haugen to Miller, 22 December 1893, 25 January 1894, in Haugen Papers.

[32]Nils P. Haugen to A. R. Hall, 10 May 1894, A. R. Hall Papers; on the gubernatorial campaign of 1894, see also Stuart Dean Brandes, "Nils P. Haugen and the Wisconsin Progressive Movement" (master's thesis, University of Wisconsin, 1965), 54–68.

[33]Nils P. Haugen to A. M. Anderson, 23 December 1893, in Haugen Papers.

[34]Nils P. Haugen to Nicolai A. Grevstad, 4 January 1894, in Haugen Papers; Haugen, *Pioneer and Political Reminiscences*, 108.

[35]Nils P. Haugen to Robert M. La Follette, 23 February 1894; Haugen to A. P. Weld, 28 February 1894; P. H. Swift to Haugen, 6 February 1894; R. J. Flint to Haugen, 10 March 1894, in Haugen Papers.

[36]Robert M. La Follette to Nils P. Haugen, 15 April 1894; Haugen to Samuel A. Harper, 19 April 1894; see also Haugen to J. W. Bradshaw, 7 April 1894; Haugen to Nicolai A. Grevstad, and to La Follette, 11 April 1894; Haugen to G. E. Bryant, 17 April 1894, in Haugen Papers.

[37]*Milwaukee Sentinel*, 23 May 1894; Nils P. Haugen to Nicolai A. Grevstad, 11 April 1894, in Haugen Papers; *Skandinaven*, 30 May 1894; W. D. Hoard to "Watrous," 15 May 1894, in William Dempster Hoard Papers, Library-Archives, Wisconsin Historical Society, Madison, WI; John C. Spooner to John C. Koch, 11 July 1894; Koch to Spooner, 21 July 1894; W. H. Phipps to Spooner, 1 May 1894, in John C. Spooner Papers, Manuscript Division, Library of Congress, Washington, D.C.

[38]George Koeppen to E. W. Keyes, 31 May 1894, in Elisha W. Keyes Papers, Library-Archives, Wisconsin Historical Society, Madison, WI; *Milwaukee Sentinel*, 24 May 1894; Nils P. Haugen to Soren Listoe, 27 May 1894, in Haugen Papers.

[39]*Skandinaven*, 30 May 1894.

[40]R. La Follette, *La Follette's Autobiography*, 177–178; Nils P. Haugen to W. H. Dick, 25 June 1896, in Haugen Papers.

[41]John M. Nelson to Nils Holm, 25 April 1894; also G. E. Bryant to W. W. Winterbotham, 2 May 1894, in Haugen Papers.

[42]Circular by Robert M. La Follette dated 15 June 1894, in Haugen Papers.

[43]Nils P. Haugen to A. R. Hall, 10 May 1894, in Haugen Papers.

[44]Robert M. La Follette to Nils P. Haugen, 15 April 1894, in Haugen Papers.

[45]Nils P. Haugen to Soren Listoe, 24 April 1894, in Haugen Papers.

[46]Nils P. Haugen to Robert M. La Follette, 18 April 1894; Haugen to Samuel A. Harper, 19 April 1894, in Haugen Papers.

[47]Nils P. Haugen to A. R. Hall, 27 May 1894, in Haugen Papers.

[48]Nils P. Haugen to Soren Listoe, 24 April 1894; Haugen to Robert M. La Follette, 18 April 1894, in Haugen Papers.

[49]Sewell A. Peterson to Nils P. Haugen, 16 February 1894, in Haugen Papers. The two Norwegian-American rivals were Charles Lewiston of Hudson in St. Croix County and Atley Peterson of Soldiers Grove, Crawford County.

[50]Sewell A. Peterson to Nils P. Haugen, 19 May 1894; Haugen to Peterson, 28 May 1894, in Haugen Papers.

[51]Nils P. Haugen to Robert M. La Follette, to A. R. Hall, and to H. O. Walseth, 10 June 1894, in Haugen Papers. The two Scandinavian Americans were Norwegian-American H. O. Walseth and Swedish-American Halford Erickson, both of Superior, Douglas County.

[52]Nils P. Haugen to A. R. Hall, to O. O. Halls, to Soren Listoe, and to Robert M. La Follette, 27 May 1894, in Haugen Papers. Haugen also saw the editors of a couple of minor German-language papers.

[53]Nils P. Haugen to Robert M. La Follette, 27 May 1894, in Haugen Papers. On 28 May 1894, Sawyer wrote Elisha W. Keyes that he did not expect Haugen's candidacy to gather much strength, and that he had told several candidates that he had no plan of interfering in the nominating process; in Keyes Papers.

[54]Robert M. La Follette to Nils P. Haugen, 29 May 1894, in Haugen Papers.

[55]C. W. Mott to John C. Spooner, 24 May 1894, in Spooner Papers.

[56]Nils P. Haugen to O. O. Halls, 9 October 1893, in Haugen Papers.

[57]Nils P. Haugen to John A. Johnson, and to Robert M. La Follette, 27 May 1894, in Haugen Papers.

[58]See page 75 in chapter 3.

[59]Sewell A. Peterson to Nils P. Haugen, 18 June 1894; Haugen to Peterson, 19 June 1894, in Haugen Papers; O. M. Kalheim to Rasmus B. Anderson, 12 June 1894, in R .B. Anderson Papers; see also "Autobiographical Rough Draft, I-II," in Halle Steensland Papers, Library-Archives, Wisconsin Historical Society, Madison, WI.

[60]*Skandinaven*, 13 June 1894; Nils P. Haugen to John M. Nelson, 6 June 1894; Haugen to T. C. Lund, 7 June 1894; Belle C. La Follette to Haugen, 2 June 1894, in Haugen Papers.

[61]Nils P. Haugen to Charles Lewiston, 30 March 1894; Haugen to F. F. Morgan, 7 April 1894; Robert M. La Follette to Haugen, 2 June, 14 July 1894; Sewell A. Peterson to Haugen, 9 June 1894; A. R. Hall to Haugen, 29 June 1894, in Haugen Papers. See also A. R. Hall to Samuel A. Harper, 9 June 1894, in Robert M. La Follette Papers, Library-Archives, Wisconsin Historical Society, Madison, WI.

[62]Nils P. Haugen to Hans B. Warner, 28 May 1894; Haugen to Robert M. La Follette, 27 May 1894; Haugen to John M. Nelson, 6 June 1894, in Haugen Papers; E. W. Keyes to Hans B. Warner, 9 March 1894, in Keyes Papers.

[63]E. W. Keyes to Henry Casson, 14 March 1894, in Keyes Papers.

[64]Haugen, *Pioneer and Political Reminiscences*, 55.

[65]Hans B. Warner to E. W. Keyes, 25 May 1894, in Keyes Papers; see also Nils P. Haugen to Nicolai A. Grevstad, 30 June 1894, in Haugen Papers.

[66]Nils P. Haugen to George V. Borchsenius, 10 June 1894, in Haugen Papers.

[67]Nils P. Haugen to Nicolai A. Grevstad, 30 June 1894, in Haugen Papers.

[68]Nils P. Haugen to Robert M. La Follette, 7 June 1894; see also F. G. Dahlberg to Haugen, 21 June 1894, in Haugen Papers.

[69]Robert M. La Follette to Nils P. Haugen, 2 June 1894, in Haugen Papers.

[70]Nils P. Haugen to G. E. Bryant, 5 June 1894; Robert M. La Follette to Haugen, 7, 10 June 1894; Haugen to John M. Nelson, 6 June 1894, in Haugen Papers; *Skandinaven*, 20 June, 4, 11 July, 1, 22 August 1894; *Amerika*, 4 July 1894.

[71]Nils P. Haugen to Hans B. Warner, 23 June 1894, in Haugen Papers.

[72]C. R. Morse to Nils P. Haugen, 3 July 1894, in Haugen Papers.

[73]Belle C. La Follette to Nils P. Haugen, "July 30, 1894," in Haugen Papers. The letter bears a wrong date: it was clearly written before the state convention, probably on 30 June.

[74]*Madison Democrat*, 19 July 1894; John M. Nelson to Nils P. Haugen, 21 June 1894, in Haugen Papers.

[75]*Milwaukee Sentinel*, 26 July 1894; "Proceedings of the Republican State Convention of Wisconsin," box 7, in Albert O. Barton Papers, Library-Archives, Wisconsin Historical Society, Madison, WI.

[76]W. J. Brier to Nils P. Haugen, 10 July 1894; Robert M. La Follette to Haugen, 14 July 1894, in Haugen Papers; *Skandinaven*, 18 July 1894.

[77]*Milwaukee Sentinel*, 26 July 1894; see also Nils P. Haugen to E. S. Reed, 10 June 1894, in Haugen Papers.

[78]Robert M. La Follette to Nils P. Haugen, 16 July 1894, in Haugen Papers; see also Horace S. Merrill, *William Freeman Vilas: Doctrinaire Democrat* (Madison, 1991), 217–218.

[79]Nils P. Haugen to Walter S. Hidden, 3 October 1895, in Haugen Papers; *Skandinaven*, 1 August 1894.

[80]Nils P. Haugen to K. Knudson, 15 June 1894; E. N. Anderson to Haugen, 14 July 1894, in Haugen Papers; Millard L. Gieske and Steven J. Keillor, *Norwegian Yankee: Knute Nelson and the Failure of American Politics, 1860–1923* (Northfield, MN), 150.

[81]*Skandinaven*, 1 August 1894.

[82]C. W. Mott to John C. Spooner, 27 July 1894, in Spooner Papers.

[83]Nils P. Haugen to Robert M. La Follette, 11 June 1894; Haugen to W. D. Hoard, 17 June 1894, in Haugen Papers.

[84]Lloyd Hustvedt, *Rasmus Bjørn Anderson: Pioneer Scholar* (Northfield, MN, 1966), 220; "Ole Olson" to the *Madison Daily Democrat*, 4 July 1894.

[85]Rasmus B. Anderson and Albert O. Barton, *Life Story of Rasmus B. Anderson, Written by Himself with the Assistance of Albert O. Barton*, rev. ed. (Madison WI, 1917), 617–618; A. Ueland to Rasmus B. Anderson, 14 October 1894, in R. B. Anderson Papers; Hustvedt, *Rasmus Bjørn Anderson*, 220.

[86]Robert M. La Follette to Nils P. Haugen, 9 June 1894, in Haugen Papers.

[87]Circular dated 7 June 1894; G. E. Bryant to Nils P. Haugen, 7 June 1894, in Haugen Papers; W. D. Hoard to G. E. Bryant, 1 June 1894, in Hoard Papers. At a personal level, Hoard helped Haugen until hampered by illness; see Robert M. La Follette to Haugen, 15 April, 3 May 1894; Hoard to Haugen, 13 June 1894; Haugen to La Follette, 20 June 1894, in Haugen Papers.

[88]Robert M. La Follette to Nils P. Haugen, 10, 18 June, 6 July 1894; Belle C. La Follette to Nils P. Haugen, "July 30," 1894 (on the letter's date, see note 73 above), in Haugen Papers; Carroll P. Lahman, "Robert Marion La Follette as Public Speaker and Political Leader (1855–1905)" (PhD diss., University of Wisconsin, 1939), 355.

[89]*Skandinaven*, 20 June, 4 July 1894.

[90]B. La Follette and F. La Follette, *Robert M. La Follette*, 1:107. As H. C. Adams, likewise a critic of the caucus and convention system, noted in 1901, "Somebody begins to hustle. Voters friendly to the candidates are urged to be present at the caucus. . . . Success depends upon activity, skill in organization, in getting the right crowd to the caucus polls." Adams's contention was borne out that same year by a recommendation to the La Follette organization of a prospective supporter: "He is a young man and a decided hustler." H. C. Adams quoted in the *Milwaukee Sentinel*, 13 February 1901; S. H. Cady to E. Ray Stevens, 1 February 1901, in La Follette Papers; see also Lahman, "Robert Marion La Follette as Public Speaker and Political Leader," 356–357; Carl R. Burgchardt, "The Will, the People, and the Law: A Rhetorical Biography of Robert M. La Follette, Sr." (PhD diss., University of Wisconsin, 1982), 72–73.

[91]Belle C. La Follette to Nils P. Haugen, "July 30," 1894 (on the letter's date, see note 73 above), in Haugen Papers.

[92]John A. Johnson to Rasmus B. Anderson, 21 January 1887, in R. B. Anderson Papers; see also John C. Spooner to George Koeppen, 7 July 1894, in Spooner Papers.

[93]R. La Follette, *La Follette's Autobiography*, 186–187.

[94]Nils P. Haugen to A. T. Torgerson, 9 August 1894; Haugen to G. E. Bryant, 17 June 1894; Haugen to A. R. Hall, 19 June 1894, in Haugen Papers.

[95]Nils P. Haugen to Robert M. La Follette, 20 June 1894, in Haugen Papers.

[96]Robert M. La Follette to Nils P. Haugen, 9 June 1894, in Haugen Papers.

[97]John C. Spooner to George C. Koeppen, 7 July 1894, in Spooner Papers.

[98]Jerre T. Murphy to John C. Spooner, 5 June 1894; Spooner to Murphy, 24 June 1894, in Spooner Papers.

[99]John C. Spooner to Horace Rublee, and to George C. Koeppen, 29 May 1894, in Spooner Papers.

[100]George C. Koeppen to Nils P. Haugen, 23 June 1894, in Haugen Papers.

[101]George C. Koeppen to E. W. Keyes, 31 May 1894, in Haugen Papers.

[102]Horace Rublee to Nils P. Haugen, 24 June 1894, in Haugen Papers.

[103]S. W. Campbell to John C. Spooner, 5 June 1894; Roger Spooner to John C. Spooner, 6 July 1894; John C. Spooner to Hans B. Warner, 12 July 1894, in Spooner Papers.

[104]John C. Spooner to W. H. Phipps, to O. W. Arnquist, and to S. W. Campbell, 11 July 1894, in Spooner Papers; Phipps to Nils P. Haugen, 10 July 1890; Haugen to Robert M. La Follette, 11 June 1894, in Haugen Papers; *Blue Book of the State of Wisconsin* (Madison, WI), 1893:628.

[105]John C. Spooner to W. H. Phipps, 8 August 1894, in Spooner Papers.

[106]H. C. Thom to John C. Spooner, 17 July 1894; Henry C. Payne to Spooner, 28 July 1894, in Spooner Papers.

[107]C. W. Mott to John C. Spooner, 27 July 1894, in Spooner Papers; Robert M. La Follette to Nils P. Haugen, 16 July 1894; Haugen to H. G. Kress, 4 October 1895, in Haugen Papers.

[108]E. W. Keyes to Spooner, 30 July 1894; H. C. Reed to John C. Spooner, 9 August 1894, in Spooner Papers.

[109]S. E. Olson to Nils P. Haugen, 4 June 1894, in Haugen Papers.

[110]Nils P. Haugen to A. T. Torgerson, 9 August 1894, in Haugen Papers.

[111]Even though in all likelihood Henry C. Payne, the third member of the triumvirate, was less involved in the outcome of the state convention than Spooner and Sawyer, he did at least give that result his blessings; see Payne to Spooner, 28 July 1894, in Spooner Papers.

[112]Nils P. Haugen to Robert M. La Follette, 20 June 1894, in Haugen Papers.

[113]Nils P. Haugen to Nicolai A. Grevstad, 25 August 1894; on Haugen's concern about the railroad companies, see also Haugen to Robert M. La Follette, 7 February 1894; La Follette to Haugen, 21 February 1894, in Haugen Papers; see also R. La Follette, *La Follette's Autobiography*, 179–180.

[114]Robert M. La Follette to Nils P. Haugen, 6 July 1894, in Haugen Papers.

[115]Robert M. La Follette to H. P. Myrick, 13 September 1897, in La Follette Papers; *Milwaukee Sentinel*, 10 September 1897.

[116]Quoted from Lahman, "Robert Marion La Follette as Public Speaker and Political Leader," 413, 662.

[117]R. La Follette, *La Follette's Autobiography*, 186.

[118]Nils P. Haugen to Peter Lewis, 2 April 1896, in Haugen Papers; *Skandinaven*, 26 August 1896.

[119]Nils P. Haugen to Robert M. La Follette, 18 January 1895, in Haugen Papers.

[120]Nils P. Haugen to George V. Borchsenius, 3 August 1894; Sewell A. Peterson to Haugen, 14 January 1895, in Haugen Papers; *Skandinaven*, 31 November 1894.

[121]*Normannen*, 29 March 1895.

[122]*The Scandinavian American*, 11, 25 March 1904.

[123]John C. Spooner to O. W. Arnquist, 7 July 1894, in Spooner Papers; Nils P. Haugen to Nicolai A. Grevstad, 19 January 1895, in Haugen Papers.

[124]Nils P. Haugen to H. P. Peterson, 3 April 1898, in Haugen Papers.

[125]*Normannen* 3, 10, 17 August 1894; Rasmus B. Anderson to O. A. Buslett, 13 August 1894, in Ole A. Buslett Papers, Archives of the Norwegian-American Historical Association, St. Olaf College, Northfield, MN.

[126]Robert M. La Follette to Nils P. Haugen, 10 June 1894; Haugen to La Follette, 20 June 1894, in Haugen Papers.

[127]Barton, *La Follette's Winning of Wisconsin*, 196; E. W. Keyes to John C.

Spooner, 30 April 1902, in Keyes Papers; S. B. Todd to Henry C. Adams, 30 July 1902, in Henry C. Adams Papers, Library-Archives, Wisconsin Historical Society, Madison, WI.

[128]*Wisconsin State Journal*, 26 May, 4 June 1894; Belle C. La Follette to Nils P. Haugen, 1 June 1894, in Haugen Papers.

[129]R. La Follette, *La Follette's Autobiography*, 208–209; D. L. Agnew et al., eds., *Dictionary of Wisconsin Biography* (Madison, 1960), 265.

[130]*La Follette's Magazine* 6 (22 August 1914), 5.

[131]Albert Erlebacher, "Herman L. Ekern: The Quiet Progressive" (PhD diss., University of Wisconsin, 1965), 19–33.

[132]Erlebacher, "Herman L. Ekern," 257, 279, 305–306.

[133]Herman L. Ekern to Lily Ekern, 16 January 1903, in Herman L. Ekern Papers, Library-Archives, Wisconsin Historical Society, Madison, WI.

[134]Letterhead of Andrew H. Dahl to Herman L. Ekern, 27 June 1908, in Ekern Papers; also the letterhead of Henry Johnson to Otto Krenze, placed under "1914, c. 7 September," in Henry Johnson Papers, Library-Archives, Wisconsin Historical Society, Madison, WI.

[135]See pages 138–140 in chapter 5; P. O. Strømme to "Kjære Ven," undated circular from 1902, in Buslett Papers.

[136]Anonymous letters from Madison to *Skandinaven*, 30 January 1901, 29 October 1902.

[137]R. La Follette, *La Follette's Autobiography*, 177–178.

[138]Nils P. Haugen to "My dear Jens," 21 July 1892, in Haugen Papers.

[139]Nils P. Haugen to Irvine L. Lenroot, 12 December 1928; Lenroot to Haugen, 21 December 1928, in Irvine L. Lenroot Papers, Manuscript Division, Library of Congress, Washington, D.C.

[140]Herbert F. Margulies, *The Decline of the Progressive Movement in Wisconsin, 1890–1920* (Madison, WI, 1968), 31.

[141]Nils P. Haugen to C. E. Estabrook, 4 July 1896, in Haugen Papers; Richard N. Current, *Pine Logs and Politics: A Life of Philetus Sawyer, 1816–1900* (Madison, 1950), 280–286. In Haugen's opinion, Scofield only won the governorship upon conferring with Philetus Sawyer, Henry C. Payne, and Roswell Miller, president of the Chicago, Milwaukee, and St. Paul Railroad Company, in the latter's private railroad wagon in the Milwaukee railway yards.

[142]Barton, *La Follette's Winning of Wisconsin*, 125; Robert C. Twombly, "The Reformer as Politician: Robert M. La Follette in the Election of 1900" (master's thesis, University of Wisconsin, 1964), 98–101.

[143]Margulies, *The Decline of the Progressive Movement in Wisconsin*, 61–79.

[144]E. W. Keyes to J. W. Losey, 24 January 1901, in Keyes Papers; Gardner P. Stickney to John C. Spooner, 8 March 1901, in Spooner Papers; Emanuel L.

Philipp, *Political Reform in Wisconsin: A Historical Review of the Subjects of Primary Election, Taxation, and Railway Regulation*, ed. and abr. Stanley P. Caine and Roger E. Wyman (1910; Madison, WI, 1973), 27–28.

[145]Barton, *La Follette's Winning of Wisconsin*, 168.

[146]E. W. Keyes to George Weeks, 12 April 1897; Keyes to Henry C. Payne, 29 November 1902, in Keyes Papers.

[147]La Follette portrayed his personal delivery of his message as precedent-breaking, yet governors George W. Peck and William H. Upham also spoke in person; see R. La Follette, *La Follette's Autobiography*, 242–243; "Korr." to *Skandinaven*, 20 January 1891; John M. Whitehead to Ralph H. Gabriel, 22 April 1914, in John M. Whitehead Papers, Library-Archives, Wisconsin Historical Society, Madison, WI.

[148]Carl R. Burgchardt, *Robert M. La Follette, Sr.: The Voice of Conscience* (New York, 1992), 53–71.

[149]Haugen, *Pioneer and Political Reminiscences*, 138.

[150]J. O. Davidson to John F. Linehan, 23 January 1906; Davidson to A. J. Klofanda, 15 February 1906, in James O. Davidson Papers, Library-Archives, Wisconsin Historical Society, Madison, WI.

[151]E. W. Keyes to Marvin Hughitt, 11 June 1905, in Keyes Papers.

[152]E. W. Keyes to Nils P. Haugen, 9 August 1894, in Haugen Papers; on the 1906 campaign, see also Padraic Kennedy, "Lenroot, La Follette, and the Campaign of 1906," *Wisconsin Magazine of History* 42 (Spring 1959), 163–174.

[153]Nils P. Haugen to Nicolai A. Grevstad, 26 March 1895, in Haugen Papers.

[154]Belle Haugen to Belle C. La Follette, 4 February 1897, in Haugen Papers.

[155]See "+ + + ‡" (the symbol La Follette sometimes used to conceal his identity to spying postmasters) to "Dear Al" (Alfred T. Rogers), undated letter placed under September 1902, in box B 103 of the La Follette Family Collection, Manuscript Division, Library of Congress, Washington, D.C.; see also Rogers's ("A.T.R.") reply to La Follette, which the Wisconsin Historical Society, Madison, WI, suggests was written before November 1902, in the La Follette Papers. On La Follette's lack of confidence in postmasters, see La Follette to R. A. Elward, 18 March 1900, in La Follette Papers; for an example of a spying postmaster, see M. A. Lien to John J. Esch, 5 April 1903, in John J. Esch Papers, Library-Archives, Wisconsin Historical Society, Madison, WI.

[156]Caine, *The Myth of a Progressive Reform*, 125–126; Agnew, *Dictionary of Wisconsin Biography*, 163.

[157]H. P. Peterson to J. O. Davidson, 23 January 1906, in Davidson Papers.

[158]On Davidson's Norwegian name, see O. A. Buslett to Ed. Emerson, 4 March 1909, in Buslett Papers.

[159]M. O. Anbolee to J. O. Davidson, 25 December 1905, in Davidson Papers.

[160]Sewell A. Peterson to Nils P. Haugen, 16 February 1894, in Haugen Papers; J. O. Davidson to J. D. Nelsenius, 3 January 1901, in Davidson Papers; O. N. Nelson et al., "Biographies of Scandinavians in Wisconsin and Iowa," in *History of the Scandinavians and Successful Scandinavians in the United States*, ed. O. N. Nelson, 2 vols., rev. ed. (1904; reprint, New York, 1969), 2:269–270.

[161]B. La Follette and F. La Follette, *Robert M. La Follette*, 1:198–199.

[162]According to "A Retabulation from the Wisconsin State Census of 1905," 14.5 percent of the family heads in Crawford County were first- and second-generation Norwegian Americans; in Soldiers Grove, 35.7 percent of the family heads were of Norwegian background.

[163]See page 130 in chapter 5.

[164]J. O. Davidson to G. N. Risjord, 4 May 1905, in Davidson Papers.

[165]Nils P. Haugen to N. M. Rockman, 2 March 1890, in Haugen Papers; Haugen to Robert M. La Follette, 2 April 1906, in La Follette Papers; see also Buenker, *The Progressive Era*, 501, note 69. Haugen also quoted in Lowell J. Soike, *Norwegian Americans and the Politics of Dissent, 1880–1924* (Northfield, MN, 1991), 135.

[166]H. P. Peterson to Nils P. Haugen, 23 May 1906, in Haugen Papers.

[167]Robert M. La Follette to John M. Nelson, 17 January 1906; see also La Follette to Isaac Stephenson, 23 June 1906, in La Follette Papers.

[168]Barton, *La Follette's Winning of Wisconsin*, 99–103; Nils P. Haugen to H. P. Peterson, 23 February 1898, in Haugen Papers.

[169]Kenneth C. Acrea, "The Wisconsin Reform Coalition, 1892–1900: La Follette's Rise to Power," *Wisconsin Magazine of History* 52 (Winter 1968–1969), 152.

[170]J. O. Davidson to J. P. Peterson, 30 March 1905, in Davidson Papers.

[171]Herman L. Ekern to Fred J. Bohri, 25 January 1905, in Ekern Papers; Herbert F. Margulies, "Robert M. La Follette Goes to the Senate, 1905," *Wisconsin Magazine of History* 59 (Spring 1976), 222.

[172]Margulies, "Robert M. La Follette Goes to the Senate," 222–224.

[173]O. G. Munson to J. O. Davidson, 18 November 1905, in Davidson Papers; E. W. Keyes to John C. Spooner, and to H. C. Adams, 16 December 1905, in Keyes Papers; *Milwaukee Sentinel*, 15 December 1905; *Milwaukee Free Press*, 16 December 1905.

[174]J. O. Davidson to J. E. Lehr, 9 December 1905, in Davidson Papers.

[175]The following biographical sketch is based on Herbert F. Margulies, *Senator Lenroot of Wisconsin: A Political Biography, 1900–1929* (Columbia, MO, 1977), 1–68.

[176]Irvine L. Lenroot to A. R. Hall, 13 December 1900, in Lenroot Papers; Lenroot's speech here quoted from Margulies, *Senator Lenroot of Wisconsin*, 47.

[177]Speech placed under "1902," box 8, in Lenroot Papers.

[178]Margulies, "Robert M. La Follette Goes to the Senate," 220–222.

[179]J. O. Davidson to G. L. Miller, and to Hugh O'Connor, 14 January 1905, in Davidson Papers.

[180]J. O. Davidson to H. P. Peterson, 7 July 1905, in Davidson Papers.

[181]J. O. Davidson to Lorenzo N. Clausen, 7 July 1905; O. G. Munson to Davidson, 18 November 1905, in Davidson Papers.

[182]H. S. Comstock to Nils P. Haugen, 21 September 1905, in Haugen Papers; Kennedy, "Lenroot, La Follette, and the Campaign of 1906," 165.

[183]Clipping from the *Racine News*, 23 October 1905, in Lenroot Papers.

[184]J. O. Davidson to John L. Erickson, 3 November 1905; Davidson to A. J. Pederson, 10 November 1905; Davidson to I. D. Hurlburt, and to J. D. Stuart, 13 November 1905, in Davidson Papers.

[185]John Strange to J. O. Davidson, 31 January, 12 February 1906; J. F. Dithmar to Davidson, 29 March 1906; James A. Stone to Davidson, 3 April 1906; Davidson to W. D. Connor, 12 June 1906, in Davidson Papers.

[186]That speaking tours were theoretically possible, if very unusual, under the caucus and convention system was demonstrated by La Follette's limited round of speeches in 1902 and his full-fledged speaking campaign in 1904. This understanding of La Follette's speaking activities is based on my complete reading of the 37-volume "La Follette Clippings: Clippings from Wisconsin Newspapers Concerning the Direct Primary, Elections, Railroad Rates, and Taxation, 1895–1910," Library-Archives, Wisconsin Historical Society, Madison, WI; see also the speech lists, box 7, in Barton Papers, and in Burgchardt, *Robert M. La Follette, Sr.*, 217–226.

[187]Robert M. La Follette to Irvine L. Lenroot, 15 January 1906, in Lenroot Papers.

[188]Irvine L. Lenroot to Robert M. La Follette, 17 February 1906, in La Follette Papers; La Follette to Lenroot, 31 May 1906, in Lenroot Papers; *Skandinaven*, 31 May 1906.

[189]Irvine L. Lenroot to Clara Lenroot, 1 September 1906, in Lenroot Papers; O. G. Munson to G. C. Peterson, 1 September 1906, in Davidson Papers.

[190]J. O. Davidson to A. J. Peterson, 16 March 1905; Davidson to R. S. Cowie, 13 June 1906; O. G. Munson to Nicolai A. Grevstad, 3 August 1906, in Davidson Papers.

[191]William D. Connor to J. O. Davidson, 31 July 1906; O. G. Munson to Nicolai A. Grevstad, 3 August 1906, in Davidson Papers.

[192]Davidson's 1906 announcement of his run for the governorship is found in box 36 in the Davidson Papers; John Strange to J. O. Davidson, 12 February 1906, in Davidson Papers; *Superior Tidende*, 11 May 1906.

[193]F. M. Jackson to Herman L. Ekern, 14 July 1907; Ekern to Jackson, 16 July 1907, in Ekern Papers.

[194]*Skandinaven*, 25 May 1906; J. O. Davidson to W. D. Connor, 22 June 1906, in Davidson Papers.

[195]J. O. Davidson to J. C. Gaveney, 19 January 1906; Davidson to Andrew Dahlstrom, 11 May 1906, in Davidson Papers.

[196]La Follette's 20 July 1906 Milwaukee speech is found in box B 212 in the La Follette Family Collection.

[197]"Hon. Irvine Luther Lenroot. Voters' Handbook – 1906," 22, box 5 in Lenroot Papers.

[198]The bill proposed to reduce the share of a laborer's wage exempt from the payment of debts; see Ed. Emerson to Robert M. La Follette, 26 November 1905, in La Follette Papers; J. S. Stack to J. O. Davidson, 9 April 1906; Charles F. Kaempfer to Davidson, 12 July 1906; O. G. Munson to D. Conger, 21 August 1906, in Davidson Papers; Herman L. Ekern to Andrew H. Dahl, 25 August 1908, in Ekern Papers.

[199]J. S. Swenson to J. O. Davidson, 11 July 1906, in Davidson Papers.

[200]See, for instance, Van S. Bennett to J. O. Davidson, 23 July 1906; J. T. Hanson to Davidson, 24 July 1906; N. F. Pierce to Davidson, 28 July 1906; E. C. Leean to Davidson, 31 July 1906, in Davidson Papers; Robert M. La Follette to A. G. Zimmerman, 17 May 1906, in La Follette Family Collection.

[201]W. D. Hoard to Davidson, 26 July 1906, in Davidson Papers; Hoard to W. D. Connor, 10 August 1906, in Hoard Papers; John M. Nelson to Robert M. La Follette, 15 January 1906; La Follette to A. G. Zimmerman, 17 May 1906, in La Follette Papers; *Skandinaven*, 25 July 1906.

[202]J. R. Bloom to J. D. Beck, 16 February 1906; Robert M. La Follette to Isaac Stephenson, 23 June 1906; W. J. McElroy to A. T. Rogers, 10 August 1906, in La Follette Papers; Irvine L. Lenroot to La Follette, 5 January 1906, in Lenroot Papers.

[203]J. O. Davidson to W. N. Fitzgerald, 9 December 1905, in Davidson Papers.

[204]E. W. Keyes to John C. Spooner, 10 January 1906, in Keyes Papers.

[205]John C. Spooner to E. W. Keyes, 18 June 1906, in Keyes Papers.

[206]Horace A. Taylor to E. W. Keyes, 31 May 1906, in Keyes Papers.

[207]David Atwood to J. O. Davidson, 24 January 1906, in Davidson Papers. Also quoted in Kennedy, "Lenroot, La Follette, and the Campaign of 1906," 169–170; see also Van S. Bennett to Davidson, 23 July 1906; W. B. McArthur to Davidson, 3 August 1906; J. T. Huntington to O. G. Munson, 25 August 1906, in Davidson Papers.

[208]W. D. Connor to J. O. Davidson, 25 May 1906; Davidson to Connor, 1 June 1906; O. G. Munson to Connor, 28 July 1906, in Davidson Papers.

[209]J. O. Davidson to Robert M. La Follette, 28 November 1905, in La Follette

Papers; Davidson to La Follette, 5, 9 February, 9 May 1906, in Davidson Papers; Willet M. Spooner to John C. Spooner, 23 August 1906; also Willet M. Spooner to John C. Spooner, 8 August 1906, in Spooner Papers.

[210]J. O. Davidson to A. J. Pederson, 23 April 1906, in Davidson Papers.

[211]Newspaper editors were quick to appreciate the new emphasis upon political advertising in the mass media; see R. J. Flint to Davidson, 23 July 1906, in Davidson Papers.

[212]W. D. Connor to J. O. Davidson, 7, 14 June 1906, in Davidson Papers.

[213]La Follette's 20 July 1906 Milwaukee speech is found in box B 212 in the La Follette Family Collection.

[214]*Skandinaven*, 26 July 1906. An editorial in *Amerika*, 3 August 1906, likewise attacked La Follette's "attorney argument."

[215]Nicolai A. Grevstad to Nils P. Haugen, 19 October 1905; Irvine L. Lenroot to Haugen, 23 October 1905, in Haugen Papers.

[216]Andrew H. Dahl to Herman L. Ekern, 3 November 1905; Ekern to Dahl, 16 November, 17 December 1905, in Ekern Papers; F. E. Tate to J. O. Davidson, 23 November 1905, in Davidson Papers; Ole G. Kinney to Robert M. La Follette, 1 March 1906; Nils P. Haugen to Robert M. La Follette, 2 April 1906, in La Follette Papers; Dahl to Haugen, 24 October 1905, 5 March 1906, in Haugen Papers; A. T. Rogers to Robert M. La Follette, 16 April 1906, in La Follette Family Collection; clipping from the "Milwaukee [Daily] News," 14 November 1905, box 16, in Lenroot Papers. Haugen later faltered in his support for Lenroot; see A. T. Rogers to La Follette, 7 May 1906, in La Follette Papers. Haugen, *Pioneer and Political Reminiscences*, 148–149, maintained that he advised against Lenroot's candidacy from the beginning, a claim that Soike, *Norwegian Americans and the Politics of Dissent*, 136, also mentions. For the view that La Follette was simply being naïve in supporting Lenroot, see Kennedy, "Lenroot, La Follette, and the Campaign of 1906," 174; Soike, *Norwegian Americans and the Politics of Dissent*, 135–136; Margulies, *The Decline of the Progressive Movement in Wisconsin*, 95–99; and David P. Thelen, *Robert M. La Follette and the Insurgent Spirit* (Madison, 1976), 48.

[217]Irvine L. Lenroot to Nils P. Haugen, 23 October 1905, in Haugen Papers.

[218]John M. Nelson to J. O. Davidson, 26 October 1905, in Davidson Papers.

[219]Andrew H. Dahl to Herman L. Ekern, 8, 20 November 1905; Ekern to Dahl, 10 November 1905, in Ekern Papers; Andrew Erickson to J. O. Davidson, 21 December 1905; Bjørn Holland to J. O. Davidson, 18 January 1906, in Davidson Papers.

[220]*Skandinaven*, 8 January 1906. Despite Ekern's urgings, *Skandinaven* did not publish the open letter until 16 February 1906: Herman L. Ekern to Nicolai A. Grevstad, 17 December 1905; Ekern to John Anderson, 20 January 1906; Andrew H. Dahl to Ekern, 23 February 1906, in Ekern Papers.

[221]J. O. Davidson to John Anderson and to Nicolai A. Grevstad, 8 January 1906; Davidson to A. J. Pederson, 24 January 1906, in Davidson Papers.

[222]Andrew H. Dahl to Nils P. Haugen, 20 November 1905, in Haugen Papers.

[223]*Amerika*, 3, 10, 31 August 1906.

[224]Robert M. La Follette to Nils P. Haugen, 16 January 1906, in Haugen Papers.

[225]Atley Peterson to *Skandinaven*, 25 May 1906, and to the *Milwaukee Free Press*, 28 May 1906.

[226]Alfred T. Rogers to the *Milwaukee Free Press*, 11 June 1906.

[227]Robert M. La Follette to Herman L. Ekern, 30 May 1906, in Ekern Papers.

[228]Herman L. Ekern to the *Milwaukee Free Press*, 13 June 1906.

[229]J. O. Davidson to G. L. Miller, 16 June 1906, in Davidson Papers.

[230]Nicolai A. Grevstad to J. O. Davidson, 25 July 1906, in Davidson Papers.

[231]*Skandinaven*, 26 June 1906.

[232]"Mr. Lenroot in Ashland," in "Hon. Irvine Luther Lenroot. Voters' Handbook – 1906," 47, in Lenroot Papers, box 5; manuscript titled "Ashland, June 23, 1906," in Lenroot Papers.

[233]Willet M. Spooner to John C. Spooner, 23 August 1906, in Spooner Papers.

[234]O. G. Munson to Nicolai A. Grevstad, 21 August 1906; also Carl K. Herried to J. O. Davidson, 21 August 1906; Davidson to Herried, 22 August 1906; Bert I. Bliss to O. G. Munson, 30 August 1906, all in Davidson Papers.

[235]J. O. Davidson to A. J. Pederson, 23 April 1906, in Davidson Papers.

[236]J. O. Davidson to Andrew Dahlstrom, 11 May 1906, in Davidson Papers.

[237]James Thompson to J. O. Davidson, 23 May 1906; circular letter from J. O. Davidson to Al Gilbertson and others, 24 May 1906, in Davidson Papers.

[238]J. O. Davidson to A. J. Pederson, 22 May 1906, in Davidson Papers.

[239]Herman L. Ekern to A. T. Rogers, 23 August 1906, in Ekern Papers.

[240]J. O. Davidson to Peter J. Smith, 31 January 1906, in Davidson Papers; Robert M. La Follette to Irvine L. Lenroot, 15 January 1906, in Lenroot Papers.

[241]Herman L. Ekern to Andrew H. Dahl, 27 August 1906, in Ekern Papers.

[242]A. T. Rogers to the *Milwaukee Free Press*, 11 June 1906.

[243]A. T. Rogers to Robert M. La Follette, 7 May 1906, in La Follette Papers; see also Herman L. Ekern to A. T. Rogers, 30 July 1906, in Ekern Papers.

[244]Jørgen Weibull, "The Wisconsin Progressives, 1900–1914," *Mid-America* 47 (July 1965), 213–215. According to "A Retabulation from the Wisconsin State Census of 1905," Burnett County was 42.1 percent Swedish-American, Price 21.0 percent.

[245]Robert M. La Follette to A. G. Zimmerman, 17 May 1906, in La Follette Papers.

[246]Theodore Kronshage to Robert M. La Follette, 4 September 1906, in La Follette Papers.

[247]Robert M. La Follette to Irvine L. Lenroot, 11 September 1906, in Lenroot Papers.

[248]O. G. Munson to F. J. Bohri, 27 October 1906, in Davidson Papers.

[249]Philip Lehner to A. T. Rogers, 30 January 1914, in La Follette Family Collection. On the absence of German Americans from Wisconsin politics, see also Charles C. McCarthy, *The Wisconsin Idea* (New York, 1912), 175; John R. Commons, *Myself: The Autobiography of John R. Commons* (Madison, WI, 1964), 106.

[250]Gieske and Keillor, *Norwegian Yankee*, 266–267.

[251]Ole A. Buslett to *Skandinaven*, 28 July 1906.

[252]See "Mr. Lenroot in Ashland," in "Hon. Irvine Luther Lenroot. Voters' Handbook – 1906," 47; also the speech manuscript, "Ashland, June 23, 1906," in Lenroot Papers.

[253]P. A. Guard to J. O. Davidson, 10 August 1906, in Davidson Papers.

[254]Ole A. Buslett to *Skandinaven*, 20 July 1910; see also "En Subskribent" to *Skandinaven*, 6 July 1910.

NOTES TO CHAPTER EIGHT

[1]Ed. Lorenzen to *Skandinaven*, 7 November 1894.

[2]See page 90 in chapter 4 and page 107 in chapter 5.

[3]For a discussion of these micro- and macro-historical perspectives, see pages 2–3 in the Introduction. It should be noted that the "ethnocultural interpretation" represents a macro-historical yet grassroots-oriented perspective.

[4]For this viewpoint, see Fredrik Barth, "Introduction," in *Ethnic Groups and Boundaries: The Social Organization of Culture Difference*, ed. Fredrik Barth (Bergen, 1969), 15; see also Milton M. Gordon, *Assimilation in American Life: The Role of Race, Religion, and National Origins* (New York, 1964), 81.

[5]Ole Skari to *Skandinaven*, 7 April 1897.

[6]On 2 November 1910, the last regular page with "Letters from the People" appeared. *Skandinaven* did not explain why the page was discontinued.

[7]*Skandinaven*, 11 November 1894.

[8]See *Skandinaven*, 1, 29 March 1893. The reader letters of the politically independent *Svenska Amerikanska Posten* are discussed in Ulf Jonas Björk, "'Folkets Röst,' The Pulse of the Public: *Svenska Amerikanska Posten* and Reader Letters, 1907–1911," *Swedish-American Historical Quarterly* 50 (April 1999), 4–17. Some published immigrant letter collections also include items printed in the press; see Theodore C. Blegen, ed., *Land of Their Choice: The Immigrants Write Home* (Minneapolis, 1955), vii; H. Arnold Barton, ed., *Letters from the Promised Land: Swedes in America, 1840–1914* (Minneapolis, 1975), 139–141; Frederick Hale, ed., *Danes*

in North America (Seattle, 1984), viii. On the relationship between private letters and letters to the press, see also Orm Øverland, "Innledning: De tidlige Amerikabrevene," in *Fra Amerika til Norge: Norske Utvandrerbrev,* ed. Orm Øverland and Steinar Kjærheim, 3 vols. (Oslo, 1992–1993), 1:26; Orm Øverland, "Innledning: En norsk-amerikansk vurdering av Amerikabrev i 1883," in Øverland and Kjærheim, *Fra Amerika til Norge,* 2:27–28; Niels Peter Stilling and Anne Lisbeth Olsen, *A New Life: Danish Emigration to North America as Described by the Emigrants Themselves in Letters 1842–1946* (Aalborg, 1994), 202, note 9.

[9]A similar analysis of the Danish-American press is hampered by the circumstance that only few issues of *Den Danske Pioneer,* by far the most influential paper, survive to this day.

[10]The depression era is defined as May 1893 through August 1897. On an average, *Skandinaven* printed 17.3 letters per week, or ca. 3,900 letters during the depression; likewise, *Svenska Amerikanska Posten* printed approximately seventeen letters per week; see Björk, "'Folkets Röst,' The Pulse of the Public," 6.

[11]328 pre-depression epistles to *Skandinaven,* beginning with January 1890, were studied, as were an additional 537 post-depression letters, the last dating from 1910. Generally speaking, two principles guided the sampling process. First, letters printed in election campaigns (defined as March through November of even-numbered years) were given high priority (amounting to 67.6 percent of the sampled letters); only for the depression years was systematic sampling outside the campaign season also undertaken. Second, generally, when a newspaper was picked for analysis, all letters were studied; in some cases, only Wisconsin letters were analyzed but then marked separately and not used, e.g., for geographical statistics (371 letters).

[12]Minnesota boasted a share of 24.5 percent of the reader letters to *Skandinaven,* Wisconsin 21.1 percent, Iowa 10.2 percent, North Dakota 9.8 percent, South Dakota 8.8 percent, Illinois 3.4 percent, and Nebraska 2.2 percent. Illinois boasted a share of 26.1 percent of the reader letters to *Hemlandet,* Minnesota 12.9 percent, Kansas 12.4 percent, Iowa 8.4 percent, Nebraska 7.6 percent, and Michigan 3.6 percent. Only 1.6 percent of *Hemlandet's* reader letters originated in Wisconsin.

[13]Whereas the *Skandinaven* letter sample contained fourteen letters from Chicago, it included twenty-eight from Trempealeau County. Combined, the letters from Chicago, the Twin Cities, and Milwaukee represented only 2.4 percent of the total *Skandinaven* letter sample but 9.2 percent of the *Hemlandet* sample.

[14]Of the 1,974 letters to *Skandinaven,* 41.1 percent were anonymous; the corresponding figure for the 249 letters to *Hemlandet* was an astonishing 71.5 percent.

[15]Among 662 letters to *Skandinaven* revealing gender, 8.2 percent bore a female signature; among fifty-five *Hemlandet* letters, the figure was an impressive 30.9 percent, but represented only nine writers; two writers, Emma Peterson of Algoma, Iowa, and "Jane" of Carlisle, Pennsylvania, were very prolific, together

submitting ten letters. On male preponderance also in *Svenska Amerikanska Posten*, see Björk, "'Folkets Röst,' The Pulse of the Public," 8. An analysis of *private* letters from Danish immigrants indicates a majority of female writers; see Anne Lisbeth Olsen, "The Immigrant Family on the Prairie as Seen through Personal Letters," in *On Distant Shores: Proceedings of the Marcus Lee Hansen Immigration Conference, Aalborg, Denmark June 29–July 1, 1992*, ed. Birgit Flemming Larsen, Henning Bender, and Karen Veien (Aalborg, 1993), 199–200.

[16]Nils P. Haugen to *Skandinaven*, 14 September 1898; John A. Johnson to *Skandinaven*, 27 August 1890; O. A. Buslett to *Skandinaven*, 28 March 1901; Bjørn Holland to *Skandinaven*, 22 February 1893; T. N. Hasselquist and C. O. Olander to *Hemlandet*, 23 October 1890.

[17]Peder Langbach to *Skandinaven*, 22 June, 14 September 1904; Odd Lovoll, *A Folk Epic: The Bygdelag in America* (Boston, 1975), 42.

[18]"Justus" to *Hemlandet*, 7 September 1898.

[19]"Løskar" to *Skandinaven*, 24 January 1894.

[20]See for instance "Skandinav" to *Skandinaven*, 24 January 1894; "En Hyrekarl" to *Skandinaven*, 2 May 1894.

[21]Among the *Skandinaven* letters, 49.8 percent dealt with politics; among the *Hemlandet* letters 55.0 percent. During political campaigns, 53.5 percent of the *Skandinaven* letters dealt with politics, outside campaigns 43.5 percent; all the *Hemlandet* letters sampled date from campaigns.

[22]N. T. Larsen to *Skandinaven*, 15 January 1895.

[23]See the guide for submission in *Skandinaven*, 4 January 1893, 7 November 1894, and the weekly guide for submission in *Hemlandet*, for instance 4 September 1890.

[24]See the answer to A. Søiseth, *Skandinaven*, 25 August 1897; see also Björk, "'Folkets Röst,' The Pulse of the Public," 11.

[25]*Skandinaven*, 21 October 1896.

[26]See the answer to Anfin Larsen, *Skandinaven*, 28 March 1893. In another case *Skandinaven* refused to publish the omitted portions; see H. M. Thorvik to *Skandinaven*, 25 August, 8 September 1897.

[27]"En gammel Farmer" to *Skandinaven*, 24 October 1894.

[28]See, for instance, Ole Erickson to *Skandinaven*, 8 July, 9 September, 16 September 1896.

[29]S. O. Rundal to *Skandinaven*, 18 April 1891; L. S. Cranemo to *Skandinaven*, 25 March 1891.

[30]S. O. Rundal to *Skandinaven*, 21 September 1892, 12 September 1894, 20 May 1896, 27 May 1896, 24 June 1896, 5 August 1896, 19 October 1898, 24 September 1902, 26 October 1904, 31 August 1910.

[31]P. G. Lindhardt, *Vækkelse og kirkelige retninger* (Copenhagen, 1959), 28.

On the use of clichés in Norwegian immigrant letters, see Orm Øverland, "Innledning," in Øverland and Kjærheim, *Fra Amerika til Norge*, 1:26.

[32]Herman L. Ekern to N. J. Hagen, 13 November 1908, in Herman L. Ekern Papers, Library-Archives, Wisconsin Historical Society, Madison, WI; Hagen to *Skandinaven*, 20 April 1892, 2 May, 15 August, 12 September, 3 October 1894, 21 October 1896, 17 February, 24 March, 12 May, 18 August 1897, 1 June 1900, 23 March 1904, 11 July, 19 September 1906, 17 August 1910.

[33]On a strict editorial policy concerning nonpolitical letters also, see Björk, "'Folkets Röst,' The Pulse of the Public," 6.

[34]Among 668 such letters to *Skandinaven*, 1890–1910, 84.7 percent expressed Republican sympathies; among 110 such letters to *Hemlandet*, 86.4 percent did so. The Democratic figures were correspondingly low, 5.1 percent and 4.5 percent, respectively; of 102 letters to *Skandinaven* and 55 to *Hemlandet* written prior to the outbreak of the 1893 depression, 18.6 percent and 14.5 percent, respectively, expressed Populist sympathies.

[35]H. Olson to *Skandinaven*, 28 March 1894; T. C. Kopseng to *Skandinaven*, 20 February 1895.

[36]John Larsen to *Skandinaven*, 28 March 1894.

[37]"Gammel Republikaner" to *Skandinaven*, 20 June 1894; see also page 195 in chapter 7.

[38]Herman L. Ekern to Irvine L. Lenroot, 14 August 1908, in Ekern Papers.

[39]Nils P. Haugen to O. O. Halls, 10 June 1894, in Nils P. Haugen Papers, Library-Archives, Wisconsin Historical Society, Madison, WI.

[40]"XXXX" to "Hr. Redaktør," 27 April 1895; on that same day, Haugen also wrote editor Grevstad of *Skandinaven* a letter; in Haugen Papers.

[41]Andrew H. Dahl to Herman L. Ekern, 3 November 1905, in Ekern Papers.

[42]Andrew H. Dahl to Nils P. Haugen, 20 November 1905, in Haugen Papers.

[43]Ed. Emerson to J. O. Davidson, 2 April 1906, in James O. Davidson Papers, Library-Archives, Wisconsin Historical Society, Madison, WI; Emerson to *Skandinaven*, 12 May 1906.

[44]"Milwaukier" to *Skandinaven*, 19 October 1892.

[45]The exact figures for *Skandinaven* and *Hemlandet*, respectively, were 19.5 percent and 22.6 percent.

[46]The exact figure for both *Skandinaven* and *Hemlandet* was 27.7 percent.

[47]J. Barkelay to *Skandinaven*, 20 February 1895.

[48]The exact figures for *Skandinaven* and *Hemlandet* were 52.7 percent and 49.6 percent, respectively.

[49]The analysis of 249 letters to *Hemlandet* (122 pre-depression letters, 101 depression letters, and 26 post-depression letters) included only 106 discussing political values and issues, too few to investigate chronological trends. In these let-

ters the main focus was on economic affairs (61.3 percent), followed by class-related matters (50.9 percent), ethnocultural matters (37.7 percent), pure politics (34.0 percent), "other" matters (5.7 percent), and Scandinavian affairs (1.9 percent).

[50]This does not, of course, refute the hypothesis that ethnocultural paradigms informed the thinking even of these Scandinavian-American letter writers.

[51]See the solid black columns in fig. 8.1, Appendix I.

[52]In 70.4 percent of these 199 letters, the Democrats were given the blame directly.

[53]Among 134 value-oriented letters written during the 1896 campaign, the currency question was discussed in 59.0 percent of the cases.

[54]"En Farmer" to *Skandinaven*, 28 October 1896.

[55]"O.L.L." to *Skandinaven*, 2 May 1894.

[56]Peter T. Engstrøm to *Skandinaven*, 7 April 1897; P. Lid to *Skandinaven*, 27 March 1895; "S." to *Skandinaven*, 10 February 1897.

[57]J. Crane to *Skandinaven*, 28 February 1894; "H.H." to *Skandinaven*, 6 June 1894.

[58]Martin Gellein to *Skandinaven*, 22 July 1896; see also "L" to *Hemlandet*, 21 October 1896.

[59]"J.H." to *Skandinaven*, 19 August 1896.

[60]"H.O.F." to *Skandinaven*, 19 August 1896.

[61]H. Olson to *Skandinaven*, 18 July 1894.

[62]John N. Romstad to *Skandinaven*, 22 August 1894.

[63]"Sverre" to *Skandinaven*, 28 April 1897; "Republikaner" to *Skandinaven*, 10 October 1894.

[64]G. O. Hough to *Skandinaven*, 6 February 1895; Hansine Hansen to *Skandinaven*, 27 March 1895.

[65]"D.O." to *Skandinaven*, 31 March 1897; S. O. Bridson to *Skandinaven*, 3 March 1897; E. P. Petersen to *Skandinaven*, 17 February 1897; "En Skatteyder" to *Skandinaven*, 3 June 1896.

[66]"Farmer matters" ranked second in the pre-depression years, fourth during the depression, and fifth after the depression, whereas "honesty and wisdom" ranked fifth, seventh, and second, respectively.

[67]For the pre-depression years, the exact figure was 53.0 percent of 100 letters; for the depression years 56.7 percent of 203 letters.

[68]The exact figure was 60.7 percent of 168 letters.

[69]"Skandinav" to *Skandinaven*, 24 January 1894; "En gammel Republikaner" to *Skandinaven*, 18 July 1894.

[70]"E." to *Skandinaven*, 6 June 1894.

.[71]N. H. Hilton to *Skandinaven*, 20 May 1896; Eli Pederson to *Skandinaven*, 15 July 1896; "Norsk Republikaner" to *Skandinaven*, 26 August 1896.

[72]The exact figure was 64.8 percent of 162 letters.

[73]The exact figure was 55.2 percent of 105 letters.

[74]"En Subskribent" to *Skandinaven*, 6 July 1910.

[75]G. W. Swenson to *Skandinaven*, 5 November 1898.

[76]J. J. McGillivray to *Skandinaven*, 27 April 1904.

[77]See, for instance, "R.S." to *Skandinaven*, 12 October 1910.

[78]General reference to ethnicity took place in 52.5 percent of the 984 political letters to *Skandinaven*; reference to ethnicity as part of a political argument took place in 36.4 percent of these letters. For the 137 political letters to *Hemlandet*, the corresponding figures were somewhat higher, i.e., 62.8 percent and 50.4 percent, respectively.

[79]Ethnic labels were employed in 52.2 percent of 163 pre-depression political letters to *Skandinaven* and in 45.9 percent of 257 letters postdating the depression, but only in 27.5 percent of 564 depression-era letters.

[80]Anti-Catholic slurs occurred in 6.2 percent of the 358 ethnopolitical letters to *Skandinaven*, anti-Jewish in 1.4 percent, and criticism of various other ethnic groups in 13.4 percent. Reference to a Scandinavian label was made in 91.1 percent of the ethnopolitical letters.

[81]Among the "Scandinavian" letters to *Skandinaven*, reference to Norwegian Americans was made in 78.5 percent of the cases, whereas the parallel Swedish-American figure was 11.7 percent, the Danish-American 9.8 percent. The corresponding figures for 61 "Scandinavian" letters to *Hemlandet* were 14.8 percent for the Norwegian Americans, 98.4 percent for the Swedish Americans, and 3.3 percent for the Danish Americans.

[82]The exact figures for *Skandinaven* and *Hemlandet* were 36.8 percent and 9.8 percent, respectively.

[83]"J.A. Edr." to *Hemlandet*, 3 November 1892.

[84]The Scandinavian label was used synonymously with just one of the three groups in only 30.0 percent of 120 letters to *Skandinaven*.

[85]"En Skandinav" to *Skandinaven*, 22 October 1890.

[86]Regional labels were employed in 4.9 percent of the 326 "Scandinavian" letters to *Skandinaven* and in 1.6 percent of 61 such letters to *Hemlandet*.

[87]S. E. Ødegaard to *Skandinaven*, 29 October 1890; "-" to *Skandinaven*, 7 September 1910.

[88]The exact figures were 56.3 percent and 72.9 percent, respectively.

[89]The exact figure was 51.7 percent.

[90]"Republikaner" to *Skandinaven*, 20 June 1894.

[91]"Tretten Towning" to *Skandinaven*, 8 August 1894.

[92]Martin Mortenson to *Skandinaven*, 27 April 1904.

[93]The exact figure was 14.8 percent.

[94]Those 170 letters include ninety-three blending organizational matters with issues and values.

[95]"En Farmer" to *Skandinaven*, 4 November 1896.

[96]R. R. Qualey to *Skandinaven*, 29 August 1894.

[97]C. W. Anderson to *Skandinaven*, 28 March 1894.

[98]John R. Romstad to *Skandinaven*, 22 August 1894.

[99]"W" to *Skandinaven*, 10 January 1894; Ole Kvæven to *Skandinaven*, 2 May 1894.

[100]Gro Hageman, *Det moderne gjennombrud, 1870–1905*, vol. 9 of *Aschehougs Norgeshistorie* (Oslo, 1997), 182–183.

[101]"B.A.B." to *Skandinaven*, 27 May 1896; N. Sæthre to *Skandinaven*, 5 August 1896.

[102]*Skandinaven*, 5 October 1892, 26 September 1894, 23 September 1896. Quite remarkably, in 1906 U.S. Representative James T. McCleary of Minnesota actually praised Norwegian tariff legislation in Congress; see *Amerika*, 7 September 1906.

[103]Tosten Lillehaugen to *Skandinaven*, 14 October 1896. This silverite view was promptly criticized by *Skandinaven's* editorship, who defended the gold standard.

[104]H. M. Thorvik to *Skandinaven*, 15 August 1894.

[105]"J.O.S." to *Skandinaven*, 16 September 1896; Lauritz Larson to *Skandinaven*, 12 August 1896; "Ludvig Holberg" to *Skandinaven*, 9 July 1890.

[106]"O. paa Prærien" to *Skandinaven*, 30 September 1896.

[107]O. O. Bergh to *Skandinaven*, 28 October 1896.

[108]"Knut" to *Hemlandet*, 27 October 1892.

[109]"En Farmer" to *Skandinaven*, 21 October 1896.

[110]"En Hader af Saloonen" to *Skandinaven*, 24 March 1897.

[111]O. R. B. to *Skandinaven*, 14 February 1897.

[112]Hauk Hobrok to *Skandinaven*, 14 April 1897.

[113]B. K. Holberg to *Skandinaven*, 1 October 1902.

[114]In the invocation of Scandinavian-American identity, the honesty-and-wisdom theme took fourth place in the pre-depression letters, second place in the depression letters, and first place in the post-depression letters.

[115]79.6 percent of the forty-nine letters dealing with Scandinavian-American

honesty and wisdom were of the type that blended the consideration of issues and values with organizational matters.

[116]Sever Rundahl to *Skandinaven*, 31 August 1910.

[117]John E. Ofstie to *Skandinaven*, 20 July 1910.

[118]Anonymous letter from Minot, North Dakota, to *Skandinaven*, 15 August 1906.

[119]"M.B.O." to *Skandinaven*, 30 October 1914. The reader did not specify what legislation he was referring to.

[120]Anonymous letter from Washington, D.C., to *Skandinaven*, 12 October 1910. According to an article in *Amerika*, 9 September 1909, "To avoid repetition it should be noted here that all senators and members of Congress of Scandinavian origins belong to the Republican Party, and within it most of them to the group now known as the 'insurgents.'"

[121]George F. Merill to John C. Spooner, 26 February 1903, in John C. Spooner Papers, Manuscript Division, Library of Congress, Washington, D.C.

[122]Douglas Anderson to Andrew H. Dahl, 14 June 1914, in Andrew H. Dahl Papers, Library-Archives, Wisconsin Historical Society, Madison, WI.

[123]J. C. Gaveney to E. W. Keyes, 15 August 1906, in Elisha W. Keyes Papers, Library-Archives, Wisconsin Historical Society, Madison, WI.

[124]*Svenska Amerikanska Tribunen*, 21 October 1910.

[125]H. C. Hansbrough to Rasmus B. Anderson, 18 July, 26 August, 3 September 1907, in Rasmus B. Anderson Papers, Library-Archives, Wisconsin Historical Society, Madison, WI.

[126]Robert M. La Follette, *La Follette's Autobiography: A Personal Narrative of Political Experiences*, rev. ed. (Madison, WI, 1913), 268; see also Bernard A. Weisberger, *The La Follettes of Wisconsin: Love and Politics in Progressive America* (Madison, WI, 1994), 20.

[127]A copy of the speech is found in box B 211 in the La Follette Family Collection, Manuscript Division, Library of Congress, Washington, D.C.

[128]R. Lien to *Skandinaven*, 13 April 1892.

[129]"N.J.K." to *Skandinaven*, 13 August 1890.

[130]Isak Wenlag to *Skandinaven*, 21 September 1904.

[131]John A. Johnson to Rasmus B. Anderson, 6 December 1885, in R. B. Anderson Papers.

[132]Nils P. Haugen to Rasmus B. Anderson, 24 October 1885, in R. B. Anderson Papers.

[133]*Skandinaven*, 24 October 1900; *Hemlandet*, 22 May 1906; see also *Skandinaven*, 8 October 1902; *Minneapolis Tidende*, 13 November 1896.

[134]See page 91 in chapter 4.

[135]*Skandinaven*, 4 July 1894.

[136]*Skandinaven*, 24 August 1898.

[137]*Skandinaven*, 19 August 1910.

[138]Roger E. Wyman, "Voting Patterns in the Progressive Era: Wisconsin as a Test Case" (PhD diss., University of Wisconsin, 1970), 269–270, 454; Allen Fraser Lovejoy, *La Follette and the Establishment of the Direct Primary in Wisconsin, 1890–1904* (New Haven, CT, 1941), 91–94.

[139]*Skandinaven*, 14 March 1901; *Superior Tidende*, 7 March 1901.

[140]*Superior Tidende*, 18 April 1901; "Norsk Republikaner" to *Skandinaven*, 6 March 1901; see also Bjørn Holland to *Skandinaven*, 9 July 1902.

[141]*Amerika*, 13 March 1901; see also Bjørn Holland to *Amerika*, 8 August 1902; on Rasmus B. Anderson, see pages 88–89 in chapter 4.

[142]R. Lien to *Skandinaven*, 13 April 1892.

[143]*Skandinaven*, 12 October 1904. A parallel argument had it that Norway's present political struggle mirrored the American Revolution: "After all, the fight that Norway's Left party is now waging is the same as that which was fought in America one hundred years ago," *Folkevennen* (quoting *Norden*), 9 June 1894.

[144]Hans Sperber and Travis Trittschuh, *American Political Terms: An Historical Dictionary* (Detroit, 1962), 337.

[145]Nils P. Haugen to Robert M. La Follette, 11 April 1894, in Robert M. La Follette Papers, Library-Archives, Wisconsin Historical Society, Madison, WI.

[146]"Republikaner" to *Skandinaven*, 10 October 1894.

[147]Jacob Steenson to *Skandinaven*, 22 August 1894.

[148]P. A. Ringheim to *Skandinaven*, 15 August 1894.

[149]Open letter by "Flere" to Den norske Arbeiderforening, *Folkevennen*, 18 August 1893.

[150]*Reform*, 22 July 1890.

[151]*Skandinaven*, 30 May 1894.

[152]*Skandinaven*, 15 July 1896.

[153]*Superior Tidende*, 16 May 1901.

[154]For an example of the use of the reactionary epithet [*Bagstræver*] in a purely Norwegian context, see the travel description from an anonymous correspondent in Søndre Hordaland to *Skandinaven*, 3 October 1894.

[155]*Posten*, 20 April 1893.

[156]*Skandinaven*, 28 March 1901.

[157]For emphasis on progressive reform's "scientific" qualities, see Frederic C. Howe, *Wisconsin: An Experiment in Democracy* (New York, 1912), x–xi; Charles C. McCarthy, *The Wisconsin Idea* (New York, 1912), 11–12, 16; Richard T. Ely, *Ground under Our Feet: An Autobiography* (New York, 1938), 215.

[158]La Follette himself bought into the "scientific" approach; see R. La Follette, *La Follette's Autobiography*, 359. For a discussion of the tension between popular democracy and commission rule, see McCarthy, *The Wisconsin Idea*, 172. On the influence of German reforms on progressive thinking, see Howe, *Wisconsin: An Experiment in Democracy*, 20, 30, 38–41; McCarthy, *The Wisconsin Idea*, 10–12, 160–161, 174–175, 186–188; Ely, *Ground Under Our Feet*, 53–54, 207–208; and Eric F. Goldman, *Rendezvous with Destiny: A History of Modern American Reform* (New York, 1952), 80–81, 87, 185–186.

[159]Clyde Griffen, "The Progressive Ethos," in *The Development of an American Culture*, ed. Stanley Coben and Lorman Ratner (Englewood Cliffs, NJ, 1970), 123.

[160]Robert M. La Follette to "Dear Al" [Alfred T. Rogers], undated letter in box B 103, in La Follette Family Collection; E. Ray Stevens to Robert M. La Follette, 9 January 1906, in La Follette Papers.

[161]*Blue Book of the State of Wisconsin* (Madison, WI), 1891:331–340, 1893:351–361, 1895:395–406, 1897:334–346, 1899:401–413, 1901:408–423, 1903:648–663, 1905:598–612, 1907:673–687, 1909:595–610, 1911:383–397, 1913:318–332.

[162]Quoted from George M. Stephenson, *John Lind of Minnesota* (Minneapolis, 1935), 38.

[163]John Lind to Nils P. Haugen, 7 June 1896, in Haugen Papers.

[164]Quoted from Stephenson, *John Lind of Minnesota*, 110.

[165]*Nordmanden* quoted in *Reform*, 12 November 1895. Interestingly, in the campaign of 1906 the temperance-minded *Reform* actually praised Robert M. La Follette: "Within his field he is undoubtedly the most formidable man Wisconsin has ever fostered"; see *Reform*, 21 August 1906.

[166]*Svenska Amerikanaren*, 31 October 1912.

[167]See pages 67, 70, and 77–78 in chapter 3.

[168]Siver G. Haugen to *Skandinaven*, 24 January 1894; "M." to *Skandinaven*, 14 April 1897.

[169]One-page typewritten manuscript dated "[1914]" in box "-1935," in Ekern Papers; *Skandinaven*, 8 March 1893. See also *Skandinaven*, 18 January, 22 March 1893.

[170]Nicolay Grevstad, "Courts of Conciliation," *Atlantic Monthly* 68/407 (September 1891), 401–406.

[171]Belle C. La Follette and Fola La Follette, *Robert M. La Follette, June 14, 1855–June 18, 1925*, 2 vols. (New York, 1953), 1:587.

[172]John Lind to Rasmus B. Anderson, 25 March 1887, in R. B. Anderson Papers.

[173]H. Olson to *Skandinaven*, 2 May 1894.

[174]O. Berg to *Skandinaven*, 12 May 1895.

[175]*Reform*, 30 April 1895 (quoting Rodhuggeren).

[176]See page 168 in chapter 7.

[177]Nils P. Haugen to A. B. Stickney, 12 October 1891, in Haugen Papers.

[178]*Skandinaven*, 15 June 1892.

[179]On 17 August 1894, Haugen wrote Hall that he was (again) planning to introduce a bill in Congress on the railroad problem along the lines suggested by Stickney. In Haugen Papers.

[180]Stanley P. Caine, *The Myth of a Progressive Reform: Railroad Regulation in Wisconsin 1903–1910* (Madison, WI, 1970), 72, note 3; speech by Irvine L. Lenroot at the Lincoln Club in Racine, 12 February 1906, box 8, in Irvine L. Lenroot Papers, Manuscript Division, Library of Congress, Washington, D.C.

[181]Jørn Brøndal, "Socialister, fagforeninger og broderskaber i skandinavisk Amerika, 1870–1914," *Arbejderhistorie* 1999/1 (1999), 33–50. Jon Wefald, *A Voice of Protest: Norwegians in American Politics, 1890–1917* (Northfield, MN, 1971), 4, 46, somewhat romantically postulates a special Norwegian-American affinity for what he boldly calls "the social democracy of Robert M. La Follette," based on Norwegian traditions of economic self-sufficiency, communalism, and cooperation.

[182]Marion Tuttle Marzolf, *The Danish-Language Press in America* (New York, 1979), 77; Henry Bengston, *Skandinaver på vänstreflygeln i USA* (Stockholm, 1955), 48.

[183]Richard B. Lucas, *Charles August Lindbergh, Sr.: A Case Study of Congressional Insurgency, 1906–1912* (Uppsala, 1974), 87; Wefald, *A Voice of Protest*, 81–84. Wefald's conclusions about Norwegian-American support for progressive legislation were methodologically flawed: he simply cited the vote of Norwegian-American members on selected roll calls without controlling even for the vote of other legislators. Kenneth C. Acrea, a historian investigating roll calls in the Wisconsin legislature, 1891–1909, without the aid of computers, actually suggested that in Wisconsin native-born assemblymen were more progressively inclined than their foreign-born colleagues. Still, he found that in the 1899 session, at least, legislators from dairying areas with large Scandinavian-American constituencies tended to support progressive measures, yet drew no wider conclusions from that single observation; see Kenneth C. Acrea, "Wisconsin Progressivism: Legislative Response to Social Change, 1891 to 1909" (PhD diss., University of Wisconsin, 1968), 327–328, 424. While suggesting the importance of ethnicity especially for interparty competition, Ballard C. Campbell's analysis of legislative behavior in Illinois, Iowa, and Wisconsin, 1886–1895, does not cover the emergence of the progressive movement; see Ballard C. Campbell, *Representative Democracy: Public Policy and Midwestern Legislatures in the Late Nineteenth Century* (Cambridge, MA, 1980), 199.

[184]For a discussion of the roll-call analysis, see Appendix III.

[185]Whereas Cook, Hall, and an additional two Republicans each scored 100 on the progressive scale, the five Scandinavian Americans each scored 93; the latter differed with the former on just one roll call.

[186]On this geographical subdivision, see Appendix II.

[187]This result is based on a calculation of the average per-session relative progressive ranking of the nine sections, varying from 1 to 9. Over the ten legislative sessions, the northwest's average progressive ranking was 3.2, that of the southwest 3.4, and that of the central west 4.0. At the other extreme, the score of both the central east and the southeast was 6.1.

[188]On that bill, see pages 151 and 158 in chapter 6.

[189]Silkworth's progressive score in 1901 was 3, Orton's 7. On Silkworth and Orton's stalwart sympathies, see the *Milwaukee Journal*, 25 March 1901; James G. Monahan to John C. Spooner, 1 February 1901, in Spooner Papers.

[190]John D. Buenker, *The Progressive Era, 1893–1914*, vol. 4 of *The History of Wisconsin*, ed. William Fletcher Thompson (Madison, WI, 1998), 535–568; Robert Asher, "The 1911 Workmen's Compensation Law: A Study in Conservative Labor Reform," *Wisconsin Magazine of History* 57 (Winter 1973–1974), 123–140.

[191]All but eight of the 113 seats taken by Scandinavian Americans in the 1895–1913 assembly bore a Republican label.

[192]*Blue Book of Wisconsin*, 1901:767. Jensen's progressive score in the 1901 session amounted to 7.

[193]In 1901, Cleophas's progressive score was 33, placing him fifty-eighth among the 100 assemblymen, alongside fellow Norwegian-American Andrew C. Hansen.

[194]Ekern's "progressive" scores were 83 in 1903, 100 in 1905, and 81 in 1907; Davidson's 88 in 1895 and 75 in 1897; Dahl's 69 in 1899, 93 in 1901, 82 in 1903, and 100 in 1905; Lenroot's 93 in 1901, 100 in 1903, and 100 in 1905; Johnson's 93 in 1901, 100 in 1903, and 100 in 1905. Except for Dahl's 1899 score, all these scores topped the average Republican progressive score of the legislative session in question; see fig. 8.3, Appendix I.

[195]On the small numbers of Scandinavian-American assemblymen, see fig. 5.1, Appendix I. Among the representatives of the various Scandinavian-American groups, Norwegian immigrant politicians proved most progressively inclined in 1895, 1897, and 1899; Danish in 1903 and 1905; and second-generation Scandinavian Americans in 1901 and 1907. Danish immigrant politicians and second-generation Scandinavian Americans tied for first place in 1909, whereas Norwegian immigrant politicians and second-generation Scandinavian Americans tied for first place in 1911. Norwegian and Danish immigrant politicians, as well as second-generation Scandinavian-American politicians, tied for first place in 1913. Since the 1895–1913 legislative sessions included only two Swedish immigrant assemblymen, nothing much can be concluded from the fact that only Ole Erickson, a farmer-merchant from Burnett County, proved fairly

friendly to reform during his single term, 1901–1902. Erickson's progressive score of 73 was well above the average Republican score that session (see fig. 8.3, Appendix I). Among those second-generation Scandinavian Americans whose national background could be verified, on the other hand, Swedish Americans came out at the top, whereas Danish Americans proved least open to reform. This second-generation Swedish-American progressive inclination, however, had to do simply with the fact that all three seats taken by members of that group belonged to one and the same person, Irvine L. Lenroot.

[196]In the 1909 session, Twesme's progressive score was 17, well below the 1909 Republican average; see fig. 8.3, Appendix I. Whereas only three of the forty-six Scandinavian-American Republicans yielded progressive scores below 50, twenty-seven scored 80 or above, including fourteen scoring 90 or above.

[197]My calculations.

[198]Such was the case in all legislative sessions save ties in 1907–1911 and a small reversal in 1913 (my calculations).

[199]Statewide, the same trend held true among non-Scandinavian-American Republicans representing constituencies at least twenty percent Scandinavian-American and less than twenty percent Scandinavian-American, respectively. In all sessions except 1911 (a reversal) and 1899 and 1907 (ties), the former proved more progressively inclined than the latter (my calculations).

[200]Among western non-Scandinavian-American Republicans representing constituencies at least twenty percent Scandinavian-American and less than twenty percent Scandinavian-American, respectively, it turns out that the former scored higher in three sessions (1897, 1905, 1913), the latter in two (1899, 1911), and the two groups tied in the remaining five. Thus, the differences between the two groups blurred. Similarly, among western Scandinavian-American Republicans representing constituencies at least twenty percent Scandinavian-American and less than twenty percent Scandinavian-American, respectively, the former came out ahead of the latter once (1905), the reverse happened once (1899), and the remaining five sessions (1897, 1901, 1909, 1911, 1913) resulted in ties. Both groups were present in only seven of the ten sessions (my calculations).

[201]Among western Republican assemblymen representing constituencies less than twenty percent Scandinavian-American, it turns out that Scandinavian-American legislators came out ahead of their non-Scandinavian-American counterparts five times (1895, 1897, 1899, 1901, 1913), the reverse happened once (1905), and ties resulted in two cases (1909, 1911). Both groups were present in only eight of the ten legislative sessions. Among western Republican assemblymen representing constituencies at least twenty percent Scandinavian-American, it turns out that the Scandinavian-American Republicans proved more progressively inclined than the non-Scandinavian-American in five sessions (1899, 1901, 1907, 1909, 1911), with the reverse being the case in one (1913), and the remaining three sessions resulting in draws (1897, 1903, 1905); both groups were present in only nine of the ten legislative sessions (my calculations).

[202]Even though the average Republican score varied from session to session, scores above ninety or below ten were remarkable in all sessions.

[203]In the sessions of 1903 through 1907, and again in 1911, the (very few) Republican legislators born in Denmark exhibited the strongest average pro-temperance attitudes, and in 1895, and again in 1899, their Norwegian-born colleagues did so. In 1913, on the other hand, the single Swedish-born member evidenced the highest pro-temperance score, whereas the three second-generation Scandinavian-American Republicans came in first place in 1909. Two of these three members were of verifiable Norwegian-American background. At the other extreme, in the sessions of 1895 and 1909, the Danish-born Republicans scored lower even than the Republican average, as did the seven second-generation Scandinavian-American Republicans in 1903.

[204]Among the Scandinavian-American Republican assemblymen, the westerners came out ahead of their non-western colleagues in 1895, 1899, 1907, 1911, and 1913, whereas the reverse was the case in 1903 and 1905, with draws resulting in 1897, 1901, and 1909 (my calculations).

[205]Among the non-western Republicans, Scandinavian-American assemblymen came out ahead of their non-Scandinavian-American colleagues in all sessions except that of 1899 (my calculations).

[206]For the years 1886–1895, Ballard C. Campbell similarly suggests that varying voting patterns applied to different policy areas, say, economic and social; see Campbell, *Representative Democracy*, 197–198.

[207]In the 1901 Assembly, Jensen and Cleophas both scored 100 on the temperance scale.

[208]In 1907, Nelson scored 83 on the progressive scale and 33 on the temperance scale, whereas in 1913 Grimsrud's scores were 83 and 13, respectively. For the Republican average scores for those sessions, see fig. 8.4, Appendix I.

NOTES TO THE CONCLUSION

[1]John D. Buenker, *The Progressive Era, 1893–1914*, vol. 4 of *The History of Wisconsin*, ed. William Fletcher Thompson (Madison, WI, 1998), 616–621.

[2]Robert S. Maxwell, *Emanuel L. Philipp: Wisconsin Stalwart* (Madison, WI, 1959), 78–79.

[3]H. G. Flieth to Henry Johnson, 9 July 1914, in Henry Johnson Papers, Library-Archives, Wisconsin Historical Society, Madison, WI.

[4]George L. Pullen to Henry Johnson, 13 July 1914, in Henry Johnson Papers.

[5]D. W. Maloney to Andrew H. Dahl, 13 June 1914, in Andrew H. Dahl Papers, Library-Archives, Wisconsin Historical Society, Madison, WI.

[6]Buenker, *The Progressive Era*, 653–654; John Higham, *Strangers in the Land: Patterns of American Nativism, 1860–1925*, rev. ed. (New Brunswick, NJ, 1988), 194–195; Higham suggests that the full-fledged revival of nativism began in 1915.

[7]Edwin L. Reese to Henry Johnson, 7 July 1914, in Henry Johnson Papers.

[8]Ole J. Eggum to Herman L. Ekern, 1, 3 August 1914; Ekern to Eggum, 3, 28 August 1914, in Herman L. Ekern Papers, Library-Archives, Wisconsin Historical Society, Madison, WI; *Skandinaven*, 27 August 1914.

[9]O. Ottersen to Andrew H. Dahl, 18 July 1914, in Dahl Papers.

[10]Herman L. Ekern to Emil Ekern, 28 August 1914; Thomas Morris to Herman L. Ekern, 4 September 1914, in Ekern Papers.

[11]The mother and bride metaphor was originally introduced by Carl Schurz and applied to the German-American element; see Jon Gjerde, *The Minds of the West: Ethnocultural Evolution in the Rural Middle West, 1830–1917* (Chapel Hill, NC, 1997), 61.

[12]"H.E." to *Skandinaven*, 17 February 1897.

[13]Higham, *Strangers in the Land*, 194–233.

[14]Those Danish Americans who did in fact organize tended likewise to sustain a sense of common national origins by quarreling with each over religious matters.

[15]Edward W. Said, *Culture and Imperialism* (London, 1993), 361–362 (italics added).

[16]See page 168 in chapter 7.

[17]See page 96 in chapter 4.

Index to Names of Persons